WOMEN, POPULAR CULTURE, AND
THE EIGHTEENTH CENTURY

Women, Popular Culture, and the Eighteenth Century

EDITED BY TIFFANY POTTER

UNIVERSITY OF TORONTO PRESS
Toronto Buffalo London

ISBN 978-1-4426-4181-5 (cloth)

Printed on acid-free, 100% post-consumer recycled paper
with vegetable-based inks.

Library and Archives Canada Cataloguing in Publication

Women, popular culture, and the eighteenth century / edited by Tiffany
Potter.

Includes bibliographical references and index.
ISBN 978-1-4426-4181-5

1. Women – England – History – 18th century.   2. Women in popular
culture – England – History – 18th century.   3. Popular culture – England –
History – 18th century.   4. England – Social life and customs – 18th century.   5. England – Civilization – 18th century.   I. Potter, Tiffany, 1967–

HQ1593.W658 2012   305.4094209'033   C2012-901078-2

This book has been published with the help of a grant from the Canadian
Federation for the Humanities and Social Sciences, through the Aid to
Scholarly Publications Program, using funds provided by the Social
Sciences and Humanities Research Council of Canada.

University of Toronto Press acknowledges the financial assistance to its
publishing program of the Canada Council for the Arts and the Ontario
Arts Council.

 Canada Council   Conseil des Arts
for the Arts   du Canada

 ONTARIO ARTS COUNCIL
CONSEIL DES ARTS DE L'ONTARIO

University of Toronto Press acknowledges the financial support of the
Government of Canada through the Canada Book Fund for its publishing
activities.

Contents

Illustrations

Editor's Preface

Recent studies of contemporary popular culture have illuminated the complex relationships that individuals and groups maintain with the larger artistic, political, and social movements around them. The theory that informs popular culture studies, however, has rarely been applied historically, and more rarely to the eighteenth century; when it has, the focus has generally been on broad (and conventionally masculine) fields of study, with limited consideration of the specific historical and cultural experiences of women.[1] Work published on popular elements of eighteenth-century women's culture has tended to address closely focused aspects of that experience, including, for example, shopping, women's work, and actress biographies.[2] This collection is designed to build upon this existing body of research: *Women, Popular Culture, and the Eighteenth Century* brings together studies on several aspects of what we would now term popular culture, as it existed in eighteenth-century England, from theatres, plays, and actresses, to novels, magazines, and cookbooks, as well as populist politics, dress, and portraiture. Through detailed analysis of women's engagements with popular culture, the essays included here collectively illuminate the historical naturalization of the association of the feminine and the popular, and the ways in which that association facilitated the trivialization and the containment of both the feminine and the popular. This collective reconsideration of the cultural and social practices of eighteenth-century women works to reclaim the trivial as a substantive cultural contribution.

It is clear, though, that the need for this reclamation of women's practice is not exclusively retroactive: modern culture widely carries on the same presumptions of the masculine nature of high art and the association of popular culture with the lightweight, the frivolous, the fashionable, and with other language that is near-universally coded as feminine. As Peter Goodall puts it, 'There is no more basic misconception in the study of culture than to see the debate about popular culture and its social effects as simply the product of our own times, the consequence of living in an era in which the media can be seen to have both democratized the audience but debased the standard of art' (1). This collection acknowledges the continuities of the popular and the feminine in its combination of essays addressing historically specific eighteenth-century cultural products and essays considering the implications of reimaginings of eighteenth-century women in modern popular culture.

The idea of the popular can be tremendously useful in contributing to long-standing debates about women and the public sphere in the eighteenth century. It is also, however, a notoriously nebulous concept, the subject of critical contest since the mid-twentieth century. As Stuart Hall, Tony Bennett, and others have long discussed, the idea of the popular is to some degree politically and ideologically determined, both in the moment of its production and in the process of scholarly contention over its implication. Too often discussions of popular culture slip into what Hall terms 'the descriptive': 'all the things that "the people" do and have done' (513).[3] Such a hugely encompassing approach clearly puts nuance in peril and tends to emphasize the momentary status of products or practices, rather than considering the significance of their creation and consumption by various social groups. Putting the descriptive aside, then, many of the existing frameworks theorized for popular culture embody to some degree the identification of popular culture as either folk culture or mass culture. Theories of mass culture tend to emphasize popular culture as a product that is imposed upon the populace from outside, an automatically inauthentic form of culture administered to those manipulated by cultural industries. This perspective is a necessary part of the puzzle, acknowledging the political and economic motives in much that can be identified as popular, but it risks overstating the control that culture producers hold over consumers: advertisers, arts boards, publishers, and entertainment companies would all dearly love for consumers of culture to be so malleable, but we are a mercurial lot. As Paula R. Backscheider's recent essay on popular culture notes, this anxiety about trickery in the cultural industries goes back to at least the eighteenth century in critics like Jeremy Collier, who in 1697 criticized the producers of popular culture for 'courting the favour of the people by undue practices,' which Backscheider identifies as 'a wonderful umbrella term for all the seductive, allegedly mind-numbing consciousness-manipulating "art" of our media-saturated society' ('Paradigms' 22).

Folk culture, on the other hand, is an even longer-standing vision of the popular as a non-commercial counterpart to elite culture, produced and consumed almost exclusively by amateurs and non-elites; this construction is problematic too, however, in its reverse exclusivity, often declining to include as folk culture popular forms of art, communication, or entertainment eventually consumed by elite or blended audiences. The folk culture sense of popular culture assumes an autonomous 'popular culture' that is separate from the spheres of social power and cultural dominance.[4] The guiding sense of the popular for this collection combines Backscheider's beautifully direct summary that 'popular culture is defined by its relationship to the dominant culture and that is one of perpetual tension, sometimes antagonistic, sometimes perpetuating, but always a site of potential critique' ('Paradigms' 20) and Jonathan Culler's suggestion for a middle ground between folk and mass culture, based on his argument that 'people are able to use the cultural materials foisted on them by capitalism and its media and entertainment industries to produce a culture of their own' (244).

As current approaches to popular culture make clear, no one of the dominant theoretical typifications of the popular alone can encompass the full range of implications of the production, consumption, and practice of popular culture in the context of eighteenth-century women. The essays in this volume take their senses of the popular from different places on this continuum, sharing an overarching sense of the popular as practices or products that – in terms of their production, consumption, or both – 'were part of the consciousness of the learned or educated as well as of the uneducated; read or seen or talked about by so many people that we can say they were taken for granted as part of the environment' (Paulson x). Some, though not all, of the contributors to this collection would add the necessity of popular culture's being 'associated with a profitable endeavor, therefore, to some extent self-consciously "manufactured," calculated to succeed because composed with high awareness of audience-pleasing elements' (Backscheider, 'Paradigms' 21).

Adding still further to the complexity of the project of historicizing popular culture is the dynamic nature of that which constitutes the popular and the elite: 'from period to period, the *contents* of each category change. Popular forms become enhanced in cultural value, go up the cultural escalator – and find themselves on the opposite side. Other things cease to have high cultural value, and are appropriated into the popular, becoming transformed in the process' (Hall 514). In fact, perhaps the single best example of this escalator phenomenon comes from the eighteenth century: the case of Jane Austen. Like many women venturing into publication before her, Austen wrote in large part out of financial necessity, publishing anonymously to preserve her reputation and privacy. Her novels were reasonably successful upon first publication, the result in no small part of word-of-mouth recommendations, as they received only a handful of reviews. As Brian Southam has documented, those reviews were generally positive, but made no claims to lasting brilliance or high art. By the mid-nineteenth century, Austen's status rose as her popularity diffused: the novels were still in print, but embraced primarily by a cultured few (Duffy 98–9). Austen's status would shift again after 1870, however, when James Edward Austen-Leigh published a biography of his Aunt Jane, which Southam suggests was a precursor to a marked increase in both the popularity and the prestige of her novels. They became widely available to popular audiences in Routledge sixpenny editions, but critics remained convinced that her work was too sophisticated for popular consumption (Trott 92–4). By the mid-twentieth century, Austen's novels were increasingly treated as examples of elite culture, classic literature taught in universities across the world as representative of great English Literature. And as recently as the 1990s, her status has shifted yet again: Austen has not lost her standing – her work remains a mainstay of college courses and scholarly study – but she has taken a curious place on Hall's cultural escalator as the only canonical literary writer whose name can virtually guarantee a profitable popular film.[5]

This dual instability, of both the idea of the popular and the evolving popular or elite status of different cultural productions, means that the essays in this volume do not take on a single critical position, or even necessarily broach the question of the triangulation of the feminine, the popular, and the eighteenth century in similarly explicit ways. Instead, they take distinct approaches to specific aspects of the relationship between eighteenth-century women and popular culture: the popularization of notions of femininity, women's participation in political and artistic portions of the public realm, and the implications of the reproduction of eighteenth-century women as subjects of modern popular culture. As the studies in this volume make clear, the significance of things popular lies not in formalizations of their status, but in the implications of their existence, performance, and consumption, and in the ways in which they communicate the tensions of their cultures of production.

The complications of the theorization of 'the popular' outlined above are put into the context of the eighteenth century in several different ways in this volume. In Part I, my chapter argues for the need to examine the intersections among the popular and the feminine in both eighteenth-century and modern contexts of popular culture, using as exemplary texts Alexander Pope's *The Rape of the Lock* and perhaps the most startling recent work linking eighteenth-century women and popular culture, Seth Grahame-Smith's adaptation of Jane Austen's novel in *Pride and Prejudice and Zombies* (2009). The nuances and overlap among the putatively elite and the identifiably popular are brought into sharp focus in Jessica Munns's discussion of the actress as fashion icon, and the ways in which actresses of middling or even low birth could foster vogues for high fashions of dress and coiffure by virtue of their theatrical imitations of aristocratic women. In discussing the practices of performance and the theatre, Paula R. Backscheider and Berta Joncus each offer detailed insights into the critical role of female performers in the evolution and implications of a specific genre, with Backscheider on political tragedy, and Joncus on that most identifiable of eighteenth-century popular art forms, the ballad opera. Elaine Chalus then pursues the political implication of women's fashion as she considers the ideological work done by women's ribbons, fans, and other conventionally frivolous adornments in eighteenth-century political and military culture.

The popular identity of women and their creation and consumption of popular cultural products goes well beyond the flamboyance of fashion and actresses, however. In Part II of this volume, Isobel Grundy identifies the shifting fashions of the letter-writing public, both in terms of the social implication of an accessible mode of private communication among women and in the ways in which the letter-writing histories of Lady Mary Wortley Montagu and Demaris Cudworth (later Masham) reflect their self-constructions and their respective senses of the place of women in private and popular discourse. Further engaging the relationships among the private, the domestic, the public, and the popular, Robert James Merrett traces the place of English women in the culture of professional cookery through their roles in the rise of the cookbook: the print embodiment of a task routinely performed by women in all but the most privileged circles, the cookbook represents a fascinating transitional space in the relationships among French and English, elite and mass, and male and female cultures. Mary Chadwick's documentation of the popular print and social forms of the late eighteenth-century vogue for riddles similarly takes what might be seen as an ungendered parlour activity and considers the cooptation of the riddle's popularity for the service of moral conservatism, demonstrating that not just the apologetic prefaces but at times the riddles themselves locate their pleasure in a feminized frivolousness and potential moral peril. Continuing the consideration of publication and popular culture into the eighteenth-century periodical, Peter Sabor documents the experiences and responses of the handful of female contributors to Samuel Johnson's *The Rambler*, as well as Johnson's own struggles with the demands of the popular as they are voiced by the women of his circle. Holly Luhning and Timothy Erwin round out the discussions of women's reading and writing with considerations of Eliza Haywood's *Love in Excess* and Jane Austen's *Northanger Abbey*. Luhning considers the ways in which Haywood's *Love in Excess* engages the tensions among popular understandings of biology and the profitable representation of the body in print, while Erwin considers the problems of perception and popular ideas of aesthetics through contemporary prints, philosophies, and devices of observation.

The essays in Part III of this volume build on the historical specificity developed in the first eleven essays. They examine the ways in which images of eighteenth-century women are used in modern fiction, film, and television, revealing some of the continuities in the associations between the feminine and the popular, and considering the implications of adaptation for our understanding of eighteenth-century texts and the women they represent. Elizabeth Kowaleski Wallace's chapter on Emma Donoghue's novel *Slammerkin* (2000), and Martha F. Bowden's on Beryl Bainbridge's *According to Queeney* (2001) examine modern historical fiction that rewrites real eighteenth-century women as fictionalized protagonists, demonstrating the continuities in the construction of women's identities and the ways in which modern literature puts these private eighteenth-century women to work as commodities for popular consumption, not at all unlike the actresses described by Backscheider, Joncus, and Munns. The last three essays of the volume are grouped around a similar translative process in their collective consideration of the implications of modern film and television adaptations of Jane Austen's fiction. Tamara S. Wagner's analysis of the depictions of the equivalencies among shopping for fashions and shopping for men in film adaptations of *Northanger Abbey* and *Pride and Prejudice* recognizes the specific intersections among the fashion trade, the commodification of the sexes in eighteenth-century courtship convention, and the market for upscale films in the twentieth and twenty-first centuries. Focusing more closely on technical and design issues, Andrew Macdonald and Gina Macdonald offer insight into the filmic process involved in literary adaptation; their comparison of three iterations of *Persuasion* on screen reveals the challenge of communicating to a modern popular audience Austen's nuanced sense of competitions among mass and elite cultures. And finally, Claire Grogan outlines the ways in which the intertextuality of two recent television adaptations of *Pride and Prejudice* alter the possible interpretations of Austen's original novel.

As the chapters in the third section of this collection suggest, the popular culture associated with women in the eighteenth century should be read not as an artefact of dated values and ideologies, but rather as evidence of a contested relationship that continues to influence modern culture and its ideas of femininity, class, and public performance of identity. More so than many other periods, the eighteenth-century continues to be rewritten in ways that attempt to use the era as a vehicle to convey specific ideologies of contemporary culture, and we hope that this volume provides a useful overview of the complex theoretical framing, the fascinating historical circumstances, and the intriguing modern iterations of the parallel formulations of the feminine, the frivolous, and the popular.

NOTES

1 The three most notable general works on eighteenth-century popular culture are Burke, *Popular Culture in Early Modern Europe*; Reay, *Popular Culture in Seventeenth-Century England*; and Harris, *Popular Culture in England, c. 1500–1850*. Backscheider's more recent 'Paradigms of Popular Culture' offers insights into several of the elements of eighteenth-century popular culture considered in the essays collected here. For an anthology of eighteenth-century popular texts, see Mullan and Reid, *Eighteenth-Century Popular Culture*. For a visual sense, see Plumb, *Georgian Delights*.

2 Several books address specific aspects of eighteenth-century popular culture, but do not take it on as their primary focus. See, for example, Sweet and Lane, whose collaboration provides an important framework on the social institution of the town, and Rogers, who offers helpful framing in his

study of Defoe and Pope. On reading and the consumption of cultural nar-
ratives of the feminine, see Justice, McDowell, Richetti, Vincent, and Wanko.
On women, money, work, and consumption, see Baudino, Kowaleski
Wallace, and Batchelor and Kaplan. On theatre, see Luckhurst and Moody,
and Backscheider, *Spectacular Politics*. On art, see Paulson, and on fashion,
Lemire, and Styles and Vickery. On popular recreations, see Malcolmson.
Wollenberg and McVeigh offer insight into musical performance, and Chico
into dressing rooms and women's space.

3 Gary L. Harmon develops his definition, but his starting point is a useful example of the convention of the descriptive: 'Popular culture may be
defined as consisting of the arts, rituals and events, myths and beliefs, and
artifacts widely shared by a significant portion of a group of people at a
specific time' (63).

4 In 'Politics,' Tony Bennett notes the parallels between folk and mass culture and the theoretical approaches used to articulate them. He suggests
that the implied oppositions of mass and folk culture might be mediated
using the work of Antonio Gramsci, which he argues can unify structur-
alist understandings of popular culture (which often regarded popular
culture as 'an "ideological machine" which dictated the thoughts of people just as rigidly and with the same law-like regularity as in Saussure's
conspectus') and the culturalist understanding, which was 'often
uncritically romantic in its celebration of popular culture as expressing the authentic interests and values of subordinate social groups and
classes' (82).

5 Backscheider makes a similar argument in terms of the relative prestige
and popularity in modern scholarship and teaching of Samuel Richardson's
Clarissa and *Pamela* ('Paradigms' 55–6).

WORKS CITED

Backscheider, Paula R. 'The Paradigms of Popular Culture.' *Eighteenth-
Century Novel* 6–7 (2009): 17–59. Print.
– *Spectacular Politics: Theatrical Power and Mass Culture in Early Modern England.*
Baltimore: Johns Hopkins UP, 1993. Print.
Batchelor, Jennie, and Cora Kaplan, eds. *Women and Material Culture, 1660–
1830.* New York: Palgrave Macmillan, 2007. Print.
Baudino, Isabelle, et al. *The Invisible Woman: Aspects of Women's Work in
Eighteenth-Century Britain.* Aldershot: Ashgate, 2005. Print.

Bennett, Tony. 'Popular Culture and the "Turn to Gramsci."' *Cultural Theory and Popular Culture: A Reader.* 4th ed. Ed. John Storey. London: Pearson, 2009. 81–7. Print.

– 'The Politics of the "Popular" and Popular Culture.' *Popular Culture and Social Relations.* Ed. Tony Bennett, Colin Mercer, and Janet Woollacott. London: Open UP, 1986. Print.

Burke, Peter. *Popular Culture in Early Modern Europe.* 3rd ed. Aldershot: Ashgate, 2009. Print.

Chico, Tita. *Designing Women: The Dressing Room in Eighteenth-Century English Literature and Culture.* Lewisburg: Bucknell UP, 2005. Print.

Culler, Jonathan. 'Doing Cultural Studies.' *The Literary in Theory.* Stanford: Stanford UP, 2007. Print.

Duffy, Joseph. 'Criticism, 1814–1870.' *The Jane Austen Companion.* Ed. J. David Grey. New York: Macmillan, 1986. 93–101. Print.

Goodall, Peter. *High Culture, Popular Culture: The Long Debate.* St. Leonards, NSW: Allen & Unwin, 1995. Print.

Hall, Stuart. 'Notes on Deconstructing "the Popular."' *Cultural Theory and Popular Culture.* 4th ed. Ed. John Storey. New York: Longman, 2009. 508–18. Print.

Harmon, Gary L. 'On the Nature and Functions of Popular Culture.' *Studies in Popular Culture* 6 (1983): 3–15. Print.

Harris, Tim, ed. *Popular Culture in England, c. 1500–1850.* New York: St Martin's Press, 1995. Print.

Justice, George. 'Poetry, Popular Culture, and the Literary Marketplace.' *A Companion to Eighteenth-Century Poetry.* Ed. Christine Gerrard. Malden, MA: Blackwell, 2006. 97–110. Print.

Kowaleski Wallace, Elizabeth. *Consuming Subjects: Women, Shopping, and Business in the Eighteenth Century.* New York: Columbia UP, 1996. Print.

Lemire, Beverly. 'Reflections on the Character of Consumerism, Popular Fashion and the English Market in the Eighteenth Century.' *Material History Bulletin* 31 (1990): 65–70. Print.

Luckhurst, Mary, and Jane Moody. *Theatre and Celebrity in Britain, 1660–2000.* Basingstoke: Palgrave Macmillan, 2005. Print.

Malcolmson, Robert. *Popular Recreations in English Society 1700–1850.* Cambridge: Cambridge UP, 1973. Print.

McDowell, Paula. 'Consuming Women: The Life of the "Literary Lady" as Popular Culture in Eighteenth-Century England.' *Genre* 26 (1993): 219–52. Print.

Mullan, John, and Christopher Reid, eds. *Eighteenth-Century Popular Culture: A Selection.* Oxford UP, 2000. Print.

Parker, Holt N. 'Toward a Definition of Popular Culture.' *History and Theory* 50.2 (2011): 147–70. *Academic Search Complete*. Web. 10 January 2012.

Paulson, Ronald. *Popular and Polite Art in the Age of Hogarth and Fielding*. Notre Dame: U of Notre Dame P, 1979. Print.

Plumb, J.H. *Georgian Delights*. London: Wiedenfeld & Nicolson, 1980. Print.

Reay, Barry, ed. *Popular Culture in Seventeenth-Century England*. London: Croom Helm, 1985. Print.

Richetti, John J. *Popular Fiction before Richardson: Narrative Patterns 1700–1739*. Oxford: Clarendon, 1992. Print.

Rogers, Pat. *Literature and Popular Culture in Eighteenth-Century England*. Sussex: Harvester, 1985. Print.

Southam, Brian C. *Jane Austen: The Critical Heritage, 1812–1870*. London: Routledge and Kegan Paul, 1968. Print.

– *Jane Austen: The Critical Heritage, 1870–1940*. London: Routledge and Kegan Paul, 1987. Print.

Styles, John, and Amanda Vickery. *Gender, Taste, and Material Culture in Britain and North America, 1700–1810*. New Haven: Yale UP, 2007. Print.

Sweet, Rosemary, and Penelope Lane, eds. *Women and Urban Life in Eighteenth-Century England: On the Town*. Aldershot: Ashgate, 2003. Print.

Trott, Nicola. 'Critical Responses, 1830–1970.' *Jane Austen in Context*. Ed. Janet Todd. Cambridge: Cambridge UP, 2005. 92–100. Print.

Vincent, David. *Literacy and Popular Culture: England 1750–1914*. Cambridge: Cambridge UP, 1993. Print.

Wanko, Cheryl. *Roles of Authority: Thespian Biography and Celebrity in Eighteenth-Century Britain*. Lubbock: Texas Tech UP, 2003. Print.

Wollenberg, Susan, and Simon McVeigh. *Concert Life in Eighteenth-Century Britain*. Aldershot: Ashgate, 2004. Print.

WOMEN, POPULAR CULTURE, AND THE EIGHTEENTH CENTURY

PART I

Performance, Fashion, and the Politics of the Popular

1 Historicizing the Popular and the Feminine: *The Rape of the Lock* and *Pride and Prejudice and Zombies*

TIFFANY POTTER

Though the theoretical concept of popular culture is a twentieth-century creation, the practices that the theory engages are long-standing. In this chapter, I address the historical typifications of the popular as feminine in eighteenth-century England, and the ways in which the feminine is imagined as popular and so excluded from the intellectual and ideological valuation of elite culture, in contexts ranging from its performance in women's social practice to its institutionalization in depictions of women in literature like Alexander Pope's *The Rape of the Lock* (1717). The implication of this naturalization is not limited to the historical, however; these same associations continue in modern culture, as can be demonstrated in an analysis of the 2009 adaptation *Pride and Prejudice and Zombies*, which uses Jane Austen's masterpiece as a device to critique twenty-first-century popular culture, the presumed pretensions of high literary culture, and the ideologies of art and gender that have carried forward from the eighteenth century to our own day.

The types of social practice that are implied by popular culture function in the eighteenth century as means by which women could participate in realms of elite culture which might normally be expected to exclude respectable women: art, public performance, philosophical debate, and politics. Women participated in these spheres in ways that often allowed both sexes to imagine that conservative boundaries were being observed: women did not, for the most part, offer militant objection to the patriarchal status quo or the masculine typification of high culture, and yet, through the devices of popular culture, they exerted influence and made their positions heard or seen. This is consistent with the twentieth-and twenty-first-century theorization of popular culture; as John Fiske explains, 'popular culture is made by subordinate peoples in their own interests out of resources that also, contradictorily, serve the economic interests of the dominant' (8), such that the popular embodies the culture produced by the subordinate as they consume the dominant culture. And while Fiske's Marxist position implies that 'subordinate peoples' are identified primarily by class, the specific historical circumstances of the eighteenth century suggest that gender is a potentially equally significant signifier of difference and subordination, similarly demanding a response that recognizes the tension between resistant individual agency and incorporation in response to prescriptive ideas of culture.

There is debate about how we can define popular culture before the twentieth century, and how we can make such a potentially slippery construction critically useful.[1] Both Barry Reay and Peter Burke begin with forms of the negative definition of 'the culture of the non-elite ... including women, children, shepherds, sailors, beggars and the rest' (Burke xiii). Since no artistic production or cultural practice has the same meaning to all people, we cannot retroactively define popular or elite culture by class, genre, form, or even audience. This becomes clear upon the recognition of the continuum of behaviours, artefacts, and audiences for nearly every aspect of culture in which the majority of women participated in eighteenth-century England. Nearly all women were involved, for example, in needlework, from the stitching of clothing to recreational embroidery; in clothing, from the functional to the fantastic; in the production and socialized consumption of food; and in culturally defined rituals of courtship, marriage, and domestic life. Women of all classes attended public performances, from Drury Lane and Covent Garden to the Haymarket and sites populated by travelling entertainers. In his work on taste, Pierre Bourdieu articulates the implications of this sort of understanding of cultural production and consumption as a continuum:

> There is no area of practice in which the aim of purifying, refining and sublimating primary needs and impulses cannot assert itself, no area in which the stylization of life, that is, the primacy of forms over function, of manner over matter, does not produce the same effects. And nothing is more distinctive, more distinguished, than the capacity to confer aesthetic status on objects that are banal or even 'common' ... or the ability to apply the principles of a 'pure' aesthetic to the most everyday choices of

everyday life, e.g. in cooking, clothing or decoration, completely reversing the popular disposition which annexes aesthetics to ethics. (6)

While Peter Burke refers to a continent-wide trend of upper-class 'withdrawal from popular culture' in the later eighteenth century (380), the observation depends upon an exclusively class-based understanding of the popular, drawing on examples of Scottish mummers and minstrel poetry, but ignoring the sorts of larger significations suggested by Bourdieu.

Widely practised social entertainments like dance and card playing provide useful examples of this continuum of the popular. Before the eighteenth century, English dance was quite firmly striated between country dance (from the maypole at the village green to the community gatherings for traditional dances in barns or public spaces) and aristocratic dance (in large homes, typified by slow processional pavanes or more energetic galliards). The phenomenon of subscription balls that began in the eighteenth century in resort spas broke this separation of popular and elite: the events were held in public spaces like assembly rooms and included both traditional country dances and more formal group dances such as the minuet. And while the expected dismay at this mixing of social groups and practices was certainly expressed, the evolution of shared culture becomes clear in both the events themselves and in the figure of the dancing master, conveying the skills required for participation in this popular cultural event to anyone who could pay. Even when the attendance at a ball was dominated by one group or the other (often depending on location and season), 'a sense of fashionable delight was common to them both. Dances for which one paid an entrance fee also broadened the range of social contact ... as with so many aspects of eighteenth-century culture, the commercialization of dancing brought great opportunities for enjoyment to greater numbers of men and women' (Plumb 34).[2] Ronald Paulson makes a similar case for the playing of cards: 'though everybody played cards (or so it seemed), whist as developed by Hoyle was initially a gentleman's game, and only people above a certain economic level were likely to read books on the subject. On the other hand, Hoyle's book embodied in words procedure which may have reached far down into the practice of the "inferior sort of people," whose popular game was taken up by their betters and then "improved" and formulated in Hoyle's book' (xi).

A theory of women's popular culture in the eighteenth century, then, must recognize this fluidity in definitions of both women's culture and popular culture. As the preface to this volume explains in more detail, the idea of the popular is paradoxical, as scholars engage that which seems easily knowable in a way that acknowledges the varied influences of economic class, intellectual hierarchies, and sheer numbers of participants, as well as the contradictions and collaborations of descriptive methodologies (what Stuart Hall critiques as 'all the things that "the people" do and have done' [513]), mass culture (popular culture as a product imposed upon the populace from outside, an automatically inauthentic form of administered culture), and folk culture (some form of ostensibly more authentic culture, outside of conventional ideas of hierarchy, produced and consumed almost exclusively by non-elites). That which constitutes the popular is also in some degree of flux: given shifts in cultural systems of valuation over time, popular can evolve into elite, and elite can be appropriated into popular, often long after the text, product, or performance has been created. The popular is not just about work created by and for the masses, but also the ways in which popular social and creative practices are incorporated into elite art, or into media arguably controlled by the elite.

Women and Popular Culture in the Eighteenth Century

Such understandings of popular culture may find some of their roots in the eighteenth century, as Paula Backscheider suggests in 'Paradigms of Popular Culture.' Backscheider describes popular culture as defined by its sometimes antagonistic, sometimes perpetuating relationship to the dominant culture, and as 'easily available, affordable, familiar to a large number of people representing several social classes, and associated with a profitable endeavor, therefore, to some extent self-consciously "manufactured," calculated to succeed because composed with high awareness of audience-pleasing elements' (21). My emphasis on the specifically gendered implications of those tensions of creation and consumption, antagonism and perpetuation, builds upon the work of Burke, Reay, Paulson, and Backscheider and their critical formulations of a specifically eighteenth-century idea of the popular, combined with Stuart Hall's influential 1981 article 'Notes on Deconstructing "the Popular"' and work that followed it, including Tony Bennett's on the politics of popular culture and that of Lana Rakow and Joanne Hollows on feminism and popular culture. These scholars and others argue for popular culture as 'simply part of the process by which texts are classified and as a result, no text or practice is inherently popular or elite in character, but may well move between the two as historical conditions change' (Hollows 27). In Hollows's articulation, popular culture is not a static construct, but rather a site 'where conflicts between dominant and subordinate groups are played out, and distinctions between the cultures of these groups are continually constructed and reconstructed' (27). This approach recognizes the power relations inherent in popular culture, but declines to identify culture as elite or popular, high or low, based merely on the social or economic standing of those who create it. As Peter Bailey describes it in terms of nineteenth-century England, popular culture is a 'hybrid, a generically eclectic ensemble or repertoire of texts, sites and practices that constitute a widely shared social and symbolic resource ... Its materials are put to specific and selective use by its consumers, who variously embrace, modify or resist its meanings under the particular conditions and relationships of its reception' (10–11).

In terms of a process of historicization, this understanding of popular culture can then be further illuminated by the recognition that prior to the twentieth century, the feminine is inherently associated with the popular. It seems essential to analyse the cultural and literary implications of the ways in which high or elite culture in the eighteenth century defaults to the male, from the explicitly masculine identity of the artist, to the masculinized genre of the early novel (as opposed to the location of the products of female writers in the gendered generic ghetto of amatory fiction).[3] Fiction by women writers such as Eliza Haywood and Mary Davys, for example, provides a sense of the equation of the devalued feminine and the disregarded popular, as well as insight into the ways in which women's culture crosses back and forth across the masculine divisions of popular and elite. Davys appears to have been low born, but was the widow of a respected Anglican clergyman when she published her novels about aristocratic life during the time that she ran a coffeehouse catering to young gentlemen at Cambridge. Haywood's circumstances are similarly complex, another woman of unimportant rank, with a mixed circle of acquaintance, writing of the travails of the gentry. Even given the relatively low literacy rates of the day, Davys's and Haywood's novels were widely consumed, though the fact that readers were primarily assumed to be women left these works outside of the scholarly discussion of even the (only marginally) higher-culture genre of novel until the late twentieth century. Samuel Richardson and

Henry Fielding would struggle mightily to establish perceived distinctions between their valuable work in the newly constructed genre of the novel and the mere amatory fiction that had long been written by women and read by so many.

Despite half a century of long pieces of prose fiction published by women, Fielding famously asserts of *Joseph Andrews* that his is a 'kind of Writing, which I do not remember to have seen hitherto attempted in our language' (3), and typifies women writers as 'those Persons of surprising Genius, the Authors of immense Romances, or the modern Novel and *Atalantis* writers; who, without any Assistance from Nature or History, record Persons who never were, or will be, and Facts which never did nor possibly can happen: Whose Heroes are of their own Creation, and their Brains the Chaos whence all their Materials are collected' (163). In his implication that women's writing is the product of mere fancy, entirely removed from the masculinized realms of nature and history, Fielding articulates a standard understanding of his day in the links between the feminine and the popular in fiction, even as he undermines it through his own literary product. Women writers, their audiences, and their inherently feminine product are in this construction all frivolous, all products of fashion. The feminine and the popular are both constituted by performance and consumption.

Andreas Huyssen theorizes this link in the context of early twentieth-century modernism as he argues for the political and ideological implications of the standardization of 'connotations of mass culture as essentially feminine' (192) in opposition to a 'male mystique in modernism' (194). He documents the extent to which hierarchical cultural divisions were cast in gendered terms, with mass culture 'somehow associated with woman while real, authentic culture remains the prerogative of men' (191). And while Huyssen's article concludes with postmodernism as possible panacea for 'the persistent gendering as feminine of that which is devalued' (196), R.L. Rutsky asserts absolute continuity of the gesture if not the form: at the end of the twentieth century, 'while contemporary theory may not explicitly characterize popular culture as feminine, it still tends to denigrate it in terms traditionally associated with women – the rhetoric of trivial, superficial (and therefore deceptive) pleasures, of conformity and commodification, of a dangerous fluidity that threatens to co-opt, absorb, adulterate or infect' more rigorous intellectual and social domains (8). Such critical contests over the twentieth-century devaluatory gendering of popular culture illuminate the historical circumstance. Where high culture defaults to male – as it does in eighteenth-century England – what is considered 'women's culture' is often intrinsically connected to the popular, with each used circularly to affirm the lesser value and cultural contribution of the other. When women read amatory fiction or consume fashionable commodities, they demonstrate their shallowness of mind; the fact that these commodities are consumed primarily by women similarly affirms the lack of importance as cultural and artistic products.

Alexander Pope's 1714 mock-epic poem *The Rape of the Lock*, for example, depends upon exactly these assumptions, wondering, as it does, 'What mighty Contests rise from trivial Things' (I 2). Although her historical original, Arabella Fermor, was Roman Catholic and thus in a relatively liminal position in the marriage market even with her family's wealth, Pope's Belinda is undoubtedly of the economic and social elite; still, the poem depicts the feminine as intrinsically frivolous, and its mapping of Belinda's social trial onto Homer's *Iliad*, Virgil's *Aeneid*, and Milton's *Paradise Lost* asserts that there is no claim to high culture even among women of privilege. Christina Knellwolf has argued that Pope's much-debated attitude toward women is important not just in itself, but in the way it illuminates what women represented in eighteenth-century England. In *The Rape of the Lock*, she suggests, 'Pope's objective is to render an image of existence that is void of meaningful life' and 'all those elements which are offensive to Pope's understanding of woman may appear like horrid perversions and parodies of that which is good and meaningful.'[4] Though I am not entirely persuaded by Knellwolf's subsequent argument that 'the abundance of half-real, half-living figures that surround Belinda challenge the notion of emptiness' (195), the suggestion that Belinda stands in for cultural emptiness is useful here.

As has been well documented over several decades, *The Rape of the Lock* both critiques epic convention by feminizing it, and mocks femininity by rendering it ridiculous through the machinery of epic convention: Helen's kidnapping becomes the theft of a lock of hair; Aeneas's journey to the Tiber is rewritten as Belinda's jaunt up the Thames; the gods become glittering sylphs and grumbling gnomes; and the arming of the hero is rendered as the toilette of a spoiled girl, right down to the description of her petticoats in the same terms as Homer's description of Achilles's shield. Belinda's primary interaction with the larger, more important world is at her toilette, as Arabia and India appear commodified as perfume, jewellery, and combs, diminished markers of the way in which association with the feminine creates even the colonial empire as mere frippery. Though Emrys Jones is not thinking of popular culture in the same way that I do (he contrasts exaggerated politeness and rationalism with the squalid and the indecent as marked features of 'the high and low in life as in literature'), he is exactly right in noting that the poem 'is full of the small objects and appurtenances of the feminine world which arouse Pope's aesthetic interest: such things as "white curtains," combs, puffs, fans, and so on ... The man of good sense might laugh at it, but he could not destroy it; and to some extent he had to recognize an alternative system of values' (16–17). The invocation of the material culture of the popular is a prominent device of Pope's mock epic – fans and puffs are insubstantial devices of the air, and they indicate the insubstantial nature of alternative cultural systems like the feminine and the popular.[5] Pope does not deny the pleasures of the pretty and the trivial, but his accounting of Belinda's world asserts emphatically that no matter what her status, Belinda is merely a woman, and that everything that she touches is rendered trivial by association.

Pope's own Dedication asserts this strategy specifically when he explains that 'the ancient Poets are in one respect like many modern Ladies; Let an action be never so trivial in it self, they always make it appear of the utmost Importance.' The assumption that women are fundamentally uninterested in the true art and learning of high culture is repeated several times in six short paragraphs: 'I know how disagreeable it is to make use of hard Words before a Lady ... The *Rosicrucians* are a people I must bring You acquainted with. The best Account I know of them is in a French Book call'd *Le Comte de Galalis*, which both in its Title and Size is so like a *Novel*, that many of the Fair Sex have read it for one by Mistake.' Before the poem proper even begins, then, Pope's equation of the feminine, the popular, and the facile is explicitly asserted.

No matter how heroic Belinda's actions might be (and, indeed, are, as she battles in drawing room games and then physical combat to collect and defend the markers of status achieved through her flirtatious sexual inaccessibility), she can never matter as anything more than a pretty object of petty gossip, a fact emphasized by the piling up of epic conventions, similes, and speeches that affirm the fundamental ridiculousness of a woman as participant in great literature, even as its object, let alone as its consumer or critic. Pope's characterization of the feminine as an embodiment of the insignificant is not in itself a trivial thing, since, as Stuart Hall argues, cultural industries 'have the power constantly to rework and reshape what they represent; and, by repetition and selection, to impose and implant such definitions of ourselves as fit more easily the descriptions of the dominant or preferred culture' (513). Pope's depiction of femininity contributes to a naturalized cultural understanding of the feminine as a pale imitation of the true elite of the masculine realm: the soldiers she commands are merely cards, and her grandfather's seal ring dwindles over generations to a lady's buckle, a baby's whistle, and finally a hairpin – the material culture of political masculinity is refashioned until it is a merely decorative imitation (V 89–96), confirming the natural progression of infantilization and trivialization of femininity that encourages the outraged Arabella Fermor to reimagine herself only within her culture's preferred descriptions of femininity.

Amid the myriad possible examples of the exclusion of the feminine from high culture, the series of speeches in Canto IV shows this work concisely. The Baron's speech after Sir Plume sputters his demand for the return of the lock begins with 'by this Lock, this sacred Lock I swear' (IV 133). The passage goes on to allude in a general way to Achilles's oath in the *Iliad* (I 233–44), but the reference to the 'sacred lock' makes clear the explicit comparison between Achilles and Belinda, and its implications. In Pope's own translation of the *Iliad*, the phrase 'sacred lock' is used to describe Achilles's cutting of his hair as a gesture of respect at the funeral of Patroclus (XXIII 189). The similarities are inverted, however: Achilles's self-inflicted act conveys devotion, honour, and heroism in the face of tragedy, while Belinda's victimization conveys its opposite: 'Honour ... Ease, Pleasure, Virtue, All ... resign[ed]' (IV 106). Instead of marking the eternal and unbreakable power of masculine friendship and honour, the Baron's cutting of Belinda's hair conveys the ephemeral nature of female identity – defined by appearance and vulnerable to erasure with the removal of the markers of the social value (and economic value on the marriage market) granted by beauty.

Belinda's speech in response similarly locates her as a parody of that with true value, modelled as it is after Achilles's lament for Patroclus: 'Curs'd be that Day when all the Pow'rs above / Thy Charms submitted to a mortal Love' (XVIII 107–8). Achilles wishes that he had never been conceived, that he might never have suffered such loss and been forced to create 'new woes, new sorrows.' Belinda cries, 'For ever curs'd be this detested Day, / Which snatch'd my best, my fav'rite Curl away!' (IV 147–8). In *The Rape of the Lock* Pope's heroine knows so little of the world and is so self-absorbed that she cannot imagine corporeal non-existence, but only the absence of admiration, clearly to her equivalent to the absence of existence:

> Oh had I rather un-admir'd remain'd
> In some lone Isle, or distant *Northern* Land;
> Where the gilt *Chariot* never marks the Way,
> Where none learn *Ombre,* none e'er taste *Bohea*!
> There kept my Charms conceal'd from mortal Eye,
> Like Roses that in Desarts bloom and die.   (IV 153–8)

Her omens are marked by clumsiness with her patch-box, rattling china, and a grumpy dog before she remembers dreaming of a Sylph. Achilles's world-changing anger becomes Belinda's bathetic fit of spleen. To be fair, Pope allows that these events are terribly important to Belinda and her future; the point is that what is important to women (even privileged women) – unlike even the private affections of men in the *Iliad* – is not actually important to anyone who matters, and has no meaning to the larger, real world.

Even such brief examples are highly suggestive: Huyssen and Rutsky's critiques of the systemic gendering of modernist art prove also to be accurate descriptors of eighteenth-century constructions of hierarchies of culture. If high culture is implicitly masculine in eighteenth-century England, then it would seem to oppose naturally both low culture and women's culture. Constructs of femininity exist across a much wider circle than just the economically and socially privileged (and indeed they exist diachronically when the eighteenth-century woman is reimagined from these sources in ways that illuminate twenty-first-century constructs of the feminine). Women from across a wide range of social standings participate in culturally trivialized popular practices in a way that allows them to engage the processes of production of femininity that were used to define them. As readers, creators, consumers, and audience members, these women contribute in a less public way than perhaps do actresses, women writers, or the women involved in politics, but the continuum of female practice, combined with the consistency of its perception and reception by male elites, prevents us from differentiating between elite and popular in women's culture, as is so clearly possible in the high and low masculine cultures of eighteenth-century England.

Eighteenth-Century Women in Modern Popular Culture

The associations among the feminine, the frivolous, and the popular are thus clear in the historically specific contexts of eighteenth-century England. Perhaps surprisingly, they are in many ways equally clear in modern popular culture, and eighteenth-century women, women writers, and feminized popular culture continue to be used as conduits for such ideological conflations, creating a continuity of historical records of popular culture as formative parts of gendered identity. The naturalization of the links among the feminine and the popular turns out to be an ongoing practice, and women's popular culture of the eighteenth century continues to be put to use in popular media as a frequent touchstone for nostalgic modern iterations of femininity, of class, and of public performance of identity. More so than many other periods, the eighteenth century continues to be rewritten in ways that attempt to use the era and its women as vehicles to convey specific ideologies of modern culture, but because of the presumptively elite nature of Literature in its historical incarnations, eighteenth-century women writers and characters must be culturally relocated to serve the demands of the popular. Given that popular texts can be argued to embody a struggle for meanings, and that they 'can ensure their popularity only by making themselves inviting terrains for this struggle' (Fiske 5), this relocation is frequently merely a matter of medium, as the shift from Literature to film or television renders the elite accessible without the labour of its reading. But in other cases, the high literary form of the long eighteenth-century novel can be brought into the popular through more surprising means and to surprisingly subtle ends.

John Fiske has argued that popular culture refuses to produce

> the deep, complexly crafted texts that narrow down their audiences and social meanings; it is tasteless and vulgar, for taste is social control and class interest masquerading as a naturally finer sensibility ... [its aim is] to produce meanings that are relevant to everyday life. Relevance is central to popular culture, for it minimizes the difference between text and life, between the aesthetic and the everyday that is so central to a process- and practice-based culture (such as the popular) rather than a text- or performance-based one (such as the bourgeois, highbrow one) ... the popular text, therefore, has to work against its difference to find a commonality between divergent social groups in order to maximize its consumption and profitability. (6)

As an example of the significance of the transliteration of the elite art of the eighteenth-century page into the vulgar text that finds commonality to maximize consumption, I shall consider the recent cross-period 'collaboration' *Pride and Prejudice and Zombies,* 'by Jane Austen and Seth Grahame-Smith.' No genre more safely fits into the most trivial category of popular culture than zombie narratives, as the book itself points out with its title page promise, 'The classic Regency romance – now with ultraviolent zombie mayhem.' And yet, intentionally or not,[6] Grahame-Smith's adaptation offers important insights into the cultural tensions raised by the modern reader's experience of reading Austen's women, the practice-based culture consuming the performance-based one.[7]

Given that Austen's novel revolves from its first sentence around the problem of marriage, it makes sense that Grahame-Smith's version both accepts and problematizes the original's foundational assumption that for a young woman in the eighteenth century, a good marriage is a matter approaching the significance of life and death. Zombies provide a literalization of the threat of a social death in spinsterhood, rewritten as a genuinely life-threatening danger, in opposition to the socially constructed life-and-death quality of the marriage plot. The device emphasizes the concurrent triviality and deep importance of the marriage plot for Austen's characters. As the adaptation explains of Mrs Bennet,

> when she was nervous – as she was nearly all the time since the first outbreak of the strange plague in her youth – she sought solace in the comfort of the traditions which now seemed mere trifles to others.
>
> The business of Mr Bennet's life was to keep his daughters alive. The business of Mrs Bennet's was to get them married. (8–9)

Like the majority of women in the historical eighteenth century, the women of Austen's novel are closely bound by conventions of conduct: what can be done and said and what cannot. Jane very nearly pays the price of spinsterhood for the combination of her observance of the rules of silence and her mother's appalling violations of them; Lydia's failures to observe the rules make her ridiculous for much of the story, and then nearly ruin her sisters' chances at respectable marriages; and Elizabeth is marked as the heroine because she manages to find the golden mean of appropriate self-determination and self-representation that is appreciated by both Mr Bennet and Mr Darcy.

Grahame-Smith's update recognizes the alien quality of this heavy social coding for modern readers, and makes concrete Austen's concern

with the social implications of the requirements of silence by establishing that the socially correct term for zombies in Hertfordshire is
'unmentionables.' This language allows them to stand in for several
of the unspoken ideas that are so important in *Pride and Prejudice*, but
particularly the unspoken rules of gendered conduct in courtship and
the realities of property marriage. In Austen's narrative, each of the
marriage plots (of Jane, Elizabeth, Lydia, and Charlotte) is to some
degree determined by the unmentionable: that which is so universally
acknowledged that to speak of it would be vulgar. Both of the two central couples, Elizabeth and Darcy and Jane and Bingley, must battle the
unmentionables of money and class (which is why the horror of the
original text is located in Mrs Bennet's acknowledgment of her ambi-
tion). In *Zombies*, Elizabeth and Darcy overcome the literal 'unmentionables' as they form their alliance through bloody physical battle rather
than pensive drawing room silences. The Grahame-Smith version
includes Darcy's slighting of Elizabeth in the first ball scene exactly as
it appears in Austen, for example, with verbatim repetition of pages of
Austen's original prose, but the origins of his later affection are not as
mysterious: the Bennet girls battle the unmentionables that attack the
gathering, 'each thrusting a razor-sharp dagger in one hand, the other
hand modestly tucked into the small of her back. From the corner of
the room, Mr Darcy watched Elizabeth ... He knew of only one other
woman in all of Great Britain who wielded a dagger with such skill,
such grace, and deadly accuracy' (14).

Similarly, Austen's Lydia nearly becomes unmentionable (the part of
the family no one talks about) through her elopement with Wickham.
From the start of the situation, Elizabeth begs that Darcy 'conceal the
unhappy truth as long as it is possible' (288); Darcy demands that his
role in the resolution remain secret; and Mr Gardiner wishes 'that the
subject might never be mentioned to him again' (318). Even when the
eventual marriage must by convention be announced, it is barely mentioned (much to Mrs Bennet's dismay) 'without there being a syllable
said of her father, or the place where she lived, or any thing' (339). We
are reminded of the pall of the unmentionable that hangs over Lydia's
happy ending when Mr Collins offers his heartfelt concern that her circumstances 'should be so generally known' (363).

Austen's most heartbreaking depiction of marriage, though, has
always been that endured by Charlotte Lucas, who accepts a marriage
to the obsequious social striver Mr Collins because she knows that she
has a social script to follow, and she dares to imagine for herself 'only

a comfortable home.' To the ears of both Elizabeth and modern readers, Charlotte offers a damning indictment of contemporary models of
marriage when she asserts, 'I am convinced that my chance of happiness with him is as fair as most people can boast on entering the marriage state' (Austen 154–5). Her marriage has only solitary pleasures in
her hours away from her husband, coming from her public standing as
wife rather than any personal affinity. Charlotte's sacrifice to unmentionable social and economic demands is reconsidered in Grahame-
Smith's adaptation, where Charlotte marries Collins because she knows
she has been 'stricken' and will soon become ill herself. With nothing
to lose, Charlotte chooses to combine the metaphorical death-in-life of
an obviously bad marriage with the literal living death of the zombie.
After the wedding – at which Charlotte's speech already 'seemed a trifle
laboured' (110) – she deteriorates slowly, losing first her social graces,
then the power to speak, until she is monstrous in both eighteenth- and
twenty-first-century terms: she violates all decorum (shovelling her
food and squatting in the corner of the room during tea) and finally
begins to decompose corporeally, left as she is to rot in the country with
her boorish husband. Throughout the depiction of Charlotte's marriage, her decline becomes the thing that is quite obvious, but no one
can comment upon. Elizabeth has known all along and has agreed to
help her friend hide her domestic deficiencies as long as possible, and
the reader eventually discovers that Lady Catherine DeBurgh has been
experimenting on Charlotte with a medical serum to slow the progress
of the plague, but everyone else has merely participated in the social
compact of silent appearances that regulates Austen's women.

The ever-status-conscious Mr Collins will not admit that he has married a zombie any more than he would admit any other social impropriety. When Lady Catherine eventually forces him to acknowledge it,
he performs his 'husbandly duty' and kills the zombie Charlotte before
she loses the final vestiges of self-control that prevent her from killing
or infecting others. The revisionist critique of eighteenth-century regu-
lations of feminine conduct is emphasized in this scene, as in Collins's
letter to Mr Bennet, where the account of Charlotte's end is followed
with this sentence:

> Be assured, my dear sir, that despite my own crippling grief, I sincerely
> sympathise with you and all your respectable family, in your present
> distress, which must be of the bitterest kind. The death of your daughter
> would have been a blessing in comparison of this, just as the beheading

and burning of my bride was a fate preferable to seeing her joining the ranks of Lucifer's brigade. You are grievously to be pitied. (237)

The pompous Collins articulates what Austen's contemporaries well knew: for the good of a respectable family, a tragic death is less problematic than a scandal.

At the end of the letter, Collins mentions that his own body is by then to be found hanging from Charlotte's favourite tree: weak and noxious as he is, Collins's character is given a depth in the frivolous adaptation that he never attains in Austen's version. He is a suicide, knowingly sacrificing his own soul so that he will not have to endure either heaven or earth without his wife, and in this he is granted a moment of self-knowledge and the reader a moment of empathy that Austen never permits. Perversely, the zombie revision of eighteenth-century marriage renders Charlotte not just a social functionary as wife, but a beloved and valuable woman.

Equally 'unmentionable' in Austen's novels is the source of certain characters' wealth in the empire. The Bingleys' family money comes from unspecified trade, and the problem of representation of empire and imperialism has been widely discussed in the wake of Edward Said's comments in *Culture and Imperialism:* 'precisely because Austen is so summary in one context, so provocatively rich in the other, precisely because of that imbalance, we are able to move in on the novel, reveal and accentuate the interdependence scarcely mentioned on its brilliant pages' (96). Said argues that Antigua and other colonial destinations in *Mansfield Park* 'stand for a significance "out there" that frames the genuinely important action *here,* but not for a great significance' (93). A great many readers have leapt to Austen's defence,[8] but what matters here is not whether or not Said's reading is correct, but rather the ways in which Grahame-Smith's adaptation once again forces the unmentionable into play in a way that illuminates usage of eighteenth-century women (here, the woman writer) as a popular medium to comment upon modern cultural preoccupations, twisting the presumptive disposability of popular fiction, women's fiction, and zombie stories in a way that articulates the intersections among that which is assumed to be of lesser artistic value in the eighteenth and twenty-first centuries, and merging the canonical and the frivolous in a self-conscious way.

Zombie-narrative convention typically relies upon an apocalyptic event,[9] and here the infestation of unmentionables represents a threat to both individual and community, as they impede travel, social discourse, and the exchange of ideas (even letters cannot travel without a vulnerable human escort). The zombie plague is a threat to England's nationhood, and the primary weapon against this plague is the martial arts, in which Mr Bennet has ensured that his daughters are highly trained (though even this is defined as fashion when enacted by women: in Grahame-Smith's revisioning, the Bennet girls may have saved their community with their Shaolin martial arts, but they have not been trained by the Japanese monks and ninjas whom Lady Catherine uses to mark her own elevated status). Marking power by proficiency in the martial arts relocates Eastern culture to the centre of the narrative, remapping political and ideological concerns through the link to marriage and femininity: it is not the girls' beauty or their good nature that allows them to overcome their lack of fortune, but their training in the philosophical and cultural knowledge of the Orient as they defend the routes and practices of social exchange that constitute the nation.

The novel's last lines bring together these two threads of the unmentionable and make clear that even happy marriages come with a price for women. Lydia is sent away to a life of cheerfully changing the adult diapers of Wickham, whom Darcy has beaten into disability as a condition of their financial agreement;[10] Mary remains with her mother, 'no longer mortified by comparisons between her sisters' beauty and her own'; Kitty returns to Shaolin to further her training; and Elizabeth and Jane are happily married. But marriage forces the sisters away from their duty to public safety, as they dwindle into wives: Jane 'could not bear to be so close to Longbourn as a married woman; for every unmentionable attack made her long for her sword.' The sisters spar to 'keep their skills sharp, though His Majesty no longer required them to do so,' and 'the sisters Bennet – servants of His Majesty, protectors of Hertfordshire, beholders of the secrets of Shaolin, and brides of death – were now, three of them, brides of man, their swords quieted by that only force more powerful than any warrior' (316–17). Whether that force is love or patriarchy is not made entirely clear, but marriage reimposes dominant modes of femininity and maternity, passivity and spectatorship, and the assurance of rightful lines of inheritance and restored order.[11]

Like so much modern popular culture linked to the eighteenth century, Grahame-Smith's text seems egregiously trivial, perhaps even mocking exactly the valuation of eighteenth-century women's popular culture that this essay seeks to assert, not least in *Pride and Prejudice and Zombies'* entirely self-conscious links to the presumed temporariness of its distraction from what the elite determine to have true, permanent

artistic value. Embodiments of the popular convey significant information, whether in their cultural moment or in revisiting that moment
centuries later. Grahame-Smith's rewriting of Austen's novel is doubly
ironic, first as it retrivializes a popular female-authored text that has
attained elite canonical and iconic status in literary history, and second,
as the very gestures that mark its triviality concurrently reassert the
deep cultural significance and powerful critiques enclosed in the spar-
kly dress of the frivolous and fashionable.

NOTES

1 For a concise, highly readable conversation on these challenges, see Briggs,
   Burke, Richards, Smith, and Yeo, 'What Is the History of Popular Culture?'
2 As the work of Terry Castle in particular makes clear, a similar pattern of
   intersection among elite and mass culture (and varying positions on Hall's
   'cultural escalator') can be observed in the cultural phenomenon of the
   masquerade.
3 See Ballaster on amatory fiction. On the practices of novel reading and the
   shifting status of the novel as literature in the early eighteenth century, see
   Warner, Clark, Vincent, and Dennis Hall. On interpreting such elements of
   the popular, see O'Driscoll.
4 Martin Price offers a gentler, but similar summary: 'The world of Belinda is a
   world of triviality measured against the epic scale; it is also a world of grace
   and delicacy, a second-best world, but not at all a contemptible one' (7).
5 On the poem's use of objects and commodities, see Nicholson, Brown, and
   Crehan for very distinct interpretations.
6 In an interview on Q, a radio program on Canada's CBC Radio, Quirk publisher Jason Rekulak named Charlotte Lucas as an example of the press's
   attempt to maintain the original text's elements of social critique.
7 In structure and content, the majority of Pride and Prejudice and Zombies is
   Austen's work. The adaptation retains not just Austen's narrative arcs, but
   her verbatim text for extended periods. The zombies are added as an unfor-
   tunate circumstance – akin to a plague or easily spread infection – that the
   Bennet girls must face as they pursue good marriages.
8 Particularly notable for this chapter is Susan Fraiman, who argues that
   Said's 'typing of Austen is . . . symptomatic of a more general gender politics
   underlying his postcolonial project' (807).
9 On zombie narratives, see Bishop, Paffenroth, Rhodes, and McIntosh and
   Leverette. Recent scholarship has particularly emphasized the use of the

zombie to interrogate ideas of identity, consumerism, gender, and post-colonial understandings of imperialism.

10 Darcy's infliction of Wickham's apparent spinal injury implies not just physical punishment, but also a restoration of rightful lines of inheritance, ensuring that he and Lydia will never have children who might seek any of either the Darcy or Bennett family money. Wickham agrees to 'allow Mr Darcy to render him lame, as punishment for a lifetime of vice and betrayal, and to ensure that he would never lay another hand in anger, nor leave another bastard behind' (260).

11 In the introduction to his arguments on the late nineteenth century, Hall suggests that in the eighteenth century, '"the people" threatened constantly to erupt; and, when they did so, they broke onto the stage of patronage and power with a threatening din and clamour ... and, often, with a striking, popular, ritual discipline. Yet never quite overturning the delicate strands of paternalism, deference and terror within which they were constantly if insecurely constrained' (509).

WORKS CITED

Austen, Jane. *Pride and Prejudice* (1813). Ed. Robert P. Irvine. Peterborough: Broadview, 2002. Print.

Austen, Jane, and Seth Grahame-Smith. *Pride and Prejudice and Zombies.* Philadelphia: Quirk, 2009. Print.

Backscheider, Paula. 'The Paradigms of Popular Culture.' *Eighteenth-Century Novel* 6–7 (2009): 17–59. Print.

Bailey, Peter. *Popular Culture and Performance in the Victorian City.* Cambridge: Cambridge UP, 1998. Print.

Ballaster, Ros. *Seductive Forms: Women's Amatory Fiction from 1684 to 1740.* 2nd ed. Oxford: Clarendon, 1998. Print.

Bennett, Tony. 'The Politics of the "Popular" and Popular Culture.' *Popular Culture and Social Relations.* Ed. Tony Bennett, Colin Mercer, and Janet Woollacott. London: Open UP, 1986. Print.

Bishop, Kyle. *American Zombie Gothic: The Rise and Fall (and Rise) of the Walking Dead in Popular Culture.* Jefferson, NC: McFarland, 2010. Print.

Bourdieu, Pierre. *Distinction: A Social Critique of the Judgement of Taste.* London: Routledge, 1984. Print.

Briggs, Asa, Peter Burke, Jeffrey Richards, Dai Smith, and Stephen Yeo. 'What Is the History of Popular Culture?' *History Today* 35.12 (1985): 39–45. Print.

Brown, Laura. *Alexander Pope.* Oxford: Blackwell, 1985. Print.

Burke, Peter. *Popular Culture in Early Modern Europe.* 3rd ed. Aldershot: Ashgate, 2009. Print.

Castle, Terry. *Masquerade and Civilization: The Carnivalesque in Eighteenth-Century English Culture and Fiction.* Stanford: Stanford UP, 1986. Print.

Clark, Anna. 'The Politics of Seduction in English Popular Culture, 1748–1848.' *Progress of Romance: The Politics of Popular Fiction.* Ed. Jean Radford. London: Routledge, 1986. 47–72. Print.

Crehan, Stewart. '*The Rape of the Lock* and the Economy of "Trivial Things."' *Eighteenth-Century Studies* 31 (1997): 45–68. Print.

Fielding, Henry. *Joseph Andrews, with Shamela and Related Writings.* Ed. Homer Goldberg. New York: Norton, 1987. Print.

Fiske, John. *Understanding Popular Culture.* New York: Routledge, 1989. Print.

Fraiman, Susan. 'Jane Austen and Edward Said: Gender, Culture, and Imperialism.' *Critical Inquiry* 21.4 (1995): 805–21. Print.

Hall, Dennis R. 'Signs of Life in the Eighteenth Century: Dr. Johnson and the Invention of Popular Culture.' *Kentucky Philological Review* 19 (2005): 12–16. Print.

Hall, Stuart. 'Notes on Deconstructing "the Popular."' *Cultural Theory and Popular Culture.* 4th ed. Ed. John Storey. New York: Pearson Longman, 2009. 508–18. Print.

Hollows, Joanne. *Feminism, Femininity, and Popular Culture.* Manchester and New York: Manchester UP, 2000. Print.

Huyssen, Andreas. 'Mass Culture as Woman: Modernism's Other.' *Studies in Entertainment: Critical Approaches to Mass Culture.* Ed. Tania Modleski. Bloomington: Indiana UP, 1986. 188–207. Print.

Jones, Emrys. 'The Appeal of the Mock-Heroic: Pope and Dulness.' *Alexander Pope's 'The Rape of the Lock.'* Ed. Harold Bloom. New York: Chelsea House, 1988. 13–18. Print.

Knellwolf, Christina. *A Contradiction Still: Representations of Women in the Poetry of Alexander Pope.* Manchester: Manchester UP, 1998. Print.

McIntosh, Shawn, and Marc Leverette, eds. *Zombie Culture: Autopsies of the Living Dead.* Lanham, MD: Scarecrow, 2008. Print.

Nicholson, Colin. 'A World of Artefacts: *The Rape of the Lock* as Social History.' *Literature and History* 5 (1979): 183–93. Print.

O'Driscoll, Sally. 'Reading through Desire: Interpretive Practices for Eighteenth-Century Popular Culture.' *British Journal for Eighteenth-Century Studies* 29 (2006): 237–51. Print.

Paffenroth, Kim. *Gospel of the Living Dead: George Romero's Visions of Hell on Earth*. Waco: Baylor UP, 2006. Print.

Parker, Holt N. 'Toward a Definition of Popular Culture.' *History and Theory* 50.2 (2011): 147–70. *Academic Search Complete*. Web. 10 January 2012.

Paulson, Ronald. *Popular and Polite Art in the Age of Hogarth and Fielding*. Notre Dame: U of Notre Dame P, 1979. Print.

Plumb, J.H. *Georgian Delights*. London: Wiedenfeld & Nicolson, 1980. Print.

Pope, Alexander. 'The Rape of the Lock' (1714). Ed. John Tilotson. *The Poems of Alexander Pope*. Ed. John Butt. 11 vols. London: Routledge, 1993. Print.

– 'The Iliad of Homer.' Ed. Maynard Mack. *The Poems of Alexander Pope*. Ed. John Butt. 11 vols. London: Routledge, 1993. Print.

Price, Martin. 'Patterns of Civility: Art and Morality.' *Alexander Pope's 'The Rape of the Lock.'* Ed. Harold Bloom. New York: Chelsea House, 1988. 7–12. Print.

Rakow, Lana F. 'Feminist Approaches to Popular Culture: Giving Patriarchy Its Due.' *Journal of Communication Inquiry* 9 (1986): 19–41. *Sage Premier*. Web. 15 November 2011.

Reay, Barry, ed. *Popular Culture in Seventeenth-Century England*. London: Croom Helm, 1985. Print.

– *Popular Cultures in England 1550–1750*. New York: Longman, 1998. Print.

Rekulak, Jason. Interview. *Q*. CBC Radio. 24 June 2010. Radio. http://www.cbc .ca/q/episodes/.

Rhodes, Gary D. *White Zombie: Anatomy of a Horror Film*. Jefferson, NC: McFarland, 2001. Print.

Rutsky, R.L. 'Popular/Theory.' *Strategies: A Journal of Theory, Culture and Politics* 12.1 (1999): 7–11. Print.

Said, Edward. *Culture and Imperialism*. New York: Vintage, 1994. Print.

Vincent, David. *Literacy and Popular Culture: England 1750–1914*. Cambridge: Cambridge UP, 1993. Print.

Wanko, Cheryl. *Roles of Authority: Thespian Biography and Celebrity in Eighteenth-Century Britain*. Lubbock: Texas Tech UP, 2003. Print.

Warner, William. *Licensing Entertainment: The Elevation of Novel Reading in Britain*. Berkeley: U of California P, 1998. Print.

Wollenberg, Susan, and Simon McVeigh. *Concert Life in Eighteenth-Century Britain*. Aldershot: Ashgate, 2004. Print.

2 'The Assemblage of every female Folly': Lavinia Fenton, Kitty Clive, and the Genesis of Ballad Opera

BERTA JONCUS

Ballad opera is one of the great secrets of British eighteenth-century popular culture. Dismissed by modern scholars until recently, in its day the genre was hugely influential. During the period of its efflorescence (1728–37), ballad opera revolutionized musical taste, built up a corpus of roughly 160 works, generated some 3,000 musical numbers, produced singing 'stars' in a recognizably modern sense, and reached a breadth of dissemination previously unknown for London theatrical productions.[1] In stage action and song, ballad opera also stereotyped, derided and censured women, and often appealed for them to be disciplined, violently if necessary. Ironically, this negative focus on women became the platform on which two sopranos, Lavinia Fenton and Kitty Clive, rose to stardom. By manipulating their performances of femininity, these two singers both shaped and popularized the works they performed. This chapter investigates the genesis of ballad opera in light of Fenton's and Clive's contributions. Their agency in their own star production, and in ballad opera generally, depended on singing techniques and methods of stage representation that allowed their own interpretations to overwrite the playbook. Fenton retired after one season of stardom, and Clive, initially marketed as the new Fenton, eventually cultivated a public persona much at odds with Fenton's. Rather than playing on sympathy – particularly male sympathy – as Fenton had, Clive impressed audiences with a vocal vigour and tart address around which ballad operas at Drury Lane, particularly those by Henry Fielding, soon came to be designed.

Each of these very different legacies imprinted itself on the content and development of ballad opera. Through Fenton, John Gay's satirical *Beggar's Opera* became a sentimental vehicle; subsequent ballad operas – starting with *The Cobler's Opera* (1729) designed around Fenton – retained this stamp. Through Clive, ballad opera later became famed for its intemperate attacks on foreigners, fops, and the faint-hearted; it encapsulated popular prejudice in the cutting remark. Whereas Gay had conceived *The Beggar's Opera* partly as a caustic commentary on Italian opera, ballad opera quickly became a valued and voluble mouthpiece of Britishness. Both Fenton and Clive con-tributed to this transformation through their 'natural' manner of sing-ing, and through print publicity that advertised their embodiment of national values. That the genre's two central works, *The Beggar's Opera* and *The Devil to Pay*, were each transformed through their principal player attests to the power of the star to guide theatrical productions as well as practices.

This study highlights how stars could exercise greater power in a genre appealing explicitly to low- as well as high-style taste. Ballad opera's 'common' airs, its half-price afterpiece tickets, and its constant presence at fair booths and fringe theatres all situated it firmly in popu-lar culture. Yet ballad opera was full of sophisticated allusion – to Italian opera, pastoral tropes, current politics, and court scandal – a command of which was requisite for full appreciation. Through an interest in celebrities that cut across social boundaries, star production was both promoted by and helped to promote ballad opera's fusion of low- with high-style taste.

Lavinia Fenton and the Invention of Ballad Opera

In writing *The Beggar's Opera,* John Gay self-consciously created a new genre, rattling normative cages by mischievously combining antitheti-cal theatrical forms.[2] The result was the most profitable and popular theatrical work that had ever been mounted, which made the fortune of Lincoln's Inn Fields's manager John Rich and an overnight star of Fenton. While the privileged worried that the interests of the lower orders had commandeered the Taste of the Town, the aristocracy flocked to the theatre no less than the audience of the pit and the gallery, whose 'depraved' taste was the alleged engine behind Gay's 'triumph.'[3] *The Beggar's Opera* was disseminated in the form of playbooks and printed music; it spawned epilogues, printed commentary, poetry, pam-phlets, and ballads; product tie-ins included playing cards, fans, and fire screens. No theatrical production had ever resonated in the public sphere to this degree.[4]

What was the secret of Gay's success? Eighteenth-century theatre personnel sought the formula for years. With hindsight, five answers suggest themselves. First was the ingenuity of Gay's satirical allusions, which mocked the powerful and the famous – among them Prime Minister Robert Walpole and the *prime donne* Faustina and Cuzzoni – by deploying referents familiar to a broad range of spectators. Second was the populist source of the story in the careers of the highwayman Jack Sheppard and the fence Jonathan Wild. Sheppard's exploits had provoked a flood of print material, and his execution in 1724 attracted record-breaking crowds;[5] in writing *The Beggar's Opera,* Gay was drawing on one unprecedented event in mass spectatorship to create another. Third was the familiarity of the music that he used for his airs. The work's roughly sixty melodies were 'common tunes,' traditional and theatrical alike, both embedded in domestic musicking based on oral and print transmission (Böker 33–102). Fourth, *The Beggar's Opera* commented, particularly in its airs, on the enduringly popular topic of how women are, and how they should be.[6] Fifth was public obsession with the seventeen-year-old Fenton, which may have been the most important factor of all.[7] Fenton bewitched audiences, not least the duke of Bolton, who, after watching her onstage multiple times – William Hogarth famously painted the duke's besotted gaze – made her his mistress, and eventually his wife. Gay was to question 'whether her fame does not surpass that of the Opera itself' (Burgess 72–3).

During ballad opera's first season, Fenton was the focus and principal mediator of its practices. Despite her youth, both her method of singing and her characterization of Polly were formative for the genre. Her untrained ('unaffected') voice and simple, comprehensible delivery were held to instantiate the putative British characteristics of rationality and lack of artifice. The press lionized Fenton's voice and singing methods, claiming her superiority over Italian *prime donne* Faustina and Cuzzoni, whose ardent supporters among the nobility were routinely ridiculed by critics for their folly. Through their vocal pyrotechnics, the *prime donne* were held to envoice luxury, corruption, and licentiousness; their supporters' scandalous 1727 riots in the presence of royalty seemed to many proof of an insidious ability to overpower spectators' common sense and decorum (Aspden).[8] Commodified for the first time in London's theatrical history, natural singing was held to make Fenton the winner in a competition between foreign and British values. Gay likely anticipated such critical reaction: the very deployment of low-style music and dramatis personae in his 'Opera' satirized, through

inversion, the conceits of Italian opera. Yet *The Beggar's Opera* unexpectedly created a middle ground between popular and elite culture; with
it, Italian opera was perhaps not so much repudiated as supplemented
by a British product whose practices were held to consolidate native
values. Fenton's interpretation of Polly itself undid much of Gay's subversive intent. To create the role of Polly, Gay drew on the practice of
farce in which a stereotype teaches audiences what conduct to avoid.
Gay's Polly was a 'Fine Lady,' who, in striving to adopt the ways of her
superiors makes these manners appear ridiculous. This was a common
character type of the period, made unusually affecting by Gay's brilliant stroke of combining it with the type of the sincere heroine who
marries only for love. Polly's mother scolds her for assuming the ways
of gentlewomen, such as wearing lace, coveting trinkets, and pretending to love, and advises her to extract what she can from her husband
Macheath while he is still alive. Polly shares her mother's cynicism,
explaining how she 'knows as well as any of the fine Ladies how to
make the most of [her] self and [her] Man too' (Fuller 11, 17).

Despite such dialogue, Fenton contrived to represent Polly as 'a natural, innocent Girl, forming Sentiment from her own heart,'[9] foregrounding those moments when the playbook allows Polly to embody the
tender maid. According to an anecdote passed down by James Boswell,
her performance of air twelve, 'O Ponder well,' transformed an initially
dubious first-night audience into enthusiasts, 'much affected by the
innocent looks of Polly.'[10] Fenton's interpretation became the bench-
mark against which Clive, who eschewed tenderness for feistiness,
would have to battle eight years later (Joncus, 'In Wit').

Much of the material published around that first run of *The Beggar's
Opera* related to Fenton. It served competing narratives: was Fenton
common, promiscuous, and scheming, or was she loyal, sincere, and
a fair model of her sex? A fake 'memoir' argued strongly for the latter interpretation, asserting that in bailing out her first lover, she had
proved herself 'the most humble, the most affable, and the least con-
ceited of any Woman' (*Life of Lavinia* 43). Among Fenton's disparagers
was Nicholas Amhurst, who, writing under the pseudonym of Caleb
D'Anvers, attacked the Walpole government by analogy with scurri-
lous readings of Fenton's putative on- and offstage behaviour.[11]

A key weapon in the armory of Fenton's publicists was her mezzotint portrait (see figure 2.1). Gay and others commented on its ubiquitous display around London, presumably at booksellers, coffee houses,
and music and print shops (Joncus, 'Clad' 92).[12] As was standard in

mezzotints, an epigram was printed under the likeness to guide the viewer's reading of the image. Fenton's epigram mapped onto her the merits of British airs. Both her ballads and her manner of singing them were interpreted to signify her innocent, home-grown allure:

> While crowds attentive sit to Polly's voice,
> And in their native Harmony rejoyce;
> Th'adversary Throng no vain subscription draws,
> Nor Affectation promts [sic] a false Applause.
> Nature untaught and Pleasing Strains supply's,
> Artless as her unbidden Blushes rise,
> And Charming as the Mischief in her Eyes.

Although Fenton here is held to embody the feminine positively – with charm, euphony, and 'artless' manner – the epigram also invites the male viewer's ardour. Invoking pastoral clichés, it yokes Fenton's innocence to an erotic adventurism unfettered by social constraints, thereby synthesizing and capitalizing on warring rumours about her character.

The epigram also pits the sincerity of 'native Harmony' against the 'Affectation' and 'false Applause' of Italian opera. That Fenton stood for the ascension of British over Italian song was also clear from George Bickham's 1728 engraving *A Stage Medley* (see figure 2.2), which decried this development. In this assemblage of printed images linked to the *Beggar's Opera*, Fenton's mezzotint portrait is positioned above an illustration of the rivals Faustina and Cuzzoni (see figure 2.3) in which each *prima donna* appeals to Apollo to crown her victor in a singing contest. Ballad verses attached to the illustration ridicule the public preference for 'Country Fair' over Italian opera, projecting this as a Folly of the Town (see verses, figure 2.3). Elsewhere, an imagined letter troped this notion: 'the Rival Queens [Faustina and Cuzzoni] in interest now combined' beg Fenton not to 'scream Us from this happy Isle' (*Letters in Prose* 13). Another soprano, Mrs Seedo, organized for her own benefit 'a BRITISH CONCERT, consisting of English, Scotch, and Irish Ballads,' led by Fenton. This was 'the first Performance of this Kind' (*Daily Journal* 25 March); that is, the first London stage concert devoted exclusively to native ballads. Fenton was the only player for this benefit whose name was given entirely in upper case in its advertisement.

Theatre managers continued to champion British ballads, not least because doing so capitalized on popular resentment toward the social privilege that Italian opera symbolized. Fenton was key to this

Figure 2.1. John Chaloner Smith. *Miss Fenton* (1728). Reprinted courtesy of the British Museum (AN136825001). © Trustees of the British Museum

Figure 2.2. George Bickham. *The Stage Medley Representing the Polite Taste of the Town and the Matchless Merits of Poet Gay Polly Peachum and Capt. Macheath* (1728). Satires Stephens Series, British Museum: London 1806. Reprinted courtesy of the British Museum (AN354915001). © Trustees of the British Museum

Figure 2.3. Detail of *The Stage Medley Representing the Polite Taste of the Town and the Matchless Merits of Poet Gay Polly Peachum and Capt. Macheath*

enterprise. Her voice, like that of the modern popular singer, was held to reveal her true nature because unmediated by professional training. This tenet is central to the draw of the pop star: fans believe that the 'grain' of the voice grants an insight into the singer's personality which the varnish of technique would only smoothen.[13] Fenton's mezzotint itself made this point, mapping personal artlessness onto vocal.

Keying off Fenton's publicity, the second ballad opera to be mounted, *The Cobler's Opera*, staged the 'loyal' Fenton who envoiced her qualities through British song. The ballad opera's title was inadvertently apropos: the production cobbled together ideas from *The Beggar's Opera* relating to Polly. Her sentiments in the celebrated air twelve of *The Beggar's Opera* ('O Ponder well') were dramatized in a climax in which Fenton ('Jenny') declares that she is unwilling to live without her lover. *The Cobler's Opera* recycled other formulae from *The Beggar's Opera*: an ugly rival's jealous pursuit of Fenton's lover; the rival's threat to poison Fenton; and a message from the king that saves the situation. Musically, this second ballad opera was of a piece with the first. Traditional ballads commingled with theatre and dance music, culminating in a finale whose density of airs increased as the action heated up. As with *The Beggar's Opera*, theatre- and dance-derived airs far outweighed the number of traditional ballads (Joncus and Rogers, 'Beyond').

The scarcity of traditional ballads in ballad opera highlights an important aspect of its production. What put the 'ballad' into ballad opera was not a specific repertory but rather a set of practices: straight tone and chest resonance, the direct exhortation to listen with which a street ballad singer – a hawker of news and moral instruction – accosted passers-by, and the recycling of a melody whose earlier verses would be known to audiences. This last practice was what gave Gay's airs their satirical bite: anticipating the listener's recollection of earlier settings, his verses twisted them into new, barbed readings. When, for instance, in air six of *The Beggar's Opera* ('Virgins are like fair Flowers') Gay has Polly tell the audience that a women's exchange value in the marriage market plummets once she is deflowered, he set it to music by Henry Purcell which, in *The Prophetess* (revived 1724), accompanied a villain's praise of the purity of the heroine for whom he lusts. By choosing this particular tune, which had circulated widely in Thomas D'Urfey's *Pills to Purge Melancholy*, Gay highlighted the hypocrisy of men who praise the virtue they seek to ruin. The impact of such musical double entendres was heightened by vocalists interrupting the dramatic action to address their audience directly, as did street ballad singers. In air six,

Polly instructs listeners how virgins 'once pluck'd' are left to 'rot, stink and die' in the brothels of Covent Garden. That Fenton could sing such advice airs while remaining credible within the persona of a sentimental heroine suggests something of the flexibility and diversity of ballad opera as a system of signification.

In the reception of *The Beggar's Opera*, Fenton's vocal technique and public image became a locus classicus for native taste and simplicity. Fenton performed femininity with such success that it caused her own removal from the theatre. Once the duke of Bolton made her his mistress he insisted that she retire at the end of her triumphant 1728 season, which deprived the London stage of its most celebrated English singer.

The Fashionable Lady: Ballad Opera and Female Foibles

From 1728 London theatres embraced ballad opera: low-cost and low-tech, it was attractive to the managers of patent and fringe theatres alike, and by the summer of 1731 fifty-two new works had been mounted. Standard procedures crystallized, becoming the butt of James Ralph's satire in his ballad opera *The Fashionable Lady* (1730).

The American-born Ralph, who later collaborated with Fielding, perceptively analysed ballad opera's characteristic content, practices, and constituencies. A rehearsal play, *The Fashionable Lady*, collated the perspectives of the dramatis personae with that of Ralph himself by having fictional characters watch and critique an entertainment. The main protagonist is Mrs Foible, a Fine Lady, who, helped by her maid Prattle, toys with suitors with similarly emblematic names – Mr Trifle (a would-be scholar) and Mr Smooth (a fop) among them. Foible's character is summarized thus:

> You know my Cousin Foible is the Assemblage of every female Folly–true she is beautiful as Venus, and would dress like one of the Graces; but that Affectation ruins her Gentility, as Pride sullies her Beauty. – Besides her Brain is as empty as a Harpsichord, and her Heart as various as its Musick; her Conversation is trifling as an Opera, and her Passions a Medley like an Entertainment. (I ix)

For Ralph, Foible was ballad opera, in which surface attraction belies emptiness (Brain/Harpsichord), unpredictability (Heart/Musick), triviality (Conversation/Opera), and inconstancy (Passions/Entertainment). Ralph allegorized Ballad Opera as a Fine Lady because ballad operas were all about women. Female nature was typically probed in musical numbers that, as in *The Beggar's Opera*, veered away from the sentimental plot to do so. Negative ascriptions far outweighed positive: jealousy, stupidity, flightiness, cupidity, concupiscence, and vanity à la Foible persistently bobbed to the dramatic surface in ballad operas. The documented subjects of ballad opera airs attest to this focus, as do ballad opera titles such as *The Wanton Countess*, *The Harlot's Progress* (after Hogarth's print series), *The Cure for a Scold*, and *Vanelia; or, The Amours of the Great* (Joncus et al. *BOPO*).

In *The Fashionable Lady*, 'Mr Ballad' represented the second, in Ralph's view deplorable, feature of ballad opera: its music. Ralph's 'Mr Modely' soundly castigates Ballad for his love of 'old English Tunes,' 'Chorusses,' and 'noble Symphon[ies] ... of Rusticks'; through dialogue and action Ballad enacts the crass stupidity of audiences who reject Italian opera amid the 'national Phrenzy' for common tunes. Ranging Foible alongside Ballad, Ralph created a tableau in which natural female vices amplify bad musical taste. Blinded by fashion, Foible buys 'all the English Operas' and organizes in her home 'an excellent Concert' in which she can 'sing over' the type of airs that indict her lack of discrimination (I xvi). In Ralph's *Fashionable Lady*, the unruly female not only exemplifies the genre's favourite topic, but also stands as a metonym for ballad opera itself.

Kitty Clive: From Theatric Nymph to Actress of Merit

Lavinia Fenton had shown that a player could subvert authorial intent to her advantage. Kitty Clive proved mistress of this art, while at the same time breaking free from the particular character type which Fenton had coined and which Clive's early promoters attempted to project onto her. Her place in Britain's popular culture, and that of her works, were secured through two seminal productions, *The Devil to Pay* (1731) and *The Mock Doctor* (1732). Both were informed by misogyny: unruly wives were savagely beaten, and this action was justified in song. Clive's stage triumphs in these punitive representations attest to her ability to eclipse the playbook with her own self-projection.

Clive's unusual vocal training and early casting show her being groomed in the art of ballad opera. Her singing teacher, Henry Carey, a champion of British ballads, designed several pioneering works around Clive. These, most notably six English cantatas and the sentimental musical comedy *The Contrivances* (1729), forged an individual style that bridged the gap between 'low' British and 'high' Italian music (Gillespie 217–34). Clive was Carey's ideal mouthpiece. While able to execute high-style works – she regularly sang the music of Handel, who later composed for her – Clive also commanded a 'voice like *London Cries*' that the delivery of low-style popular ballads demanded.[14]

At Drury Lane, Clive was deployed to win back audiences from *The Beggar's Opera* at Lincoln's Inn Fields. Clive's vocal prowess was tested in her stage debut, for which she sang an interpolated air; thereafter she was cast in practically every ballad opera Drury Lane ever mounted. Success was not, however, immediate. Manager Colley Cibber botched Drury Lane's initial foray into the genre by trying to elevate it, writing, mounting, and leading an execrable ballad-opera-cum-pastoral titled *Love in a Riddle* (Cibber 1729). Cibber's singing was terrible, and reportedly only Clive's charms saved the cast from being hissed off the stage.[15] Carey probably arranged the music, as was claimed in 1765 and is suggested by the fact that Clive's Phillida, a secondary role, was given an extended musical scene.[16] Following its near-failure, *Love in a Riddle* was immediately abridged by lopping off its high-style scenes; re-titled *Damon and Phillida*, and based solely around the comic subplot, the work was now led by Clive – as were two other pastoral 'Operas' in which she represented a nymph in the tradition of Fenton.[17] The point was underlined in Clive's first mezzotint portrait (1729), which was not a likeness of her but rather reproduced a seventeenth-century oil painting of a bare-bosomed shepherdess (see figure 2.4). To this the engraver attached her then name 'Miss Rafter'[18] and the following epigram, redolent of the naive eroticism previously attributed to Fenton:

See native Beauty clad without disguise,
No art t'allure a paltry Lovers Eyes,
No stiff, sett Airs, which but betray the mind,
But unaffected Innocence we find:

Happy the Nymph with charms by Nature blest,
But happier Swain, who of the Nymph possest,
Can taste the Joys, which she alone can bring,
And live in Pleasures which alternate spring.

The Devil to Pay (1731) was the unlikely means by which Clive freed herself from Fenton's shadow, 'breaking forth on the Public in a Blaze of Comic Brightness,' and causing her salary to be doubled. Reviewing her

G. Schalken Pinxit.   MISS RAFTER *in the Character of* PHILLIDA *th*
See native Beauty clad without disguise, | *Happy the* Nymph *w. charms by Nature blest.*
No art'fallure a paltry Lovers Eyes, | *But happier* Swain. *who of the* Nymph *possest.*
No stiff.sett Airs,which but betray the mind, | *Can taste the Joys,which she alone can bring,*
But unaffected Innocence, we find: | *And live in Pleasures which alternate spring.*

Figure 2.4. John Chaloner Smith. *Miss Rafter in the Character of Phillida* (1729). Reprinted courtesy of the British Museum (AN601212001). © Trustees of the British Museum

career in 1764, David Baker would emphasize how she 'established her own Reputation with the Audience' through this work.[19] In some ways, *The Devil to Pay* turned out to be even more influential than *The Beggar's Opera*: not only did it become a staple afterpiece, but it was speedily translated, seeding productions in France and Germany, and the new genres of opéra comique and Singspiel (van Boer 119–39; Gluck, Forward). Clive was critical to this legacy: it was the revised version designed around her which was exported, and, as Baker pointed out, *The Devil to Pay* would likely never have become a stage staple had she not been in it.

The playbook tells us why. An 'operatiz'd' farce from 1686, *The Devil to Pay* omitted the extended musical scenes of more sophisticated ballad operas and focused obsessively on the need to beat termagant wives. The play's author, Thomas Jevon, had circumvented the social decorum that banned wife abuse in polite society by having a magician transform Lady Loverule into the wife of a member of the lower orders, the cobbler Jobson, who in response to her 'impertinences' whips her until she begs for mercy. Restored to her natural form, she thanks Jobson for correcting her former conduct.[20]

How did this violent farce become the vehicle for Clive's breakthrough? Clive played the minor role of Nell, the cobbler's wife, whose form is exchanged with that of Lady Loverule. In Jevon's play, Nell is a drudge who passively accepts her fate, good and bad. The interpretation of Nell by Clive, who for the first time 'exerted those comic Powers' for which she was soon famous, flatly contradicted this characterization. Nell became a character of 'sprightly innocence' informed by the 'saucy and unnatural familiarity' and 'self-sufficiency' which were to become Clive trademarks.[21] In *The Rosciad* (1761), Charles Churchill characterized Clive's comic genius thus: 'Original in spirit and in ease, / She pleased by hiding all attempts to please' (12). Injecting Nell with spirit and sympathy, Clive animated a character whose rags-to-riches fortune likely appealed to less privileged spectators' desire to escape from their own social and economic constraints.

Clive's airs helped her to overwrite Jevon's playbook. In air thirty-one, Nell asserts her will over that of her husband ('For hence I will not, cannot, no nor must not buckle to'), and in air twenty-nine, she claims that simplicity is more attractive than artifice ('Fine Ladies with an artful Grace / Disguise each native Feature') (Coffey 49–50). Both airs resonated with Clive's existing stage persona, established by Carey's *Contrivances* and her shepherdess roles. Because radically different from Jevon's original, however, Clive's Nell suggested drastic revision to the piece once she became a sensation. Dialogue and characters were cut

Figure 2.5. Engraved frontispiece (after the 1731 original) for the playbook for Charles Coffey's *The Devil to Pay: or, The Wives Metamorphos'd. An Opera. As it is Perform'd at the Theatre-Royal in Drury-Lane, by His Majesty's Servants. With the Musick Prefix'd to Each Song.* Printed for J. Watts: Wild Court, London. 1748. Reprinted by permission of The Bodleian Library, University of Oxford (Harding D637)

to focus the action on Nell's transformation into Lady Loverule, and on her exchanges with Lord Loverule in this form. An aria from Handel's opera *Ottone* ('No, non temere') was made into a duet. In this new musical climax, Nell and Lord Loverule declare eternal affection ('O may it last for life!') [22] – a scene completely at odds with the original, in which the two characters' confusion distances them from each other, thereby safeguarding the distinction between their stations. For audiences, the revised 1731 love scene may have resonated with Clive's earlier performances of Handel's 'Son confus' pastorella' (from *Poro*), as an interlude song (Joncus, 'Handel'). Now, however, low-style presentation helped to mask the high-style source out of which a popular hit tune was created.

Nell became as iconic for Clive as Polly had been for Fenton: using the frontispiece of the playbook, the scene-painter Francis Hayman painted Clive as Nell, in an oil displayed publicly in a supper-box of Vauxhall Pleasure Gardens, one of the first public spaces in Europe where social stations could mingle. Engravings of Hayman's oil were issued separately, and frontispieces to *The Devil to Pay* continued to circulate with the design used by Hayman (see figure 2.5).[23] Clive's talent for projecting her own image, rather than the character on the page, would serve her well throughout her career, as she described to her protégée Jane Pope many years later:

> I am sorry to hear you have an indifferent part in the new Comedy ... however I charge you to make a good part of it[;] let it be never so bad, I have often done so myself therefore I know it is to be done turn it & wind it & play it in a different manner to his intention and as hundred to one but you succeed.[24]

Although *The Devil to Pay* was her breakthrough, it was Henry Fielding's vehicles for Clive that formed the bedrock of her pre-eminence in ballad opera. As Fielding's first biographer noted, 'The LOTTERY, the INTRIGUING CHAMBERMAID, and the VIRGIN UNMASKED served to make early discoveries of that true comic genius ... of Mrs Clive ... [and] he, in his turn, reaped the fruits of success from her abilities' (Murphy 15). That Clive finally exorcized Fenton's ghost through Fielding was acknowledged in a puff of 1732:

> By HINT [Fielding] and KEYBER [Colley Cibber] form'd to please the Age,
> See little RAFTOR mount the Drury stage.

FENTON outdone with her no more compares,
Than GAY's best Songs with HINT'S *Mock Doctor's* Airs.
Lament, O Rich! Thy Labours all are vain,
HINT writes and RAFTOR acts in Drury Lane.[25]

Yet Clive had to fight against Fielding's characterizations, just as she had against Jevon's, to represent herself as she chose. Writing her earliest epilogues – an audience address seemingly in 'her' voice – Fielding tried to shoehorn Clive back into the 'nymph' persona of her bare-bosomed 1729 mezzotint, first in the epilogue for their first big hit, *The Lottery* (1732), and then more aggressively for *The Covent Garden Tragedy* (1732):

In Various Lights this Night you've seen me drest.
A virtuous Lady [Kissinda in *The Covent Garden Tragedy*], and a Miss
confest [Isabel in the afterpiece, *The Old Debauchees*],
Pray tell me, Sirs, in which you like me best?
Neither averse to Love's soft Joys you find,
'Tis hard to say, which is the best inclin'd . . .
For you we dance, we sing, we smile, we pray;
On you we dream all Night, we think all Day.

Here, the male gaze is not only what Clive is made to serve ('tell me Sir, in which [dress] you like me best?') but is her sole preoccupation ('On you we dream all Night, we think all Day').

As her first spoken mainpiece, *The Covent Garden Tragedy* should have ushered in a new phase in Clive's career. Instead the play outraged critics, who accused Fielding of implying through its stage action that all women were 'arrant whores.'[26] Set in an infamous Covent Garden brothel – where Fielding himself was probably no stranger[27] – this burlesque tragedy depicted the procurement of a 'keeper' by Kissinda/Clive, a story whose parallels to unfavourable press about Fenton are striking.

The *Mock Doctor* (1732) which opened on 23 June, was Drury Lane's answer to the debacle of *The Covent Garden Tragedy,* and brought the Clive-Fielding collaboration to bear on a theme of proven popularity: wife-beating. About a month earlier, Clive had led the cast of the short-lived ballad opera, *The Comical Revenge; or, A Doctor in Spight of his Teeth* (unpublished). Advertised as being 'after Moliere,' it was based on Susannah Centlivre's treatment of *Le medecin malgré lui* (titled *Love's*

Contrivance, 1703), a play in which spousal abuse figured prominently (Lockwood 408). The bookseller, John Watts, London's most prestigious publisher of ballad operas, was poised to issue in early July a new translation of *Le medecin malgré lui*. Drury Lane had Fielding quickly throw together a ballad opera version of this comedy, and Fielding, in his preface, puffed Watts's forthcoming edition.[28] *The Mock Doctor* was therefore a promotional taster as well as a Clive vehicle, and Watts himself may have suggested using this comedy to enhance sales of his Molière volumes.

Because originally authored by Molière, *The Mock Doctor* possessed a cultural capital that *The Devil to Pay* had lacked. As in *The Comical Revenge*, Clive played a wily wife who tricks others into drubbing her husband after he attacks her, neatly allowing audiences to merge Fielding's latest Clive vehicle with her earlier breakthrough role of Nell.[29] Not only does *The Mock Doctor*'s first scene, of a quarrel between man and wife of the lower orders, conveniently echo that in Jevon's play, but one of its earliest lines ('A Wife is worse than a Devil') seems to invite being read through *The Devil to Pay* (Molière I i). Clive profited in three ways: from leading a stage classic, from playing a fictional character whose qualities – loyalty, wit, and ingenuity – were congruent with her established stage manner, and from singing almost all of a small number of airs. *The Mock Doctor* included only nine airs, half of what was standard for one-act ballad operas, and all but one of which in the original version were sung by Clive. In the revised version, first performed 16 November 1732, she sang all but two of nine songs.

Fielding's largest addition to Molière's original comedy was his ballads, and two scenes to enlarge Clive's part (Lockwood 410). Clive's airs were perniciously antifemale, circling around female cupidity and reinforcing male sexual prerogatives. Air one implies a man's right to sex ('Who gives him – what's Meat for his Master?'); airs two and eight justify wife-abuse ('One tender Smack, / More sweet than Sack / Can quell all her fury'); air four asserts that all women cuckold their husbands ('No horned Brother dares make Sport / They're Cuckolds all arow'); air six counsels men in the workings of the sex market ('A Woman at St James's / With Hundreds you obtain / But stay till lost her Fame is/ She'll be cheap in Drury Lane'), air nine asserts greed is typically a woman's ideal ('She is most happy, who well knows how to hold/ At once her dear Virtue, and her Lover's dear Gold').[30] In Fielding's additional scenes, Dorcas/Clive outwits her husband's ploy to prove her infidelity; her triumph is, however, undone by her husband convincing another doctor to cure his wife of imputed madness by letting her blood, shaving her hair, starving her, and strapping her twice daily. This last scene, together with her ballads, militated against Clive's preferred self-representation, as well as giving the lie to Fielding's playbook introduction claim to 'preserve the spirit of Molière.' Arguably, Fielding was aiming to balance high-style packaging against low-style popular themes; his additions were, however, also redolent of a personal penchant for representing 'arrant whores.'

'The Success of the *Mock-Doctor* [was] more ow'd to the extraordinary good action of [Theophilus Cibber] and Miss Raftor than to the Merit of the Writer,' wrote the critic Thomas Cooke (39), who recognized that Fielding's 'translation' might fail to charm audiences. When left alone by Fielding, however, Molière's discursive strategies offered Clive new means with which to emancipate herself from the playbook. Dorcas shares with the theatre audience knowledge which is being denied to onstage characters. Based on *commedia dell'arte* practices, this type of representation allowed Clive to do in spoken words what she was already doing in ballads: address spectators outside the dramatic narrative.[31] Clive's excellence in this Janis-faced form of representation became legendary; to capitalize on it, Drury Lane mounted many more productions featuring 'characters of this kind,' in which Clive was deemed 'perfect.'[32]

Fielding finally caught up with Clive, penning the witty, tart-tongued roles in which her skills could fully unfold.[33] He also began to publicize Clive's acting skills. To this end, he asserted in the playbook of *The Mock Doctor* that Clive's 'Capacity is not confined to a Song, and I dare swear [critics] will shortly own Her able to do Justice to Characters of much greater Consequence' (Fielding, *Mock ... Dumb* Preface; Lockwood 430). He followed this plug with the lengthy 'Epistle to Mrs Clive,' which appeared in editions of one of her most popular musical vehicles, *The Intriguing Chambermaid*, 'taken from' Jean-François Regnard's *Le retour imprévu* (1700). The 'Epistle' was devised in part to justify falling attendance at Drury Lane, where an actors' rebellion had left the house deserted of all top players apart from Clive. Why Clive had elected not to follow the rebel players is mysterious. The revolt was led by Theophilus Cibber, who had robustly supported Clive's career; manager Charles Fleetwood, against whom the actors were rebelling, not only grossly mismanaged the company but also persistently cheated actors of wages, a practice that was sure to affect Clive at some point.[34]

Perhaps her antagonism towards Cibber, which three years later would become a *cause scandale* (Joncus, 'In Wit') was already on the rise, or perhaps she welcomed the chance to rid herself of rival actresses. Whatever Clive's reasons, the decision proved a tactical misstep when attendance at Drury Lane plunged.

In his 'Epistle' Fielding alleged that the Town had deserted Drury Lane because Italian opera had vitiated its taste. Although nonsensical – London's Italian opera productions were floundering – Fielding's claim once more pitted English 'opera' against Italian by claiming, against all evidence, that Italian and ballad opera audiences were the same. In contrast to the triumphant Fenton, Clive was, in this view, an innocent victim of the Town's foolish preference for 'foreign Musick':

> It is your Misfortune to bring the greatest Genius for acting on the Stage at a Time when the Factions ... among the Players have conspired with the Folly, Injustice, and Barbarity of the Town to ... sacrifice our own native Entertainments to a wanton affected Fondness for foreign Musick; and when our Nobility seem eagerly to rival each other, in distinguishing themselves in favour of *Italian* theatres, and in neglect of our own.

Clive's skills and reception clearly shaped Fielding's writing for her. While his early works for Drury Lane had actively worked against her own self-representation, commercial pressure eventually forced Fielding to acknowledge and promote the gifts that Clive possessed.

The contributions of Fenton and Clive to the production of popular theatre, because based in performance, have tended to elude the historian's gaze. As the eighteenth-century critic John Hill observed, 'we give to the author the praise which belongs to her [Clive]' (Hill 230). This tendency is nowhere clearer than in studies about Gay and Fielding's ballad operas, in which the female star's impact – through her practices, reputation, and reception – receives only glancing mention. Yet Fenton and Clive contributed significantly to the success, meaning, and development of the works they performed; they also, through publicity engendered by their interpretations, helped guide discourse about women in popular culture. Their achievements are particularly impressive in light of the negative female stereotyping that dogged both their ballad operas and their publicity. By projecting the personae they wished to embody, Fenton and Clive changed the direction, and aided a broad-base reception of, ballad opera. Only by reading ballad operas through the lens of the principal player, as eighteenth-century audiences did, can we recapture the dynamics which made them so popular.

NOTES

1 For data about the titles, musical numbers, and cast members of ballad operas, see Ballad Operas Online (*BOPO*) (Joncus, Burden, Rogers, and Lipinski).

2 Mixing genres was standard procedure in eighteenth-century satire; scholars of John Gay routinely credit Jonathan Swift with suggesting Gay's peculiar mix of pastoral and criminal literature in *The Beggar's Opera:* 'The Pastoral Ridicule is not exhausted ... what think you of a Newgate Pastoral, among the Whores and Thieves there?' (Fiske 94–5). Gay also did not name the genre: the term 'ballad opera' crept into advertisements during 1732 (Joncus et al., *BOPO* Advertisements 1728–32).

3 'Yesterday I was at the rehearsal of the new opera composed by Handel: I like it extremely, but the taste of the town is so depraved, that nothing will be approved of but the burlesque. *The Beggar's Opera* entirely triumphs over the Italian one.' Letter of Jan. 1728 from Mary Pendarves to her sister Ann Granville (Deutsch 220). See also *The London Journal* 23 March 1728: 'There is nothing which suprizes all true Lovers of Music more, than the Neglect into which the Italian Operas are at present fallen ... *The Beggar's Opera* I take to be a touch-stone to try British taste on ... Our English audience have been for some time returning to their cattish nature; of which some particular sounds from the gallery have given us sufficient warning' (qtd in Deutsch 223).

4 The most thorough account of the play's reception remains Schultz's 1923 *Gay's* Beggar's Opera: *Its Content, History and Influence.* For an evaluation of its later production, see Barlow. On Fenton's reputation, see Wanko's 'Eighteenth-Century Actress,' 'Three Stories of Celebrity,' and *Roles of Authority.*

5 'Not since ... seventy-five years earlier ... [at] the execution of [the] leader of the Bishopsgate mutiny [Robert Lockyer] against service in Ireland had such a vast proportion of the London population assembled' (Linebaugh 39).

6 Although verses about females dominate Gay's airs, modern scholars have largely overlooked this point. Constructions of gender are, however, discussed in Dugaw 166–96. Modern criticism of Gay's *Beggar's Opera* is extensive: see Kidson and Rogers; Empson; Bloom; and Nokes 401–44.

7 Olive Baldwin and Thelma Wilson only recently established Fenton's extreme youthfulness. See 'Fenton, Lavinia' in the online version of the *Oxford Dictionary of National Biography.*

8 Critics of Italian opera routinely accused *prime donne* of exciting their supporters beyond the boundaries of decorum, mapping misconduct of followers onto the singers themselves. The riot between Cuzzoni and Faustina

supporters was a prime example. In *The Devil to Pay in St James's, or A full and true Account of the most Horrid and Bloody Battle between Madam Faustina and Madam Cuzzoni* (1727) not only is the 'Polite World' castigated for their 'Warm Disputes' over singers, but an onstage cat-fight between the sopranos is imagined to have taken place. Handel scholars have cited this fictional report as fact. I am grateful to Dr Aspden for sending me her article before its publication.

9   *Daily Journal* 13 November 1736.

10 See the entry for Tuesday, 18 April 1775, in Boswell (630). I would like to thank Jeremy Barlow for calling my attention to this passage.

11 Amhurst typically issued his polemics against Fenton in *The Craftsman*, the opposition publication that he founded and directed from 1726; his attacks on Fenton were also reprinted elsewhere. He was by no means the only writer to impute that she was promiscuous. See, among others, *Polly Peachum*. See also Wanko.

12 This article gives a full history of the illustrations mentioned in this chapter, as well as of Clive's iconography.

13 'The effects of the "the body in the singing voice" have been explored most famously by Roland Barthes, in his essay on the "grain" of the voice ... This point is usually taken up in rock criticism as a celebration of the "materiality of the body speaking its mother tongue"' (Frith 191).

14 'A cousin too she has, with squinting eyes, / With wadling gait, and voice like *London Cries*.' Epilogue written by a Friend, spoken by Mrs CLIVE' [pencil MS note '1756'], anonymous newspaper cutting in Harvard Theater Collection, Box File of Newspaper Clippings, 'Kitty Clive.'

15 See *The Laureat* 110. Cibber blamed the failure of this work on a cabal organized against him (Cibber 243–4).

16 A 1765 edition of *Damon and Phillida* in the New York Public Library states: 'The Songs adapted and arranged by Mr Carey' (Gillespie 87).

17 *Phebe, or The Beggar's Wedding* and *Patie and Peggy*, first performed at Drury Lane on 13 June 1729 and on 20 April 1730 respectively.

18 When she married in 1732, Clive took her husband's family name.

19 'In 1730 [1731], however, she had an Opportunity afforded her, which she did not permit to pass unemployed, of breaking forth on the Public in a Blaze of Comic Brightness. This was in the Part of Nell, in the *Devil to Pay, or the Wives Metamorphos'd*, a Ballad Farce, written by Coffey, in which she threw out a full Exertion of those comic Powers, which every Frequenter of the Theatre must since have received with such infinite Delight. Her Merit in this Character occasioned her Salary to be doubled, and not only established her own Reputation with the Audience, but fixed

the Piece itself on the constant List of acting Farces, an Honour which perhaps it would never have arrived at, had not she been in it' (Baker, 'Clive, Catherine' n.p.).

20 The 'operatiz'd' version of this farce left Jevon's original dialogue virtually unchanged. Compare Jevon's original to Coffey.

21 See *The Theatre Turned Upside Down* 7. On Clive's 'sauciness,' see Hill 151, 222.

22 See Rubsamen 2:1–35. This duet has been recorded on *Handel in the Playhouse* (Ozmo). It may be accessed as an audio sample on *BOPO* (Joncus et al.)

23 For a reproduction and further details about Hayman's oil painting, see Joncus 'His Spirit.'

24 See Clive, Letter of 15 Dec 1774 (no. 8).

25 See 'To Miss Raftor.' 'Wm Hint' was the name used to stand for Fielding in the paper war about *The Covent Garden Tragedy* (1732). On the *ad hominem* allusion of 'Keyber' for Colley Cibber, see Woods.

26 This argument formed the centre of a paper war conducted principally between the *Grub Street Journal* and Fielding (Hume 139–41; Lockwood 341–59). Many of the exchanges between *Grub-Street Journal* and Fielding are reprinted in Paulson and Lockwood 41–68.

27 'Thus formed and disposed for enjoyment, he launched wildly [from 1727] into a career of dissipation' (Murphy 9). On Fielding's dissolute lifestyle, see Battestin 143–51.

28 Lockwood 408, 430. Lockwood estimates that Fielding wrote the play between 5 and 16 June 1732; Fielding complained about the speed at which he had to work (Lockwood 406).

29 The cultivation of a stereotypical character, or 'line,' to capitalize on a principal player's renowned skills was fundamental to seventeenth- and eighteenth-century stage productions (Stern 152–3).

30 These airs are in the first version. In the second version, Clive sang four of her eight original airs. A reproduction of the play's first version, later revised, is available on Eighteenth-Century Collections Online. On Fielding's revisions to his original, see Lockwood 411–12. Fielding's ballads in both versions of *The Mock Doctor* defamed women (Joncus and Rogers, forthcoming).

31 This method of address was endemic to *commedia dell'arte,* and Molière also drew on it routinely (see Vinti).

32 'There is hardly a scene in which the truth of the action is more difficult: and this Mrs Clive does perfectly. In many characters of this kind [i.e. the scheming servant in *The Intriguing Chambermaid*], all that we admire is in this actress' (Hill 230).

33 See *The Miser* (1733), *Deborah; or, A Wife for you all* (1733), the revised *Author's Farce* (1734), *The Intriguing Chambermaid* (1734), *An Old Man taught Wisdom* (1735), *Eurydice* (1737), and *Miss Lucy in Town* (1742). On Clive's influence on these works, see Hume 150–4, 169–73, 222–5, 265–6.

34 Among several accounts of this episode, one of the best is in Hume 173–80.

WORKS CITED

Aspden, Suzanne. 'Identità in scena sul palco lirico loninese: Faustina Bordoni versus Francesca Cuzzoni.' *Händel e il dramma per musica*. Florence: Leo S. Olschki. Forthcoming.

Baker, David Erskine, and Pre-1801 Imprint Collection (Library of Congress). *The Companion to the Play-House ... down to the present year 1764*. London: T. Becket and P.A. Dehondt, 1764. Print.

Baldwin, Olive, and Thelma Wilson. 'Fenton, Lavinia.' *Oxford Dictionary of National Biography*. Ed. Colin Matthew, Brian Harrison, and Lawrence Goldman: Oxford UP, 2009. Web. 5 Jan. 2010.

Barlow, Jeremy. 'The Beggar's Opera in London's Theatres, 1728–1761.' *The Stage's Glory: John Rich (1692–1761)*. Ed. Berta Joncus and Jeremy Barlow. Newark: U of Delaware P. In Press.

Battestin, Martin. *Henry Fielding: A Life*. London: Routledge, 1989. Print.

Bloom, Harold, ed. *John Gay's The Beggar's Opera*. New York: Chelsea House, 1988. Print.

Böker, Uwe. 'John Gays The Beggar's Opera und die soziahistorischen Kontexte: Satire, Kriminalität, Ballade, Oper, Kommerzialisierung.' *John Gay's The Beggar's Opera 1728–2004: Adaptations and Rewritings*. Ed. Ines Detmers and Anna-Christina Giovanopoulos. Amsterdam: Rodopi, 2006. 33–102. Print.

Boswell, James, R.W. Chapman, and J.D. Fleeman. *Life of Johnson*. Oxford and New York: Oxford UP, 1980. Print.

Burgess, C.F., ed. *The Letters of John Gay*. Oxford: Clarendon, 1966. Print.

Carey, Henry. *The Contrivances*. London: W. Mears, 1729. Print.

Churchill, Charles. *The Rosciad*. Dublin: n.p., 1761. Print.

Cibber, Colley. *An Apology for the Life of Mr Colley Cibber*. 2nd ed. London: J. Watts, 1740. Print.

– *Love in a Riddle*. London: J. Watts, 1729. Print.

Clive, Catherine. *Collection of Letters to Jane Pope, 1769–85*. Folger Library. US-Ws W.b.73. Manuscript.

Coffey, Charles. *The Devil to Pay; or, The Wives Metamorphos'd*. London: J. Watts, 1731. Print.

Cooke, Thomas, ed. *The Comedian, or Philosophical Enquirer*. No. 7 [October 1732]. London: J. Roberts, 1732. Print.

Deutsch, Otto Erich. *Handel: A Documentary Biography*. London: Adam & Charles Black, 1955. Print.

Dugaw, Dianne. *Deep Play: John Gay and the Invention of Modernity*. Newark, DE; London: U of Delaware P; Associated University Presses, 2001. Print.

Empson, William. 'Some Versions of the Pastoral.' *Twentieth-Century Interpretations of* The Beggar's Opera. Ed. Yvonne Noble. Englewood Cliffs, NJ: Prentice-Hall, 1975. 5–36. Print.

Fielding, Henry. *The Covent Garden Tragedy*. London: J. Watts, 1732. Print.

– *The Intriguing Chambermaid*. London: J. Watts, 1734. Print.

– *The Mock Doctor . . . Done from Molière*. 1st ed. London: J. Watts, 1732. Print.

– *The Mock Doctor; or, The Dumb Lady Cur'd*. 2nd ed. Dublin: Reprinted by George Faulkner, 1732. Print.

Fiske, Roger. *English Theatre Music in the Eighteenth Century*. 2nd ed. Oxford: Oxford UP, 1986. Print.

Frith, Simon. *Performing Rites: On the Value of Popular Music*. Cambridge, MA: Harvard UP, 1996. Print.

Fuller, John, ed. *The Beggar's Opera*. Vol. 1. 2 vols. Oxford: Clarendon, 1983. Print.

Gillespie, Joseph Norman. 'The Life and Work of Henry Carey (1687–1743), vol. 1 of 2.' Dissertation. University of London, 1982. Print.

Gluck, Christoph Willibald, et al. *Le diable à quatre, ou, La double métamorphose*. Kassel and New York: Bärenreiter, 1992. Sämtliche Werke. Abteilung IV, Französische komische Opern / Christoph Willibald Gluck. Print.

Hill, John. *The Actor; or, A Treatise on the Art of Playing*. London: R. Griffiths, 1755. Print.

Hume, Robert D. *Henry Fielding and the London Theatre, 1728–1737*. Oxford: Clarendon, 1988. Print.

Jevon, Thomas. *The Devil of a Wife, or a Comical Transformation*. London: J. Heptinstall, 1686. Print.

Joncus, Berta. '"Clad without Disguise": Imagining Kitty Clive (1711–1785).' *Music in Art* 34.1–2 (2009): 89–106. Print.

– 'Handel at Drury Lane: Ballad Opera and the Production of Kitty Clive.' *Journal of the Royal Musical Association* 131.2 (2006): 179–226. Print.

– '"His Spirit is in Action Seen": Milton, Mrs Clive and the Simulacra of the Pastoral in *Comus*.' *Eighteenth-Century Music* 2.1 (2005): 7–40. Print.

– '"In Wit Superior as in Fighting": Kitty Clive and the Conquest of a Rival Queen.' *Huntington Library Quarterly* 73.4 (2010): forthcoming.

Joncus, Berta, et al. *Ballad Operas Online*. 4 Nov. 2009. Web.

Joncus, Berta, and Jeremy Barlow, eds. *The Stage's Glory: John Rich (1692–1761)*. Newark: U of Delaware P. In Press.

Joncus, Berta, and Vanessa Rogers. 'Beyond *The Beggar's Opera:* John Rich and English Ballad Opera.' *The Stage's Glory: John Rich (1692–1761)*. Ed. Berta Joncus and Jeremy Barlow. Newark: U of Delaware P. In Press.

– 'Ballad Opera and British *double entendre:* Henry Fielding's *The Mock Doctor.*' *Die Praxis des Timbre in verschiedenen europäischen Kulturen: Eine musikalische Praxis zwischen Oralität und Schriftlichkeit.* Ed. Herbert Schneider. Hildesheim: Georg Olms Verlag, Forthcoming.

Kidson, Frank, Bruce Rogers, and Pforzheimer Bruce Rogers Collection (Library of Congress). *The Beggar's Opera: Its Predecessors and Successors.* Cambridge: Cambridge UP, 1922. Print.

The Laureat; or, The Right Side of Colley Cibber, Esq. London: J. Roberts, 1740. Print.

Letters in Prose and Verse to the celebrated Polly Peachum. London: A. Millar, 1728. Print.

The Life of Lavinia Beswick, Alias Fenton, Alias Polly Peachum. London: A. Moore, 1728. Print.

Linebaugh, Peter. *The London Hanged: Crime and Civil Society in the Eighteenth Century.* 2nd ed. New York: Verso, 2003. Print.

Lockwood, Thomas, ed. *Plays: Henry Fielding, 1731–1734.* Vol. 2. Oxford: Clarendon, 2007. Print.

Molière. '*Le Médecin Malgré Lui,* Comédie, Par Monsieur De Molière. *A Doctor and No Doctor,* A Comedy.' *Select Comedies of Mr. de Moliere.* Vol. 2. London: J. Watts, 1732. Print.

Murphy, Arthur. 'An Essay on the Life and Genius of Henry Fielding, Esq.' *The Works of Henry Fielding, Esq; with the Life of the Author.* London: A. Millar, 1762. Print.

Nokes, David. *John Gay: A Profession of Friendship.* Oxford: Oxford UP, 1995. Print.

North, Roger, and John Wilson. *Roger North on Music: Being a Selection from His Essays Written during the Years c. 1695–1728.* London: Novello, 1959. Print.

Ozmo, Zak, Director. *Handel in the Playhouse.* Oppella Nova Records, 2009. CD.

Paulson, Ronald, and Thomas Lockwood, eds. *Henry Fielding: The Critical Heritage.* London: Routledge & Kegan, 1969. Print.

Polly Peachum on Fire, The Beggar's Opera Blown Up, and Capt. Mackheath Entangled in his Bazzle-strings. London: A. Moore, 1728. Print.

Ralph, James. *The Fashionable Lady; or, Harlequin's Opera. In the Manner of a Rehearsal. As it is Perform'd at the Theatre in Goodman's-Fields.* London: J. Watts, 1730. Print.

Rubsamen, Walter H. 'Mr Seedo. Ballad Opera and the Singspiel.' *Miscelánea En Homenaje a Monseñor Higinio Anglés.* Vol. 2. Barcelona: Consejo Superior de Investigaciones Cientoficas, 1958–61. 1–35. Print.

Ryan, Lacy. *The Cobler's Opera.* London: J. Roberts, 1729. Print.

Schultz, William Eben, Oliver Baty Cunningham Memorial Publication Fund, and Elizabethan Club (Yale University). *Gay's Beggar's Opera: Its Content, History, and Influence.* New Haven: Yale UP, 1923. Print.

Stern, Tiffany. *Rehearsal from Shakespeare to Sheridan.* Oxford: Oxford UP, 2000. Print.

The Theatre Turned Upside Down, or the Mutineers. A Dialogue. Occasioned by a Pamphlet, Called the Theatric Squabble. London: A. Dodd, 1733. Print.

'To Miss Raftor.' *Grub-Street Journal* 17 August 1732. Print.

van Boer, Bertil H. 'Coffey's *The Devil to Pay:* The Comic War and the Emergence of the German Singspiel.' *Journal of Musicological Research* 8.1–2 (1988): 119–39. Print.

Vinti, Claudio. 'L'Addresse au Publique.' *Molière à l'École Italienne: Le Lazzo dans la Création Moliéresque.* Ed. Claude Bourquoi and Claudio Vinti. Turin and Paris: L'Harmattan, 2003. Print.

Wanko, Cheryl. 'The Eighteenth-Century Actress and the Construction of Gender: Lavinia Fenton and Charlotte Charke.' *Eighteenth-Century Life* 18.2 (1994): 75–90. Print.

– *Roles of Authority: Thespian Biography and Celebrity in Eighteenth-Century Britain.* Lubbock: Texas Tech UP, 2003. Print.

– 'Three Stories of Celebrity: *The Beggar's Opera* Biographies.' *Studies in English Literature, 1500–1900* 38.3 (1998): 481–98. Print.

Wilson, John, ed. *Roger North on Music: Being a Selection from His Essays during the Years c. 1697–1728.* London: Novello, 1959. Print.

Woods, Charles B. 'Cibber in Fielding's *Author's Farce:* Three Notes.' *Philological Quarterly* 64 (1965): 145–51. Print.

3 Politics and Gender in a Tale of Two Plays

PAULA BACKSCHEIDER

This chapter is a contribution to the ongoing effort to understand how performances of history – both national and theatrical – release the dynamic relationships between the present and the past. By broadly developing the contexts of productions and closely analysing their receptions, I continue the exploration of popular culture, especially of plays that arouse competition for ownership of interpretation that become what theorists term 'sites.' As such, they make tensions discernible and meaning arises from the forces that intersect. By popular culture, I mean 'works that were read or seen by almost everybody; were part of the consciousness of the learned or educated as well as of the uneducated; read or seen or talked about by so many people that we can say they were taken for granted as part of the environment' (Paulson, *Popular* x). Although every play enters a popular culture venue, it has to pass a high bar – known to the learned and uneducated, the elite and the masses – to qualify as true popular culture. With that status, plays become available for volatile interpretations over time because of what Mikhail Bakhtin described as 'tastes of the context and contexts in which it has lived its socially charged life.' Words, and therefore texts, are never neutral but 'shot through with intentions and accents' (293). When revived they contribute to the work of maintaining or contesting the status quo.

Popular culture theorists have long known that imitative texts and performances have the potential of laying bare unrecognized aspects of canonical works. In this essay, I will analyse the results of late eighteenth-century revivals of a respected, reliable repertory play, Thomas Otway's 1682 *Venice Preserved* (with special emphasis on the great actresses who played the female lead) and a nearly unknown play, George Watson's 1795 *England Preserved* (and a forgotten actress with an impossible name, Tryphosa Wallis). Both plays can be used to illustrate some fundamental, deep structural possibilities always latent in popular culture. Potentially subversive and even incendiary, popular culture's power to transform spectacle into recognition or even sudden, revelatory insight makes it volatile and unpredictable. As such, groups have always claimed especially pertinent texts and performances, attempted to control interpretation, and insisted upon unintended symbolic value.

In my discussion of these plays, I will describe, compare, and contrast the most famous actresses, pointing out that they fall into two categories. One group privileged the horrifying nature of tragedy and one the pathetic, thereby releasing the potential for fear and pity that tragedy has always held. I will also argue specifically that the women's parts and the popular understandings of the actresses who created them increasingly came to represent the duties of women in times of turmoil and, more insistently, to highlight the ways the political inevitably invades the domestic. As we know, opinions about women's nature and capacities were becoming more conservative at the end of the eighteenth century, and these plays, I believe, also suggest how disciplining discussions of the very nature of women were carried out. Representations of Woman, as much as acting ability and interpretation, came to influence popular judgment.

Venice Preserved and Casting Belvidera

On the first night of the Covent Garden production of Thomas Otway's *Venice Preserved* in February 1794, John Thelwall, one of the most prominent of the men who would be charged with treason in May,[1] and his reformist friends vigorously applauded and demanded encores of parts of the play that highlighted government corruption and the hardships of ordinary people. He and other reformers had published and continued to publish sections of the play as expressions of their cause.[2] *The Life of John Thelwall* reads, 'The conspicuous figure Thelwall made in promoting the applause of ... passages ... was not forgotten on his trial' (H. Thelwall 286).[3] The latent political ideas of *Venice Preserved* are built into the very fabric of the play. A reliable repertory piece from the time of its first performance in 1682, by the end of the century it was both a classic and a popular culture play.[4] It had a noble history as one of the great plays written during the Exclusion Crisis, the time of the attempt to bar

King Charles II's Catholic brother James from the throne. It is the story of a man, Jaffeir, who is torn between joining a rebellion and revealing it to the government, who is proselytized by his best friend and his wife, and who cradles both idealistic and mean personal motives. This recitation of the plot shows that there was almost no time when it could be stripped of political applications. Upon production, the play was quickly claimed by the monarchy,[5] thereby assuring that its lesson would come from the horrific deaths of the rebels, from the murder-suicide on the stage upon a stage (the scaffold), and from the madness of the heroine Belvidera, whose last vision is Jaffeir and Pierre rising from Hell. Jaffeir was a wonderful representative of many people in 1682; he is fully aware of the suffering caused by revolutions and also of the corruption of the government and of his country's 'tatter'd fleet,' 'Bankrupt nobility,' 'factious' 'divided Senate' (II iii 69–91), and hungry citizenry. A century later, Thelwall and the reformers highlighted the play's applicability to 1794, and the Covent Garden production was closed after only two performances.

In spite of this theatrical debacle and the ongoing treason trials, John Philip Kemble chose to revive the play in October 1795 as part of his parade of classic British plays staged to celebrate the opening of the new Drury Lane theatre. Sarah Siddons had been playing Belvidera since 1782; Kemble, Jaffeir since 1786; with Bensley and Palmer both playing Pierre since 1784. For them, it was truly part of their reliable, predictable, classic repertoire. On the first night of Kemble's production, however, the audience competed for ownership of the play. The lines, 'Domestic traitors, / Who make us slaves, and tell us 'tis our Charter' received sustained applause, but other audience members loudly cheered for the rebels and even associated their cause with the 'liberal' and Jacobin cause, universal suffrage. *The Oracle and Public Advertiser* described 'contending parties.'[6] Just as the press had done during the Covent Garden production, they quickly began to take sides at Drury Lane. The *Times*, always supportive of the ministry, observed, 'Among other strange coincidences let it be ranked, that this Play was revived at the very moment when the same parts are acting on the great stage of *Paris*... one should be tempted to suppose the *whole National Convention* sat for the picture' (27 October 1795). The *Times* and other papers noted how well Renault's blood-thirsty speeches fit the French mood. Their motive was to read the play as condemning *the French* and the direction the Revolution was taking. In fact, as Elizabeth Inchbald (who witnessed the event) observed, the earlier Covent Garden production had been associated with the French National Convention, but the Drury Lane one was 'applied . . . to certain men or assemblies in the English state.' She also alludes to the fact that this was not the only time such associations had been made.[7] Historians have come to agree that the 'most serious threat to the conservative order in Britain in the 1790s would have come from a radical politicization of the plight of the poor, from food rioters' (Eastwood 162).

Kemble responded to crowd reaction by removing most of the speeches about food shortages and unrest. In tense times, it had always been dangerous to cast a charismatic actor in the part of Pierre. Kemble replaced Robert Bensley, who was described as performing the part with 'manly energy,' with John Palmer, who emphasized Pierre's personal suffering. Newspapers reported that the audiences attempted to 'repress' 'party tokens of approbation and censure' so that the elaborate production with sets by Marinari and costumes 'such as . . . never witnessed in any previous representation' could continue.[8] Kemble's well-known dedication to 'a *favourite system*' of reviving 'excellent plays, with suitable embellishment,' the fact that the play severely punishes rebels, and praises for the brilliant acting were much repeated. That did not work. Audience members once again cheered Pierre's greatest, most defiant lines, and the Lord Chamberlain ordered the play closed. Many journalists on both sides regretted the audience's conduct, the closing of the play, and even the authorities' not allowing the contention for ownership of interpretation. As is always possible with popular culture, *Venice Preserved* had become a site of ideological and aesthetic conflict.

Venice Preserved is also the story of Belvidera, a woman with a terrible secret who must decide where her duty lies: husband, father, or countrymen. The conspirators whom her husband has joined plan to kill her father and other senators, and she knows that innocent citizens will die in the rebellion. She persuades her husband to reveal the rebellious plot, the government reneges on its promises to him, and he dies a murderer and a suicide; Belvidera goes mad, imagines him rising from hell, and dies. Her part has the most interesting history of the three leads and, perhaps, became the most socially significant as the potential of popular culture to reveal ideological undercurrents was released. Written for Elizabeth Barry, the greatest tragic actress of the Restoration, the part passed to Susannah Cibber and then to Ann Barry, perfect Belvideras for their times after the threat of civil war died. Cibber began playing the part in the 1740s, the key decade for the rise of sensibility, and

Barry in the 1760s when the movement was dominant. In striking contrast, their strength was pathos, not the commanding fear and awe of Elizabeth Barry and, later, of Siddons. Otway, for example, described Elizabeth Barry: 'Her Eyes black, sparkling, spiteful, hot, and piercing,' and she was known for having a 'talent for noble wretchedness' (Hume 220), something quite different from pathos. Siddons, of course, was a large woman with a pronounced and masculine Roman nose; contemporaries often commented on 'the piercing brilliance' of her dark brown eyes (Asleson 43). Perhaps the greatest tragic actress of all time, she carefully studied her signature parts and introduced innovative, deeply affecting scenes. As Lady Macbeth, for instance, she could bring an audience to hysteria. A witness to her 1786 performance of Belvidera commented on Siddons's 'absolute control' of every emotion and on her performance of 'great resentment' of the insults 'to a highborn Senators daughter' and contempt for 'that assembly, all made up of wretches' (*Beauties* 4, 6), interpretations perhaps not present in other actresses' performances.[9]

In part after part, all four actresses triumphed by portraying an exceptionally wide range of strong emotions, but the balance of pity and horror differed for each pair. Speaking lines (later cut) that emphasized Belvidera's sexuality, Elizabeth Barry made Belvidera a dangerous seductress, one of the many women who threatened a man's honour in Exclusion Crisis plays. Siddons was said to chill the audience's blood when she spoke famous lines. Susannah Arne Cibber, the beautiful and beloved former singer for whom Handel wrote arias, was recognized as 'the most pathetic of all actresses' (Lynch 281). She was a small woman with large dark eyes and combined acting styles learned from the rhetorical performers like James Quin and the 'natural' ones like David Garrick. She was the first to play Belvidera as a delicate and adoring wife. The great Quin, a large, intimidating man praised for 'statuesque dignity' and gravity, played Pierre opposite the small, delicate Cibber whose speaking voice was not strong but deeply moving; the two crushed several capable but unequal Jaffeirs between them. In these productions, Belvidera's paramount femininity was opposed to Pierre's ultimate masculinity. Reviews ubiquitously mention how she brought audiences to 'melt' in tears repeatedly throughout her performance (Marsden 154).

Ann Barry, later Mrs Crawford, was 'a perfect beauty.' Her light auburn hair, graceful, slim, taller-than-average figure, and her lovely voice opened the way to the eighty-two parts she played in her forty-six years on the stage. At the end of her career, she overlapped with

Sarah Siddons. An eye-witness described her as retaining 'the symmetry of her person and the sweetness of her voice' and as 'the *lover*' on the stage whose dominion was 'the tender, the confiding, and impassioned' (Bernard 1:279–80), strengths that feminized Anne Barry's Belvidera and made her both seductress and sufferer. The *Gazetteer* of 30 November 1784 said that Siddons 'cannot, so powerfully as Mrs Crawford assail at intervals the heart' and compared Crawford's effect to 'an electrical machine . . . the effect is instantaneous on every part of the theatre.'[10]

When Cibber began playing to Garrick's Jaffeir, she dominated scenes, especially the one in which she drew out the secret of the conspiracy and then persuaded Jaffeir to reveal it to the senate (Taylor 171–2). The way Cibber played on Jaffeir's affections and took centre stage with representations of feminine devotion to her husband, vexed by her compassion for her father and the innocent citizens who would be murdered, reconfigured her part into the mid-century ideology of the domestic woman. Cuts and revisions to the text reinforced this interpretation by decreasing her sexual attractiveness and agency. Cibber moved to Covent Garden and played Belvidera to Spranger Barry's Jaffeir. By all accounts, they played the parts as passionate lovers. As *The Connoisseur* complained, it was fashionable for tragic couples playing love scenes to take 'every opportunity of heightening the expression by kisses and embraces . . . the hero and heroine are continually flying into each other's arms.'[11] Ann Barry replaced Cibber and played opposite her husband Spranger Barry as Jaffeir, thereby pushing the play further toward becoming about Belvidera and Jaffeir's relationship rather than the competition between her and Pierre and what they symbolize. Her performance, like Cibber's, emphasized the private sphere over, for instance, Elizabeth Barry's and Sarah Siddons's attention to the public issues. Described as 'tender' and 'confiding,' Ann Barry was also described as sometimes languid, an affectation of lassitude with posed reclining. As Charlotte Lennox wrote in *The Art of Coquetry* (1747), 'The languid Nymph enslaves with softer art' (142). Each actress, then, represented for her time the central conception of tragic womanhood, and the play as popular culture reinforced each even as, collectively, performances left a record of changing demands on women in times of crisis.

England Preserved and Casting Lady Surrey

In between these two revivals of *Venice Preserved*, one of the most heavily subsidized plays of the decade was produced, George Watson's *England Preserved* (performed 21, 23, 24, 26, 28 February, 2 March, and

23 April in 1795). Its title points out a relationship to *Venice Preserved*, and its star was the ward of the Lord Chancellor, who was part of a group of powerful men who believed that the British theatre could be used as effectively as the French stage to solidify political positions. In France, plays often provided (and interpreted) the latest news, while other plays were written and produced as pure propaganda (Cox 241–7). Leonard Connolly provides evidence that some argued 'by implication at least, that government should make more effective use of the propaganda value of the theater' (83). Some dramatists agreed with the playwright John Haggit that the English government was not learning from the French National Assembly that 'by the pieces which they have ordered to be acted, as well as *those composed for the purpose* ... [they] have gained an astonishing increase of popularity to their cause' (qtd in Cox 245–6, emphasis mine). Evidence survives that a cabal did indeed exist. John Larpent's diary, for instance, notes times when he consulted William Windham and plays were banned or ordered drastically revised. The Lord Chamberlain himself was sometimes directly involved.[12] Playwrights recognized propaganda beyond ideological alignment in Watson's play. The *Tribune* reported that it was 'pushed upon the stage, we are told, with a weight of patronage at its back. *It could not be refused by any means whatever*' (J. Thelwall 310, emphasis mine). It was also lavishly mounted. As the *Whitehall Evening Post* said, 'Every aid that the Manager could give was liberally bestowed. The dresses were costly and appropriate, and in scenery as well as decoration the *costume* was carefully attended to.'[13]

The play is set shortly after the death of King John I, one of the most controversial kings in English history.[14] In the last years of his reign, the barons had objected to his excessive use of force and coercion, raised a force to oppose him, and asked for help from the French. In 1215 King John was compelled to swear to the Magna Carta, the most important document in British constitutional history. Although opposition periodical writers objected to Watson's application of history, he used the facts and gender effectively to control interpretation. He begins after John's death, and a major line in the plot is the earl of Surrey trying to escape the French. Unlike in *Venice Preserved*, the 'rebels' have no cause and the enemies, notably the French, have been isolated. Pembroke, Protector of England during Henry's minority, is entirely exemplary. Lady Surrey, Pembroke's daughter, enters in Act III and takes over the play. The scene opens with her joyous anticipation of her husband's arrival, but a knight tells her he has been captured by the French as he tried to return to the king. An emotional scene ensues in which she shrieks, nearly faints, feels her judgment disturbed, and then resolves to find him. She asks Pembroke to keep her son while she disguises herself and goes to her husband. She finds him, there is an emotional reunion, and a sympathetic guard helps her escape with the promise of following with Surrey. She returns to the castle and hears he has been recaptured, providing another scene in which she is wild with grief and worry.

Unlike Belvidera, Lady Surrey is able to be loyal both to her father and her husband, and the character was widely interpreted as representing the 'horrors and miseries incident to a country in a state of civil war' (*Whitehall Evening Post* 21–4 February 1795). For three acts, the audience is treated to the scales of emotions that Belvidera and she-tragedy heroines had long performed. As a few comparisons will show, Watson hoped to make Lady Surrey's part a success in two ways: by recreating some of Siddons's signature scenes and by modelling the part on the domestic Belvideras in vogue before Siddons. With both strategies, he hoped to make her the loving wife and trusting daughter *but also* the perfect war-time mother. In one of her first speeches, she exults to her son who has wished he were old enough to fight: 'O! may thy manly prime fulfil the hopes / Thy childhood gives! . . . To think I've given to my native land / A guardian hero' (III i p. 329). Part of Siddons's carefully developed persona was that of a devoted mother, and she often appeared on stage and was portrayed in prints with her son and other child actors. Henry Siddons, then eight, appeared with his mother in her debut return to the London stage in 1782. Her doting, worried gaze at him helped establish her reputation as a domestic woman at heart and became one of the defining moments in her performances. Lady Surrey has a major scene of this kind (which even the *Times* labelled 'a stage trick' [23 February 1795]). Watson borrows as well from Siddons's performances in John Home's *Douglas* (1756), one of the most popular pathetic tragedies of the century. Both Home's Lady Randolph and Watson's Lady Surrey have emotional dungeon scenes that include shrieks of agony and near-madness.

In spite of scenes of the sort that Siddons performed regularly, the part of Lady Surrey was designed for the kind of feminine, domestic heroine Crawford and her replacement Elizabeth Younge Pope had been. An important part of the background to the casting of Lady Surrey was the fact that Covent Garden had been struggling to replace the declining Pope, who, although unequal to Siddons, could be counted on for 'reliable excellence in an extraordinary variety of roles' (*Biographical Dictionary* 12:71).[15] Pope was a tall, lovely woman with a soft, delicate complexion and elegant figure; she was compared to Greek statuary and was particularly skilled at pathos. Thomas Harris was basically a businessman but a very experienced theatre manager. As Frederick Reynolds notes, in contrast to actor-managers like Kemble, Harris assigned parts 'to that performer, whom he thought, would best amuse the town' (2:126), and he was usually creative and successful in recruiting talent for tragic roles. Faced, however, with Drury Lane's tragedy juggernaut, Siddons, and the talent of the vivacious Elizabeth Farren who made the part of Lady Teazel her signature, Harris showed a little desperation.

Rather than along a gender continuum, up to this point the actresses who played Belvidera fell into two categories represented by emphasis on feminine pathos or on striking ability to arouse tragic fear and awe. Interestingly, Covent Garden's replacements and Watson's play would come to introduce into the discussion a stronger emphasis on the very nature of Woman, and that, as much as acting ability and interpretation, determined judgment. Harris's first try was Charlotte Ann Wattle Twisleton, whose first role at Covent Garden was Belvidera in February 1794. She had performed at private theatricals, at Westminster School, and in the summer at Cheltenham and Liverpool. 'Her figure is neat, her action is free and unembarrassed . . . though not beautiful, has a pleasing and intelligent countenance,' the *Morning Post* reported. All agreed that she was pretty, elegant, quite petite, and stage-struck (*Morning Post* 3 February 1794; *Whitehall Evening Post* 1–4 February 1794; *St. James Chronicle* 1–4 February 1794). One review compared her to Ann Crawford and another mentioned the symmetry of her figure, but the mostly chivalrous and politely complimentary reviews contrasted her unfavourably to Siddons, and by the next season she was back performing at Bristol, Bath, Birmingham, and the like.[16]

Next Harris paid an inflated salary to lure Tryphosa Jane Wallis from Bath, a major, provincial theatre, where he rediscovered the formerly unsuccessful London actress.[17] She was the oldest of strolling players' eight children and, after her mother died when she was eleven, Wallis was taken into the home of Alexander and Charlotte Wedderburn, Lord and Lady Loughborough, who had been her patrons when she acted in Harrogate. *A Biographical Dictionary of Actors, Actresses . . .* notes that her 10 January 1789 Covent Garden debut was 'through the influence of her benefactors,' and reviewers sniped that her roles, salary, and position were sustained through patronage. In 1797 after her return to London, the *Monthly Mirror* began its biographical sketch of her: 'It was ever our opinion that Miss Wallis possessed no well-founded claim to the rank she held on the London boards; but she had the good fortune to be patronized by the Lord High Chancellor of Great Britain.' For her first London debut as Sigismunda in *Tancred and Sigismunda*, Lady Loughborough bought her a dress reputed to have cost £100. She played Belvidera on 21 January in another new dress. Wallis suffered from bouts of stage fright in London, and, in the fall of 1789, she began acting at Bath and enjoyed success there for five years.

Harris saw her perform there and re-engaged her for Covent Garden. At her final performance in Bath, Wallis addressed her audience, pleading that, because of her responsibilities for her seven brothers and sisters, she needed the London income and opportunities. This act gave her a lasting reputation for virtue and sacrifice, and it somewhat softened London reviews. Back at Covent Garden in the fall 1794, she played the major parts she had at Bath, including Calista in *The Fair Penitent*. Throughout her career she was known for her beautiful dresses, and her life with the Loughboroughs associated her with the aristocracy, an identification that critics have argued replaced identifications with prostitutes and available women common to earlier decades.[18] In fact, one retrospective noted, 'Patronage carried her into the drawing room, and there she learnt some of the inelegancies, but none of the graces of fashion. Miss Farren [who married the Earl of Derby after his wife's death] made a different use of her opportunities; she stole all its graces, and left the rest behind her' (*Monthly Mirror*, September 1797).

The philosophies of the two theatres were different; Kemble preferred classical modes, and players in his *Venice Preserved* 'appeared in the *costume* of their various Countries.'[19] Having better figures than Siddons, the Covent Garden actresses increased the interest in their performances with contemporary clothes, although they sometimes erred. Mrs Twisleton's white satin dress with crepe and silver was described as 'extremely elegant' but 'much too rich, considering the alledged distress and poverty of' Belvidera (*Times* 3 February 1794). Classical touches elevated but distanced the heroines, while currently fashionable dresses worked to make the women and their dilemmas more immediate and timely. Wallis's dresses invariably received favourable comments such as 'elegantly simple, and admirably suited both to the character and her own person,' and sometimes she was praised for 'giving consequence to characters.'[20] Rather than blending historical touches with current

fashion as Siddons and many actresses did (Ribiero 105–27), she fell
into the category of actresses whose dresses replicated and set fashion
for aspiring women in the audience. In an attempt to keep the play
going, new dresses for her were advertised for the 28 February performance. Scholars have theorized that clothing and behaviour could
'foster the notion that they were worthy of audience appreciation, both
on the stage and off it' (Crouch 71).[21] Whether an actress is identified by
her last name or with a title such as 'Miss Wallis' is telling. Unlike these
performers whose gender was always under surveillance, actresses like
Pope and Siddons were almost always identified by their last names as
the male players were, thereby granting them full professional status.

England Preserved, the Nature of Woman, and Casting War-time Women

Watson, thus, knew that Wallis would play Lady Surrey and, in spite
of the Siddons-style touches, wrote within the tradition of the Covent
Garden actresses. Many reviews said that Wallis was not up to the
part of Lady Surrey, and a few questioned whether any actress was,
a topic perhaps suggested by the role itself. The *Star* said that 'the
incessant labour requisite to fill the part of *Lady Surrey* is actually
beyond the bodily powers of the female frame' (23 February 1795).
Somewhat surprisingly, 'muscle' was beginning to be prominently
discussed. Elizabeth Farren was criticized as 'not sufficiently mus-
cular,' and Siddons, the ideal, was described as having 'sufficient
muscle to bestow a roundness upon the limbs, and her attitudes are,
therefore, distinguished equally by energy and grace.' One of the genteel code words was 'en bon point,' meaning plump or fat in a soft,
'fleshy' way; such actresses were also criticized for body shape and
lack of effective movement. Siddons, although heavy, was sometimes
cleared of the charge: 'not at all inclined to the *em-bon-point*' (West
159–61). Twisleton apparently was 'inclining to the *en bon point*' (*Sun*
3 February 1794). In the huge theatres of the time, both voice and
movement had to be robust; Wallis and a line of Covent Garden
actresses could deliver neither but elicited fascinating comments on
female nature and capacity.

Part of the context for *England Preserved* was the popularity of
Shakespeare's *King John,* which had been played every year except the
1793–4 season and which was so in vogue that Jane Austen had wished
to see it instead of *Hamlet.*[22] Siddons's performance of Constance was

a *tour de force* of 'maternal love and intrepidity ... of proud grief and majestic desolation.'[23] Conceptions of the nature and capabilities of women were strong, and part of the success of Siddons's interpretation of Lady Macbeth and other characters was her ability to move, suddenly or gradually, from the elevated and noble to the feminine and, therefore, to reinforce these gender requirements. She did not always succeed, however, and was occasionally criticized for 'too masculine a tone' in, for instance, Act I of *Venice Preserved*; the *Sun's* 22 October 1795 review compares her unfavourably to the more feminine, 'tender' Belvideras. The vulnerable woman strongly marks some of Siddons's scenes, however, as with Lady Macbeth in the sleepwalking scene and at the moment she sees her father in Duncan and cannot kill him. As she moves from more masculine resolve than her husband to vulnerability to regret, her feminine nature seems to suffuse the character.

Watson appears to have tried to take advantage of the perception of the nature of women and these highly successful theatrical transitions. In a parallel to Volumnia in *Coriolanus*, Lady Surrey rises above what women were thought capable of because of her loyalty to her husband and the nation. She is aroused repeatedly to such actions by the situation of her husband and displays contradictory characteristics that are the product of the times and, therefore, seem to indicate an attempt to modernize her. She displays bursts of courage described as beyond women's nature, and then collapses into end-of-the-century feminine debilitation, physical and mental. In Act III, she says, 'This sudden death of hope / Disturbs my judgment' (III i p. 331). Speeches promising to 'for a husband, rise above my sex' (III i p. 332) and 'I'm prepared for all; / . . . and cannot now be moved' (III ii p. 336) alternate with 'Where doth my frenzy hurry me?' (IV iii p. 347). With references to the 'brain grows feverish' (V i p. 354), she conjures up the formulaic images of madness, a state of mind much in fashion for tragic women. Siddons was a master of it and recognized for her ability to create different images of madness as appropriate for different characters and situations. Unlike tragic women whose madness inevitably precedes death, Lady Surrey, being guiltless, always returns, as a needle to true north, to the characteristics identified with ideal women in the period. Watson has her summarize this theory of wartime women:

Woman, aroused by pure and virtuous love,
Defies all Nature's obstacles combined:

Her soul, exalted even above itself,
Over hill, and precipice, and rocky glen,

. . .

Swift as the winds she'll wing her fearless flight,
Snatch, amidst death, her great inspiring prize;
Then, struck with what she's past, her courage lose,
Her dangers swell, and sinking on herself,
Be all the timid female o'er again.   (IV iii p. 346)

Ronald Paulson has pointed out the dominance of female allegorical figures in the Revolutionary period. In France, Reason, Nature, Truth, and even Fraternity were women. He agrees with Lynn Hunt that '"the collective violence of seizing liberty and overthrowing the monarchy were effaced behind the tranquil visage and statuesque pose of an aloof goddess" the female figure of Liberty' (Paulson, *Representations* 21–2). On both sides of the Channel iconic figures of women were depicted leading men (and citizens) into battle. Siddons had posed as Tragedy and Britannia and could be the iconic allegorical figure, but, tellingly, prints were already showing French liberty as a Medusa-haired wild woman with a head impaled on a pitchfork.[24] When Lady Surrey seizes her brother's sword and shouts, 'Follow me, brother, I can brave the field!' she performs the parts of Liberty and Britannia. Rising to express Britishness – male and female – to send men to battle and willing to go herself, sometimes greater than herself and womankind, sometimes on the edge of surrendering to the hysteria of the day, she was intended to be a fascinating spectacle of the time.

The final tableaux in *Venice Preserved* and *England Preserved* suggest how important gender is and why neither play worked in 1795. By depicting the misery war causes women – the impact on the domestic front – Watson's play was opportune as he hit the notes of his conflicted times. Swinging from hysteric to domestic, dove to amazon, Lady Surrey shrieks and sobs at one moment, and then seizes a sword and heads out of the domestic space where she has earlier caressed her son. She and Siddons were images of their time, which demanded both allegoric performances and symbolic stances for its survival. In *Venice Preserved*, the aged, formerly vengeful Priuli walking with the child off the stage that is haunted by his dead father, and Pierre, and the mad, then dead Belvidera was an image straight out of English print representations of events in France. They walk into the unknown and, despite Priuli's pledges, are a reminder of the threatening unknown into which Britain was entering with the war against France. The happy tableau at the end of *England Preserved* had even less credibility. Reassuringly, the need for heroics passes, and father, brother, husband, and son are safe around Lady Surrey. Again, an old man and a child (the unseen King Henry) are the hopes of the future. Like Francis Aickin who played Priuli, the actor Alexander Pope who played the earl of Pembroke was more journeyman than star. Reviews consistently labelled him mediocre and described his tendencies to both whine and declaim. Joseph Holman, who played Surrey, was Pope's age, played many of the same tragic leads, and was similarly reviewed. He, too, had interpretation faults and fell into rants. According to the *Biographical Dictionary of Actors, Actresses...*, he deliberately attempted to set his acting style apart from Kemble's and employed 'extravagance of action' and energetic movement, which was sometimes described as 'agitation.' None, then, produced a reliable, confident masculinity to satisfy the popular imagination.

Wallis, a rather ordinary woman and ordinary actress who, because of her background, united both a lower-class and an aristocratic body, as Lady Surrey was surrounded by family, with peace restored. Rather frighteningly, neither play shows a wise, powerful male in the full power of midlife. Watson was attempting to restore order with his patriarch and the configuration of an intact, multigenerational family. In fact, as some writers saw, this conclusion actually highlighted the contrasts between 1217 with its celebration of Magna Carta and the end of a war, and the late eighteenth-century loss of civil rights that included the suspension of habeas corpus and the long, harrowing war in which the British found themselves. In 1798 when *England Preserved* was revived, it was even more of a fairy tale, as the British were now coping with the Irish Rebellion, Napoleon on the march, Spain joining the French in the war against Britain, women in Kent being taught to fight a feared invasion, and news of such difficulties funding the war so that the gold standard was suspended. Because of the power of popular culture to release the dynamic relationship between past and present, *Venice Preserved* was too threateningly prophetic and *England Preserved* too fancifully reassuring for the late 1790s, and the women's performances of female nature too vivid a record of domestic stress.

NOTES

1 Thelwall's major offences were membership in reformist organizations, leading the organization of Conventions, and writing and giving political

lectures. Reporting his arrest, the *Times* said that he was 'a Member of the different seditious Societies, and known by giving democratic Lectures' (14 May 1794). Charged with high treason along with him were eleven others including Thomas Holcroft and John Horne Tooke. Thelwall was acquitted of treason on 5 December 1794. See also Barrell, 392–401, 567–9.

2 As Paul Keen notes, Daniel Eaton frequently used *Venice Preserved* quotations as epigraphs and examples in his reformist writing and had already been tried twice for seditious publishing.

3 Henrietta Cecil Thelwall's *The Life of John Thelwall* quotes lines 144–64 and 205–15 from Act I.

4 See my essay, 'Paradigms of Popular Culture' and my forthcoming 'Male, Female, History, and a Tale of Two Plays.'

5 King Charles II attended on the third night, thereby financially rewarding Otway. The play was also performed on 21 April 1682 as part of the Tory celebrations over the duke of York's return from Scotland and again on 31 May for the duchess of York at her first appearance at the theatre since returning from Scotland.

6 *Morning Post and Fashionable World* 22 October 1795; *Oracle and Public Advertiser* 27 October 1795. On competing cheers, see also the *Sun* 23 October 1795, the *Times* 27 October 1795, and *General Evening Post* 24–7 October 1795.

7 'Remarks on *Venice Preserved*,' *Remarks* 3. Inchbald's distinction is supported by periodical reports: the *Times*, for instance, calls those who applauded Pierre in 1794 'Jacobinical spirits' (3 February 1794), and the *Sun* on 22 October 1795 described them as giving 'violent approbation of the democratic remarks.'

8 *Morning Chronicle* 22 and 27 October 1795; Review of Bensley 22 October 1795.

9 On Siddons's power to 'wear the lightnings of scorn in her countenance,' see also Bate, 'Shakespeare and the Rival Muses,' quoting James Boaden, 97.

10 The review refers to the playing of Euphrasia in *The Grecian Daughter*, one of Siddons's signature roles.

11 *Connoisseur* 14 March 1754. This essayist quotes *Venice Preserv'd* but does not specifically complain about the performance of Belvidera and Jaffeir.

12 Connolly gives examples, 93, 104–5. On Loughborough and the cabal, see Hilton 62–7, 94, and Christie 217–22.

13 *Whitehall Evening Post* 21–4 February 1795.

14 Terence Hoagwood, one of the few critics to mention the play, erroneously locates the play in 1422, when Henry VI was an infant king (30). Historians today recognize that the reputation of John has been unfairly tarnished by hostile accounts, and his fight with the barons was based on his disregard for traditional feudal relationships between the crown and the nobility. See Carpenter, *The Minority of Henry III*, and Mortimer, *Angevin England*.

15 Pope was in ill health and died slowly (her last original role, January 1797).

16 The *Times* and the *Sun* for 3 February 1794; *Whitehall Evening Post, St. James Chronicle, London Chronicle* all for 1–4 February 1794; quotation from *Morning Post* 3 February 1794. See also *Biographical Dictionary of Actors, Actresses,* s.v. 'Twisleton.'

17 Information about Wallis comes from the *ODNB, A Dictionary of Actors,* and periodical reviews and essays cited in this essay.

18 See especially Crouch 58–78, and Ribeiro 105–27.

19 *Morning Post and Fashionable World* 22 October 1795, and see Ribeiro, 118–22, especially the illustrations.

20 Respectively, *Morning Chronicle* 26 September 1795, and *Monthly Mirror* January 1797.

21 See also Perry 62–6. On actresses as influencing fashion and even being consulted by noble women, see Crouch 72–4, and Munns in this volume.

22 Bate describes the play as 'central to the canon of Shakespeare's plays between 1792 and 1820' (*Shakespearean Constitutions* 204).

23 Quoted from Siddons's biographer Thomas Campbell, in Bate, 'Rival Muses' 89 (and see 90–4). See also Burwick 137–9, and Keen 173, 177–8.

24 See Thomas Rowlandson, *The Contrast 1793;* iconic representations of British and French Liberty in which France is associated with madness, cruelty, injustice, ingratitude, among other negative qualities, abound from the period, cf. Donald 142–83.

WORKS CITED

Asleson, Robyn. '"She was Tragedy Personified": Crafting the Siddons Legend in Art and Life.' *A Passion for Performance: Sarah Siddons and Her Portraitists.* Ed. Robyn Asleson. Los Angeles: J. Paul Getty Museum, 1999. 41–95. Print.

Backscheider, Paula. 'Paradigms of Popular Culture.' *Eighteenth-Century Novel* 6–7 (2009): 20–59. Print.

– 'Male, Female, History, and a Tale of Two Plays.' Forthcoming. Bakhtin, Mikhail. *The Dialogic Imagination.* Trans. Caryl Emerson and Michael Holquist. Austin: U of Texas P, 1981. Print.

Barrell, John. *Imagining the King's Death: Figurative Treason, Fantasies of Regicide, 1793–1796* Oxford: Oxford UP, 2000. Print.

Bate, Jonathan. *Shakespearean Constitutions: Politics, Theatre, Criticism, 1730–1830* Oxford: Clarendon, 1989. Print.

– 'Shakespeare and the Rival Muses: Siddons versus Jordan.' *Notorious Muse:*

The Actress in British Art and Culture, 1776–1812. Ed. Robyn Asleson. New Haven: Yale UP, 2003. 81–103. Print.

The Beauties of Mrs Siddons: or a Review of her Performance of the Characters of Belvidera, Zara, Isabella, Margaret of Anjou, Jane Shore, and Lady Randolph; in Letters from a Lady of Distinction to a Friend in the Country. London, 1786. Microfilm.

Bernard, John. *Retrospections of the Stage*. 2 vols. London, 1830. Microfilm.

Biographical Dictionary of Actors, Actresses, Musicians, Dancers, Managers, and Other Stage Personnel in London, 1660–1800. Ed. Philip H. Highfill, Kalman A. Burnim, and Edward A. Langhans. 16 vols. Carbondale: Southern Illinois UP, 1973–93. Print.

Burwick, Frederick. 'The Ideal Shatters: Sarah Siddons, Madness, and the Dynamics of Gesture.' *Notorious Muse: The Actress in British Art and Culture, 1776–1812*. Ed. Robyn Asleson. New Haven: Yale UP, 2003. 129–50. Print.

Carpenter, D.A. *The Minority of Henry III*. Berkeley: U of California P, 1990. Print.

'Characteristics of Living Authors and Players.' *Monthly Mirror* (September 1797). 172–5. Microfilm.

Christie, Ian. *Wars and Revolutions, 1760–1815*. Cambridge, MA: Harvard UP, 1982. Print.

Connolly, Leonard. *The Censorship of English Drama, 1737–1824* San Marino: Huntington Library and Art Gallery, 1976. Print.

Cox, Jeffrey N. 'Romantic Drama and the French Revolution.' *Revolution and English Romanticism: Politics and Rhetoric*. Ed. Keith Hanley and Raman Selden. Hemel Hemstead, Hertfordshire: Harvester Wheatsheaf, 1990. 241–60. Print.

Crouch, Kimberly. 'The Public Life of Actresses: Prostitutes or Ladies?' *Gender in Eighteenth-Century England: Roles, Representations and Responsibilities*. Ed. Hannah Barker and Elaine Chalus. London: Longman, 1997. 58–78. Print.

Donald, Diana. *The Age of Caricature: Satirical Prints in the Reign of George III*. New Haven: Yale UP, 1996. Print.

Eastwood, David. 'Patriotism and the English State in the 1790s.' *The French Revolution and British Popular Politics*. Ed. Mark Philp. Cambridge: Cambridge UP, 2002. 146–68. Print.

Hilton, Boyd. *A Mad, Bad, and Dangerous People? England 1783–1846*. Oxford: Clarendon, 2006. Print.

Hoagwood, Terrence. 'Romantic Drama and Historical Hermeneutics.' *British Romantic Drama: Historical and Critical Essays*. Ed. Hoagwood and Daniel P. Watkins. Madison, NJ: Fairleigh Dickson UP, 1998. 22–55. Print.

Hume, Robert. *The Development of English Drama in the late Seventeenth Century*

Oxford: Clarendon, 1977. Print.

Inchbald, Elizabeth. *Remarks for the British Theatre*. Introduction by Cecilia Macheski. Delmar, NY: Scholars' Facsimiles & Reprints, 1990. Print.

Keen, Paul. *The Crisis of Literature in the 1790s*. Cambridge: Cambridge UP, 1999. Print.

Lennox, Charlotte. 'The Art of Coquettry.' Ed. Paula Backscheider and Catherine Ingrassia. *British Women Poets of the Long Eighteenth Century: An Anthology* Baltimore, MD: Johns Hopkins UP, 2009. 141–4. Print.

Lynch, James. *Box, Pit, and Gallery: Stage and Society in Johnson's London*. Berkeley: U of California P, 1953. Print.

Marsden, Jean. *Fatal Desire: Women, Sexuality, and the English Stage, 1660–1720*. Ithaca: Cornell UP, 2006. Print.

Mortimer, Richard. *Angevin England, 1154–1258*. Oxford: Blackwell, 1994. Print.

Otway, Thomas. *Venice Preserved Lincoln:* University of Nebraska Press, 1969. Print.

Paulson, Ronald. *Popular and Polite Art in the Age of Hogarth and Fielding*. Notre Dame: U of Notre Dame P, 1979. Print.

– *Representations of Revolution (1789–1820)*. New Haven: Yale UP, 1983. Print.

Perry, Gill. 'Ambiguity and Desire: Metaphors of Sexuality in Late Eighteenth-Century Representation of the Actress.' *Notorious Muse: The Actress in British Art and Culture, 1776–1812*. Ed. Robyn Asleson. New Haven: Yale UP, 2003. 57–80. Print.

Reynolds, Frederick. 1827. *Life and Times of Frederick Reynolds*. 2 vols. New York: Benjamin Blom, 1969. Print.

Ribeiro, Aileen. 'Costuming the Part: A Discourse of Fashion and Fiction in the Image of the Actress in England, 1776–1812.' *Notorious Muse: The Actress in British Art and Culture, 1776–1812*. Ed. Robyn Asleson. New Haven: Yale UP, 2003. 104–28. Print.

Taylor, Aline. *Next to Shakespeare: Otway's Venice Preserv'd and The Orphan*. Durham, NC: Duke UP, 1950. Print.

Thelwall, Henrietta Cecil. *The Life of John Thelwall*. 2 vols. London, 1837. Microfilm.

Thelwall, John. 'The Second Lecture on the Political Prostitution of our Public Theatre.' *The Tribune* (15 April 1795): 309–18. Microfilm.

Watson, George. *England Preserved: A Tragedy in Five Acts. Modern Theatre*. Vol. 4. Ed. Elizabeth Inchbald. 1811; New York: Benjamin Blom, 1968. 309–62. Print.

West, Shearer. 'Body Connoisseurship.' *Notorious Muse: The Actress in British Art and Culture, 1776–1812*. Ed. Robyn Asleson. New Haven: Yale UP, 2003. 151–70. Print.

4 Celebrity Status: The Eighteenth-Century Actress as Fashion Icon

JESSICA MUNNS

Their best Cloaths, best Looks, shining Jewels, sparkling Eyes, the Treasure of the World in a Ring. Then there's such a hurry of Pleasure to transport us, the Bustle, Noise, Gallantry, Equipage, Garters, Feathers, Wigs, Bows, Smiles, Oggles, Love, Music and Applause. I cou'd wish that my whole Life long were the first Night of a New Play. (Farquhar V.i.13–18)

The theatre, as Mirabel, the playboy hero of George Farquhar's *The Inconstant* (1702) enthusiastically indicates, was a place of glamour and fashion where the glitterati of the late seventeenth and eighteenth century met to see and be seen. As Gill Perry puts it, theatres represented 'a public culture of social exchange and spectatorship' (2) which went well beyond the process of watching a play, although the play was an essential part of the process, gathering people together to participate in communal acts of looking at the stage and at each other. In 1752, for instance, Horace Walpole wrote to Sir Horace Mann of the Gunning girls that 'there are mobs at their doors to see them get into their chairs; and people go early to get places at the theatre when it is known they are there' (Postle 5). There were increasing numbers of sites for celebrity and fashion in the eighteenth century, from the court to operas, clubs, assembly rooms, masquerade balls, and art exhibitions. Such leisure events, the people who attended them, and the costumes they wore were much described in journals and newspapers that disseminated fashion and social trends into the wider realms of popular culture.[1] However, few areas of leisure activity brought celebrity and fashion together so entirely as the theatre, where the actresses portraying women of fashion and the actual women of fashion in the audience were engaged in an endless process of exchanging roles and clothes. It was, indeed, customary for court ladies to donate robes worn on special occasions (which could not be worn again without eliciting comment) to the actresses, and in time, and actresses in their turn set the fashion trends that all must follow.

As is widely recognized, various factors came together in the late seventeenth and eighteenth centuries to elevate the status and fame of actors and move them, especially actresses, into a celebrity status with their 'performance' on- and offstage closely scrutinized and commented on (Luckhurst and Moody 3). Felicity Nussbaum has cogently characterized many of these factors:

> The expansion of print culture in the eighteenth century, along with the rise of mercantilism, the lessening power of the aristocracy, the secularization of society and the increase in leisure gave rise to a media apparatus that was essential to the construction of celebrity. ('Actresses' 148)[2]

The increase in internal and external trade that fuelled the economy of the eighteenth century also encouraged and was encouraged by the increasing availability of luxury goods.[3] Elegant and rich clothing had always been available to the very wealthy. However, the attenuation of the sumptuary laws that had helped to mark out the aristocracy as unique, combined with the spread of wealth and the rise in luxury goods, made fashionable clothing widely available, much desired and much admired. The actress – largely engaged in impersonations of the lifestyles of the rich and titled, highly visible, and usually very attractive – was a natural subject for the nascent machinery of publicity and for the display of the luxury phenomena of high fashion. As Fred Inglis has recently insisted there is a close connection between 'celebrity and art' with the theatre standing out as an institution through which one can trace the rise of celebrity in popular culture (41).

By the opening years of the eighteenth century, the actress (along with other female public entertainers, such as opera singers and dancers) was an established figure on the stage, though still retaining much of her novelty value in a society where few women were open to a general public gaze. The other group of notable women who were also to some extent open to a public gaze were the great women of fashion and the court. Their activities and appearances, and especially their scandals, were increasingly reported in popular media and their pictures engraved and distributed – all characteristics the great women of the realm had in common with actresses. However, an actress was both more easily subject to public scrutiny and more likely to become a 'celebrity' than a great lady. Unless, that is, the great lady very markedly transgressed normal rules of aristocratic behaviour, as did the duchess of Kingston who was tried for bigamy (1776), or Georgiana, duchess of Devonshire when she campaigned in the Westminster elections (1784).[4] The actress in general was more open to comment, and much less protected by her status than were the great ladies, and yet there was a complex interdependence between actresses and great ladies that confirmed actresses' emergence as celebrities and as icons of fashion. Samuel Pepys's brief excited comments on the actresses such as 'Nell in her boy's clothes, mighty pretty' (7 May 1668) are indicative of the interest the actresses and their clothes aroused, especially when their clothes involved showing their legs. Nevertheless, by the eighteenth century the mere fact of a woman on stage ceased in and of itself to be astonishing; through the circulation of biographies, memoirs, and paintings, and their cheaper print forms, the appearance of the actress made an impact on a wider popular culture. Indeed, as Laura Rosenthal notes, where once the actress had been associated with prostitution, by the eighteenth century writers were 'likely to see [actresses] as social performers, trendsetters, and even fashion plates' ('Entertaining Women' 161).

The theatre and drama that re-emerged following the restoration of the monarchy in 1660 was not a restoration of the previous popular theatre replete with city comedies, but a much more limited, and to a large degree a court-controlled and elite affair.[5] The plays that were revived or written for the two restored playhouses ranged from the dreamy tragi-comedies of Beaumont and Fletcher (works that initially had been written for the private theatres), Spanish intrigue plays, and, increasingly, heroic tragedies on the one hand, to comedies of upper-class courtship and sex games on the other. Whether in comedies or tragedies, the roles that the newly recruited women actors were called upon to portray were generally those of great ladies: in tragedies, empresses, queens, and duchesses, and in comedies, members of the gentry and upper bourgeoisie.[6] The royal fiat that women must now perform female roles led to the rapid recruitment of women with good enough speaking voices to perform the roles of noble ladies and queens.[7] The actresses had preferably to be literate so that they could read their lines, or failing that, intelligent so that they could memorize them. Ideally they were good-looking, and could act, dance, and sing – or had the ability to be trained to do these things. They also had to be sufficiently poor and desperate to perform on stage and so enter the no-man's land (or no-woman's land) of the déclassé. Such women inevitably proved to be an attractive novelty. Famously some, such as Nell Gwyn, Moll Davis, and Margaret Hughes, became royal mistresses with, in Gwyn's case, her children ennobled. The 1680 portrait of Nell Gwyn by Simon Verelst with the top of her left nipple showing above the loose and negligent décolleté of her bodice certainly indicates that she is not a lady; on the other hand, the pearls wound in her hair and around her neck indicate that she is not a common prostitute either. The actress who became a mistress of the very great, no matter how humble her origins, moved into a sphere close to that of the lady she had portrayed on stage and certainly, as in the case of Nell Gwyn, became a figure of public speculation and satire, as well as raunchy appreciation. The famous anecdote of her response to the crowd who mistook her for the duchess of Portsmouth and gathered angrily around her carriage when she drove into Oxford in 1681 – 'Pray good people be civil, I am the protestant whore' – whether true or not, indicates a high degree of popular recognition.[8]

Much has been written about the interchangeability of the terms 'actress' and 'whore'[9] and Kimberly Crouch has remarked that 'actresses associated with characteristics of both the prostitute and aristocratic women could choose which model of behaviour to follow' (78). In terms of fashion and elegant lifestyle, the choice was surely easy. Actresses professionally engaged in lives of spectacle and display had every reason to imitate aristocratic women off-stage as well as on-stage. Quite early on and apart from actresses forming liaisons with noblemen, one Restoration actress, Mary Lee, married a baronet. Unfortunately the marriage was probably not entirely legal; however, although obliged to return to the stage when her husband/partner fled the country to avoid his debts, Lee kept the title, Lady Slingsby.[10]

The connection between the actress and the female aristocrat was not just a matter of forming sexual liaisons, or role-playing. Female aristocrats and lower-class actresses were mutually involved in circuits of representation in which they drew on each others' manners and appearance. The great ladies whom the actress mimicked on stage were also engaged in an endless interchange between pictorial representations of themselves which borrowed from dramas, just as dramas borrowed from pictorial representations. This interchange has been studied by Angelica Goodden in her book *Actio and Persuasion* with reference to the French stage. However, if less formally encoded, a similar process can be observed in England with painting and stage representations drawing on each other in terms of setting, costume, and formalized gestures. Both actresses and ladies were busy fashioning themselves from similar sources, including significant imports from France. The interchanges between the elegant representations of the visual and active arts, and between the actress and the noblewoman, were given further resonance by that ubiquitous figure of the age, the French dancing master, such as St André. St André visited England in the 1660s and taught actresses to move and dance like ladies, and ladies to move and dance like actresses. Restoration actresses were perhaps figures of curiosity and notoriety rather than entirely celebrities but by the eighteenth century with her position secure on the stage, the actress very much comes into her own.

Paula Backscheider has noted that popular culture is 'associated with profitable endeavor' and 'therefore to some extent self-consciously manufactured,' and the eighteenth-century actresses provided profit both for themselves and others via imitation and tie-in marketing (21). Lavinia Fenton (1708–60, see figure 2.1 on p. 30), for example, became one of the first superstars after she created the role of Polly Peachum in John Gay's *The Beggar's Opera* (1728) and was rapidly commodified into a variety of saleable objects. Her portrait was painted on screens and fans, and accounts both laudatory and abusive circulated about her (*Oxford Dictionary of National Biography*). Charles Paulet, third duke of Bolton fell in love with her and in 1751 (when his estranged first wife died) they were married. Famously, William Hogarth's painting *The Beggar's Opera, Act III* (1728/9) depicts a scene from the final act of the play, with Fenton as Polly on her knees begging for MacHeath's life, and the duke of Bolton in a stage-box gazing at her with admiration. Such was Fenton's fame that John Gay wrote in humorous self-deprecation to Jonathan Swift of 'a Mezzo-tinto Print publish'd to day of Polly, the Heroine of the Beggar's Opera, who was before unknown, & is now in so high vogue, that I am in doubt, whether her fame does not surpass that of the Opera itself' (72–5).[11]

Hester Santlow (c. 1690–1773), a dancer as well as an actress, was famous for her appearances as a female Harlequin and also for her long curly hair, which she would loosen when dancing. Hair 'à la Santlow' became a fashion. Santlow's dress in her most famous role as a female Harlequin was not only a feminization of the popular male harlequin costume but an example of the type of dress a fashionable woman might well wear to a masquerade ball.[12] Santlow was also sanitizing and upgrading the harlequin figure which was strongly associated with fairground booths and strolling players.[13] While 'legitimate' theatre might seek to distance itself from the performances of strollers there was always a significant cross-over between the popular and elite performance arenas, which fed into the market for portraits and prints.[14] A famous portrait of Santlow as a female Harlequin by John Ellys was frequently copied and widely circulated. Indeed, this role and this costume were so well known that in his travel memoirs published in 1710, a German visitor, Zacharias Conrad von Uffenbach, noted of Santlow, 'She is universally admired for her beauty, matchless figure and the unusual elegance of her dancing and acting and she is visited by those of the highest fashion in England ... They make such a to-do about her that her portrait in this costume is painted on snuff boxes and frequently sold' (Lewis 94).[15]

Among the many actresses who made their mark as both celebrities and fashion icons, Mary Robinson (c. 1756–1801), however, stands out. She was born into genteel circumstances in Bristol, but the family fortunes suffered a major decline when her father deserted his family. Robinson was hurried into marriage at fifteen by her anxious mother, but this was a disaster as the law clerk she married turned out to be a gambler, womanizer, and general ne'er do well. The stage was an obvious alternative for a beautiful, well-spoken, and impecunious young woman and Robinson made her debut at Drury Lane in 1776. Three years later she attracted the attention of the young Prince of Wales when performing Perdita in *The Winter's Tale* and left the stage to become his mistress. Although the liaison was very short lived, Robinson did not return to the stage. Jonathan Bate has gallantly remarked that 'she went on, with extraordinary fortitude, to remake herself as a novelist, poet and feminist pamphleteer' (94). Nevertheless her stage name, Perdita, remained with her for the rest of her life.[16] The famous portrait of her by Thomas Gainsborough (1781), which shows her circumspectly holding a miniature of the Prince of Wales, was entitled 'Mrs. Robinson' but rapidly gained the addition 'Perdita.'

Like many actress celebrities, Mary Robinson wrote her memoirs, in her case in the last years of her life, and they are remarkable not only for the liberality of her political and social sentiments, but also for the many descriptions of the clothes she wore on various occasions. For instance, on her first visit to a Pantheon concert she remembers that she wore a 'habit composed of pale silk satin, trimmed with broad sable'

(96), on her second visit to the Pantheon she wore 'white and silver' and 'was followed with attention' (103), and on a visit to Ranelagh Gardens she recalls she wore a 'plain and simple' gown 'composed of pale lilac lustring' with a 'wreath of white flowers' on her head (160). Robinson is equally attentive to the appearances of other celebrity women, noting that the actress Frances Abington was 'bewitching,' her manners were 'fascinating, and the peculiar tastefulness of her dress excited universal admiration' (117). Robinson's attention to appearance was repaid in that in her turn her dress excited universal admiration too. Laetitia Hawkins remarked (a trifle grudgingly),

> To-day she was a *paysanne* with her straw hat tied at the back of her head, looking as if too new to what she passed to know what she looked at. Yesterday she perhaps had been dressed as the belle of Hyde Park, trimmed, powdered, patched, painted to the utmost power of rouge and white lead. Tomorrow she would be the cravatted Amazon of the riding horse. But be she what she might, the hats of the fashionable promenaders swept the ground as she passed. (qtd in Fyvie 301)

Robinson's memoirs are full of descriptions of her horror at the public notice taken of her at the height of her fame. 'Whenever I appeared in public' she remarks, 'I was overwhelmed by the gazing multitude. I was frequently obliged to quit Ranelagh, owing to the crowd which staring curiosity had assembled round my box' (*Memoirs* 67–8). However, the care she took over her public appearances, as indicated by Hawkins, suggests that like many of today's celebrities, she also courted public attention. The large number of prints of pictures of Robinson, as well as cartoons, attest to the popular pleasure in following what she did (and with whom) and what she wore (and where).

Frances Abington (1737–1815), the actress whom Robinson so admired, led a much longer life and was more professionally successful on the stage, particularly admired as a comedic actor. Tragedies tended to be set in exotic places or in classical times: the costumes required for these performances (although usually modernized) might also tend toward classical draperies, or feathers and turbans. Comedies, on the other hand, were generally set in the here-and-now, in fashionable London, and among fashionable people. An actress who excelled in comic roles was also, therefore, likely to be an actress who excelled in presenting herself as a part of the *bon ton*, a creature of elegance, grace, and style. Moreover comic dramas invited extravagant displays of high fashion in a delightfully contradictory way: the plays frequently satirized excess in fashion, even as actors and audiences relished the display. The absurdly fashionable character is frequently male – Sir Fopling Flutter in Sir George Etherege's *Man of Mode* (1676) and his heirs, Sir Novelty Fashion and Lord Foppington in Colley Cibber's *Love's Last Shift* (1696) and *The Careless Husband* (1704). Absurdity in fashion is more forgivable (on stage at least) in women than in men; however, overly fashion-conscious women are also to be found in drama. In *The Way of the World,* William Congreve's Mirabel famously warns Millamant against 'tight-lacing' during pregnancy (IV.i.264–7). Frances Abington was to make two rather frivolous and fashionable characters, Lady Betty Modish from *The Careless Husband* and Lady Teazle from *School for Scandal* (1777) very much her own. Through the year 1777, prints of her in both roles circulated, as Lady Betty in an astonishing hooped dress, sprigged with ropes of braid, and as Lady Teazle at the moment of discovery in the final act, in an anonymous print and a painting by James Roberts. In both painting and print she has a tall hair style with the feathers widely associated with Abington in the mid-70s.[17] Perry has argued that Abington's success and charm lay in her ability to present herself as chastely flirtatious rather than as a flirt – removing the latter's implication of looseness (9–12, 107). Whether a flirt or merely flirtatious she certainly appears both fashionable and lovely in the many portraits of her by the great artists of the period.

Joshua Reynolds, in particular, painted many portraits of Abington and one of the most famous is his 1771 portrayal of her in the role of Miss Prue in the revival of William Congreve's *Love for Love* (1695). Despite the informality of her posture, leaning over the back of a chair, Abington is dressed very fashionably. Aileen Ribeiro notes of this portrait that Abington is in a 'fashionable pink silk dress trimmed with embroidered net and black silk bracelets,' a revival of a Jacobean fashion item that emphasized whiteness of skin, only in broader silk in their eighteenth-century incarnation (Riberio, 'Costuming' 108). In this portrait Abington/Miss Prue has her thumb rather sexily against her lips as she gazes thoughtfully at the spectators. Miss Prue is described in the personae dramatis of *Love for Love* as 'a silly, awkward Country Girl,' and Reynolds's portrait is a tribute to Abington's skills as a comic actress whom he presents as both fashionable and *louche*, and sexy and innocent – as, indeed, the admired Mrs Abington *and* the 'silly, awkward Country Girl.'[18] Like Mary Robinson, Abington took great care

Figure 4.1. Sir Joshua Reynolds. *Mrs Abington as the Comic Muse* (1764–1768, 1772–1773 sections repainted). 2304. Reproduced by permission of Waddesdon, The Rothschild Collection (The National Trust). Photo: Gordon Roberton. © The National Trust, Waddesdon Manor

over her appearance, going to the trouble of having portraits repainted when fashions had changed. For instance, the portrait by Reynolds of Abington (see figure 4.1) as the Comic Muse was painted in 1768 and the hair and face were retouched in 1773 to bring the hair style up to date (Penny 247). According to James Boaden, Abington was the 'peculiar delight of the fashionable world' (1:363), and another contemporary commentator, Georg Christophe Lichtenberg, remarked, 'She seldom appears on the stage, when the mode in genteel society does not follow her lead' (qtd in Ribeiro, 'Costuming' 108). A head-dress she pioneered during her period acting in Ireland was not merely admired, copied, and displayed in shop widows, but became known as 'the Abington Cap.' Abington was one of the actresses who advised fashionable ladies on their attire and deportment. D'Archenholz described Frances Abington as a kind of fashion doctor, 'called like a physician' and 'driving around the capital to give her advice concerning the modes and fashions of the day' (qtd in Crouch 72). Such advice was profitable and Nussbaum points out that Abington was reported to 'supplement her stage income by nearly £1500 annually' through these activities (*Rival Queens* 231). Highly fashionable clothing took some management, and Crouch notes that actresses were well placed to advise 'elite women not just on fashionable dress but on how to wear the elaborate and complicated styles – the lengthy trains, large hoops, and multiplicity of accessories – dictated by occasions of great formality' (70).

By the 1770s, indeed, the renowned actresses of the age were undoubtedly celebrities and fashion gurus whose images were widely circulated in print form. Prices for prints varied from one shilling to several guineas, with the successful printer John Boydell pioneering the cheaper print form in the 1770s. As John Brewer points out, 'prints empowered the purchaser as well as the printseller.' The pleasures of collecting and arranging artworks, once the privilege of wealthy aristocrats were now 'possible for much humbler collectors' (461).

Given such wide circulation of their image, which went well beyond the stage itself, the concern actresses had with regard to their appearance is understandable. This concern is illustrated in an anecdote of George Anne Bellamy's (1727–88) over her costume for a revival of Nathaniel Lee's *The Rival Queens* in which she was to play Stairia opposite a Roxana played by Margaret Woffington (c. 1720–60). Bellamy's intense rivalry with Woffington is notable throughout her *Apology*, and frequently revolves around, or is expressed through, jewels and fashionable clothes. Thus on this occasion Bellamy, who had arranged for

Drury Lane to give her an allowance toward clothing, describes sending her hairdresser's wife to Paris to buy her two 'French tragedy dresses, the most elegant she could purchase' (249) and was happy that in those purchased 'taste and elegance were never so happily blended' (249). The moment was coming, but had certainly not been reached when performers' costumes would make some approximation to the period of the play in which they were acting.[19] However, in this case, *'robes de cour'* – that is the formal dress of the (French) court – was considered an appropriate costume. Tragedies were, after all, set in courts, and so court dress captured the essential mood of a play if not the period. Meanwhile, Woffington, who had arranged instead to be clothed by the company, was given robes donated by the Dowager Princess of Wales. These were not soiled, Bellamy adds kindly, just not suitable for candlelight: they appeared a 'dirty white' – 'especially when my splendid yellow was by it' (249). Bellamy tells us she wore a purple cloak with this 'splendid yellow' dress and although the mind boggles a bit at the colour combination, it probably looked good by candlelight and certainly would have eclipsed 'dirty white.'

Undoubtedly the cultural status of the actress was enhanced following the Royal Academy Spring Exhibitions which began in 1769. Actresses and ladies of birth and fashion alike were displayed, painted by the same painters, in much the same clothes and in much the same postures. Reynolds was renowned for painting women of fashion be they aristocrats, courtesans, or actresses. Indeed, it has been noted that 'it was through theatrical personalities, in particular, that Reynolds exploited the cult of personality and made the greatest inroads into allying his portrait practice to high art' (Postle 20). Reynolds's 1775 portrait of Georgiana duchess of Devonshire (see figure 4.2) is remarkably similar to his portrait of Abington as the comic muse (see figure 4.1). The duchess of Devonshire was, of course, also a renowned fashion icon, known as the 'Empress of fashion' and 'the beautiful duchess,' or in her mother's words 'one of the most showy girls I ever saw' (*Reynolds*, qtd by Mannings 311).[20] Not surprisingly, these two avatars of fashion, the 'showy' duchess and the elegant show girl, knew each other, and similarities in their images are not coincidental since they borrowed fashion motifs from each other. In Reynolds's portrait of the duchess, exhibited in the spring of 1776, for instance, the duchess is depicted with a plumed coiffure – a fashion which had been pioneered by Abington in the winter of 1774 (Penny 273). Both women are dressed in white, and lean elegantly on classical masonry, garnished with antique emblems of

Figure 4.2. Joshua Reynolds. *Georgiana, Duchess of Devonshire* (1775). Reproduced courtesy of the Huntington Art Collections, San Marino, California

comedy for Abington and more severely classical ones for the duchess. Abington's posture is more coquettish than the duchess's and with her head cocked to one side she gazes quizzically at the spectator while the duchess looks out more warily and indirectly. However, in essence here are two ladies of high fashion and great beauty, both fashion leaders, and both painted by the same great (and highly fashionable) artist. The paintings of the actresses and great ladies displayed at the Exhibition were rapidly engraved and displayed at print shops and in magazines so that these images of elegance and fashion circulated widely and the modes displayed could be copied and fed into the accelerating fashion consumerism of the eighteenth century.

Pictures of scenes from plays became increasingly fashionable, especially from the hands of George III's favourite painter, Johann Zoffany. For instance, in 1771 at the king's request, Zoffany painted a picture of Sophia Badderley, a beautiful actress-singer in the Garrick and Coleman comedy *The Clandestine Marriage*. The king was, indeed, particularly amused by the fact that Badderley was acting a love scene opposite her estranged husband, but the point is that from literally the highest in the land down to those who could afford a cheap print, the well-known actresses, their clothes, their 'private' lives, their powdered or un-powdered curls, fans, drapes, smiles, and postures were all grist to the celebrity mill.

By the later eighteenth century, we are a long way from the actress/whore dyad. Instead we have reached the point at which the fashionable actress and lady of fashion are barely distinguishable from each other. This situation was implicit from the very moment actresses appeared on the stage portraying ladies of high fashion, who were also portraying themselves in dramatic roles and postures.[21] The closeness, even at times merging of the world of what Gillian Russell has called 'fashionable sociability' and the world of theatre is clearly evident. Masquerade balls were held at the Drury Lane or Covent Garden theatres, and as we have seen, society painters painted fashionable ladies and fashionable actresses (and fashionable courtesans) alike. Nowhere is this closeness more clearly seen than in the Drury Lane performance of General Burgoyne's and David Garrick's play *The Maid of the Oaks* in the late autumn of 1774, based on the much admired *fête champêtre* organized by the general to mark the engagement of Lord Stanley and Lady Elizabeth Hamilton in the summer of that year. Not surprisingly, Frances Abington, perhaps the most posture-perfect impersonator of the women of the leisure class, played a leading role as Lady Bab

Figure 4.3. Thomas Hickey. *Mrs Abington as Lady Bab Lardoon in The Maid of the Oaks* by John Burgoyne (1775). Reproduced by permission of The Garrick Club

Lardoon.[22] A charming if rather stiff portrait of her in this role painted by Thomas Hickey in 1775 depicts her in a white, wide-hooped dress, decorated with knots of flowers, standing by a series of pastoral signifiers – Greek urn, Greek temple, elegant foliage – which gives one a strong sense of the high society 'pastoral' dress and decorated garden fashionable in the mid-1770s (see figure 4.3).[23] At this point, Abington/ Lady Bab and the aristocratic reasons for the original fete have surely merged in the public consciousness – with Abington/Lady Bab rather eclipsing the originals. As Nussbaum remarks, actresses, 'even in the 1750s and 1760s became competition to women of elevated standing' (*Rival Queens* 19).

For the actress, however, the very period – the 1770s – that saw the leading ladies of the stage, such as Frances Abington, Sophia Badderley, and George Anne Bellamy, assume roles as celebrities and leaders of fashion, also saw another trajectory open for the celebrated leading lady, one that encompasses fame but not particularly fashion. Most studies of eighteenth-century actresses conclude with Sarah Siddons and I see no good reason to break with this tradition, for indeed Siddons marks the end of one era and the start of another.

Siddons (1755–1831) is often credited with the achievement of respectable professionalism for actresses. Her husband might remark ruefully that he was not quite up to the task of being Mr Siddons, but no one accused her of any sort of sexual impropriety with the very improper aristocracy and royalty of the late Georgian era. Rather, as Pat Rogers notes in a helpful essay, a particular type of aesthetic language was employed when describing Siddons. As he points out, '[M]ore important,' in the many descriptions, 'than sheer physical looks were the qualities of dignity and majesty' and 'words like "noble" are commonly employed' (52).[24] Rogers goes on to demonstrate how often her performances were referred to in supernatural terms, as preternatural, and, indeed, sublime. Siddons certainly was a beautiful woman, and yet it was her sublimity and not her beauty that was emphasized. Significantly this was at a time when, thanks to Edmund Burke's 1755 essay *The Sublime and the Beautiful*, there was a strong sense of the way in which the sublime dwarfed the merely beautiful. As Reynolds put it in his last *Discourse* (1790), sublimity overpowers the 'little elegancies of art' (qtd in Rogers 55), and so in many ways did Siddons overwhelm the 'little elegancies' of the fashion queens of Drury Lane and Covent Garden. In Reynolds's renowned portrait of Siddons as the Tragic Muse (1784, see figure 4.4), her seated posture, as many have noted, is taken from Michelangelo's depiction of the prophet Isaiah in the Sistine Chapel. Her draped clothing is indeed theatrical, or more precisely, drawn from Reynolds's wardrobe of artistic robes.[25] This personification goes well beyond fashion and beauty (as Reynolds's portrait of Abington as Comic Muse did not), for here indeed we see instead the enthroned actress, concentrated, attentive, listening to the sad and terrible sounds of tragedy coming from the figures behind her.

The fame, success, and admiration given to Sarah Siddons opened the way forward for female actors to be regarded as professionals, gifted interpreters of the finest works of Western civilization, and not just lovely and skilful actresses who also knew a great deal about how to design and manage fans, scarves, hats, and hoops. Beauty and fashion continued to cling to the figure of the actress; nevertheless, Siddons opened a way to detach an actress's fame from fashion and to develop a language of praise and admiration separate from that of fashion and beauty. By the nineteenth century, theatre itself, of course, was altering, dividing more strictly into popular theatricals with bareback riding, dancing dogs, and human cannonballs at places such as the Pantheon and the more staid legitimate stage elsewhere. And while high society continued to be a subject of drama, increasingly dramas with a more distinctly middle-class setting emerged. The great stage actresses of later generations, such as Ellen Terry, Eleonore Duse, Sarah Bernhardt, and Mrs Patrick Campbell, were all remarkably handsome women, who dressed with care and flair, but it was their stage presence, their interpretation of particular roles – in short, their artistry – for which they were primarily famous.[26]

By the early twentieth century, however, with the development of cinema, the actress resumed her position as popular celebrity and fashion icon with closely observed glamorous film stars representing the height of fashion. Nowadays, supported by a wide range of celebrity magazines, television programs, blogs, and social networking venues, the dissemination of the image of the fashionable actress is far wider than when people crowded around print shop windows to gaze at the images of Mrs Robinson or Mrs Abington. As in the eighteenth century, the actress does not reign alone. She is displayed on the same page, or screen with the other celebrity fashion icons, such as popular singers, aristocrats, and princesses whose interchangeability with each other was implicit from the moment actresses entered the stage in the Restoration to stand in for their wealthier and titled sisters. The newer modes of marketing the image of the female celebrity are more intense

Figure 4.4. Joshua Reynolds. *Sarah Siddons, as the Tragic Muse* (1784). Reproduced courtesy of the Huntington Art Collections, San Marino, California

and aggressive than the fans, snuff-boxes, and fire-screens of the eighteenth century, but the distinction is merely one of amplification of the media in which actresses become the subjects and objects of fashion and popular culture.[27]

NOTES

1 On pleasure and leisure activities in Georgian England, see Brewer, Russell, Castle, and Ribiero, *Dress*.
2 See also Nussbaum, *Rival Queens* 13.
3 On luxury and consumerism, see Berg, and McKendrick, Brewer and Plumb.
4 For a description of the duchess of Kingston's trial and the popular interest accorded it, including a satiric play by Samuel Foote, see Russell, chapter 7, and Moody 65–89.
5 The members of the two patent companies were enrolled as royal servants and the companies took the names of their royal patrons: the King's and Duke's Companies.
6 There are remarkably few roles for women of middling or lower status in Restoration and eighteenth-century drama. Kept women and courtesans, such as Angellica Bianca in Aphra Behn's *The Rover* (1677), would have been finely dressed.
7 The royal patent issued in 1662 to Sir Thomas Killigrew, patentee of the King's Company, expressly commanded that women should now act female roles. See Beecher, *The London Stage*, Part 1, xxiv. See also Maus 595–617, and Howe 23–6.
8 The remark may well be apocryphal; see MacLeod and Alexander 168.
9 See Straub for a sophisticated discussion of the actress/whore dyad and also Bush-Bailey 15–32.
10 See Fisk's biography of Mary Lee in the *Oxford Dictionary of National Biography*.
11 Hilton's popular 2005 biography of Fenton is the most recent account.
12 For a lively description of a John James Heidegger masquerade, see Fielding, *Tom Jones* (1749), book 13, chapters 6 and 7. There is now a large body of work on the significance of the masquerade in eighteenth-century English (and indeed European) culture; see especially Castle's pioneering work on the topic, *Masquerade and Civilization*.
13 See, for instance, 'A Letter from an Actress of the Play-House to a Stroler in the Country, Concerning Reformation of Manners and the Supressing of Drolls in Bartholomew Fair,' addressed to 'My dear Harlikin,' in Mullan and Reid.

14 On the movement of personnel between booth theatres and strolling companies, see for instance, Brooks 73–95.

15 See also Goff's new biography, *The Incomparable Hester Santlow.*

16 Mary Robinson's sobriquet 'Perdita' was, of course, to be later joined by her poetic Della Crusca pseudonym 'Laura Maria'; with both names, Robinson showed great ability in using the media to shape and enhance her image.

17 On James Roberts's painting of the last act, see Russell 207–9.

18 Roach offers a rather different interpretation of this image, seeing it as a 'dirty joke' on the actress by the painter (162). However, I find this unlikely. Reynolds was very fond of Abington, and they were good friends. He painted her frequently and, 'despite his reputation for meanness with money, took forty places in the front boxes for her benefit performance on the snowy evening of 27 March 1775' (Penny 246). See also *The Life of Mrs Abington* 78.

19 See *The Morning Chronicle* 23 Sept. 1791: 'it is a general fault that all the performers [at Drury lane] seem to dress merely according to their own whim . . . and some in the top of present fashion' (qtd in Beecher lxix).

20 Lady Spencer refers to her daughter as a 'showy girl' in a letter to Lord Nuneham in September 1773 (qtd by Mannings 311).

21 As in, for instance, Reynolds's portrait of a gentlewoman such as Mrs Hale as Euphrosyne (handmaiden to Venus and personification of good cheer). See also Crouch, on the ubiquity of the allegorical figure, 75.

22 *The Maid of the Oaks* is frequently referred to nowadays as scholars look for theatre beyond the theatres. See Russell 141–52.

23 Perry states of this portrait that it is 'carefully coded to suggest a liminal status between lower-class actress and aristocratic icon' (121). However, I suggest that at this point in her career, Abington has successfully transcended her status origins. If not the thing itself – a great lady – she *appears* as a great lady would like to be depicted: charmingly elegant, artlessly artful.

24 See also Rosenthal, 'The Sublime.'

25 The 1784 painting can be seen in the Huntington Art gallery in California; there is also a 1789 replica in Dulwich Picture Gallery which was essentially carried out by Reynolds's studio under his direction (Mannings 324–5).

26 See Gale and Stokes, *Cambridge Companion to the Actress.*

27 I thank my sister and frequent collaborator, Penny Richards, for commenting very helpfully on more than one draft of this essay and Anne Greenfield for reading and proofing the essay.

WORKS CITED

Backscheider, Paula. 'The Paradigms of Popular Culture.' *Eighteenth-Century Novel* 6–7 (2009): 17–59. Print.

Baldwin, Olive, and Thelma Wilson. 'Lavinia Fenton.' *Oxford Dictionary of National Biography Online*. Web. 4 Feb. 2010.

Bate, Jonathan. 'Shakespeare and the Rival Muses: Siddons versus Jordan.' *Notorious Muse: The Actress in British Art and Culture, 1776–1812*. Ed. Robyn Aeleson. New Haven: Yale UP, 2003. 91–103. Print.

Beecher, Charles, ed. *The London Stage, Part 5, 1776–1786*. Carbondale, IL: Southern Illinois UP, 1968. Print.

Bellamy, George Anne. *Apology for her Life*. Vol. 2. London, 1785. 6 vols. *Eighteenth Century Collections Online*. Web. 4 Feb. 2010.

Berg, Maxine. *Luxury and Pleasure in Eighteenth-Century Britain*. Oxford: Oxford UP, 2005. Print.

Boaden, James. *Memoirs of Mrs. Siddons*. 2 vols. London: Henry Colburn, 1827. Print.

Brewer, John. *The Pleasures of the Imagination: English Culture in the Eighteenth Century*. New York: Farrar Straus Giroux, 1997. Print.

Brooks, Helen M. 'Women and Theatre Management in the Eighteenth Century.' *The Public's Open to Us All: Essays on Women and Performance in Eighteenth-Century England*. Ed. Laura Engel. Newcastle-Upon-Tyne: Cambridge Scholars Publishing, 2009. 73–95. Print.

Bush-Bailey, Gilli. 'Revolution, Legislation and Autonomy.' *Cambridge Companion to the Actress*. Ed. Maggie B. Gale and John Stokes. Cambridge: Cambridge UP, 2007. 15–31. Print.

Castle, Terry. *Masquerade and Civilization: The Carnavalesque in Eighteenth-Century English Culture and Fiction*. Stanford: U of California P, 1986. Print.

Cibber, Colley. *Three Sentimental Comedies*. Ed. Maureen Sullivan. New Haven: Yale UP, 1975. Print.

Congreve, William. *The Way of the World*. *The Broadview Anthology of Restoration and Early Eighteenth-Century Drama*. Ed. J. Douglas Canfield. Peterborough: Broadview P, 2001. Print.

Crouch, Kimberly. 'The Public Life of Actresses: Prostitutes or Ladies?' *Gender in Eighteenth-Century England: Roles, Representations, and Responsibilities*. Ed. Hannah Barker and Elaine Chalus. London: Addison Wesley Longman, 1997. 65–86. Print.

Farquhar, George. *The Inconstant*. *The Works of George Farquhar*. Vol. 1. Ed. Charles Stonehill. 2 vols. New York: Gordian P, 1930. 2 vols. Print.

Fielding, Henry, *Tom Jones*. Ed. Sheridan Baker. New York: W.W. Norton, 1973. Print.

Fisk, Deborah Payne. 'Lee, Mary (*fl.* 1670–1685).' *Oxford Dictionary of National Biography Online*. Web. 4 Feb. 2010.

Fyvie, John. *Comedy Queens of the Georgian Era*. London: Constable, 1906. Print.

Gale, Maggie B., and John Stokes, eds. *Cambridge Companion to the Actress*. Cambridge: Cambridge UP, 2007. Print.

Gay, John. *The Letters of John Gay*. Ed. C.F. Burgess. Oxford: Clarendon, 1966. Print.

Goff, Moira. *The Incomparable Hester Santlow: A Dancer-Actress on the Georgian Stage*. Burlington, VT: Ashgate, 2009. Print.

Goodden, Angelica. *Actio and Persuasion: Dramatic Performance in Eighteenth-Century France*. Oxford: Clarendon, 1986. Print.

Hilton, Lisa. *Mistress Peachum's Pleasure*. London: Weidenfeld and Nicolson, 2005. Print.

Howe, Elizabeth. *The First English Actresses: Women and Drama 1660–1700*. Cambridge: Cambridge UP, 1992. Print.

Inglis, Fred. *A Short History of Celebrity*. Princeton: Princeton UP, 2010. Print.

Lewis, Elizabeth Miller. 'Hester Santlow's Harlequine: Dance, Dress, Status and Gender on the London Stage, 1706–1734.' *The Clothes That Wear Us: Essays on Dressing and Transgressing in Eighteenth-Century Culture*. Ed. Jessica Munns and Penny Richards. Newark: U of Delaware P, 1999. 80–101. Print.

The Life of Mrs. Abington (by the Editor of the Life of Quinn). London: Reader, Orange Street, Holborn, 1888. *Google Books*. Web. 4 Feb. 2010.

Luckhurst, Mary, and Jane Moody, eds. *Theatre and Celebrity in Britain, 1660–2000*. Basingstoke: Palgrave Macmillan, 2005. Print.

MacLeod, Catharine, and Julia Marciari Alexander, *Painted Ladies: Women at the Court of Charles II*. London and New Haven: National Portrait Gallery and Yale Center for British Art, 2001. Print.

Mannings, David. 'Paintings by Reynolds (with prints after his works).' Section 139. *Reynolds*. Ed. Nicholas Penny. New York: Abrams, 1986. Print.

Maus, Katharine Eisaman '"Playhouse Flesh and Blood": Sexual Ideology and the Restoration Actress.' *ELH* 46.4 (1979): 595–617. Print.

McKendrick, Neil, John Brewer, and J.H. Plumb. *The Birth of a Consumer Society: The Commercialization of Eighteenth-Century England*. Bloomington: Indiana UP, 1982. Print.

Moody, Jane. 'Stolen Identities: Character, Mimicry and the Invention of Samuel Foote.' *Theatre and Celebrity in Britain, 1660–2000*. Ed. Mary Luckhurst and Jane Moody. Basingstoke: Palgrave Macmillan, 2005. 65–89. Print.

Mullan, John, and Christopher Reid, eds. *Eighteenth- Century Popular Culture: A Selection*. Oxford: Oxford UP, 2000. Print.

Nussbaum, Felicity. 'Actresses and the Economics of Celebrity, 1700–1800.' *Theatre and Celebrity in Britain, 1660–2000*. Ed. Mary Luckhurst and Jane Moody. Basingstoke: Palgrave Macmillan, 2005. 148–68. Print.

– *Rival Queens, Actresses, Performance, and the Eighteenth-Century British Theatre*. Philadelphia: U of Pennsylvania P, 2010. Print.

Penny, Nicholas, ed. *Reynolds*. New York: Abrams, 1986. Print.

Pepys, Samuel. *The Diary of Samuel Pepys*. Ed. Robert Latham and William Matthews. 11 vols. Berkeley: U of California P, 1970-1983.

Perry, Gill. *Spectacular Flirtations*. New Haven: Yale UP, 2009. Print.

Postle, Martin. *Sir Joshua Reynolds: The Subject Pictures*. Cambridge, UP 1995. Print.

Ribeiro, Aileen. 'Costuming the Part: A Discourse of Fashion and Fiction in the Image of the Actress in England, 1776–1812.' *Notorious Muse: The Actress in British Art and Culture,1776–1812*. Ed. Robyn Aeleson. New Haven: Yale UP, 2003. 105–27. Print.

– *The Dress Worn at Masquerades in England, 1730 to 1790, and Its Relation to Fancy Dress in Portraiture*. New York: Garland P, 1984. Print.

Roach, Joseph. *It*. Ann Arbor: U of Michigan P, 2007. Print.

Robinson, Mary. *The Memoirs of the Late Mary Robinson*. 1801. *Women's Theatrical Memoirs*. Ed. Sharon Setzer. Part 1. 5 vols. London: Pickering and Chatto, 2007. Print.

Rogers, Pat. '"Towering Above her Sex": Stature and Sublimity in the Achievement of Sarah Siddons.' *Curtain Calls: British and American Women and the Theater,1660–1820*. Ed. Mary Anne Schofield and Cecilia Macheski. Athens: U of Ohio P, 1991. 48–67. Print.

Rosenthal, Laura. 'Entertaining Women: The Actress in Eighteenth-Century Theatre and Culture.' *The Cambridge Companion to British Theatre, 1630–1830*. Ed. Jane Moody and Daniel O'Quinn. Cambridge: Cambridge UP, 2007. 159–73. Print.

– 'The Sublime, The Beautiful, "The Siddons."' *The Clothes That Wear Us: Essays on Dressing and Transgressing in Eighteenth-Century Culture*. Ed. Jessica Munns and Penny Richards. Newark: U of Delaware P, 1999. 56–79. Print.

Russell, Gillian. *Women, Sociability and Theatre in Georgian London*. Cambridge: Cambridge UP, 2007. Print.

Straub, Kristina. *Sexual Suspects: Eighteenth-Century Players and Sexual Ideology*. Princeton, NJ, Princeton UP, 1992. Print.

5 Fanning the Flames:
Women, Fashion, and Politics

ELAINE CHALUS

For *Parties* do not only *split* a Nation, but every Individual among them ... I speak not here of the Leaders, but the insignificant Crowd of Followers in a *Party*, who have been the Instruments of mixing it in every Condition and Circumstance of Life. As the *Zealots* among the *Jews* bound the *Law* about their Foreheads and Wrists, and Hems of their Garments; so the *Women* among us have got the distinguishing Marks of Party in their *Muffs*, their *Fans*, and their *Furbelow's*. The *Whig* Ladies put on their *Patches* in a different manner from the *Tories*. They have made *Schisms* in the *Play House*, and each have their particular sides at the *Opera*: And when a Man changes his *Party*, he must infallibly count upon the Loss of his *Mistress*.

Swift

For Jonathan Swift, animadverting in *The Examiner* upon the evils of Party at the beginning of March 1710/11, as the Sacheverell mobs spilled out to riot in the streets of London, women's use of fashion to proclaim party allegiances and their concomitant politicization of social spaces was simultaneously symbolic and deplorable. In *The Spectator*, Joseph Addison was similarly inspired to write an admonitory essay on fashionable women's ability to imbue their patches – the smallest female fashion item – with political meaning (131–2). By placing their patches strategically (Whigs to the right; Tories to the left), they subverted fashion, adapted it to serve their political purposes, and effectively turned themselves into political canvasses. Through fashion, they proclaimed their personal political opinions and made a collective statement, politicizing the public, ostensibly social space of the Opera. In so doing, they fostered the spirit of party by 'mixing it in every Condition and

Circumstance of Life' (Swift, *Examiner* 1) – and all without having to say anything.

As they were profoundly conservative men, Swift's and Addison's responses to this conjunction of women, fashion, and politics were both typical and telling. Swift dismissed the women as the 'insignificant Crowd of Followers' of party (*Examiner* 1), but Addison saw them as more worrying, because more influential. He reprimanded them sharply, drawing implicitly on centuries-old assumptions about women as agents of chaos whose meddling in politics exacerbated 'the hatreds and animosities that reign among men' through their presumptively natural tendency to excess and 'party-rage' (132). True Englishwomen should, he charged, be exemplars of restraint and familial domesticity, 'tender mothers, and faithful wives' (132), above reproach and, importantly, above political partisanship. Both men saw women's political use of fashion (itself problematic due to its close association with women, luxury, and corruption)[1] as a lamentable trivialization of politics. Swift, however, also identified it as symptomatic of a deeper change in English political culture. By the 1710s, politics had already escaped the control of politicians and hacks. The cumulative effect of frequent elections and years of entrenched Tory-Whig animosity was, as Geoffrey Holmes has argued, that 'party strife . . . took possession of the very lives of the politically-conscious' (20–1) – and those numbers were rising rapidly. The vibrant, vocal, and influential extra-parliamentary nation that would play such an important part in later Georgian politics was already taking shape.[2]

By concentrating on eighteenth-century women's use of fashion for political ends, this chapter continues the process of writing women back into the history of the extra-parliamentary nation and, by extension, calls attention to the importance of material culture, visual impact, and the use of space in explaining the viral nature of politics in the eighteenth century. It highlights strategies used to secure support for men and measures, and it suggests that the creation of visual impact through the use of colours, clothes, accessories, and objects provided opportunities for appropriation and subversion by the unenfranchised, including women of various ranks, who were intent on expressing their political opinions. By turning their dress and accessories to advantage, women could make discreet or obvious political statements. They became participants in, as opposed to spectators of, political life, and contributed to the creation of a larger public sphere.

The Political Context

Eighteenth-century correspondence frequently employs metaphors of contagion to describe the way that politics could capture public attention. While party faded into faction by mid-century, politics remained viral, periodically sweeping through London and somnolent rural boroughs, promiscuously infecting all those in its path (Chalus, 'Epidemical'). Thus, Swift complained in 1707 that politics in Leicester had polarized society down to the chambermaids and schoolboys (*Correspondence*, 62) and the dowager Lady Spencer fretted in 1784 that her daughters, Lady Duncannon and the duchess of Devonshire, were too inflamed by the 'strong delerium' of the Westminster election to take her advice.[3]

One of the reasons for this feverish excitement was that eighteenth-century elections could generate passion even when boroughs did not go all the way to the poll. While the electorate as a percentage of the population in England and Wales averaged around 19 per cent of adult males between 1689 and 1832,[4] this figure can be deceptive. At its peak in 1715, 23.9 per cent of adult males were enfranchised, which meant that almost one in four adult men was enfranchised. Although somewhat lower in 1832, at 18.4 per cent, the 'reach' of enfranchisement was still substantial, extending to friends, relatives, and connections. It also included voters' womenfolk, who were often deemed politically influential, and other women who had more direct interests in electoral politics through property ownership, inheritance, or customary practice. As Zoë Dyndor's recent examination of the Northamptonshire election of 1768 has revealed, female householders used their status to political (and occasionally, financial) advantage by making men into voters, or by serving as witnesses during and after the poll to validate men's votes (4).[5] As I have argued at length elsewhere, as repositories of political memory, these women also made valuable contributions to the electoral process (Chalus, 'Electoral').

While neither enfranchisement nor the possession of political interests were synecdoches for involvement, party fervour and incessant electioneering at the beginning of the century, and a rising number of elections from the later eighteenth century onward were important in defining allegiances and heightening the awareness of men and women alike. Moreover, the century saw the development of a political continuum, with the traditional political elite challenged by the growing influence of the middling classes and, toward the end of the period, by the radicalization of a section of the labouring sort. Political excitement was also fostered throughout the century by an assortment of intersecting and cross-cutting personal, familial, factional, and ideological differences; a liberal scattering of national and international issues, crises, and events; and the emergence of a number of charismatic but highly divisive politicians.

The popular political use of colours, clothes, and accessories therefore emerges from a period of remarkable transition and cultural change, but as Bob Bushaway notes, this is rooted in a long history of ritualistic behaviours and highly symbolic visual displays. Like their forefathers, eighteenth-century women and men paraded, processed, and perambulated for institutional, vocational, or civic reasons, often wearing specially coloured clothes, decorated with ribbons and cockades, in order to make personal or collective statements of identity and allegiance. Thus they used their appearance and actions to turn the physical locations, the 'places,' where they lived, worked, and socialized into the more abstract 'spaces' (Flather 2) where politics could be performed. These spaces could be public or private, formal or informal, inclusive or exclusive, masculine or feminine. The eager appropriation of these older models of public participation and personal statement, and their use for political ends, needs to be seen as a significant contributory factor in the generation of contagious political excitement in the eighteenth-century. They also add to our understanding of the construction of the extra-parliamentary nation, by emphasizing the importance of visual political statements in fostering group awareness and cohesion long before fashion was radicalized by the French Revolution. Whether it was the sea-green ribbons worn by thousands of Leveller men and women at Robert Lockyer's funeral in London in 1649 (Woolrych 445; Fissell 112), or the use of crape-draped apples to protest the cider tax in Exeter in 1763 (*Gazetteer and London Daily Advertiser* 13 May 1763), it is clear that contemporaries understood the importance of visual symbolism. In the hard-fought election contest for Newcastle-under-Lyme in 1790, the candidates poured money into the purchase of cockades and ribbons, flags, flowers, garlands, and highly decorated chairs. Cockades made of the best China ribbon at 1s. 4d. each formed only part of a strikingly large outlay on items for display: for every pound spent on printed paper, £14–£15 was spent on purchasing visual materials (Barker and Vincent xxvii–xxix). By the 1820s, cockades and ribbons had come to symbolize the exorbitant cost of elections and politicians' rising concerns about corruption; consequently, parliament in

1826/7 made it illegal for a candidate or his agent to distribute 'any cockade, ribbon or other mark of distinction' on pain of a £10 fine, or for returning officers to allow anyone who was wearing them to vote.[6]

Historians of eighteenth-century popular politics have long recognized the value of spectacle and political theatre to group action and the creation of collective identity.[7] Best known, perhaps, are the Foxites' adoption of blue-and-buff in support of the American colonists and depictions of the duchess of Devonshire bedecked with foxes' tails and Foxite favours during the Westminster election of 1784 (BM, AN 102402001; V&AM, E. 1238–1990). On the whole, however, British historians have not paid the politicization of clothing or accessories the same kind of analytical attention as their French counterparts.[8] Notable exceptions include historians such as Beverly Lemire and Chloë Wigston Smith, who have explored the politics of women wearing calico in the early eighteenth century; James Epstein, whose careful reading of the symbolism of the liberty cap and its use by radicals has proved highly influential;[9] and Katrina Navickas, whose recent overview of political clothing, 1780–1840, emphasizes the 'mutable semiotics' (564) of clothing that enables groups and individuals to 'adapt emblems to their own needs, arguably more immediately than language' (564), making it possible for 'all classes to voice their opinions about their place within the constitution' (541).

The Material Culture of Politics

On the whole, we still know very little about the material culture of women's involvement in popular political culture prior to the French Revolution. The surviving textual evidence is anecdotal and scattered, and the physical evidence was often ephemeral or contextual. Ribbons, bandeaux, cockades, and clothing in political colours could, moreover, be put to other uses after their immediate political purpose was met. Similarly, the political meaning of everyday fashion items – handkerchiefs, garters, lappets, and fans – which survive in museums and collections, often has to be blatant to be recognized.

Context frequently transformed ordinary fashion items into political statements (Navickas 544). Even the basic white handkerchief could be used to proclaim loyalty, support, or allegiance. Thus, when George II stopped in Ipswich in January 1737 on his return to England, the crowd that stayed up until midnight to meet him included 'the Ladies, who shak'd their Handkerchiefs at some Windows in the Market Place'

(*Daily Gazetteer* 25 January 1737). Waving a handkerchief was an elegantly simple, but not always a patriotic, statement: 'At the proclamation [of the Pretender in Edinburgh in 1745] there was a good many of the Tory and Papist Ladies present; who shew'd a great Deal of Zeal by Huzzas and waving their white Handkerchiefs and fair Hands' (*Penny London Post* 8 November 1745).

By the time that John Trusler published *The Country Election*, in 1768, women's collective presence at election-related activities was deemed so much a part of the crowded, politicized street scene that he pointedly included them in his stage directions: 'Windows full of ladies, holding out their handkerchiefs' (Trusler 2: vi). While it might be tempting to see their participation, literally, as window-dressing for the electoral scene, this was certainly not always the case, as contemporaries often singled out women's participation, and candidates claimed political allegiance from their actions. In a fulsome description of Sir George Warren's canvass in Lancaster in October 1785, a correspondent to the *Morning Chronicle* took pains to point out that Warren had the support of the ladies: 'In the procession round the town, the streets were lined with an amazing number of people, and the windows of all the houses were crowded with ladies, who, by waving their handkerchiefs, testified their wishes for the success of Sir George Warren' (12 October 1785).

Assessing women's involvement in popular politics is complicated by the use of generic labels like 'the Croud' (*Daily Gazetteer* 25 January 1737); nor is it always easy to ascertain the social status of the 'ladies' when they are identified. At times, they were unquestionably elite women (aristocrats and gentry), who rented, or had rented for them, the upstairs rooms in houses lining the most important processional routes, so they could watch the proceedings safely and comfortably from above (Harding 562). In most cases, however, the designation was complimentary, owing less to rank than to genteel dress and behaviour. The women adorned with 'true blue' badges who crowded in to the windows around the hustings in Darlington in August 1832 were simply identified as 'the most respectable ladies of Darlington' (*Electors' Scrap Book* 45). Occasionally, as in this description of a colourful, symbolic post-election scene in Worcester in 1773, the social differences between 'ladies' and 'women' was echoed in their use of space:

One of the noblest sights that was ever exhibited in this country, was after the close of the poll: the independent, the honest, and the free voters, insisted that Sir Watkin Lewes was their legal Member, and would not acknowledge Mr. Rous, as they said he had procured his majority by b – y and c – n [bribery and corruption]; they provided a chair, with a triumphal arch decorated with laurel gilt with gold, and a cap of Liberty pendant...he was carried on the shoulders of twelve persons, through the city...preceded with colours and streamers flying, a band of musick playing...The principal gentlemen of the town went before him sing- ing...accompanied by an immense concourse of people: the old people brought out their children in their arms, dressed in white with blue sashes, as emblems of innocence, thereby testifying their just abhorrence of cor- ruption, and presented him with garlands and wreaths of laurel, gilt with gold; the ladies and women of all conditions crouded [*sic*] to the windows and doors, clapping their hands and waving handkerchiefs in the air. (*General Evening Post* 9 December 1773)[10]

Half a century later, one of the successful candidates in the 1826 Northumberland election met with a similarly exuberant reception when he arrived at Haltwhistle. There, the 'ladies' crowding the win- dows, waving handkerchiefs and blue ribbons, may have been the womenfolk of the leading political families but, just as readily, they may have been the neatly dressed mothers, aunts, and sisters of the blue- clad 'junior female members' of freeholders' families who marched in the procession (*Pollbook* 76).

The 1826 Northumberland election provides records of enthusiastic female support for all the candidates: they crowded the streets, win- dows, and rooftops, adorned with candidates' favours, waving hand- kerchiefs and flags (*Pollbook* 24, 129, 141, 203). T.W. Beaumont, speaking in Hexham, reflected a typically ambivalent male response to female zeal. While quick to claim female backing, depicting women as a moral force in politics and a testimony to his personal integrity, he was also equally swift to distance himself from them by invoking the stereotype of the noisy, unruly female (Howard 680): '(Here the cheering and wav- ing of handkerchiefs continued so long, particularly from the fair sex, that Mr. B. smiled and good-humouredly observed) [*sic*] that when the female tongue is once set a-going, it is very difficult to be stopped' (203).

Coloured or printed handkerchiefs were more purposefully political than the ubiquitous white handkerchief (Atkins 27). While the codifica- tion of colours as political symbols was not yet fixed in the eighteenth century, and candidates often campaigned in the colours of their (or their patron's) livery, the Whigs tended to be associated with orange, in commemoration of William of Orange and the Glorious Revolution, and the Tories with 'True Blue'[11] (Hoppit 284; Navickas 544). The Jacobites' colour was white; their emblem a white rose. During the '45, Lord Chesterfield used this symbolism in his famous epigram on Miss Eleanor Ambrose, a beautiful young Catholic who wore an orange favour to a gala event at Dublin Castle:

Say, lovely traitor, where's the jest,
Of wearing orange in your breast;
While that breast, upheaving, shows
The whiteness of the rebel rose?[12]

In the 1790s, when the United Irishmen made green the colour of Irish nationalism, their female adherents wore green openly and provocatively, as well as intimately and subversively. Green handkerchiefs were the most common symbols, adopted by men and women; however, as Reverend James Gordon later recalled, women also displayed green-striped handkerchiefs, green ribbons, bonnets, petticoats, and shoes (68). Some, like their Jacobite predecessors,[13] even politicized their garters (68; Lecky 348). One Irish woman, whose green handkerchief had been forcibly removed, unwisely taunted the soldiers that they could not stop her from wearing green garters. For this, she was sent home with her petticoats tied around her head, presumably by the garters themselves (Lecky 348). Gordon recounts a similar anecdote: two young women wearing green garters were tied to each other, back-to-back (again, possibly with their garters), and held under guard on the street for several hours (Gordon 68). While these particular stories may be apocryphal, they underline several important points about women's politicization of fashion: that they and their male counterparts saw their actions as political; that at least some women were willing to risk public indignity or violence for their beliefs; and, additionally, that women's outward conformity could be deceptive, as women might literally wear their personal politics next to the skin.

A more public accessory, fans were one of the century's most enduring female fashions. By the eighteenth century, they were, according to Elizabeth Montagu, 'an ensign of our order' (71), carried by women across the country with any pretensions to gentility. They ranged from exquisite works of art down to bright, printed paper fans on inexpensive wooden mounts (Alexander 17), produced by entrepreneurial local printers. Like modern men's ties, eighteenth-century women's fans served as statement accessories and talking points. The images on women's fans served as effective non-verbal claims to character, fashionable sentiments, and cultured taste, as well as to patriotism and political opinion.[14] This last was made possible by the development of inexpensive printed fans:

> The topical fan, having reference to royal and distinguished personages, or recording public events, was entirely the product of the eighteenth century...During this period, the engraved fan became a purveyor of history, a kind of running commentary on the affairs of the hour. It was the fan of the people – the poor relation of the more aristocratic painted fan. (Rhead 206)

Topical fans enabled women to comment upon or celebrate domestic and international achievements, to make public their allegiance (or not) to the monarch or government of the day, and to participate in the excitement generated by politicians or political events. As women carried their fans visiting, shopping, socializing, or promenading, they personalized women's appearance and politicized their personal space. The royal family and royal events provided plenty of scope for enterprising fan-makers across the century and numerous opportunities for women to display their loyalty (*Fan Museum: Royal Fans*). Fans, for instance, marked George II's coronation in 1727 (MoL 88.96a) and the death of Frederick, Prince of Wales in 1751 (V&AM, T.202–1959), and proclaimed the recovery of George III in 1789 (V&AM, T.203–1959; MoL 48.109/1. See figure 5.1). Occasionally, royal events, like the wedding of Princess Anne, the Princess Royal, to William Prince of Orange and Nassau in March 1734, caught the public imagination and fast-acting fan-makers vied with each to meet the demand for fans on the subject. By July 1733 Jonathan Pinchbeck, fan-maker at the Fan and Crown in the Strand, was already peppering the newspapers with aggrieved advertisements for his 'Nassau Fan: or, Love and Beauty Triumphant' (*Fog's Weekly Journal* 14 July 1733); or, as he later deemed it, 'The ORIGINAL, LOYAL, NASSAU FAN' (*The Craftsman* 3 November 1733). He reminded potential purchasers to 'Beware of Counterfeits, the true Original Nassau Fans having the Name Pinchbeck prefixed to the Mount' (*Fog's Weekly Journal* 14 July 1733).[15] His competition, Mary Gamble at the Golden Fan in St Martin's Court, serenely continued to advertise her version of the fan: '(For all Loyal LADIES) THE True, Original ORANGE FAN'. At 1s. 6d. the mount and 2s. 6d. mounted (*Daily Journal* 27 September 1733), her fans would have been affordable to women well down the social ladder.[16]

Figure 5.1. Fan – *'The Recovery of George III from Illness'* (1789); Victoria & Albert Museum T.203-1959. The celebrations for George III's recovery in 1789 were very carefully planned and women made a statement of their loyalty through their adoption of a loyal costume, including fans such as this one. The mottos read: 'On the King's / Happy Recovery'; and 'Health is restored to ONE and happiness to Millions.' Photo © Victoria and Albert Museum, London

Fans honouring military and naval men were also popular in a century which saw the development of the cult of the hero.[17] For those with Jacobite tendencies, a fan with Jacobite symbols or portraits was a pointed, if daring, way of declaring political allegiance (*Fans: War and Peace*, no. 54; V&AM, T.204–1959). Those women whose Jacobitism was more circumspect (or less courageous) might carry double-sided fans, floral on one side and Jacobite on the other (V&AM, T.160–1970), allowing the choice of which side to display, where, and in what company. Conversely, women could also rejoice at Jacobite defeat with fans celebrating the duke of Cumberland's victory at Culloden (*Fans: War and Peace*, no. 55; V&AM, T.205–1959. See figure 5.2). Not all fans were this uncomplicated, though. Those representing Admiral Vernon's capture of Porto Bello in 1739 (BM, AN361123001) or his attempted capture of Cartagena in 1740 (BM, AN361124001) were, on one level, straightforward expressions of support for a popular naval hero. Their meaning was complicated when Vernon became the figurehead for opposition to Robert Walpole's foreign policy in 1740.[18] Thus, the

Figure 5.2. Fan – '*Surrender of the Jacobite Leaders to the Duke of Cumberland* after the Battle of Culloden' (c. 1746), Victoria and Alberta Museum T.205-1959. Photo © Victoria and Albert Museum, London

celebrations that sprang up across the country for Vernon's birthday in November took on deeper significance and the women who disported Vernon fans in the streets or at the evening's entertainments may well have done so with several purposes in mind (*London Evening Post* 18 November 1740).

The importance of understanding a fan's political context is well illustrated by a fan which survives in the British Museum in both expensive hand-coloured and cheaper uncoloured versions (BM, AN361783001; BM, AN358347001). Dating from September 1782, it has a central medallion of Victory driving a chariot and horses, flanked by classical ornaments and smaller medallions containing an owl and an eagle, respectively.[19] In the hand-coloured version, the medallions are strikingly blue and some of the multicoloured trim appears to be buff. At first glance, the fan is a simple, innocuous statement of educated classical taste. It becomes substantially more interesting when put into its political context. In September 1782 Britain had lost the American War of Independence and government representatives were negotiating the preliminary articles of peace with France. The Foxite Whigs, who had championed the American colonists against the king and his government, were celebrating the Americans' victory. This fan, designed by

Harriet, Lady Duncannon (a noted Foxite herself and the sister of the Foxite Whigs' leading hostess, the duchess of Devonshire) was a barely coded Foxite proclamation. The women who carried her fan – elite and otherwise – used it to celebrate the American victory and to claim a place in the larger extra-parliamentary Opposition public.

Significantly more research remains to be done on politicized fans in order to determine the range of meanings attached to them and the responses they generated, especially from men, but it appears that they provided women with an additional way of expressing political opinions, commenting upon national and international developments, and adding to the overall politicization of the spaces through which they moved. A woman carrying a fan of Bishop Sacheverell's 1710 trial (BM, AN354233001) to an evening of cards, or her granddaughter unfurling one of Warren Hastings's 1788 trial (BM, AN361082001), may only have been boasting of her attendance or indicating that she was au fait politically: we can only speculate upon the bearer's political allegiance, or how often display turned into debate, as the fans gave women entrée into the furious discussions that whirled around these much-publicized events.

The Excise Crisis of 1732–3 gives us a brief glimpse into the development of and women's use of the popular fashion of fans to express their political opinions. The Excise scheme saw Robert Walpole establish increasingly efficient means of taxation, especially through the growing use of inland duties to tax domestic consumption. By the 1730s, excise taxes had been in use as an effective way of raising revenue for nearly a hundred years; moreover, Walpole had himself successfully extended the scheme in 1723 to cover tea, coffee, and chocolate – luxuries that were fast becoming staples. As Paul Langford points out, his proposal to extend the excise to include wine and tobacco in 1732–3 was an unmitigated, but also an unexpected, failure. Interpreted by opponents and the press as an insidious attack on the rights and liberties of the freeborn Englishman, particularly the Englishman's right to private property (Linebaugh 179), the Excise Crisis marks the moment an organized opposition emerged 'that looked to some element of the excluded public for support' (Price 259). Wild and ungrounded fears about the consequences of the bill were whipped up by the 'regular Infatuation from daily and weekly Papers' and that other manifestation of eighteenth-century print culture, the hand-bill:

> little *Hand-Bills* . . . dispersed by thousands all over the City and Country, put into Peoples [*sic*] Hands in the Streets and Highways, dropped at their Doors, and thrown in at their Windows: all asserting that Excisemen were

(like a foreign Enemy) going to invade and devour them, and ready to enter their Houses; into all Houses, private or public, at any time, by Day, or by Night. (*A letter from a member of Parliament* 5)

As a result, the Excise became the 'Theme of Coffee-Houses, Taverns, and Gin-shops, the Discourse of Artificers, the Cry of the Streets, the Entertainment of Lacquies, the Prate of Wenches, and the Bugbear of Children' (6).

Printers flourished. Graphic satires and prints displaying the doom-ridden consequences of the Bill were quickly available for sale.[20] Nor did it take long for the Excise to appear on fans. On 2 June 1733, *Fog's Weekly Journal* proudly announced:

> This Day is Publish'd,
>
> An Excise Fan for all Loyal Ladies; Or, The Political Monster, as described in Fog's Journal, May the 5th, Curiously Delineated, being a Memorial for Posterity. In this most agreeable Fan, is Represented, I. A Picture of Cardinal Wolsey, the first Excise Master of England, done from an Original Painting. II. His Feats on one Hand, and those of his Successor on the other. III. A Lawyer with two honest Briefs. IV. That famous Monster, Monger, Ferdinando Ferdinandi, Drawn from the Life. V. The Death of this Monster. VI. The Modern Inquisition, with an Assembly of many Spectators, as Vintners, Tobacconists, &c.
>
> 'Tis in the Power of every British Fair
> 'To turn Excises of all Kinds to Air.
>
> Sold by M. Gamble at the Golden Fan in St. Martin's Court, near Leicester Fields. Price 2s. 6d.

This fan survives in two forms in the British Museum collection: one solely of the central section of the fan, which portrays a male figure holding papers that read 'Liberty and Property,' 'No Dutch Politiks. Down with the Excise,' above and to the left of the above-mentioned couplet to the 'British Fair' (BM, AN354263001); and another of the full, unmounted fan paper (BM, 1891,0713.379). The fan's popularity can be traced through newspaper advertisements. Martha Gamble advertised it widely in *Fog's Weekly Journal*, the *St. James's Evening Post*, the *Daily Journal*, and *The Craftsman*, until at least the beginning of May 1734, which suggests that she profited from the Excise Crisis for a year. Moreover, the fan must have been popular, for she was already advertising it as 'The famous excise Fan' by September 1733, and apparently charging more for it: 'Price 2s. 6d. the Mount, 3s. 6d. mounted' (*Daily Journal* 27 September 1733).

The newspaper reports of Lord Mayor Day that autumn testify to the fan's continued popularity and give some insight into how women used it. Women joined in to acclaim the outgoing Lord Mayor, who had been a staunch opponent of Excise:

> The Behaviour of the People upon this Occasion is an Instance that they are not unmindful of Benefits receiv'd, and will not be ungrateful to those who endeavour to serve them; for in return from Westminster the late *Lord Mayor's Coach* was perfectly carried by the Populace, the better Sort from the Windows and Balconies saluting him with the Cry of, *No Excise;* even the Ladies making their Compliments with their Fans – Such will the Reception be of all those who endeavour to serve their Country without Fee or Reward. (*Fog's Weekly Journal* 3 November 1733)

The Craftsman also drew attention to the women's actions, noting that 'the Ladies in the Balconies and Windows shew'd their Zeal by shaking their Fans and joyning in the Cry of No Excise' (3 November 1733). While some of these fans would undoubtedly have been found in the hands of those women who attended the 'Ball for the Ladies' at the end of the day, newspaper reports suggest that this display of political spirit extended substantially beyond the ball-going civic elite. If, as Richard Price has argued, the Excise Crisis illustrates the emergence of the extra-parliamentary nation as a political force, then it also was an important demonstration of women's willingness and ability to participate in that process and to claim their place through both their presence and their use of fashion.[21]

Women's politicization of space through the use of fashion needs to be seen in the context of a society that could draw on historical traditions of popular public involvement and popular statements of allegiance and loyalty through the well-established use of ritual, symbols, and activities that often included clothing and accessories. The appropriation of these older models of public participation and personal statement, and their use for political ends, helps to explain the viral nature of political excitement that was such a feature of eighteenth-century electoral politics and political crises. It also adds to our understanding of the development and gendering of the extra-parliamentary nation by highlighting some of the strategies of inclusion and appropriation used by women who were intent on expressing their political opinions. The use of fashion for political ends made politics a participatory, as well as a spectator, sport. It made politics visual and undeniably public; it fostered a sense of political awareness and allegiance (individual and/or group); it heightened political excitement and rivalry by emphasizing distinctions and factional and party differences, even for those who were not a part of the formal political nation; and it contributed to the creation of a richly complex political world where a multiplicity of formal and informal spaces could be, and were, politicized. Finally, it reminds us as historians of the need to pay more heed to material culture when studying political history. We need to remember to put fashion into its political context – we may never know who, circa 1710 when the Marlboroughs' star was on the wane, wore the expensive lappets of fine Honiton lace bearing the carefully worked portraits of the duke and duchess that now survive in the Victoria and Albert Museum (V&AM, T.212&A–1989), or where or why she wore them, but their existence is itself telling of politicization. We, therefore, need to have a better understanding of what politicized fashion items may lurk in collections around the country. Not only will this help to extend our understanding of the politicization of space through the use of clothing, adornment, accessories, and ornament, but it will also ensure that we move beyond simplistic divides between elite and popular politics to achieve a more graduated, holistic understanding of women's political involvement.[22]

NOTES

1 See Berg and Eger, and Lemire, 'Second-hand beaux.'
2 For a rethinking of the Habermasian public sphere, see Lake and Pincus.
3 Lady Spencer to Lady Duncannon, 2 May 1784. British Library (BL), Altp.
   F. 38, f. 307v. Further references to archival and special collections are as follows: British Museum (BM), Museum of London (MoL), Victoria and Albert Museum (V&AM).
4 Figures obtained from averaging O'Gorman 179, Table 3.
5 Thanks to Zoë Dyndor for allowing me to consult her article prior to publication.
6 *A bill [as amended on the report] to make further regulation for preventing corrupt practices at elections of memberts to serve in Parliament, and for diminishing the expense of such elections.* 1826–7 (367) 7/8 Geo IV. Sess. 1826/7.

7 See, for example, Brewer, *Party Ideology* and *Common People;* Clark; Epstein, 'Cap of Liberty'; Rogers, *Crowds;* Shoemaker; and Wilson.

8 See Hunt, Ribiero, and Wrigley.

9 'Cap of Liberty.' See also his 'Rituals of Solidarity' in *Radical Expressions.*

10 This letter was also published in *St James's Chronicle* (9 December 1773).

11 See, for instance, *True Blue: Or, A Letter to the Gentlemen of the Old Interest in the County of Oxford* (1754), where supporters of the Old [Tory] Interest in the county are challenged about the ideology behind their colour and label. If being a 'True Blue' meant supporting the crown and the liberties of the freeborn Englishman, then, the author claimed, the Old Interest was actually no different than the New [Whig] Interest; if, however, it did not, then it could only be a disguise for the Old [Jacobite] Interest (12).

12 William Lecky claims that she wore an orange ribbon to the annual drawing room celebrating William III's birthday in November (178); however, earlier texts, such as *The Polyanthea* (1804) and *La Belle Assemblée* (December 1807) claim that she wore an orange lily to the celebrations in July at the Dublin viceregal court commemorating the Battle of the Boyne.

13 Just how likely women were to wear politically specific garters is understandably difficult to determine. Examples survive from the early eighteenth century. See V&AM, T.139–1932: woven silk garter from 1714, bearing the motto, 'George Lewis by the Grace of God . . .'; also T.107–1938 and T.107A–1938: woven silk garters, c. 1745, inscribed 'God Bless the Prince' and 'Whiggs and Rumps,' respectively. The British Museum collection includes a striped Jacobite garter, woven in red, blue, yellow, green, and white, with a tartan pattern at each end, the motto reading, 'GOD BLESS PC AND DOWN WITH THE RUMP': BM, AN216167001.

14 Eighteenth-century fans survive in significant numbers in collections around the country but, as objects of eighteenth-century female material culture, they are still surprisingly understudied by historians. Even Styles's *The Dress of the People* and Vickery's *Behind Closed Doors,* two most recent (and outstandingly comprehensive) studies of eighteenth-century domestic material culture, make little mention of them.

15 Pinchbeck repeats his advert in the *Daily Post* 19 July and 7 August; in *Fog's Weekly Journal,* 28 July; then, slightly modified in the *London Evening Post* 16 October 16, and *Daily Post* 8 November 1733.

16 The British Museum holds several fans celebrating this wedding, although they are not designated by the titles used in the papers of the day in the online catalogue. A sample of 'The Orange Fan' can be found at BM, AN361118001; for a version of what appears to be 'The Nassau Fan: or, Love and Beauty Triumphant,' see BM, Reg. 1893,0509.1 [Schreiber 325 mounted].

17 On the hero, see McNairn and Nicholson. Admiral Lord Nelson and the
   duke of Wellington appear on numerous fans. For Nelson's victories, see
   Fans: War and Peace, no. 60; for Nelson's death, no. 61. For Wellington, see
   BM, AN361748001. General Wolfe, hero of the battle for Quebec, however,
   appears on transfer-printed household goods. By 1780, the patriotic housewife could readily have displayed Benjamin West's famous *The Death of
   General Wolfe* (1770) on a Staffordshire pottery jug: V&AM, 3630–1901.
18 News of the capture of Porto Bello only reached England in March 1740.
   See Rogers, *Whigs and Cities* 235. See also Shoemaker 116.
19 Fans also welcomed peace, such the peace of Aix-la-Chapelle in 1748 (BM,
   AN18911001; MoL, 83.239), or the outbreak of peace in 1801, prior to the
   Treaty of Amiens (BM, AN361125001).
20 See, for example BM, AN354993001, 'Excise in Triumph' (1733), upon
   which 'Dejected Trade hangs down its drooping Head.'
21 More research remains to be done to recover where possible the sartorial
   political involvement of this group of women at other political pinch-
   points of the eighteenth century. While the Regency Crisis of 1788–9 saw
   elite women use their clothing and accessories to politicize and divide
   society, and the social events they attended, the Regency caps vaunted by
   the Prince of Wales's supporters were far out of the reach of a middling-
   sort woman at a cost of 7 guineas each. The elaborate gowns and decorations devised by the supporters of the king for the celebratory balls held
   in his honour were similarly prohibitive. It seems highly unlikely, though,
   given the degree of social division that the Crisis created and the out-
   burst of patriotic fervour (real or manufactured) that swept the country
   on the king's recovery, that the women of the extra-parliamentary nation
   remained chastely uninvolved. For women's use of clothing in the Regency
   Crisis, see Chalus, *Elite Women* 100–5; Navickas 547–8.
22 I would like to thank Beatrice Behlens at the Museum of London and
   Susan North, Louisa Collins, and Matthew Storey at the Victoria & Albert
   Museum, and the staff at the Fan Museum in Greenwich. Jacqueline
   Collier shared with me her knowledge of fan-makers, especially in
   Georgian Bath. Katrina Navickas was serendipitously working on 'That
   Sash Will Hang You' at the same time that I was writing this essay and
   was kind enough to share it with me prior to publication and to comment
   on my work. I recommend her excellent work on radical women's use of
   political clothing. Finally, women and the material culture of eighteenth-
   century politics requires much more space than this essay can allow.
   Footnotes have been minimized here to give more space to the text; anyone
   requiring additional references should feel encouraged to contact me at

e.chalus@bathspa.ac.uk. For a fuller sense of women's use of colour and clothing in electoral politics, see my *Elite Women*. Special mention to Jon, Cate, Bobby, and Tiffany for their advice and patience.

WORKS CITED

Addison, Joseph, and Richard Steele. *The Spectator: with notes and a general index*. 2 vols. Philadelphia: J.J. Woodward, 1836. Print.

Alexander, Helene. *Fans*. Princes Risborough: Shire, 2002. Print.

Atkins, Jacqueline M. 'Wearing Propaganda: Textiles on the Home Front in Japan, Great Britain, and America during the East Asian War, 1931–45.' *Textile* 2.1 (2004): 24–45. Print.

Barker, Hannah, and David Vincent. *Language, Print and Electoral Politics, 1790–1832: Newcastle-under-Lyme Broadsides*. Cambridge: Boydell, 2001. Print.

Berg, Maxine, and Elizabeth Eger, eds. *Luxury in the Eighteenth Century: Debates, Desires and Delectable Goods*. Basingstoke: Palgrave, 2002. Print.

Brewer, John. *Party Ideology and Popular Politics at the Accession of George III*. Cambridge: Cambridge UP, 1981. Print.

– 'Theatre and Counter-Theatre in Georgian Politics: The Mock Elections at Garrat.' *History Today* 33.2 (1983): 14–23. Print.

Bushaway, Bob. *By Rite: Custom, Ceremony and Community in England, 1700–1880*. London: Junction, 1982. Print.

Chalus, Elaine. *Elite Women in English Political Life: 1754–1790*. Oxford: Oxford UP, 2005. Print.

– '"That epidemical Madness": Women and Electoral Politics in the Late Eighteenth Century.' *Gender in Eighteenth-Century England: Roles, Representations and Responsibilities*. Ed. Hannah Barker and Elaine Chalus. Harlow: Longman, 1997. 151–78. Print.

– 'Women, Electoral Privilege and Practice in the Eighteenth Century.' *Women in British Politics, 1760–1860: The Power of the Petticoat* Ed. Kathryn Gleadle and Sarah Richardson. Basingstoke: Palgrave, 2000. 19–38. Print.

Clark, Anna. *The Struggle for the Breeches: Gender and the Making of the British Working Class*. Berkeley: U of California P, 1997. Print.

Curtin, Nancy J. *The United Irishmen: Popular Politics in Ulster and Dublin, 1791–1798*. Oxford: Oxford UP, 2004. Print.

Dyndor, Zoë. 'Widows, Wives, and Witnesses: Women and Their Involvement in the 1768 Northampton Borough Parliamentary Election.' *Parliamentary History*. Forthcoming. Typescript by permission of author.

Electors' Scrap Book: being a Re-Publication of the Addresses and Speeches of the Several Candidates, for the City, and the Northern and Southern Divisions of the County of Durham. Durham: George Walker, 1832. *Google Books.* Web. April 2010.

Epstein, James. *Radical Expression: Political Language, Ritual and Symbol in England, 1790–1850.* New York: Oxford UP, 1994. Print.

– 'Understanding the Cap of Liberty: Symbolic Practice and Social Conflict in Early Nineteenth-Century England.' *Past & Present* 122 (1989): 75–118. Print.

The Fan Museum Presents Fans: War and Peace, 20 Oct. 2009–28 Feb. 2010. Rochester: Fan Museum, 2009. Print.

The Fan Museum Presents Royal Fans, 5 March – 7 July 2002. Greenwich: Fan Museum, c. 2002. Print.

Fissell, Mary E. *Vernacular Bodies: The Politics of Reproduction in Early Modern England.* Oxford: Oxford UP, 2004. Print.

Flather, Amanda. *Gender and Space in Early Modern England.* Woodbridge: Boydell and Brewer, 2007. Print.

Gordon, James. *History of the Rebellion in Ireland, in the Year 1798.* 2nd ed. London: T. Hurst, 1803. *Google Books.* Web. April 2010.

Harding, Vanessa. 'Space, Property, and Propriety in Urban England.' *Journal of Interdisciplinary History* 32.4 (2002): 549–69. Print.

Holmes, Geoffrey. *British Politics in the Age of Anne.* Revised ed. London: Hambledon, 1987. Print.

Hoppit, Julian. *A Land of Liberty? England, 1689–1727.* Oxford: Oxford UP, 2000. Print.

Howard, Sharon. 'Riotous Community: Crowds, Politics and Society in Wales, c.1700–1840.' *Welsh History Review* 20.4 (2001): 656–86. Print.

Hunt, Lynn. *Politics, Culture, and Class in the French Revolution.* Berkeley: U of California P, 1984. Print.

La Belle Assemblée. London: J. Bell, 1807. Print.

Lake, Peter, and Steven Pincus. 'Rethinking the Public Sphere in Early Modern England.' *Journal of British Studies* 45. 2 (2006): 270–92. Print.

Langford, Paul. *The Excise Crisis: Society and Politics in the Age of Walpole.* Oxford: Oxford UP, 1975. Print.

Lecky, William Edward Hartpole. *A History of England in the Eighteenth Century.* 5th, 6th impr. 2nd ed, revised. 8 vols. London: Longmans, Green & Co., 1879–90. Print.

Lemire, Beverly. 'Domesticating the Exotic: Floral Culture and the East India Calico Trade with England, c.1660–1800.' *Textile* 1.1 (2003) 65–85. Print.

– 'Second-hand beaux and "red-armed Belles": Conflict and the Creation of Fashion in England, c.1660–1800.' *Continuity and Change* 15.3 (2000): 391–417. Print.

A letter from a member of Parliament for a borough in the west, to a noble lord in his neighbourhood there, concerning the excise-bill, and the manner and causes of losing it. London; republished in Dublin, 1733. Print.

Linebaugh, Peter. *The London Hanged: Crime and Civil Society in the Eighteenth Century.* 2nd ed. London: Verso, 2003. Print.

McNairn, Alan. *Behold the Hero: General Wolfe and the Arts in the Eighteenth Century.* Montreal and Kingston: McGill-Queen's UP, 1997. Print.

Montagu, Elizabeth. *The Letters of Mrs. Elizabeth Montagu, with Some of the Letters of Her Correspondents.* Ed. Matthew Montagu. 3 vols. Boston: Wells and Lilly, 1825. Print.

Navickas, Katrina. '"That Sash Will Hang You": Political Clothing and Adornment in England, 1780–1840.' *Journal of British Studies* 49.3 (July 2010): 540–65.

Nicholson, Adam. *Seize the Fire: Heroism, Duty, and the Battle of Trafalgar.* New York: HarperCollins, 2005. Print.

O'Gorman, Frank. *Voters, Patrons, and Parties: The Unreformed Electoral System of Hanoverian England, 1734–1832.* Oxford: Clarendon, 1991. Print.

Pollbook of the Contested Election for the County of Northumberland from June 20th to July 6th, 1826, including a Complete Collection of the Addresses and Speeches &c. Alnwick, 1827. *Google Books.* Web. 6 Feb. 2010.

The Polyanthea: or, a Collection of Interesting Fragments, in Prose and Verse. 2 vols. London: J. Budd, 1804, 268–9. *Google Books.* Web. 15 Mar. 2010.

Price, Richard. *British Society, 1680–1880: Dynamism, Containment and Change.* Cambridge: Cambridge UP, 1999. Print.

Rhead, G. Woolliscroft. *History of the Fan.* London: Kegan Paul, Trench, Trübner & Co., 1910. Print.

Ribiero, Aileen. *Fashion and the French Revolution.* London: Batsford, 1988. Print.

Rogers, Nicholas. *Crowd, Culture and Politics in Georgian Britain.* Oxford: Oxford UP, 1998. Print.

– *Whigs and Cities: Popular Politics in the Age of Walpole and Pitt.* Oxford: Clarendon, 1989. Print.

Schoeser, Mary. 'A Secret Trade: Plate Printed Textiles and Dress Accessories, c.1620–1820.' *Dress* 34 (2007): 49–59. *Ebsco.* Web. 20 Jan. 2010.

Shoemaker, Robert. *The London Mob: Violence and Disorder in Eighteenth-Century England.* London: Hambledon and London, 2004. Print.

Smith, Chloë Wigston. '"Calico Madams": Servants, Consumption, and the Calico Crisis.' *Eighteenth-Century Life* 31.2 (2007): 29–55. Print.

Styles, John. *The Dress of the People: Everyday Fashion in Eighteenth-Century England*. London: Yale UP, 2007. Print.

Swift, Jonathan. *The Correspondence of Jonathan Swift, D.D.* Ed. Francis Elrington Ball and John Henry Bernard (1910). *Google Books*. Web. 3 Sept. 2009.

– *The Examiner* 1.32 (1–8 March 1710/11). *ECCO*. Web. October 2009.

True Blue: Or, A Letter to the Gentlemen of the Old Interest in the County of Oxford. London, 1754. Print.

Trusler, John. *The Country Election*. London, 1768, 1788. Print.

Vickery, Amanda. *Behind Closed Doors: At Home in Georgian England*. New Haven and London: Yale UP, 2009. Print.

Wilson, Kathleen. *The Sense of the People: Politics, Culture and Imperialism in England, 1715–1785*. Cambridge: Cambridge UP, 1995. Print.

Woolrych, Austin. *Britain in Revolution, 1625–1660*. Oxford: Oxford UP, 2004. Print.

Wrigley, Richard. *The Politics of Appearances: Representations of Dress in Revolutionary France*. Oxford: Oxford UP, 2002. Print.

PART II

Women, Reading, and Writing

6 The Culinary Art of Eighteenth-Century Women Cookbook Authors

ROBERT JAMES MERRETT

Between 1700 and 1799, 435 British cookbooks were published. With print runs and reprints tallied, the book trade produced 531,250 volumes of 'receipts' in the period. Seventy editions appeared in the 1780s (Lehmann 63). Most cookbooks appeared anonymously or pseudonymously, but by 1800 women nominally dominated the genre. While the century saw the rise of haute cuisine (Trubek 3–4), women spurned culinary elitism to promote and popularize middle-class culture. Yet, in creating discursive spaces by associating haute cuisine with professional chefs and seeking gender solidarity, they fell subject to social dialectic: their dependence on the book trade advanced class formation and fashionable consumerism while their bourgeois aesthetics were snared within the polarities of imperial ideology.[1]

Patriarchy and Culinary Traditions

On ascending the throne in 1661, Louis XIV presented himself as a demigod. Court feasts ritualized his transcendence. The night-long festival of 2 May 1668 celebrating military victories dazzled six hundred guests. Such glorious feasts displaced feudal gift-exchanges: by entertaining aristocrats at Versailles with unmatchable ostentation, Louis turned hospitality into state strategy and nobles into mere courtiers. By regimenting aristocratic manners and haute cuisine, he rendered the bureaucracy, academies, army, and church instruments of apotheosis (Apostolides 318–20). His Revocation of the Edict of Nantes in 1685, the acme of absolutism, created a diaspora of 200,000 Protestants and the conversion of many more by persecution (Stanton 358–64).

The cookbook heralding this new order was *Le Cuisinier français* (1651) by François Pierre de La Varenne (1618–78). Preparing meals for courtiers helped him record the changes in 150 years of French cooking. Thus, he favoured herbs over spices and discarded medieval olios. To his publisher, La Varenne taught 'how to correct the vitious qualities of meats by contrary and severall seasonings' and afforded 'unto man a solid nourishment, well dressed, & conformable to his appetites, which are in many the rule of their life, and of their looking well.'[2] Fine cooking obviates medicines since 'it is sweeter by farre to make according to one's abilitie an honest and reasonable expence in sauces, and other delicacies of meats, to cause life and health to subsist, [than] to spend vast summes of money in drugs, medicinall herbs, potions, and other troublesome remedies for the recovery of health.' La Varenne's cuisine is linked to nationalism and urban grandeur: France is superior to 'all other nations in the world in point of civilitie, courtesie, and comelinesse in every kind of conversation' and is esteemed for its 'comely and dainty fashion of feeding' ([A8r–9r]).

Since Louis relished epicurean meals, courtiers invented dishes to please him. The representative cook here is François Massialot (1660–1733). He was *chef de cuisine* to the dauphin, to the king's brother, to the duke of Orléans (the king's nephew), and to the duke of Chartres (the future regent). Admired across Europe, Massialot's *Le Cuisinier royal et bourgeois* appeared in 1691. The English version, *The Court and Country Cook*, came out in 1702. Besides detailing the structure of court meals, Massialot arranges recipes alphabetically, providing cross-references and a detailed index. To the English publisher, the book exemplifies the cuisine that 'may only be said to Preside in *Europe*, where the best Ways of Seasoning and Dressing all sorts of Provisions, which that Continent affords are well known; and where Justice is done, at the same time, to the wonderful Productions, caus'd by the happy Situation of other Climates.' Seeing cuisine as a European achievement, he insists that, while Massialot's dishes are served at 'the Court of France, or in the Palaces of Princes, and in the Houses of Persons of great Quality,' they may serve all but 'the meaner sort of Country-People' ([A2v–3r]).

Despite the influence of French fashions after Charles II's restoration, the Civil War had accustomed Britons to resist both the absolutism and the culinary modes of France. Monsieur Marnettè dedicates *The Perfect Cook* (1656) to wives of the mayor and sheriffs of London by deriding French confectionery: 'every Matron and young damsel are so well vers'd in the Pastry Art' that they 'out-vie the best Forreign pastry

Cooks in all the World.' His treatise, containing 'nothing save Out-landish Cates and Junkets,' will divert patrons with the 'Forreign Cates and Delicacies, happily never as yet tasted within her walls' ([A4r–v]). This satire relies on the culinary sophistication of female citizens.

French cuisine is no more advanced in *The Accomplisht Cook* (1660), the period's fullest cookbook by Robert May (1588–1665?). Aware of La Varenne's cuisine from having studied in Paris, May caters to small and large budgets in order to help readers treat 'Kindred, Friends, Allies and Acquaintance' to a 'handsome and relishing entertainment in all seasons of the year' ([A5r]). This social inclusiveness became a watch-word of female cooks. Perpetuating dishes going back to Edward III, May drew on manuscripts as well as Italian, Spanish, and French cook-books. His patrons were Catholic aristocrats whom he served in the 'Golden Days of Peace and Hospitality, when you enjoy'd your own, so as to entertain and relieve others' (A3r). In the Civil War, he worked for Elizabeth, countess of Kent, who is linked to two books on household management published after her death in 1651. One, *A Choice Manual* (1653), discusses medicines; the other, *A True Gentlewomans Delight* (1653) by W.I. Gent, is a cookbook from which May drew. These titles reveal the countess's centrality to the culinary manuscript culture of women. May produced a second edition in 1664, his book reaching a fifth edition in 1685, because of the fullness of its one thousand recipes and innovative illustrations. May influenced female cooks by oppos-ing monopolistic guilds and promoting puddings, pies, and roasts but not French 'made dishes.' His appreciation of aristocratic patronage for social cohesion is a tenet that female cookbooks often imitate.

Rivalries between the cities of London and Westminster in the absence of a dominating court led to distinct urban and rural culinary modes and to advances in estate management by landowners whose housekeepers reflected their practices in cookbooks. One exemplary landowner was William Russell (1613–1700), the 5th earl of Bedford. In 1641, he inherited dilapidated Woburn Abbey along with Bedford House and Covent Garden. A Parliamentary general, he surrendered his post in 1642; the chattels of Bedford House were seized as a pen-alty. Inigo Jones built him a ninety-room mansion on the abbey site. Educated as a Puritan, Russell became a royalist: in the Civil War, Charles II stayed three times at Woburn, the earl riding in the cavalcade that led the king into London and playing a role at his coronation in Westminster Hall on 23 April 1661. He obtained a royal pardon for his Parliamentary sympathies. When Covent Garden grew fashionable in the 1640s and 1650s, he garnered good rents, and in 1671, the Crown granted him the right to open a fruit and vegetable market there.[3] When William III appointed him duke of Bedford in 1694, Woburn had become a cynosure of civic well-being, as records of the estate's food consumption attest.

Woburn was a model of mixed economy: while Russell drew from urban and local markets, he was also self-sustaining. Buying poultry and dairy produce from tenants, he purchased mutton, pork, veal, calves' heads, sheep's feet, neat's tongue, tripe, capons, pullets, pigeons, lobsters, and flounders locally. He stocked Woburn's ponds with pike and perch from Thorney, his Cambridge estate. Barrels of oysters came from Colchester. He made bulk purchases of nutmeg and cloves from London grocers and bought dried and candied fruits from French confectioners in Paris and London. For his orchards and kitchen gardens, he acquired stock and seeds from London nurseries. He cultivated many kinds of pears, plums, and cherries along with peaches, nectarines, and apricots. He imported Westphalia hams from Germany. He acquired six or seven fat bullocks each summer so that salt meat was available during the winter. His Cambridge estate yielded hundreds of ruffs, reeves, quails, knots, dotterels, and swans. Improvements on that estate supplied corn, oats, hemp seed, and cole seeds, the latter producing colza oil for cooking (Thomson 218–20).

Woburn's varied foodstuffs represent what housekeepers prepared for landed gentry. Yet, if they necessarily ignored the vegetarianism of Thomas Tryon, John Evelyn, and George Cheyne (Stuart 64–5, 80–1, 166–8), they also shunned the haute cuisine of chefs employed by Whig peers in the Georgian era. Lord Chesterfield (for whom Vincent La Chapelle cooked) and the duke of Newcastle (whom Monsieur de St Clouet served), embodied their rank in the elaborate culinary modes, the court no longer setting fashions by 1730, its banquets distant from the refinement of Versailles (Mennell 119). The decline in English court cookery is manifest in the works of Patrick Lamb, Robert Smith, Henry Howard, and Charles Carter, whose recipes female cooks found whimsical and impractical, even while suspecting the authors of holding back recipes. As Eliza Smith wrote: 'I cannot but believe, that those celebrated Performers, notwithstanding all their Professions of having ingenuously communicated their Art, industriously concealed their best Receipts from the Publick' ([A5r]). Since most court cookery books were published at the end of careers, they did not keep pace with haute cuisine.

Lamb published *Royal Cookery; or the Complete Court-Cook* (1710) after serving Charles II, James II, William III, and Queen Anne. Upholding '*the* Grandeur *of the* English *Court and Nation*,' he notes the '*publick* Regales' he designed for regal accessions, ambassadorial receptions, installations of peers, and aristocratic nuptials. Yet hyperbole about Britain is unmatched by culinary invention, his recipes simply traditional French and English dishes. When the fifth edition of Howard's *England's Newest Way in all Sorts of Cookery, Pastry, And All Pickles that are fit to be used* appeared in 1726, the author admits supplementing his recipes from the '*Choice Manuscripts of several Ladies*' ([A2v]). Smith, who worked under Lamb in William's reign, says in *Court Cookery: Or, The Compleat English Cook* (1723) that his receipts appear in 'a plain *English* Dress' from concern for frugality. Excluding bills of fare, table design, medicines, and preparations of beverages, he imagines readers as members of the gentry, not as courtiers.

Changed tones in Carter's *The Complete Practical Cook: Or, A New System Of the Whole Art and Mystery of Cookery* (1730) and *The Compleat City and Country Cook: Or, Accomplish'd Housewife* (1732) confirm the decline of court cookery. His 1730 preface, in addressing gentlemen, defines cooking as requiring 'Variety *and* Novelty' ([A1r]): chefs are ingenious artists who make 'New Experiments *to gratify the Taste*' of men whose '*splendid Circumstances make them emulous to excel in the Delicacies of this Mystery, especially when they exert their Wealth and the Magnificence to entertain their Friends with* grand *and* sumptuous *Repasts.*' Cookery, not having '*reach'd Perfection*,' is degraded by publishers who vamp up 'Old Books' and pay artists to lend their names to title-pages. Haute cuisine, insists Carter, is a noble profession: '*he that can excellently perform in a* Courtly *and* Grand *Manner, will never be at a Loss in any other*' ([A2r]). The art's '*noble Mysteries*' are beyond a 'Tavern-bred Dabbler *in the Science.*' To Carter's mind, French chefs come to England because of scarce produce in France and quick-changing culinary fashions there. But he does not despise haute cuisine, having befriended Mr Austin, master of Pontack's, the famous French restaurant.[4] His 1732 preface, while more sharply criticizing publishers' degradation of cookery, admits gentlemanly demands for elegant table service, lauds housekeepers, specifies the duties of housewifery, and decries epicurean luxury in favour of dishes suitable to everyone from princes to country gentlemen since they are not '*unreasonably chargeable to the Pocket*' (vii). Carter patriotically claims that French cooks rack '*Invention to disguise Nature and lose it in Art*,' puzzling rather than pleasing the palate. That this changed tone reflects the influence of female readers and cooks is confirmed by an appendix of recipes collected by a noble lady, chosen by experts in housewifery, and added in 1732. The posthumous third edition, *The London and Country Cook: Or, Accomplished Housewife* (1749), is revised by a housekeeper to a London merchant. Whether a real person or a publisher's device, she reflects the growing influence of female readers: simplifying the preface, she replaces many recipes with economical and practicable ones.

Early cookbooks by men who were not professional chefs saw women as originators of recipes and recognized in manuscript collections their up-to-date culinary principles (Lehmann 32). Key examples that honoured this popular culture of food, beverages, cosmetics, and medicines are Gervase Markham's *The English Hus-Wife* (1615), a ninth edition appearing in 1683, and the posthumous, privately published *The Closet Of the Eminently Learned Sir Kenelme Digbie Kt Opened* (1668), which also had a long afterlife. Both men saw themselves as compilers, Digby the paramount collector. At age fourteen he began gathering receipts in Spain and from his grand tour to France, Germany, and Italy from 1622 to 1625, building his collection. Digby's international culinary knowledge and openness to female culture influenced May, whom he patronized.

Women's Cookbooks and the Book Trade

Some cookbooks by women perpetuated manuscript culture. Mary Kettilby's *A Collection Of Above Three Hundred Receipts In Cookery, Physick and Surgery; For the Use of all Good Wives, Tender Mothers, and Careful Nurses* (1714) upholds collective female authorship, Kettilby content to be an anonymous compiler. The military metaphors she applies to her compilation shrewdly appropriate gendered terms. There is nothing so easy, she says, '*as the raising whole Regiments of Nostrums and Recipes, if we will admit all the Voluntiers*' who rush to be enlisted. But as fast as they crowd in, '*these forward Ones are generally found to fail us in the Time of Trial.*'[5] Success in cooking as in battle depends '*upon such, as with great Trouble and Expence are press'd and dragg'd into the Service*' ([A3v]). If choosing recipes is like press-ganging soldiers, she praises the 'Noble Charity and Universal Benevolence' of 'the Fair Sex,' urging that, by serving cheap recipes to the poor, ladies will imitate their '*Great Master*' ([A6r]). Kettilby combines piety, '*Splendid Frugality*,' and praise of the 'Delicate House-wives' who formed her collection '*for the*

Service of Young and Unexperienc'd Dames' in '*the Polite Management of their Kitchins'* ([A7v]). Her nexus of concerns marks later cookbooks by women: a protofeminist stance, verbal wit, lady-like refinement, economy, and charity.

Male commentators on economic developments keenly propounded women's roles in popular culture. Richard Bradley, whose *The Country Housewife, And Lady's Director* of 1736 reached a sixth edition in 1763, urged women to manage dairies, orchards, and kitchen gardens, advising them how to operate outside the market economy. The ladies' 'Amanuensis' rather than 'Instructor' ([A1v]), he draws recipes eclectically from taverns (including Pontack's), European correspondents, and English and French cooks, the wide range of women he cites motivated by opposition to 'the imaginary receipts of our modern Books of Cookery' ([A2]). Another theorist who addressed women in charge of small and large rural properties is William Ellis whose *The Country Housewife's Family Companion* appeared in 1750. A culinary conservative, he draws recipes from Digby, William Rabisha, and Richard Bradley.[6] He ignores cookbooks aimed at urbanites in his commitment to self-sufficient, profitable farming. A proponent of the agrarian revolution, he stresses productive roles for women which were being made necessary by the rising value of farm land.

Economic need led Hannah Wolley (1622–74) to become the first professional woman cookbook writer. Her titles address women: *The Ladies Directory* (1661); *The Cook's Guide* (1664); *The Queen-like Closet* (1670); *The Accomplish'd Lady's Delight* (1672); and *A Supplement to the Queen-Like Closet* (1674), completed just before her death. A conscious publicist who ignored manuscripts, she self-published her first but used publishers for later volumes, redrafting early works while drawing on English, French, and Italian sources as well as on May. To gain readers, she stretched the genre: receipts for physic, surgery, cosmetics, preserving, candying, and cooking are combined with instructions on ladies' deportment and servants' duties. Telling how to store and repair clothes and how to decorate rooms, she advertises lessons in embroidery and offers conserves for sale, implying that publication earned no sufficiency. She was angered by the book trade's commercial patriarchy when Dorman Newman published *The Gentlewoman's Companion* (1673), an unauthorized but successful compilation of her work (Lehmann 49–50; Considine 994). '*The Epistle Dedicatory*' addresses '*all Young Ladies, Gentlewomen, and all Maidens whatever,*' the compendium intended as '*a Universal Companion and Guide* to the Female Sex, in all

Relations, Companies, Conditions, and *states* of *Life,* even from *Child-hood* down to *Old-age;* and from the Lady at the *Court,* to the Cook-maid in the *Country'* (A3–[v]). A 'Compleat Book' of 'Universal Usefulness,' it invites 'our Sex' to be 'useful in their Generation by having a competent skill in Physick and Chyrurgery, a competent Estate to distribute it, and a Heart willing thereunto' ([A4v–5r]). Newman's textual mediation renders Wolley's inclusive feminism questionable. Claiming that women's brains would be as fruitful as their bodies were they to have 'the same Literature' as their 'insulting Lords and Masters' (1–2), the text prescribes a young gentlewoman's deportment toward her governess and servants; how she should walk, govern her eyes, converse in company, address superiors, and conduct herself in courtship and marriage. After alphabetizing recipes from '*Artichoaks Fried'* to '*Warden Tarts,'* the text gives bills of fare for each month. Then follow prescriptions for pregnancy, delivery, and lactation as well as for childhood illnesses. A woman's culinary habits are given social ramifications, the act of carving, for instance, heightening her significance in her family and the world. When it reports having seen 'the good Gentlewoman of the House sweat more in cutting up a Fowl, than the Cook in rosting it' (65), the text insists that women must serve the best parts to guests and be self-effacing hostesses who never speak as epicures. While Wolley is a gentlewoman adapting aristocratic fashions for the gentry, she does so as one suffering financial hardship, and she teaches lower-class women how to serve as nursery-, chamber-, cook-, dairy-, scullery- and laundry-maids. If she established a feminist voice in cookery, she also formalized tasks for female servants, directing culinary knowledge down the social hierarchy.

While later female cooks similarly claimed unique authorship, the intertextuality imposed on them by the book trade eroded their voices. Eliza Smith's *The Compleat Housewife: Or, Accomplished Gentlewoman's Companion* (1727), a best seller, reached an eighteenth edition in 1773. But, her name not appearing on the title-page until the posthumous fifth edition of 1732, she did not authorize later editions (Lehmann 84, 96). Her preface was displaced from the seventeenth edition of 1766 by a supplement of foreign dishes that undermines the patriotism otherwise conveyed through devices such as assertive preferences for English produce, wine, and practices. The problem of authorship and intertextuality is demonstrated particularly nicely in the serial plagiarisms of Smith's project. While her preface copies images of fashion and biblical anthropology from John Nott's *The Cooks and Confectioner's Dictionary*

(1723) and she takes her bills of fare from Lamb (Davidson 727), she was plagiarized in turn. *The Complete Family-Piece: And, Country Gentleman, and Farmer's, Best Guide* (1736) stole her receipts for cookery and confectionery. *The Lady's Companion* (1740) took receipts from her as well as from Richard Bradley, Carter, and La Chapelle (Lehmann 101). Hannah Glasse's *The Art Of Cookery* (1747) lifted its chapter on creams from Smith, while stealing many recipes from Howard and *The Lady's Companion* (Lemann 111). That later editions of Smith and Glasse stole from one another (Willan 100) and weakened their authorship confirms that the book trade's commercialism degraded as much as it facilitated popular culture.

A housekeeper from Devon, Smith addresses 'rural and urban gentry who had a taste for entertaining but whose budgets were not elastic' (Colquhoun 198). Her recipes from manuscript collections favour wine-gravy-anchovy sauces, while others are cheap versions of grand dishes. Unusually, given her promotion of native wines, twenty-one receipts stipulate claret in dishes and as a pharmacological menstruum. Conforming for 'Fashion-sake' to write a preface which is like a lady wearing '*a Hoop-petticoat*' to a ball (A2r), she claims that its topic, the antiquity of cookery, is new.[7] Before the '*Art of Cookery,*' a vegetable diet dominated, '*Apples, Nuts, and Herbs*' serving as '*both Meat and Sauce,*' since '*Mankind*' stood in '*no need of any additional Sauces, Ragoos, &c.*' and since '*Food and Physick were then one and the same thing*' ([A2v]–3). In Esau's time, soups and savoury dishes were invented for declining palates. In Samuel's time, cookery became a science; '*Luxury had not brought it to the height of an Art,*' although the Israelites were becoming '*Fashionists.*' Cookery has so improved that, having reached its acme, it is now declining. Current inventions '*are only the Sallies of a capricious Appetite*' that debauch '*the Art it self*' (A4r). Including naturalized French dishes in her 500 recipes, she offers '*English Constitutions and English Palates*' receipts for frugal and sumptuous tables since they are '*wholesome, toothsome, all practicable and easy to be performed*' ([A5r]). Scorning French modes, she promotes English produce, since foreign foods detract from national identity.

Jean-Francois Revel holds that 'bourgeois' cuisine melds traditional, 'unexportable' peasant food with fashionable, erudite cuisine (53–4). Cookbooks by Smith's followers such as Sarah Harrison, Glasse (1708–70), and Elizabeth Raffald (1733–81) bear Revel out. Their scorn for haute cuisine is uneasy since they cannot evade it. The 'feminisation of cooking' (Colquhoun 214) is also at issue here. Cultivating female readers and correspondents, they would eliminate the dichotomy between eating from necessity and luxury by severing consumption from social aspiration. But their books show that cooking entails cultural appropriation and imperial commerce. Yet, they offset their unease by associating haute cuisine with the insensibility and decadence of men.

In *The House-Keeper's Pocket Book, And Compleat Family Cook* (1733), Harrison remarks how men belittle the *'Feminine Arts of Government'* that are *'of much more intrinsick value than some admired branches of Literature,'* for what can be *'of greater Use'* than *'by Prudence and good Management, to supply a Family with all things that are Convenient'* (ix)? Housewifery supplies the *'deficiency of Wealth, by dressing and disposing all things Elegantly,'* making a *'well dress'd Entertainment'* finer than a *'Dish of Beef Stakes'* (x–xi). The 400 receipts added to her second edition along with textual modifications made as late as the ninth edition of 1777 (by which time a conger owned her title) reveal her gendered stance to have been long promoted as a marketing strategy. Underselling her competition by 50 per cent (her book costing half the average price of 5s.), she urges readers to replace 'Common Receipt-Books' with her 'compleat System of a House-keeper's Duty' because, in uniting 'Frugality unto Elegance in Eating,' it leaves time for 'the more weighty Affairs of [their] Families' (vi–vii). In addressing ladies, Harrison degrades culinary labour, confirming that women authors of cookbooks did not necessarily uphold a popular sense of a female solidarity.

Glasse's wish to teach 'the Generality of Servants' and 'the lower Sort . . . in their own Way' ([Ar]) together with her 281 genteel subscribers dignify class formation and demean kitchen work. Decrying the 'high Way' in which 'Great Cooks' speak, she opts for plain English, rejecting terms like 'Lardoons' used by *The Lady's Companion* from which she lifted 287 recipes.[8] Cost governing her, she outlines the *'French* tricks' of *'French* Cooks' who dupe grandees into extravagance: a chef in France will 'dress a fine Dinner of twenty Dishes and all genteel and pretty, for the Expence he will put an English Lord to for dressing one Dish.' Shunning the 'Esteem of those Gentlemen' for 'the good Opinion of my own Sex,' her book excludes medical receipts and directions on 'the Oeconomy of the Family': there is no need to offer 'Nonsense of that Kind' nor 'impertinent' rules for table design and plate setting since English ladies ought not to follow modish rules ([Av]).

Besides scorning the generic inclusiveness favoured by most women authors, Glasse's book is poorly organized and uninventive (Davidson 339–40). Her claim to make cheap sauces as 'rich and high' as a French

'Cullis' of a 'Leg of Veal and a Ham' is untenable. Her complicated and crude recipes are oblivious to 'the centuries of pride in the slow refinement of a perfect sauce' (Colquhoun 220). Retaining French terms for 'Mutton à la Royale,' 'Mutton in Epigram' (24), 'Veal à la Bourgoise' (28), 'Veal à la Piemontoise' (29), and 'Veal à la Dauphine' (30), she, like contemporaries, is open to foreign modes such as 'Mutton the Turkish Way' (26); 'A Pillaw of Veal' (28); and 'Currey the India Way' (52). However, while opposing 'profess'd Cooks' by emphasizing basic techniques of roasting and boiling, she recommends such tricks as dressing a fowl to look like a pheasant and applying beaten ginger to sweeten rank venison and hare (8). In calling for truffles and morels to be on hand in the kitchen (12), she is hardly single-minded about extravagance.

Having served Lady Elizabeth Warburton as housekeeper, Raffald, like Glasse, was impelled by an entrepreneurial drive. After marrying her employer's gardener, she became a publicist in Manchester where she opened a confectionery shop, ran a school of cookery and domestic economy, and established a register office for servants. She self-published her Experienced English Housekeeper in 1769 with the aid of 800 subscribers, having proofed her own copy and ensured its plain language. Her book sold in London as well as Manchester. Her second edition grew by 100 recipes donated by ladies. Six more editions appeared in her lifetime, probably because she sold the product of her recipes in her shop. Thirty-three editions, many unauthorized, appeared by 1834. Since she expects ladies to pass her book onto housekeepers 'of the meanest Capacity' ([A2v]), she confirms the trend that saw cooking descend the social scale. That, like Glasse, she excludes medical receipts indicates that she expects householders to seek professional help rather than rely on popular lore. Her money-saving recipes for sauces and catsups were labour-intensive; the 'Lemon Pickle and Browning' she substitutes for 'Cullis' (iii) requires pickling for three months. Her copious instructions for spinning sugar, an arduous process of making table decorations and ornamental desserts (163ff.), and her copper-plate engravings illustrating grand tables (361–2) aim to gratify the eyes of ladies who increasingly lacked culinary skill, thanks to the labour of female servants.

Their cookbooks' popularity could not have gratified Glasse and Raffald. The former, widowed before her second edition appeared in 1747, declared bankruptcy in May 1754, Andrew Miller then buying the sheets of the fifth edition and the copyright. Self-publication brought her neither financial rewards nor authorial security. So, too, with Raffald whose sudden death led her ne'er-do-well husband to sell her copyright and rival congers to adapt her text. Far from upholding the two women's culinary authority, the book trade's expansion of readership exposed their inconsistencies and contributions to social hierarchy.

When Mary Cole, housekeeper to the earl of Drogheda, published *The Lady's Complete Guide; Or Cookery In All Its Branches* in 1788, she admitted taking receipts 'from every reputable English Book of Cookery now extant.' Lacking the 'Vanity to pass herself as an Author,' she calls herself a compiler. The proliferation of treatises on the 'useful art' makes her book 'absolutely necessary.' It is, she declares, a library of cookery. Voicing truisms that her language is accessible to every class of reader, that frugal and uncomplicated dishes are the best, and that she offers a 'great number of Original Receipts,' she is unique in naming authors, often citing page references and plural sources. However, besides renewing interest in French cuisine, her citations problematize cookbook history. Glasse is cited fewer than twenty times, Raffald less than eighty, while Charlotte Mason's *The Ladies' Assistant* (1773) is named ninety times.[9] Curiously, John Farley's *The London Art of Cookery* (1783) is cited 150 times. Principal cook at the London Tavern, Farley did not write his book but lent his name to the work of a hack who took recipes from Glasse and Raffald (Lehmann 79, 148). That Cole names Monsieur Clermont fifty-four and George Dalrymple fifty-three times is suspicious: in 1769, Clermont published *The Professed Cook,* his translation of Monsieur Menon's *Les Soupers de la Cour* (1769), while Dalrymple self-published *The Practice Of Modern Cookery* in Edinburgh in 1781, copying Clermont word for word. That Cole thinks the two are distinct saps her culinary authority. Fraud is likely since six French cooks listed on her title-page are neither verifiable nor cited in her text. Cole is likely a publishing figment (Lehmann141). Still, she exposes prejudices against female authors by citing William Verral's self-published *A Complete System Of Cookery* (1759) twenty-one times but Martha Bradley's *The British Housewife* ([1758]) not once. Both authors promoted French cuisine in the Seven Years' War, xenophobia probably explaining why they were not reprinted (Lehmann 125–6).

Why does Cole favour Verral when Bradley's is the most encyclopedic and personally engaged cookbook of the century? Verral's recipes fill only 240 pages. While he prefers the 'old English way' of roasting (231), he celebrates '*the most modern and best French Cookery*' learned from St Clouet, Newcastle's chef (ii).[10] Giving recipes bilingual titles and cooking with Champagne and Rhine wines, Verral organizes his book according to the size of plates on which dishes are served, their relative positions in table settings, and their location in first and second courses. His theory of sauces and marinades and his light use of garlic show up in such dishes as truffles in claret or burgundy (189–90), pears cooked in port (209), and turtle with madeira (235–40). Doubtless, his preface upset middle-class readers by exposing their ignorance of kitchen hygiene and modern equipment. He mocks clients who enjoy *soupe maigre* as a meat soup when it consists of carrots, turnips, onions, and herbs *'boiled to a sort of porridge and strained through a cullender to a large quantity of toasted bread'* (xvii–xviii). He relishes duping clients' 'depraved' tastes with gross ingredients (xx). His ultimate target is the truism that haute cuisine is wasteful: St Clouet provided *'a table of twenty-one dishes at a course, with such things as used to serve only for a garnish round a lump of great heavy dishes before he came here'* (xxx). That his French master used tongues, pallets, eyes, brains, and ears proves that haute cuisine's utilization of organ meats requires efficiency and invention.

Drawing on Lamb, La Chapelle, and Glasse, Bradley transforms their recipes with her sense of French aesthetic modes: the 'best Dinner in the World will have an ill Aspect if the Dishes are not properly disposed on the Table.' The English, having 'learned a great deal of the Art of Cookery' from the French, should follow them in 'this finishing Article, the Arrangement of the Dishes upon the Table,' because, if to 'please the Palate is one Design' of cookery, 'to please the Eye is the other' (69). Since imitating 'grand Feasts' will improve 'our common Tables' (70), housekeepers must grasp the congruence between number of covers, shape of tables, and disposition of platters, French rules on these matters leading to 'Freedom, Ease, and Prettyness' (200). Their table manners are less subject to fashion than the English, for the French 'have the Art of preserving good Manners with less Ceremony than our Ancestors used to do' (73). Unsurprisingly, Bradley will not limit herself to national foodstuffs but calls for anchovies, capers, caviar, cayenne pepper, ginger, all-spice, mangoes, olives, truffles, morels, and soy, explaining how they are produced and warning of adulteration: traders to the East Indies beat down the price of soy so that producers make it 'carelessly' and of poorer ingredients (113); London shops sell sprats as anchovies (6–7); and capsicum pods grown in England being inferior to chili pepper, shops adulterate them with salt (9).

That Menon's *La Cuisinière bourgeoise* (1746) appeared in 1793 as *The French Family Cook: Being A complete System of French Cookery* confirms renewed interest in French cuisine, despite the Revolution. Menon's book, the most reprinted in France, addressed women, emphasized hearty country recipes, cut costs, and simplified methods to bring refined culinary practice within reach of the bourgeoisie (Willan 89). Menon's outlook found British admirers. Arthur Young praised French cuisine in his *Travels* of 1793 when he contrasted Britain's five distinctive dishes – turbot and lobster sauce, ham and chicken, turtle, haunch of venison, turkey and oyster – with the hundreds dressed by French cooks, even poor families enjoying varied diets. While an English dinner of a joint of meat with a pudding or '*pot luck*' is bad luck, French cookery allows average families to put four dishes on the table for every one in England (1:290). Concluding that 'trifles' of food and wine better indicate 'the temper of a nation' than 'objects of importance,' Young holds that French tables symbolize 'good temper' (1:75).

The most reprinted eighteenth-century cookbooks by women decried French cuisine and male chefs. Promoting cookery as an art compatible with domestic economy, they aimed to detach it from upper-class fashion. Yet, in invoking female solidarity, they undervalued the provenance of recipes in manuscript culture and the public domain because they could not avoid imitating aristocratic modes. In collectively failing to construct female solidarity, they did not stabilize the cookbook's generic features. In 1800, what cookbooks contain and how they relate to conduct books and to medical, management, and horticultural manuals remains unclear. In contextualizing commercially successful titles, this chapter attends more to authors' voices than to their recipes, since they sought financial reward and recognition as artists.[11] These women treated food as more than a physiological necessity. If they did not always acknowledge its synaesthetic appeal, they regularly differentiated domestic space by ranking scullery, kitchen, office, and dining-room in an ascending order of womanly refinement. This bourgeois ideology in female culinary discourse was seized on by the book trade as highly profitable. In promoting women's literacy even as it co-opted manuscript culture and the social networks which constructed their culinary practices, the publishing industry exploited the economic necessity imposed on lower-class females partly as a result of agrarian and industrial progress. The popularization of their work as housekeepers, cooks, and cookbook writers demeaned that work, even as it fortified the aspirations of middle-class women as they set about rising up the social hierarchy. This dialectical tension between popularization and disparagement means that cookbooks, far from being trivial or marginal texts, are important testaments to the struggles of eighteenth-century lower-class women in popular culture. By succumbing to the book trade's capitalistic practices and nationalistic prejudices, female cookbook authors contributed to the stratification that disadvantaged their gender. In largely ignoring the developments being made by French cuisine while relegating food preparation to the servant classes, cookbooks addressing middle-class women impeded the thoughtful amalgamation of erudite and peasant cooking that leads to great cuisine. Still, eighteenth-century cookbooks by women manifest the discursive modes by which their hopeful entrepreneurship sought to resist the culinary imperialism that was codified by Louis XIV and that may be seen to flourish more than two hundred years after the French Revolution.

NOTES

1 I follow Stephen Mennell's critique of Pierre Bourdieu's view of the static superficiality of food: 'Within a developing social figuration, modes of individual behaviour, cultural tastes, intellectual ideas, social stratification, political power and economic organisation are all entangled with each other in complex ways which themselves change over time in ways that need to be investigated' (13). I find Mennell's 'developmental perspective' on the integration of French and English culinary systems persuasive (18). On his attitude toward bourgeois 'stylization' of food, see Bourdieu 77. On differentiating French and English modes of eating, see Mennell 131. For current views of 'strained relations between authors and booksellers,' see Merrett 55n1 and passim.
2 *The French Cook*, the translation of La Varenne by I.D.G., was published in 1653, 1654, and 1673. My citations are from the 1654 edition.
3 On the Bedfords' development of real estate, see Rudé 12–15.
4 Pontack's opened in Abchurch Lane in 1666, serving French food and Bordeaux wines. Its renown is mirrored in cookbooks. 'Mutton Cutlets from Pontack's,' 'Veal Cutlets from Pontack's,' and 'How to stew Carp from Pontack's' appear in Harrison's *The House-keeper's Pocket Book* and in James Jenks's *The Complete Cook* (1768).
5 Isabella Beeton's 1861 comparison of a cook to an army commander is not as original as Nicola Humble claims (xxiv).
6 Rabisha's book was *The whole Body of Cookery Dissected* (1661).
7 Nott refers to the 'Hoop-petticoat' before giving a biblical account of food (A2–[3v]).

8 See *The Lady's Companion* 309. On Glasse's plagiarism, see Davidson
   339–40.
9 Mason's title-page describes her as housekeeper to families of fashion for
   thirty years. The seventh edition of her book appeared in 1793, a new one
   coming out in 1800.
10 On Clouet's high-handed treatment of Newcastle, see Wheaton 163–7.
11 'It is precisely because they are an ephemeral, market-led form of writing
   that cookery books reveal so much about the features of a particular historical
   moment ... Cookery books are always interventions in the nation's diet, rather
   than an accurate reflection of its current state: they represent an attempt to
   popularize new foods, new methods, fresh attitudes' (Humble xxv–xxvi).

WORKS CITED

Apostolidès, Jean-Marie. 'From Roi Soleil to Louis le Grand.' *A New History
   of French Literature*. Ed. Denis Hollier et al. Cambridge: Harvard UP, 1989:
   318–20. Print.
Bourdieu, Pierre. 'Taste of Luxury, Taste of Necessity.' *The Taste Culture
   Reader: Experiencing Food and Drink*. Ed. Carolyn Korsmeyer. Oxford: Berg,
   2005. 72–8. Print.
Bradley, Martha. *The British Housewife: Or, The Cook, Housekeeper's, And
   Gardiners Companion*. London: S. Crowder & H. Woodgate, [1760?].
   Eighteenth Century Collections Online (ECCO). Web. 21 Sept. 2009.
Bradley, Richard. *The Country Housewife, And Lady's Director*. 6th ed. London
   and York: W. Bristow & C. Etherington, 1762. ECCO. Web. 16 Sept. 2009.
*Carter, Charles. The Complete Practical Cook: Or, A New System Of the Whole Art
   and Mystery of Cookery*. London: W. Meadows, C. Rivington, and R. Hett,
   1730. ECCO. Web. 21 September 2009.
– The *Compleat City and Country Cook: Or, Accomplish'd Housewife*. London:
   A. Bettesworth, C. Hitch, C. Davis, T. Green, and S. Austen, 1732. ECCO.
   Web. 21 September 2009.
– *The London and Country Cook: Or, Accomplished Housewife, Containing
   Practical Directions and the best Receipts In all the Branches of Cookery and
   Housekeeping*. London: Charles Hitch, Stephen Austen and John Hinton,
   1749. ECCO. Web. 21 September 2009.
Cole Mary. *The Lady's Complete Guide; Or Cookery In All Its Branches*. London:
   G. Kearsley, 1788. ECCO. Web. 16 November 2009.
Colqhoun, Kate. *Taste: The Story of Britain Through Its Cooking*. New York:
   Bloomsbury, 2007. Print.

Considine, John. 'Wolley, Hannah.' *Oxford Dictionary of National Biography*. Ed H.C.G. Matthew and Brian Harrison. Oxford: OUP, 2004. Volume 59, page 994. Print.

Davidson, Alan, ed. *The Oxford Companion to Food*. New York: Oxford UP, 1999. Print.

Glasse, Hannah. *The Art Of Cookery, Made Plain and Easy*. 2d ed. London, 1747. ECCO. Web. 19 Oct. 2009.

Harrison, Sarah. *The House-Keeper's Pocket Book, And Compleat Family Cook*. London: T. Worrall, 1733. ECCO. Web. 14 Oct. 2009.

Hollier, Denis, et al. *A New History of French Literature*. Cambridge, MA: Harvard UP, 1989. Print.

Howard, Henry. *England's Newest Way in all Sorts Of Cookery, Pastry, And All Pickles that are fit to be used*. 5th ed. London: J. Knapton, R. Knaplock, J. & B. Sprint, D. Midwinter, B. Lintot, A. Bettesworth, W. & J. Innys, J. Osborn, R. Robinson, and A. Ward, 1726. ECCO. Web. 14 October 2009.

Humble, Nicola, ed. *Mrs Beeton's Book of Household Management*. Oxford: Oxford UP, 2000. Print.

Kettilby, Mary. *A Collection of Above Three Hundred Receipts In Cookery, Physick and Surgery; For the Use of all Good Wives, Tender Mothers, and Careful Nurses*. London: Richard Wilkin, 1714. ECCO. Web. 25 Nov. 2009.

Korsmeyer, Carolyn, ed. *The Taste Culture Reader: Experiencing Food and Drink*. Oxford: Berg, 2005. Print.

Lamb, Patrick. *Royal Cookery; or, the Complete Court-Cook*. London: Abel Roper, 1710. ECCO. Web. 14 October 2009.

La Chapelle, Vincent. *The Modern Cook*. 3 vols. London: Printed for the Author, 1733. ECCO. Web. 14 October 2009.

La Varenne, François Pierre de. *The French Cook*. Trans. I.D.G. London: Charles Adams, 1654. *Early English Books Online* (EEBO). Web. 17 Aug. 2009.

Lehmann, Gilly. *The British Housewife: Cookery Books, Cooking And Society In Eighteenth-Century Britain*. Totnes, Devon: Prospect Books, 2003. Print.

Marnettè, Monsieur. The Perfect Cook. London: Nath. Brooks, 1656. EEBO. Web. 17 August 2009.

Massialot, François. *The Court and Country Cook*. Trans. J.K. London: W. Onley, A. & J. Churchill, and M. Gillyflower, 1702. ECCO. Web. 23 Nov. 2009.

May, Robert. *The Accomplisht Cook, Or The Art and Mystery Of Cookery*. London: Nath. Brooke, 1660. EEBO. Web. 13 Aug. 2009.

Mennell, Stephen. *All Manners of Food: Eating and Taste in England and France from the Middle Ages to the Present*. 2nd ed. Urbana and Chicago: U of Illinois P, 1996. Print.

Merrett, Robert James. 'Problems of Self-Identity for the Literary Journeyman: The Case of Alexander Bicknell (d. 1796).' *English Studies in Canada* 28 (2002): 31–63. Print.

Nott, John. *The Cooks and Confectioners Dictionary: Or, the Accomplish'd Housewives Companion*. London: C. Rivington, 1723. ECCO. Web. 16 Nov. 2009.

Raffald, Elizabeth. *The Experienced English House-keeper*. Manchester, 1769. ECCO. Web. 16 Nov. 2009.

Revel, Jean-François. 'Retrieving Tastes: Two Sources of Cuisine.' *The Taste Culture Reader: Experiencing Food and Drink*. Ed. Carolyn Korsmeyer. Oxford: Berg, 2005. 51–6. Print.

Rudé, George. *Hanoverian London 1714–1808*. London: Secker & Warburg, 1971. Print

Smith, Eliza. *The Compleat Housewife: Or, Accomplished Gentlewoman's Companion*. London: J. Pemberton, 1727. ECCO. Web. 10 Nov 2009.

Smith, Robert. *Court Cookery: Or, The Compleat English Cook*. London: T. Wotton, 1723. ECCO. Web. 14 October 2009.

Stanton, Domna C. 'Religious Controversies.' *A New History of French Literature*. Ed. Denis Hollier. Cambridge: Harvard UP, 1989: 358–64. Print.

Stuart, Tristram. *The Bloodless Revolution: A Cultural History of Vegetarianism from 1600 to Modern Times*. New York: W.W. Norton, 2007. Print.

Thomson, Gladys Scott. *Life in a Noble Household, 1641–1700*. London: Jonathan Cape, 1937. Print.

Trubek, Amy B. *Haute Cuisine: How The French Invented The Culinary Profession*. Philadelphia: U of Pennsylvania P, 2000. Print.

Verral, William. *A Complete System Of Cookery*. London, 1759. ECCO. Web. 9 Nov. 2009.

Wheaton, Barbara Ketchum. *Savoring The Past: The French Kitchen and Table from 1300 to 1789*. New York: Simon & Schuster, 1983. Print.

Willan, Anne. *Great Cooks and Their Recipes From Taillevent to Escoffier*. London: Pavilion, 2000. Print.

Wolley, Hannah. *The Gentlewoman's Companion; Or, A Guide To The Female Sex*. London: Dorman Newman, 1673. EEBO. Web. 10 Aug. 2009.

Young, Arthur. *Travels During the Years 1787, 1788 & 1789*. 2 vols. 2nd ed. London: W. Richardson, 1794. Print.

7   Women and Letters

ISOBEL GRUNDY

During the eighteenth century, almost everyone who was literate wrote letters, as we can see from letter-writing manuals aimed at the relatively uneducated. And though estimates of the literate population of the British Isles differ, and though it was in any case more male than female, it probably included even at the beginning of the eighteenth century at least a million actual or potential women letter-writers, and at the end of the century something approaching four times that number.[1]

Over the whole period the exchange of familiar letters was booming, partly as a result of improved systems for delivery. The London penny post was firmly established, after several false starts, before the century began. A nationwide penny post was considered as early as 1659, but was not to become a reality until 1840.[2] Outside the capital, nevertheless, the exchange of letters (paid for not by the sender but by the recipient) became steadily more practicable for those who could not afford a private messenger. Signposts were set up; road surfaces improved. In 1720 Ralph Allen established cross-posts, opening for the first time the possibility of sending a letter from anywhere to anywhere without routing it via London, and in 1784 the first mail coach rumbled out of Bristol, signalling the beginning of the end for the mounted post-boy.[3]

Profusion of letters was thus a new aspect of popular life in England at the beginning of the long eighteenth century, and developments in systems and techniques ensured that letters both reflected and made news as the century progressed. Letters provide an unequalled window for observing the shifting cultures of dress, entertainments, social practices, politics, indeed every aspect of changeful human lives. Styles in letters themselves change too: in the material they incorporate, the language in which they clothe it, and the voice and persona adopted for various purposes by the letter-writer.

Within this welter of letters sent and received, no selection chosen for comment here can claim to be in any way representative. Letters of the period, especially women's letters, have been a frequent topic for analysis.[4] The many literary studies of women as letter-writers have recently been joined by studies of women who wrote letters as an activity of practical, not literary life.[5] This essay will centre on shifting fashions in the English female letter-writing subject, her voice and her self-construction, largely through the topic of fashion in its most basic sense (styles of clothing) and resistance to that kind of fashion.

All letters reflect something of their writers' personalities, aspirations, and relationships with their correspondents and with epistolarity itself, and reflect also the way that fashions in these concepts change. Popular considerations of gender, which help to shape all these elements, shift perhaps most widely of all. Letters of personal feeling or social obligation have often been seen as particularly women's work (eighteenth-century urban myth had it that women wrote better letters than men), while letters of business, of practical or scholarly information, or of literary aspiration each made up a gendered field in which the onus was on women to justify their presence there and to conform to specific gendered expectations and assumptions.

Women's letters of religious exhortation and of scientific or philosophical learning, for example, are both transformed over the course of our period. In the Restoration years, close to the heyday of the radical religious groups, some sectarian Christian women continued as they had done during the Interregnum to indite letters on religion and politics to individuals and to groups, some of which inculcate a militant other-worldliness and resistance to secular authority, with an often fiery style that is indistinguishable from that of their male comrades.[6] These texts, treading directly in the footsteps of St Paul's Epistles, were genuine letters sent and received, but also public documents speaking with authority to an entire community. Later women writers of religious advice in the epistolary mode, issuing their works with commercial publishers and addressing a wider audience through an original, personal recipient, typically urged more submissive, less obtrusive private devotion, and sought to reflect those qualities in the tone of their writing.[7]

Early in this period women writing letters about science or philosophy (like Anne Conway, Damaris Masham, and Catharine Trotter

Cockburn) often assume the role of junior interlocutor addressing some male expert in a version of his own specialized language, while at the end of the eighteenth century they often (like Catharine Macaulay and Priscilla Wakefield) write or publish to instruct young students of their own sex about the natural or the human world. Though here as elsewhere in the range of epistolary forms, there are no hard and fast dividing lines, the emphasis that each group lays on the gender of the author and that of her audience is differently inflected by the different roles played by each group of writers.

Travel letters were another popular vehicle for women throughout the period. The prospect of an unusual journey led many to set pen to paper, and some did so with publication at least potentially in mind. Lady Mary Wortley Montagu's *Letters . . . Written during her Travels*, first written in 1716–18, recast in book form by 1724, and published in 1763, scored an instant, fashionable success with readers who clearly did not feel that the content had dated damagingly over the nearly fifty years since composition. Nevertheless, changing fashions can be traced in the self-presentation of women travellers. It was apparently not unmodish in 1716–18 for a young woman to boast of physical courage, for example. Montagu twice contrasts her own fearlessness during storms at sea with the terror of someone else – on one occasion the captain of the vessel (Montagu 1:248–9, 443–4). At night on the edge of a precipice, observing that the postilion in charge of the galloping horses has dropped asleep, she reports coolly that she 'thought it very convenient to call out to desire 'em to look where they were going.' She feels free to boast of her bravery, albeit in ironical terms, to her sister and to a foreign virtuoso, the Abbé Conti (Montagu 1:281–2).

Eighty years on, in *Letters Written During a Short Residence in Sweden, Norway, and Denmark,* Mary Wollstonecraft too asserts more than once that she is not afraid in frightening situations, as befits a disciple of rationality. But she freely confesses the weakness of sensibility. As a solitary, perhaps weary, female she draws interested enquiry in Norway, 'as if they were afraid to hurt, and wished to protect me' (Wollstonecraft 65). This sympathy and concern moves her painfully, especially since the Norwegians apparently sensed her suffering at being parted for the first time from her daughter, to whom, 'as a female,' she is more attached than a man could be. This passage, which leads into another about her fears for her daughter, presents women as an inherently, necessarily fearful group: 'With trembling hand I shall cultivate sensibility, and cherish delicacy of sentiment, lest, whilst I lend fresh blushes to the rose, I sharpen the thorns that will wound the breast I would fain guard' (Wollstonecraft 65). It is as if Wollstonecraft buys her readers' permission for her own fearlessness by performing exaggerated anxiety for her daughter. Montagu, in contrast, had breezily assured her sister that travel had not harmed her own health or the – naturally far dearer – health of her child (Montagu 1:259).

Even the category of business letters, instruments designed to produce movement of people, material, and cash – which proved a versatile tool for myriads of women striving to maintain or to advance their position in an increasingly competitive world – reflected historically changing attitudes to women's roles. Archives of business letters left by women tend to negotiate the gendered expectations of their correspondents by means of occasional, formulaic allusion to their gender as an anomaly in business dealings, without allowing it to affect the pitch of their business-epistolary voices or to sap their confidence as users of the discourse common to the sphere of money and exchange.

These articulate business women, trespassers in a masculine sphere, often initiated new fashions in business practices. Elizabeth Beighton (de facto manager and joint editor of *The Ladies' Diary*) exploited and forwarded a modish retooling of the ancient genre of the almanac, and Elizabeth Montagu (colliery magnate as well as patron and bluestocking) gestured toward the age of sensibility and of reform with her annual entertainments for chimney-sweeping children.[8] Other practical letter-writers who lack these women's power still reflect, willy-nilly, changing fashions in gender. Paula McDowell has noted how in petitions (a subgenre of the letter) early eighteenth-century book-trade women, when they ran afoul of authority, were less likely to plead for mercy as feeble women than to assert a professional standing, no matter how lowly (McDowell 58, 104–5, 108–9). At the other end of the century, Jennie Batchelor has shown how supplicants crowding the mailbag of the Royal Literary Fund espoused the role of the weaker sex laying claim to protection, even rescue, from the stronger. Their rhetoric of humility is a tactical approach of powerless female to powerful male (disguised as expression of innate femininity), as they emphasize their neediness rather than their literary contribution, and exploit their gender (a handicap in earning) as a useful tactic in their indigence.

A more self-aware writer of business letters, the novelist Charlotte Smith, constructs a more nuanced and conscious self in addressing her publishers and the trustees of her father-in-law's estate. She dissociates her persona either as a parent responsible for her children, or as a productive novelist with a professional track record, from her unwilling role as a helpless victim of society's actively misogynist institutions. She presents a subjectivity full of conflict among shifting, incompatible expectations and demands (Smith, passim).

Case Studies: Cudworth/Masham and
Pierrepont/Wortley Montagu

Letters of social exchange, of family bonding, kinship, or personal self-expression also shifted with the shifting zeitgeist. I will focus here on a few groups of letters, mostly to friends with a few to relations, whose authors were seeking not only to keep their relationships in repair but also to participate in the literary – authors who thought of their letters as artefacts, as something they fashioned out of words for their own pleasure and that of their readers. These literary letter-writers seek explicitly and centrally to construct a self in their letters, a self shaped by the fashion of its moment in cultural history.

The idea of fashion in selfhood is not particularly startling (see, for instance, Rorty). Nor would it have surprised the first two writers I shall discuss here, Damaris Masham and Lady Mary Wortley Montagu. Born a generation apart, in 1658 and 1689 respectively, each of these was shaped by the Restoration culture in which wit was an element of female attractiveness and both disguise and self-display were accepted parts of upper-class social relations. Yet each of them, in claiming (with varying degrees of irony and self-deprecation) the character of female intellectual, finds it useful to abjure any interest in fashion as usually understood.

When Damaris Cudworth (later Masham) apparently suspects she is getting the worst of a debate with John Locke about philosophical-theological opinions, she has recourse to threats of taking the correspondence in a different, specifically feminine direction: 'were you not affraid that in Revenge I would have asked your advice about makeing me a New Petticoate? Have sent you an Account of all the new Fassions that have beene since you left the Towne? Told you what my new Manto is made of?' (Locke 2:489). Her following fashion seems to have been a joke between them: another time she reassures him that at this time she is paying no heed to the London fashions and has not 'once sat in Councell about that Matter' with women friends – though she has also not adopted the plain dress of the Quakers (Locke 2:679).

Similarly, Lady Mary Pierrepont (later Wortley Montagu) is at pains to explain how eccentric are her preferences for solitude and study.

'You see, my dear, in making my pleasures consist of these unfashionable diversions, I am not of the number who cannot be easy out of the mode . . . Nature is seldom in the wrong, custom always; it is with some regret I follow it in all the impertinencies of dress.' She professes herself amazed at the way that otherwise sensible people obey the dictates of fashion even in important matters, as well as in 'furniture, clothes, and equipage,' so that they 'make their happiness consist in the opinions of others, and sacrifice every thing in the desire of appearing in fashion' (Montagu 1:6). Aged twenty, she uses 'fashion' as a shorthand for a feminized worldliness which she resolutely condemns.

Each of these young women was writing to someone whose opinion, if not the basis of her happiness, was at least of importance to her. Damaris Cudworth addressed the first of her extant letters to John Locke on 6 January 1682, three and a half years before she married Sir Francis Masham. A quarter-century later Lady Mary Pierrepont was exchanging letters with Anne Wortley, an apparently frivolous and fun-loving contemporary. By the time of the passage quoted above, however, their correspondence had come under the surveillance and concealed management of Anne's elder brother Edward, and Edward Wortley Montagu was a serious-minded, perhaps strait-laced man of some intellectual reputation, whose good opinion Lady Mary desired just as much as Damaris Cudworth desired that of Locke.

For a young woman to present herself to an older male as not primarily a siren or a marriage prospect was a tricky exercise. The Cudworth-Locke correspondence begins 'under the sign of romance,'[9] since Cudworth adopts the pen-name of Philoclea, apparently from Philip Sidney's *Arcadia*. Her first letter answers one in which Locke expressed anxiety about being misinterpreted, and her opening sentence is not only elaborate (as her style often is) but tortured: 'Be it under whatever pretence you please that you have sent me a letter, you ought not to feare that it should be ill taken, since nothing can be liable to a Misinterpretation that you say, who as I beleeve you would not really Deceive, so perhaps should you designe it you might not find it very easie, there being something necessarie besides Witt to make one succeed in it.' With a main verb awkwardly bracketed between subordinate clauses both fore and aft, this sentence is indeed quite hard to interpret. It introduces a letter full of indirection and involution, balancing the demands of wit and love: is it possible for a lover to be sensible and witty? Is a 'good' letter (an intellectually impressive one) better than one expressing love or admiration? Cudworth, it appears, is striving mightily to impress (Locke 2:472–3). To a modern reader she seems to be trying much too hard, though perhaps such a judgment underestimates the late seventeenth-century fashion for decorated style.

By the time of the second surviving letter, about six weeks later, Locke has appointed her his 'Governess,' a flattering title which evokes curlicues of gratitude: 'of which I assure you she is not a little Proud, and which (how great Friend soever she be to Truth on other occasions) rather then lose she would very willingly owe to your too advantageous opinion of her' (Locke 2:484). Much of this series of letters is taken up by the exchange of abstruse opinion about John Smith's 1660 philosophical-theological work *Select Discourses*. But in other letters (like that of 20 March 1685, only three months before Cudworth's marriage), the verbal duelling turns not on mental exchange but on physical attraction. She tells Locke how a lady visitor had 'Maintain'd with all the Confidence of Inspiration that You Love me Exceedingly,' and represented him as the object of rivalry between herself and two other women. This produces jovial guesses at the identity of the 'Happy Gentleman' who was so sought after by ladies. Cudworth says she expects soon to find herself 'in a Ballade for your sake,' and only hopes it will not be a ballad 'Sett to the Tune of the *Forsaken Maid*' (Locke 2:703).

The verbal style of these letters recalls the models set by gurus of French *précieux* writing like Vincent de Voiture. Cudworth is perfectly capable of directness – for instance, 'I onely write to you now to let you know you have a Governess who cannot forget you' (Locke 2:517) – but she generally chooses to show her wit by elaboration. Ornamentation and conscious artistry serve her alike for explicating points of theology (seeking, for instance, to convince Locke that not all enthusiasm is incompatible with reason) or her own emotional or psychological state, the inner workings of the heart: 'you may always conclude that I am certainly in a bad Humor whenever I tell you so, since I never accuse my self falsly of things which I cannot beleeve it should be to my advantage to be thought Guiltie of' (Locke 2:521).

Within about a year after the correspondence began, Cudworth was using poetry as well as prose to unpack the complexities of the relationship. She makes great play with her alleged ill temper, speculates about other lives she might have lived through in the past if metempsychosis were true, and so on. Both her prose and her pastoral or mock-pastoral poetry serve to construct herself as a qualified player of the game of love who, however, is not just now playing that game. Bargaining reminiscent of proviso scenes in Restoration comedy and debate reminiscent of scientific discourse are here adapted as vehicles for discussion of friendship and of opinion. Cudworth presents herself as an intellectual, whose potentially handicapping gender she flaunts rather than concealing it. She writes to Locke, she insists, as a friend – and she boldly claims that women are better at friendship than men – but she permits herself an occasional giddiness and frequent, fantastical inventiveness which construct her as that unusual species, the philosopher as eligible young woman.

This correspondence spans her marriage, the passage from maid to wife, from one female role to another, each equally unlikely as a combination with the role of thinker or intellectual. She presents her married self as transformed from sovereign power to humble subject (Locke 2:723), and seems to reject both her former, unmarried name and her new married one. 'Mademoiselle C:' no longer exists in this world, yet 'Lady Masham' seems to be somebody else (Locke 2:726, 728). It is household affairs, 'the Opium of the Soul' (Locke 2:757), rather than the frivolities of fashion, which bar the married woman from the life of the mind. 'Though I was Always Dull, I find that I am now a thousand times more so then formerly; And the little Knowledge that I once had, is now exchanged for Absolute Ignorance' (Locke 2:757).

Yet this self-depreciation cannot be read at face value. Apparently by this stage in her relationship with Locke, Masham had the confidence for undiluted irony: she professes dullness, yet not long afterwards sends him a dazzlingly witty poem of argument, and even boasts that 'perhaps you may see me in Print in a little While' (Locke 2:762). In fact another decade was to elapse before her first published work, and in the meantime, correspondence became unnecessary when Locke took up residence with her and her husband.[10] Meanwhile she invokes the fashion to justify this first hint at plans for authorship. Publishing, she writes, has 'growne much the Fasion of late for our sex.' Though she professes ambivalence about this fashion, 'because (Principally) the Mode is for one to Dye First' (Locke 2:762), she is acknowledging a real and crucial shift in social practice. The new fashion for women to publish has force enough to overpower the effects of her decline into matrimony. A change of mode like this one may be not feminine frivolity but social progress.

As a very young woman who passionately loved both reading and parties, Lady Mary Pierrepont was similarly concerned to present herself to her often-censorious suitor as having no interest in fashion. Even in her letters to female friends (and the idea of her conveyed by her correspondence to today's readers is radically different from the idea of Damaris Masham precisely because letters to her peers survive) she rarely chats about petticoats or manteaus. Instead she presents herself and her friends as having minds above the frivolities of ornament so dear to human butterflies of both sexes. Sitting in rural retirement on the date of Queen Anne's 1712 birthday celebrations at court, she pictures in her mind 'all the Beaux and Belles dressing in a Hurry to make their Bows, and Cursies to the Queen; Your Paradise, and several other paradises [that is, favoured suitors, heart-throbs], in Fring'd Gloves, embroidier'd Coats, and powder'd wigs in irresistable Curl ... while we, my Dear, in our several little Cells are perhaps more happy than they, at least more easy' (Montagu 1:115–16).

In Montagu's letters, then, fashion is for beaux and belles. When poets wear 'Embrodier'd Coats and pink colour'd Top knots' then poetry, she implies, is in a parlous condition (2:24). To her sister, Montagu expresses casual contempt first for a male cousin ('a consummate puppy as you'l perceive at first sight') and then for apparently over-dressed female cousins who 'blaze' or 'brille' (2:36, 74). Yet the style of her 'Beaux and Belles' letter to her friend Philippa or Phil, with its visual detail and drama, its evocation of feeling ('Hurry,' 'irresistible,' 'Cells'), is quite different from that of the 'Nature is seldom in the wrong, custom always' letter to Anne Wortley and Anne's brother. In the earlier letter she writes of the fashionable world like a philosopher who has never entered it, in the later one like a former fashionista.

Items of dress figure frequently in her letters to her sister in connection with gifts or errands, but they are usually mentioned, not described in detail: black or coloured 'lutestring,' 'narrow minunet,' a ready-made nightgown – that is, an evening gown – a 'pritty Cap' for her daughter, and, yes, a mantua and petticoat (2: 8–9, 10, 19, 21, 25, 46, 53). Her pose of contempt for fashion, though its sincerity is impossible to gauge, was not merely something assumed to impress a man whose good opinion she desired. It was part of her self-construction as an intelligent woman, carried over from one correspondence to another, but often expressed with a modishly witty eye for fashion detail.

When she is travelling abroad, on the other hand, and has unfamiliar fashions to describe, she relishes painting those fashions in words. This is true both of the Viennese court dress which she finds equally a torment to the wearer and the observer, and of the Islamic women's garb which she sees as offering delightful freedom of movement to the wearer and beauty to the beholder. Her word-picture of her Turkish dress – the gold-embroidered white kid slippers, the light, full, brocaded damask 'drawers,' the fine white embroidered gauze 'smock' with its wide sleeves and diamond fastening, the waistcoat, the kaftan, the broad girdle, the fur-lined outer robe, the tasselled head-dress and lavish ornaments in the hair – (1:326–7) is probably one of the best-known passages about dress in the literature of the period. In alien cultures Montagu's Enlightenment interest in the vagaries of human manners allows her to give free rein to describing fashion.

The same interest ensures that her letters to her early girl-friends and a few years later to her sister, while they give scant attention to petticoats or manteaus, are rich in detail about the opportunities for proving herself in the swing and up to the minute. In these letters she seeks out and passes on controversial printed texts (Delarivier Manley's *The New Atalantis,* the 'Bath lampoons') and oral or epistolary gossip (the latest jilting or elopement or adultery, the arrest of Manley and her publisher) (1:18–19). Even at the end of her life she writes that she is 'much diverted with the Adventures of the three Graces lately arriv'd in London' (the Wynne sisters), and the likelihood that they will 'produce very glorious Noveltys' (3:226). Her scorn of fashion is not, either in youth or age, a scorn of novelty.

It is, however, in youth a scorn for materialism. 'Apartments, Table etc. are things that never come into my head' (1:30). When as a young woman she tells a contemporary that she despises 'the silly shine of Equipage' (1:120) and assures Edward Wortley Montagu that women as a group are not, as he supposes, easily dazzled by the 'charms of show, and all the pageantry of Greatnesse' (1:24), it is materialism that she disavows. She claims to speak here for her sex: while philosophers despise these things through care and study, young women despise them naturally.

To her suitor fashion meant not so much materialism as changeful-ness and hypocrisy. He insults her writing skills by likening them to skill in fashion. Her corresponding with him, he maintains, does nothing to indicate that she holds a special value for him, but is merely self-display. 'Every woman wou'd write instead of dressing for any lover she had not resolv'd to strike out of her list, that coud persuade herselfe she did it halfe so well as you. I know that when you write you shine out in all your beauty' (Montagu 1:52). Her indignant reply picks up the fashion metaphor: for her to wear Spanish dress in England would be extravagantly silly, she writes, no matter how much it flattered her beauty. Fashion has its place as part of custom, a real but insignificant place in human life, and both are subject to the dominion of reason (1:55–6).

Her courtship letters reflect a greater need for approval than the letters of Cudworth (later Masham) to Locke, and heavier pressure from her correspondent's sense of admissible female identity. Each party to this correspondence works at self-presentation; each diagnoses and comments on the character expressed in the other's letters, but there is less exchange, less reciprocal self-presentation, than between Cudworth and Locke. Writing as an intellectual, Pierrepont expresses greater humility of gender than Masham. Writing as a friend, she is ready to concede that most women are incapable of friendship, and so falls back on exceptionalism in her presentation of herself (rather like the derogatory assessment of other women implied in Cudworth's threatening Locke with discussion of petticoats).

For both these writers, a strong interest in dress is the mark of a presumptively feminine frivolity that they are determined to disavow. Their attitudes illuminate the way that, for an intellectually energetic and ambitious woman seeking male mentoring, it was tactically necessary to separate herself from her mentor's conception of popular feminine culture (popular rather than elevated or rational, although it was upper-class, just because it was feminine). Biographical details about Masham are too sparse to reveal to what extent, aside from her relationship with Locke, she lived her life within this culture. But Montagu's correspondences situate her in a succession of women's worlds: from the young women's world of courtships (both desired and detested), parties, jokes, secrets, and exchange of information about the latest in clothes and books; through a middle-aged world centred on children and servants, health issues, and gossip; to a world evoked in late letters which make constant references to the past, to earlier generations, and to her own advancing years. Montagu's latest correspondence charts a version of female old age which contrasts markedly with that promulgated by the dominant male culture.

Letters of Fashion

The evidence of contemporary publication does not suggest that fashion or the mode featured as a topic in the correspondence of contemporary circles of women like that of Mary Astell, Elizabeth Thomas, and Mary, Lady Chudleigh (nor between Thomas and her fiancé Richard

Gwinnett). But the state of knowledge about these women's lives, even after energetic and admirable scholarly efforts, does not allow us to assume a negative. Catharine Trotter, later Cockburn, has appeared from the letters included in Thomas Birch's edition of her works (published in 1751, two years after her death) as an austere theologian or philosopher in her maturity, with little attention to spare for the frivolities of female popular culture. Indeed, her letters to Locke are not personal in the way that Damaris Masham's had been. But her biographer, Anne Kelley, has now shown from the manuscripts of those letters that this impression is mistaken. In September 1740, with one of her daughters about to be married, Cockburn describes for her niece a list of what was to be ordered from London, had a sisterly gift not provided most of it: 'a compleat Suit of Cambrick, head, handkerchief, & double Ruffles, with a pretty broad & fine Edging; a plain white silk for a Gown, & a good flowerd silk, a quilted Coat' (Kelley 209).

Other female circles went further in delight in fashion, though their members also had a stake in cultural and intellectual life. A few years later Lady Mary Pierrepont, Mary Pendarves (later Delany) wrote to her sister, Anne Granville, of another queen's birthday which she likewise was not going to attend (that of Queen Caroline in 1728): 'Great preparations are made for it: abundance of embroidery' (Delany 1:159). Pendarves was born eleven years later than Montagu, and as a champion embroiderer herself (and a frequenter of high society) she takes – or reveals – a closer interest in dress than the other letter-writers discussed here.[11] As a young woman she never presents herself as too intellectual for an interest in fashion, although by the date of this letter (with her painful first marriage behind her) she was already discussing theology (among other topics) in correspondence with John Wesley, and had been suspected by an acquaintance of 'set[ting] up for a poet' (1:197). Her correspondence with Wesley (which is silent on modes of dress) is not concerned with seeking approval in the manner of the less established and matured Damaris Cudworth or Lady Mary Pierrepont. Her letter to her sister, quoted above, promises not only 'the new plays,' but also 'a tippet of my own making and invention.' It goes on to the kind of report on the modes which those other letter-writers would have eschewed. 'After the birthday I believe everybody will go into colours, except at Court; if there is any alteration in the fashions I will tell you. The *curly murly* fashion of the hair is not much worn now' (1:159).

Such reports are common currency in this correspondence. A couple of years later Pendarves reports to her sister, 'Gauze heads are now the top mode: I will send you one exactly in the fashion and charge you to wear it without any alterations. You will think it strange coarse stuff, but it is as good as the Queen's, and sure that's good enough for you' (1:220). The wit and worldliness of this correspondence defines itself through critical engagement, not disengagement, with the popular upper-class topic of fashion. She regularly flags a sense of amusement at the vagaries of the mode – all her life she comments tirelessly on this or that fashion as ridiculous, ugly, or overdone – but such individual criticisms are the accompaniment of a steady interest.

In 1734, after a full account of clothes at a family wedding, she moves on to describe in detail the dress she plans to wear at another such occasion, an approaching royal one: 'I have got my wedding garment ready, 'tis a brocaded lutestring, white ground with great ramping flowers in shades of purples, reds and greens. I gave thirteen shillings a yard; it looks better than it describes, and will make a show: I shall wear with them dark purple and gold ribbon, and a *black hood* for decency's sake' (1:428). As herself an unmatched artist in embroidery, she can write like a connoisseur and dismiss inferior work. On one grand occasion in February 1741 she finds Lady Scarborough's gown magnificent enough but of 'a very unmeaning pattern,' its 'petticoat embroidered with clumsy festoons of *nothing at all's supported by pillars* no better than posts' (2:147).

She reports herself best pleased with the outfit worn by the duchess of Queensberry, whose embroidery featured at 'the bottom of the petticoat *brown hills* covered with all sorts of weeds, and *every breadth* [of fabric] had *an old stump of a tree* that run up almost to the top of the petticoat, broken and ragged and worked with brown chenille,' around which were worked 'all sorts of twining flowers' (2:147). The future Mary Delany shows her scientific interests by enumerating the several species of flower, and her craftswoman's interests by noting that the small size of the flowers and leaves 'made them look very light,' while gold thread was contrived to look 'like the gilding of the sun.' She concludes, 'I never saw a piece of work so prettily fancied, and am quite angry with myself for not having the same thought, for it is infinitely handsomer than mine' (2:147–8). These indulgences in fashion talk, over which her intelligence plays like the gilding of the sun, have an artistry far from the dismissive phrases of Masham or Montagu (though they are of the same genre with Montagu's description of the Turkish dress). It seems no great stretch to call Delany a woman-identified woman, enjoying a discourse of female community, in which she shows her wit not by rejecting fashion but by discriminating among different manifestations of fashion.

Nevertheless in her late seventies, writing a letter which is also an essay on conduct for the use of a young great-niece, Delany takes the role of a censor of fashion. She invokes the benevolent power of Propriety to defend the girl against Vanity and Assurance. She now distances herself from simple pleasure in fashion as she had never done in years past, remarking wryly not on bad taste in dress but on the defect of caring too much for dress: 'I have given *less offence* by observing on a *moral failing*, than setting a cap in *better* order!' Here Delany downgrades the fashion (in dress) as comparatively insignificant. Yet her attitudes differ in several ways from those of most moralists on this topic. First, she has lost nothing of the clarity and firmness of judgment which as a younger woman she regularly applied to dress. A cap may still be better or worse ordered, even though other questions may be of more moment than caps. Secondly, though she does not say so, Delany had earned her right to comment on clothes through her own membership in women's clothes culture. Moralists' age-old diatribes against this culture had by now expanded to take in the rising fashion industry and the direction of style by commercial interests. Women were attacked as consumers of dress, in parallel with the well-known attacks on them as passive consumers of fashionable literature, primarily the novel. Delany, no passive consumer of either clothes or books, exercised her individual talent both in designing and describing. This upper-class woman is a representative, no matter how unlikely, of that female popular culture which saw needlework not only as a task (in her case as a money-saver) but also as an art form, an opportunity for self-expression and for competitive excellence. She also understood how mainstream attitudes to this women's culture shift with time: 'in my youth it was reckon'd *very vulgar* to be *extravagantly* in the fashion' (Delany 2nd series 2:310). During her older years the pink of fashion was more often reckoned immoral than vulgar.

Letters from women to women are perhaps our primary means of understanding such women's cultures. Letters contain multitudes: the genre actively resists generalization. Letters that Masham wrote to other people besides Locke do not survive to illuminate her self-presentation in any other relationship. And this adept and sparkling letter-writer was capable of pettish dismissal of the genre. What, she demands, 'Signifies an Absent Friend? One sees them not; One Converses not with them, but by the Tedious way of Letters' (Locke 3:49). When not constructing herself as above the fashion, or reporting delightedly on exotic dress, Montagu tried on the fictional epistolary guises of a predatory serial widow (for her essay in the *Spectator*) and a male Turkey merchant (for her pro-inoculation polemic), and the real-life role of passionate lover for whom the world is well lost (writing to Francesco Algarotti). Delany turned her descriptive talents in other letters to intellectual rather than sartorial novelties: the avant-garde music of Handel, advances in botany, and the geology of the Giants' Causeway as investigated by Joseph Banks and Daniel Solander.

Nevertheless, it seems possible that the serious thinking of women in Delany's generation (she was in later life a member of the bluestocking circle) ran in different channels from those of its immediate predecessors; that for them an intelligent woman of the world felt less need to conform to the standards expected by male intellectuals, less need to dazzle by her 'wit,' and greater freedom to include in her self-presentation a specialized interest in the details of female popular culture such as dress. The letters of Pendarves/Delany look forward to those of Jane Austen, who shares her enjoyment of critiquing the fashion and relating her own responses to it in making and (in Austen's case) renovating.

Letters of different generations provide a lens through which to glimpse the changing tone of relationships between correspondents. This snapshot of three intellectual letter-writers over a span of about half a century reveals something of the way they constructed themselves through letters, and sought to embody for their correspondents the currently admired or accepted traits of 'woman' while asserting a claim to critical intelligence and the role of commentator on the changing zeitgeist as that was reflected in the adornment of their own sex.

NOTES

1 For estimates of population at 5 million in 1688, nine million in 1801, and female literacy rates as 25 per cent in 1714, 40 per cent or more in 1750, and 51 per cent in 1839–40, see Stanton 248; Brewer 167; Hunter 72; and Altick 380.
2 Altick 380; *Oxford Dictionary of National Biography* under William Dockwra; *Encyclopaedia Britannica*, 1911.
3 *Oxford Dictionary of National Biography* under Ralph Allen; Ellis 102.
4 See, for instance, Perry, Earle, and Brant.

5 Amanda Vickery's influential 1998 study of letter-writing networks among
   women of the English propertied class has been followed by Susan E.
   Whyman's study of letter-writing by both sexes, and Dena Goodman's
   monograph on the rather different culture of gentlewomen's epistolarity
   in France.
6 For instance, Margaret Fell Fox, Anne Audland, Barbara Blaugdone, and
   Joan Vokins.
7 For instance, Hester Mulso Chapone, Jane Warton, Susanna Haswell
   Rowson, Helena Wells, and even the evangelical Mary Bosanquet Fletcher.
8 See Miegon 162ff, 168, 172, 175, 183–4; and Brown, Clements, and Grundy
   (Montagu entry).
9 Brown, Clements, and Grundy (Damaris Masham entry).
10 Locke spent more and more time at Oates (at High Laver in Essex), from
   1690, when he made his first extended visit. He was there again for the
   Christmas holidays and stayed several months (paying for his keep). In
   1691 they invited him to make Oates his permanent home, which he did
   (Locke 2:470).
11 She also recalls another meaning of the word 'fashion' – the highest and
   most visible ranks in society. Like Montagu she belonged in those highest
   ranks, and unlike Montagu embodied their social code. In the words of
   Edmund Burke, 'She was a *truly great* woman of fashion . . . the woman of
   fashion of all ages' (Delany 2nd series 2:12).

WORKS CITED

Altick, Richard D. *The English Common Reader: A Social History of the Mass
   Reading Public, 1800–1900*. 1957. Columbus: Ohio State UP, 1998. Print.
Batchelor, Jennie. 'The Claims of Literature: Women Applicants to the
   Royal Literary Fund, 1790–1810.' *Women's Writing* 12.3 (October 2005):
   505–21. Print.
Brant, Clare. *Eighteenth-Century Letters and British Culture*. Basingstoke:
   Palgrave Macmillan, 2006. Print.
Brewer, John. *The Pleasures of the Imagination: English Culture in the Eighteenth
   Century*. New York: Farrar Straus Giroux, 1997. Print.
Brown, Susan, Patricia Clements, and Isobel Grundy, eds. *Orlando: Women's
   Writing in the British Isles from the Beginnings to the Present*. Cambridge UP
   Online. June 2006. Web. 17 April 2010. http://orlando.cambridge.org/.
Delany, Mary. *The Autobiography and Correspondence of Mary Granville, Mrs.
   Delany, with interesting reminiscences of King George the Third and Queen*

Charlotte. Ed. Augusta Hall, Baroness Llanover. London: R. Bentley, [1st series] 1861, 2nd series 1862. Print.

Earle, Rebecca, ed. *Epistolary Selves: Letters and Letter-Writers, 1600–1945*. Aldershot: Ashgate, 1999. Print.

Ellis, Kenneth. *The Post Office in the Eighteenth Century: A Study in Administrative History*. London: Oxford UP, 1958. Print.

Goodman, Dena. *Becoming a Woman in the Age of Letters*. Ithaca: Cornell UP, 2009. Print.

Hunter, J. Paul. *Before Novels: The Cultural Contexts of Eighteenth Century English Fiction*. New York: W.W. Norton, 1990. Print.

Kelley, Anne. *Catharine Trotter: An Early Modern Writer in the Vanguard of Feminism*. Aldershot: Ashgate, 2002. Print.

Locke, John. *The Correspondence of John Locke*. Ed. Esmond Samuel De Beer. Oxford: Clarendon, 1976–89. Print.

McDowell, Paula. *The Women of Grub Street: Press, Politics, and Gender in the London Literary Marketplace, 1678–1730*. Oxford: Clarendon, 1998. Print.

Miegon, Anna E. '"The Ladies' Diary" and the Emergence of the Almanac for Women, 1704–1753.' PhD dissertation. Vancouver, BC: Simon Fraser University, 2008.

Montagu, Mary Wortley. *The Complete Letters of Lady Mary Wortley Montagu*. Ed. Robert Halsband. Oxford: Clarendon, 1965–7. Print.

Moore, Lisa L. *Sister Arts: The Erotics of Lesbian Landscapes*. Minneapolis: U of Minnesota P, 2011. Print.

Oxford Dictionary of National Biography. Ed. Henry Colin Gray Matthew, Brian Harrison, and Lawrence Goldman. 2004. Web. 22 April 2010.

Perry, Ruth. *Women, Letters and the Novel*. New York: AMS Press, 1980. Print.

Rorty, Richard. *Contingency, Irony, and Solidarity*. Cambridge: Cambridge UP, 1989. Print.

Smith, Charlotte. *The Collected Letters of Charlotte Smith*. Ed. Judith Phillips Stanton. Bloomington: Indiana UP, 2003. Print.

Stanton, Judith Phillips. 'Statistical Profile of Women Writing in English from 1660 to 1800.' *Eighteenth-Century Women and the Arts*. Ed. Frederick M. Keener and Susan E. Lorsch. New York, Westport, CT, and London: Greenwood P, 1988. 247–54. Print.

Vickery, Amanda. *The Gentleman's Daughter: Women's Lives in Georgian England*. New Haven and London: Yale UP, 1998. Print.

Whyman, Susan E. *The Pen and the People, English Letter Writers 1660–1800*. Oxford: Oxford UP, 2009. Print.

Wollstonecraft, Mary. *Letters Written During a Short Residence in Sweden, Norway, and Denmark*. London: Joseph Johnson, 1796. Print.

8 Writing Bodies in Popular Culture: Eliza Haywood and *Love in Excess*

HOLLY LUHNING

Eliza Haywood was one of the most popular and prolific writers of the early eighteenth century, and in the 1720s her output alone accounted for a significant percentage of all writing being published in English by women. This achievement is doubly impressive when considered in the cultural context of the period in which she began to write. At the beginning of the eighteenth century, women who wrote were stigmatized; as Alexander Pettit puts it, 'Female authorship was widely considered to be the literary equivalent of prostitution' (9). Yet Haywood was prolific, well-known, and a best-selling author. The topics that she often wrote about – women, love, sex, the body, marriage, mental illness, and money – were common to a growing body of medical and political writings, and periodicals at the time. She generated the plots and characters of her texts from popular interests and concerns; this sort of public knowledge provided a basis from which she could comment on, challenge, and even produce cultural beliefs.

Haywood's work deserves to be examined for its literary merit, but also as an artefact of how the most prolific early woman writer of the English language managed a highly successful career in a business that did not traditionally include women. Aphra Behn and Delarivier Manley both had commercial success before Haywood, but both suffered arguably more negative public feedback and had shorter-lived careers. Her work, both business and literary, contributes to an understanding of eighteenth-century culture and history in a manner that cannot be explained solely by studies limited to more canonical literary figures such as Alexander Pope, Jonathan Swift, or Daniel Defoe. London and England in general underwent rapid social change in the early part of the century, and the marketplace that Haywood dealt with would have afforded different possibilities than the one in which Behn and Manley participated. Additionally, as products of one of the most popular women writers in English literary history, and one of the first to make writing a commercially viable occupation, Haywood's work and career differ from those of her male counterparts. She was writing from a time and culture that questioned the social propriety of women writing and publishing, yet Haywood not only wrote, but published widely. Paula Backscheider suggests that '[o]ne of the great mysteries of literary history is the artistic and social dynamic that gives rise to an artistic configuration that becomes formulaic and had mass appeal, that engages the attention of a very large, very diverse audience, and that stands up to itself' (27). Haywood's work and career fit this description. She established and managed her career and authorial persona in an unprecedented manner. Her career epitomizes the possibilities available to writers, male and female, who capitalized on the changing marketplace. As Catherine Ingrassia documents, Haywood's overall 'production of texts was unmatched between 1719 and 1728' by any writer, man or woman (79). Her work, which both confirms and challenges societal norms, attracted and sustained the attention of a large, popular audience.

Haywood's activities as writer, bookseller,[1] and overall cultural player reflect what Paula McDowell refers to as a 'synthetic' model for the study of the literary marketplace, in which women printworkers, writers, and consumers are linked in a 'communications circuit' (136). This model challenges the idea that authorship (or for that matter, reading) is a solitary activity; the model 'broadens the class spectrum of women we study, and it also opens up women's involvement in a broader variety of texts' (136). Many women were writing during this period, such as Jane Barker, Mary Astell, Catherine Cockburn, Elizabeth Thomas, Susannah Centlivre, and Elizabeth Rowe; others, such as Haywood and Manley were involved in several commercial aspects of the book trade. Viewing the marketplace as a web that connects authors to bookbinders,[2] to the upper classes, and to the increasingly literate middle class not only opens up the class spectrum that identifies the popular, but also reveals a powerful network of women who were a part of shaping literary tastes, cultural habits, structures of feeling, and public opinion.

Haywood's career epitomizes the possibilities open to a writer who capitalized on the existence of the sort of communications circuit that McDowell describes. As Ingrassia posits, Haywood 'depended on her ability to produce, manipulate, and circulate symbolic instruments –

literary commodities – that demonstrate her credit on paper' (Ingrassia 78). This 'paper credit' or economic gain relied on Haywood's ability to interpret topical subjects and cultural trends and then weave such elements into compelling narrative. She turned her intangible skills of intelligence, creativity, and acute social insights into a product – her writing – and in doing so created for herself a position of authority in which she possessed significant cultural currency. Haywood prolifically produced popular texts that circulated through a booming book trade and among a growing reading public. She capitalized on the legal and subsequent economic changes in print culture, and in the process eroded gender and class barriers surrounding the profession of author. She also produced work that was and has been consistently described as scandalous or transgressive; she both reflected and challenged the culture from which she was writing. Though at the beginning of the eighteenth century, booksellers rarely equated women's writing with economic value, Haywood's popularity helped to propel both the novel and women writers into a position where they were viewed by publishers and the reading public as both viable commodities and cultural players, shaping popular understandings of the nature of fiction, the feminine, and the often devaluatory codes that defined them.

As James Raven notes, bookselling was 'obviously different from most other consumer trades in that it was not simply commercial but intrinsically artistic and political' (208), and the economic success that *Love in Excess* (1719) provided for its publisher, William Chetwood, influenced the perception of what he, and other booksellers, considered to be marketable. Cultural tastes and economic interests were engaged in a mutually influential relationship. Sarah Prescott posits that 'Haywood's success can be said to have changed the face of the marketplace for fiction dramatically. The decade following the publication of *Love in Excess* saw a remarkable increase in the publication of women's fiction' (106). Haywood's work during this period – literary and commercial – not only established her success as a popular writer, but contributes to English iterations of popular culture in its creation of a space for the potentially positive reception of future women writers participating in the literary marketplace.[3]

Haywood and Amatory Fiction

Haywood's early novels conflate sentimental and erotic literature; this style, termed amatory fiction, is well-suited to house both racy narratives and social critique. Paula Backscheider and John Richetti assert that amatory fiction before 1740 presents 'a powerful articulation of female identity and self-consciousness available nowhere else in the culture of the time' and that this writing 'revises and subverts traditional masculinist constructions of the feminine' (xiv). And though the genre of sentimental literature is often located as a product of the middle part of the eighteenth century and connected to the cult of sensibility that emerged later in the century, sentiment is distinct from sensibility and was not uncommonly utilized in writing of the early eighteenth century. Sentiment as defined as emotional affect is certainly concurrently in play as a part of amatory genres: as Janet Todd remarks, 'the mark of sentimental literature' is the 'arousal of pathos through conventional situations, stock familial characters and rhetorical devices ... It is a kind of pedagogy of seeing and of the physical reaction that this seeing should produce' (4). And although amatory literature is to some degree defined by its erotic elements, Ros Ballaster notes differences between pornographic and amatory writing; she suggests that the 'primarily anatomical, procreative and instructional emphasis of [pornographic] literature bears little relationship to the erotic-pathetic drive of the seduction and betrayal narratives of Behn, Manley, and Haywood' (29). Ballaster posits that it is the mix of the erotic and sentimental that defines amatory literature, 'a particular body of narrative fiction by women which was explicitly erotic in its concentration on the representation of sentimental love' (29). The conflation of the emotional and the physical produces a genre of writing that is particularly suitable to exploring and questioning social power systems such as gender, economics, and class.

At this same time, as Janet Todd documents, the popular cult of sensibility was in its inchoate stages. The body was becoming increasingly socially acknowledged as a space to express emotion, delicacy, and sensitivity; later in the century, the popular rise of the cult of sensibility would further position the body as a powerful, public site of communication. Haywood, as part of the culture producing these concepts, writes about, relies upon, and shapes this emerging, broad cultural understanding of the relationships between body and emotion. Her texts reflected, anticipated, and developed perceptions about the body that were relevant to readers in the context of social and cultural discourse. As John Fiske notes, this sort of relevance 'is central to popular culture, for it minimizes the difference between text and life' (6). *Love in Excess* discusses and presents bodies in a manner that both entertained and challenged readers, and was also becoming increasingly familiar to a reading public. However, the novel is not simply comprised of characters who signal emotion through their bodies and who are involved in a sexually titillating narrative; Haywood exploits amatory and sentimental conventions to produce a text that at once produces a racy story and social critique. Her writing relies on a popular understanding of the relationships among bodies, sentiment, and emotion to draw attention to the restrictive social world her characters inhabit. Haywood depends on corporeal evidence to construct and complicate the emotional and social journeys of her characters. In particular, she challenges cultural assumptions that men and women have fundamental differences in regard to physical and emotional experiences of desire. Specifically, she chronicles the transformation of Count D'Elmont from rake to sensitive lover in part through the description of his body[4] as he comes to experience physical symptoms of love similar to those of the women in the novel. Haywood moves toward collapsing her culture's naturalized understandings of difference in male and female physiology and emotion, rendering subversive social critique accessible to the women who constituted the presumed audience of her presumably trivial medium.

Writing the Body

Through most of the eighteenth century, the body and mind were conceptualized as causally linked. Illness and health were thought to be joint matters of the mind (Hamlin 71). Strong emotions such as fear or love could put women at risk of illness: as Michel Foucault writes of the perception of women's sensibilities: 'the sympathetic sensibility of her [woman's] organism, radiating through her entire body, condemns woman to ... diseases of the nerves' (qtd in Vila 228). Nervous disorders were frequently blamed for a cornucopia of symptoms such as lethargy, spasms, nausea, headaches, and blockages. They were also an indication of a gendered bifurcation of the understanding of the relationship between body and emotion that emerged in the eighteenth century. Women were perceived as most often afflicted with disorders of the nervous system and this perception contributed to, as Ludmilla Jordanova expresses it, the 'feminization of the nervous system' (14). Excessive expressions of emotion, or physical ailments thought to be caused by emotion, were thought to be experienced almost exclusively by women.

Despite this association of the feminine with the nervous system,[5] however, the popular interest in sentimentality, and the eventual popular emergence of the cult of sensibility created a cultural space that cast displays of feeling, in both men and women, as acceptable and even desirable. Paul Goring suggests that there was a 'preoccupation in British culture of the period with the human body as an eloquent object, whose eloquence arises from the performance of an inscribed system of gestures and expressions. This preoccupation is manifest in various eighteenth-century projects which, at some level, were engaged in training the body – in shaping and directing ways in which bodies, both male and female, should appear in public' (5). The body, or description of the body in literature, functions as a canvas on which to express experience; the concept of a sensible body 'is to claim, if only by implication, an experiencing body' (Van Sant 89). As sensibility emerged as a popular concept it was connected to the idea of delicacy, but Van Sant argues that although the sensible body was 'an instrument of the feminization of culture, this body was not a woman's body. The feminized delicacy of the body of sensibility runs counter to its eroticized sensitivity' (89). Although a sensible body could sometimes denote excess of emotion, the body that displayed visible signs of feeling was an active, responsive body. There were elements of physical and social agency in such displays.

In this way, the body functions as a social canvas in a way that has significance to popular culture and its place in the naturalization of the feminine; Haywood employs this canvas – her characters' bodies – to express plot, emotional development, and personal change. Goring suggests that the body 'provides an inescapable textual surface . . . because of the very resilience of its claims to being natural' (19). The understanding of the body as 'natural' allows the body to occupy a position of cultural authority: what is 'natural' is understood to be authentic and powerful. Haywood cites her characters' physicality as evidence that indicates sincere and significant emotional change and personal development. The bodies of Haywood's characters perform both physically and socially; as Judith Butler explains, this performativity acts as 'a reiterative power of discourse' (236). The body exists as a physical entity, but the social understandings of the body influence how the physical body is read by one's self and others. In *Love in Excess* Haywood uses and produces social understandings of sentiment and the expressive body to construct and communicate the emotional journeys of her characters.

Haywood relies on the cultural intersections between emotion and the body to articulate her characters' experience of love. She often includes a description of a character's beating heart, or panting breath, or describes the experience of 'burning,' 'raging,' or 'swooning' with emotion. The descriptions of the corporeal responses serve as proof of the sincerity and magnitude of the characters' emotions. Barbara Stafford suggests that 'early modern aesthetics and biology shared a relational praxis and a detecting theory that focused on the puzzle of the feeling and thinking person ... As diagnostic disciplines, their purpose was to discover and exhibit the inarticulable relationship of interior to exterior, idea to form, private pathos to public pattern' (2). Near the beginning of the novel, Alovisa is conscious that the public reads the body, as Stafford says, like a 'pattern'; when Alovisa attends the ball and sees the object of her love, D'Elmont, fraternizing with Amena,

> disdain, despair, and jealousie at once crowded into her heart, and swelled her almost to bursting ... and at length threw her into a swoon ... The ladies ran to her assistance ... and were a great while before they could bring her to her self; and when they did, the shame of having been so disordered in such an assembly, and the fears of their suspecting the occasion, added to her former agonies, and racked her with the most terrible convulsions. (41)

She understands that cultural codes of modesty dictate that she should not express her emotions, but even though she is verbally silent, her body does not allow her to conceal her desire. Alovisa's agonies grow worse as she realizes her swoon may be publicly understood as a reaction to desire. In this scene, Haywood illustrates both the rigidity of behavioural codes directed at women and also the codes' lack of ability to control physical and emotional desire. Alovisa attempts to adhere to social codes, but her desire is unabated and her physical symptoms communicate both the force and authenticity of her attraction to D'Elmont.

Haywood's dependency on female characters' physical symptoms to indicate their desire repeatedly highlights and critiques the highly restrictive social world in which women lived. Again, this pattern of Haywood simultaneously reflecting, challenging, and shaping popular social codes is related to her public identity as an author who interpreted and manipulated popular subjects and trends in the context of an engaging narrative. For example, conduct literature and cultural codes promoted restraint regarding how women presented themselves and their bodies in both the public and private spheres. This popular conduct literature, like popular culture itself, 'is obvious and superficial, refusing to produce the deep, complexly crafted texts that narrow down their audiences and social meanings' (Fiske 6). These texts simultaneously reflected and defined popular, normative eighteenth-century upper-class courtship rituals; women were expected to remain modest and feign indifference regarding men's advances and defer to the judgment of their parents or guardians in the selection of a suitor. As the conduct manual, *Mysteries of Love Reveal'd* asserts:

> They ought not to shew at first . . . Rigour; for that rather chases away than gains a Lover. Nor ought they to yield their Hearts as soon as they are solicited; for that is rather the Effect of a foolish Pity, than of the Merit of their Suitors; and he will not be apt to esteem that much, which costs him so little, and is aquired with so much ease. It is thus that these . . . Fair-ones captivate Hearts by a noble Pride: For in despising Love at the first, they at last triumph with the greater Power. (iii)

Women were expected to conceal their amorous interests in order to secure a man's esteem and affections. Haywood draws attention to this restrictive environment when D'Elmont first returns to the Paris court; women were attracted to D'Elmont but 'in secret, cursed that custom which forbids women to make a sudden declaration of their thoughts' (37). Haywood portrays several female characters in *Love in Excess* as torn between their attempts to maintain the illusion that they follow proper conduct and their responses to contradictory emotional and corporeal experiences. Alovisa, unable to resist expressing her emotions for D'Elmont, at first writes him a letter to explain his mistaken identification of her first love note; she is about to send him the correspondence when she says, 'No, let me rather die . . . to pieces with this shameful witness of my folly, my furious desires may be the destruction of my peace, but never of my honour, that shall still attend my name when love and life are fled' (44). The rigid conduct codes do not allow for women to follow their 'furious desires' while maintaining 'honour'; Alovisa must pick one or the other.[6] Eventually, Alovisa manages to navigate the codes of conduct and satisfy her desires, but she dies by accidentally falling on D'Elmont's sword at the conclusion of part one of the text. Through this death, Haywood illustrates that the social and cultural framework of the time often prohibited women from successfully navigating both the demands of social viability and the realization of emotional and corporeal desires.

As a man, D'Elmont is not constrained by the strict codes of conduct to which women were expected to adhere, but he also eventually experiences powerful physical manifestations of his emotions. At the beginning of the novel the narrator makes several references to the fact that D'Elmont has never truly been in love. When D'Elmont asks Amena to dance at the ball, he does so 'not that he was in love with her, or at that time believed he could be touched with a passion which he esteemed a trifle in it self, and below the dignity of a man of sense' (42). When Brillian tells D'Elmont the story of his love for Ansellina, Brillian is moved to tears; the narrative then moves into a paragraph which outlines in detail D'Elmont's inexperience with and attitude toward love, and the narrator's opinions on what constitutes sincere desire:

> The Count had never yet seen a beauty formidable enough to give him an hours uneasiness (purely for the sake of love) . . . those little delicacies, those trembling, aking transports, which every sight of the beloved object occasions, and so visibly distinguishes a real passion from a counterfeit, he looked on as the chimera's of an idle brain, formed to inspire notions of an imaginery bliss, and make fools lose themselves in seeking; or if they had a being it was only in weak souls, a kind of disease with which he assured himself he should never be infected. (75–6)

While rejecting the merits of the idea of being in love, D'Elmont still characterizes love in terms of physical manifestations; he terms it a disease, something that infects bodies. Haywood carefully choreographs D'Elmont's evolution through how she characterizes his disdain for love: not only does she reveal D'Elmont's belief that such an emotion is below a man of sense, but also she illustrates his negative perception of love in physical terms of disease and infection.

Later in the text, Haywood again uses physical evidence to support D'Elmont's transformation to sincere lover. When he meets Melliora, 'this insensible [man] began to feel the power of beauty . . . [T]he first sight of Melliora gave him a discomposure he had never felt before' (86). His body reacts in a way that, like Alovisa's, can be publicly read; when Melliora faints he responds with 'a wildness in his countenance, a trembling horror shaking all his fabrick in such a manner, as might have easily discovered to the spectators (if they had not been too busily employed to take notice of it) that he was actuated by a motive far more powerful than that of compassion' (87). Here, D'Elmont experiences 'those trembling, aking transports' (75) that he previously believed were a 'chimera' (76). D'Elmont's physical experience illustrates to readers, himself, and eventually Melliora that his emotions are genuine. Further, his new-found understanding for those who love stems from his personal, physical feelings.

Because D'Elmont experiences the emotional, and the emotionally motivated physical effects of love, he is then able to gain insight and evolve into a more sensitive being. It is only after D'Elmont falls in love with Melliora that he is able to feel compassion for Amena's unrequited love; her letter 'now filled him with remorse and serious anguish' whereas before falling for Melliora 'he would have laughed at, perhaps despised' her letter and her actions (92). The experience of love, which D'Elmont previously characterized as silly and beneath him, becomes a powerful influence and is responsible for his evolution into a more self-aware character. For example, D'Elmont sees Incognita in her garden, where she 'threw her self down on a carpet which was spread upon the floor; and after sighing two or three times, continued to discover the violence of her impatient passion,' and he hears her exclaim 'Oh D'Elmont ... Little doest thou guess the tempest thou hast raised within my soul, nor know'st to pity these consuming fires!' (177). He is moved to reveal himself because 'no consideration was of force to make him neglect this opportunity of undeceiving her' (177).

D'Elmont again demonstrates his kindness and self-awareness when he deals with Violetta. Her body articulates her love for him; he recognizes her trembles, blushes, and difficulty in conversing with him as evidence of her love. He is concerned about inspiring yet another case of unrequited love: 'here was a new cause of disquiet to D'Elmont; the experience he had of his too fatal influence of his dangerous attractions gave him sufficient reason to fear this young lady was not insensible of them and that his presence was the sole cause of her disorder' (234). Haywood may be poking a bit of fun at D'Elmont's almost fairy-tale-like transformation from rake to introspective, sensitive, handsome, and irresistibly attractive gentleman. But D'Elmont does develop into a much nobler man after he loves and thus experiences the physical symptoms that in women would be attributed to their delicate nervous systems and feminine physiology.

If Haywood subverts the popular image of the masculine rake by exposing him to feminine disorders, she also creates, by the narrator's

account, a better version of D'Elmont as a human being. His unbeliev-
able irresistibility calls attention to the perceived difference between
male and female physiology and social and cultural roles that were
prominent in textual dialogues regarding the body and gendered
social behaviour. D'Elmont functions as a fairy-tale figure, one who
bridges the difference between male and female. Through D'Elmont,
Haywood creates a sexualized version of the sentimental mode of
masculinity articulated in writing such as Richard Steele's Spectator
essays. Haywood complicates the performance of gender in a novel
that also achieved wide popularity; her own popular identity as an
author, along with her economic success and her text's engagement
with a wide reading public created for Haywood an opportunity to
present an innovative interpretation of gender performance within
the context of, as Fiske denotes it, 'obvious and superficial' (6) popular culture.

While Haywood uses some of her characters, like D'Elmont and
Melliora, to suggest progressive ways to negotiate popular concerns
surrounding gender roles and sexual desire, she also contrasts these
positive models with characters who conform to rigid mainstream ste-
reotypes. One charge commonly levelled against Haywood is that her
fiction is often formulaic, repetitive, and involves stereotypical characters. As Backscheider points out, however, 'popular culture theorists ... recognize that where numerous variations on the same issue
emerge, writers are obsessively modeling a problem and testing solutions' (38). Haywood examines and deconstructs various 'problems'
through her employment of stereotypical characters and situations in
terms of forwarding the plot, and as a contrast to her nuanced, complicated central character. For example, in Love in Excess, she constructs
some characters who unwaveringly adhere to the role of a heterosexual
aggressor; these characters advocate only for their own interests and
are also often cast as villains. Baron D'Espernay is wealthy, titled, and
acts as D'Elmont's advisor regarding Melliora; he encourages D'Elmont
to rape her. When D'Elmont relates that Melliora has rejected his
advances, D'Espernay replies,

'What,' said he, 'a man of wit, and pleasure like Count D'Elmont, a man
who knows the sex so well could he let slip so favourable an opportunity
with the finest woman in the world; one for whose enjoyment he would
die, – Could a frown, or a little angry coiness (which ten to one was but
affected) have the power to freeze such fierce desires?' (113)

D'Espernay reads D'Elmont's gender, position in society, and ability to gratify his sexual desires as constitutative of D'Elmont's masculinity. He expects that D'Elmont should not let 'a little angry coiness' obstruct his desire for Melliora. D'Espernay goes on to explain to D'Elmont that by not possessing Melliora physically, 'you do not only injure the dignity of our sex in general, but your own merits in particular ... a little resolution on your part would make her all yours' (113). He equates D'Elmont's manliness with the employment of sexual force, and chides him when he attempts to reject this version of masculinity. D'Espernay is invested in establishing his authority over D'Elmont. As Karen Harvey notes, 'manhood was not made or lost through men's exercise of patriarchal authority over women: manhood was also forged through men's relationship with other men' (127). Haywood reveals the cultural codes among men that work to edify misogyny.

While D'Elmont does not succumb to D'Espernay's influence, he also does not enjoy a seamless, or perhaps even complete, transition into a reformed and sensitive man. When Ciamara attempts to seduce D'Elmont, even though he is emotionally disinterested in her, he still 'gave his hands and eyes a full enjoyment of all those charms, which had they been answered by a mind worthy of them, might justly have inspired the highest raptures, while she, unshocked, and unresisting, suffered all he did, and urged him with all the arts she was mistress of, to more' (225). The narrator explains D'Elmont's behaviour by noting that he is 'still a *man!*' (225): ultimately, he is characterized as possessing an underlying, essential phallic nature. These two modes of male being – emotionally sensible and essentially phallic – operate fictionally together to allow Haywood to write a racy yet socially meritorious text. Her ability to combine predictable elements of amatory fiction with social commentary and criticism, along with her popular position in print culture and the print marketplace, allows her to be simultaneously publicly successful and subversive: she replicates, challenges, and influences popular tastes, testing variations on the problem of the physical body and the gendering of popular fiction.

Haywood emphasizes that the feeling, sensitive, corporeally expressive man is very desirable and successful in realizing his own desires. In part three, D'Elmont, who previously believed that '[a]mbition was ... the reigning passion in his soul' (76), relinquishes some of his rakish ways, and becomes Melliora's devoted (albeit adulterous) lover. By engaging in an emotional as well as a physical attachment to Melliora, D'Elmont moves from the stereotype of the aggressive rake toward the emerging stereotype of the sensitive man of feeling.[7] Haywood, however, marks this departure from the older stereotypical masculine behaviour as a positive change in D'Elmont's character. D'Elmont is 'inconsolable' (250) when Melliora is kidnapped and he sets out on an expedition to find her. He is no longer satisfied with the person of just any woman; he must have Melliora in particular. As Tiffany Potter has argued and as Stephen Ahern subsequently has suggested, D'Elmont represents 'the differences but also the continuities between two dominant models of masculinity: the amoral rake-hero of the Restoration and the sentimental man of feeling of mid-Georgian England' (Ahern 76). D'Elmont has evolved into a more modern, effective man.

Haywood punishes male characters who have not embraced feeling and who embody the old, hyperaggressive masculine ways, notably in the Baron D'Espernay, who dies at the end of part one. The Baron attempts to procure sex from Alovisa and encourages D'Elmont to rape Melliora, and it is this self-entitled, insensitive attitude that leads D'Espernay to his death. While Haywood punishes the supposedly sinful Alovisa in the same scene, Alovisa dies quickly but D'Espernay, 'mortally wounded,' suffers for two days before he dies (158). D'Espernay's once virile but now wounded body becomes a site of suffering and of social justice; Haywood's narrator comments that 'there appeared so much of justice in the Baron's death' that Brillian and D'Elmont 'found it no difficult manner to obtain their pardon' from the king (158). Haywood's narrative reflects a changing social ideal of masculinity. At several points in the text, Haywood pointedly privileges an alternative type of masculinity that does not adhere to more patriarchal, aggressive, sexually commodified models.

D'Elmont not only becomes more aware, understanding, and attractive because he has loved, but he uses his corporeal manifestations of love as powerful evidence of his sincerity when he courts Melliora. Their courtship is highly transgressive; she is his ward, and he is married. In popular romantic fiction, their story could easily fall into a seduction narrative cliché, where the older man sexually capitalizes on his position of authority over a young, vulnerable woman. Yet both Melliora and the reader are convinced of D'Elmont's sincerity not necessarily because of his words, but because of his body. His body marks him not as predator, but as a person who has genuine feelings and respect for Melliora. D'Elmont entreats Melliora to listen to his profession of love by explaining that

[a] thousand times you have read my rising wishes, sparkling in my eyes, and glowing on my cheeks, as often seen my virtue struggling in silent tremblings, and life-wasting anguish to suppress desire ... by all my sleepless nights and restless days, by all my countless burning agonies; by all the torments of my galled, bleeding heart, swear, that you shall hear me. (111)

D'Elmont cites his visible physical disorder as proof that his love is sincere and that he is worthy of an audience with her. Additionally, D'Elmont's speech to Melliora is similar to women's discussions of their love for D'Elmont. He admits freely that he is seriously afflicted by his love and explains that he can suppress his emotion no longer. His appeal to Melliora gains him some ground as a lover, but Melliora is aware that

whatever his pretences were [she] could look on his designs no otherwise than aimed at the destruction of her honour, and was fired with a virtuous indignation. But then she saw in this married man, the only person in the world, who was capable of inspiring her with a tender thought; she saw him reduced to the last extremity of dispair for her sake. (112)

D'Elmont's words and body tell Melliora that she holds power over his emotions. D'Elmont's emotional sincerity is not divorced from his sexual desire; Haywood does not signal that he is a sincere suitor by having him privilege emotional over sexual intimacy. Rather, she presents emotional and physical intimacy as connected, necessary components for a sincere, realized love. She also illustrates the commonality in the ways that Melliora and D'Elmont experience desire. D'Elmont tells Melliora, 'Did'st thou but know the thousandth part of what this moment I endure, the strong convulsions of my warring thoughts, thy heart steeled as it is, and frosted round with virtue, would burst its icy shield and melt in tears of blood to pity me' (124). The image of a bursting, bloody heart is of course a reference to Melliora's surrender of her virginity, and D'Elmont's earlier mention of his 'rising wishes' (111) references his phallic desire. But instead of being offended that D'Elmont has made this reference, Melliora identifies with his sufferings and says, 'Oh have I not a heart? A most susceptible, and tender heart? Yes, you may feel it throb, it beats against my breast, like an imprisoned bird, and fain would burst it's cage' (124). Like D'Elmont's, Melliora's love involves sexual desire. Through this pair, Haywood undermines the common courtship dynamic of male pursuit and female resistance and instead illustrates that an ideal love involves emotional and physical desire and agency in both partners.

Love in Excess marked two particular, related, and equally important successes for Haywood: the text itself became popular and flourished, and Haywood the author became well-known and recognized as a marketable writer. After *Love in Excess*, she was extremely prolific. In the 1720s, she produced, on average, a novel every three months; her rapid rate of production led her publishers to view her and her work as commercially viable investments. This high rate of production also signals that a large reading public was interested in her writing. Haywood's novels, along with 'many more like them during these years, [in which] women (in current critical parlance) write women and women's bodies' (Backsheider, *Popular* xvi), and also men's bodies, repetitively and selectively reflect and define a popular understanding of the text of the body. Although Haywood's work from this period may be viewed as repetitive in terms of her discussion about bodies and sexuality, as Backsheider argues, when a writer or genre creates several versions on a single theme, they may be seen to be 'testing solutions and, if they become popular, we know that the culture may share their active engagement' (38). Haywood's writing reflected and responded to this popular interest in bodies, while it also capitalized on the opportunities the changing marketplace allowed new writers, especially novelists, to engage with and influence a reading public. She achieved a high profile presence, became an example that women's writing could be a lucrative product, and moved into a position to interpret and produce popular tastes about sexuality, the body, gender, and social behaviours.

NOTES

1 Haywood opened a bookshop at the Sign of Fame in 1741; the store operated for approximately a year. She was also a trade publisher, a bookseller who would assemble and sell texts to preserve the anonymity of the printer or author. Haywood was arrested, but never prosecuted for seditious libel for assembling and distributing a pamphlet, *A Letter from H– G – g, Esq . . . To A Particular Friend* (1750) which contained lightly veiled criticism of George II.
2 Women were often employed in bookbinding because it entailed sewing; plus, the job paid poorly.

3 Chetwood's risk of publishing a first novel by an unknown woman writer
   paid off handsomely. Though there is controversy over exact sales and
   numbers of editions and printings, the novel clearly sold well at its debut
   and was reprinted several times throughout the century. Patrick Spedding
   accuses Chetwood of inflating the rate of sales for the book by skipping
   editions and making it look like the book was selling better than it actually
   was (88). But, in an industry where '[n]umbers counted more than prestige'
   (Raven 207), it is perhaps no surprise that Chetwood would choose to create an illusion of extremely high sales. According to Spedding, the first
   edition was issued twice, but Chetwood advertised the second issue as the
   third edition, and he referred to the second printing as the fourth edition.
   However, other critics such as Christine Blouch believe there could be eight
   or more editions. The controversy over the number of editions has led to
   a misinterpretation of how well the novel actually sold: Spedding's recent
   bibliographic work concludes that 6000 copies of the novel were printed
   'over a 23-year period' (88). While this is a very impressive number of copies, *Love in Excess* was not, along with *Robinson Crusoe*, the best-selling novel
   of 1719, as has been erroneously reported by W.H. McBurney and repeated
   by others.
4 D'Elmont's character changes through the course of the novel; however,
   the transformation from rake to reformed lover is not entirely smooth.
   For example, he is prevented from engaging in intercourse with Ciamara
   only because of Frankville's interruption, not because of his personal will.
   D'Elmont does transform, but he sometimes backslides into rakish behaviours along the way.
5 See Vila.
6 Melantha, however, does manage to both satisfy her desire and escape
   negative social consequences; she engages in intercourse with D'Elmont,
   becomes pregnant, and yet 'had the good fortune not to be suspected by
   her Husband even though she brought him a Child in seven Months after
   the Wedding' (159). Melantha's fate is representative of Haywood's contradictions that illustrate cultural anxieties surrounding the fallen woman
   figure.
7 The construct of the Man of Feeling did not fully emerge until the later
   eighteenth-century, and was not a popular cultural concept when Haywood
   wrote *Love in Excess*. However, I argue that D'Elmont represents a sexualized version of the sentimental mode of masculinity that was popularized
   by Steele's essays in the *Spectator* periodical, and his play *The Conscious
   Lovers*.

WORKS CITED

Ahern, Stephen. *Affected Sensibilities: Romantic Excess and The Genealogy of the Novel 1680–1810*. New York: AMS, 2007. Print.

Backscheider, Paula R. 'The Paradigms of Popular Culture.' *The Eighteenth-Century Novel* 6–7 (2009): 19–59. Print.

Backscheider, Paula R., and John J. Richetti. Introduction. *Popular Fiction by Women 1660–1730: An Anthology.* Ed. Paula R. Backsheider and John J. Richetti. Oxford: Clarendon, 1996.

Ballaster, Ros. *Seductive Forms: Women's Amatory Fiction from 1684 to 1740.* Oxford: Clarendon, 1992. Print.

Blouch, Christine. '"What Ann Lang Read" Eliza Haywood and Her Readers.' *The Passionate Fictions of Eliza Haywood.* Ed. Kirsten T. Saxton and Rebecca P. Bocchicchio, Lexington: Kentucky UP, 2000. 300–26. Print.

Butler, Judith. 'Bodies that Matter.' *Feminist Theory and the Body: A Reader.* Ed. Janet Price and Margrit Shildrick. New York: Routledge, 1999. 235–45. Print.

Fiske, John. *Understanding Popular Culture.* New York: Routledge, 1989. Print.

Goring, Paul. *The Rhetoric of Sensibility in Eighteenth-Century Culture.* Cambridge: Cambridge UP, 2005. Print.

Hamlin, Christopher. *A Science of Impurity.* Berkeley: U of California P, 1990. Print.

Harvey, Karen. *Reading Sex in the Eighteenth Century.* Cambridge: Cambridge UP, 2004. Print.

Haywood, Eliza. *Love in Excess* (1719). Ed. David Oakleaf. 2nd ed. Peterborough: Broadview, 2000. Print.

Ingrassia, Catherine. *Authorship, Commerce, and Gender in Early Eighteenth-Century England.* Cambridge: Cambridge UP, 1998. Print.

Jordanova, Ludmilla. *Sexual Visions: Images of Gender in Science and Medicine between the Eighteenth and Twentieth Centuries.* Madison: U of Wisconsin P, 1989. Print.

McBurney, William H. 'Mrs. Penelope Aubin and the Early Eighteenth-Century English Novel.' *The Huntington Library Quarterly* 20.3 (1957): 245–67. Web. 9 June 2010.

McDowell, Paula. 'Women and the Business of Print.' *Women and Literature in Britain, 1700–1800.* Ed. Vivien Jones. Cambridge: Cambridge UP, 2000. 135–54. Print.

Mysteries of love reveal'd: or, rules for the conduct of ladies and gentlemen in their amours. London, [1740?]. *Eighteenth Century Collections Online.* Web. 7 May 2008.

Pettit, Alexander, ed. *The Collected Works of Eliza Haywood*. London: Pickering and Chatto, 2005. Print.

Potter, Tiffany. 'A God-Like Sublimity of Passion: Eliza Haywood's Libertine Consistency.' *Eighteenth-Century Novel* 1 (2001): 95–126. Print.

– 'The Language of Feminized Sexuality: Gendered Voice in Eliza Haywood's *Love in Excess* and *Fantomina*. *Women's Writing* 10.1 (2003): 169–86. Print.

Prescott, Sarah. *Women, Authorship and Literary Culture, 1690–1740*. New York: Palgrave Macmillan, 2003. Print.

Raven, James. *The Business of Books*. New Haven: Yale UP, 2007. Print.

Spedding, Patrick. *A Bibliography of Eliza Haywood*. London: Pickering and Chatto, 2003. Print.

Stafford, Barbara. *Body Criticism: Imaging the Unseen in Enlightenment Art and Medicine*. Cambridge, MA: MIT Press, 1991. Print.

Todd, Janet. *Sensibility: An Introduction*. New York: Methuen, 1986. Print.

Van Sant, Ann Jessie. *Eighteenth-Century Sensibility and the Novel*. Cambridge: Cambridge UP, 1993. Print.

Vila, Anne C. *Enlightenment and Pathology: Sensibility in the Literature and Medicine in Eighteenth-Century France*. Baltimore: John Hopkins, 1998. Print.

9   Women Reading and Writing for *The Rambler*

PETER SABOR

On 14 March 1752, Samuel Johnson brought out the 208th and final number of his periodical *The Rambler*, which had appeared every Saturday and Tuesday since 20 March 1750. Sales had been disappointing; no more than 500 copies of each number were printed, although the total readership was considerably larger since entire numbers or substantial excerpts were regularly reprinted in other periodicals and newspapers (Johnson, *Rambler* 3:xxii). Yet Johnson remained undaunted. *Rambler* 208 begins with a defiant epigraph, attributed to Diogenes Laertius, printed in the original Greek and in English translation:

> Be gone, ye blockheads, Heraclitus cries,
> And leave my labours to the learn'd and wise:
> By wit, by knowledge, studious to be read,
> I scorn the multitude, alive and dead.   (5:315)

Heraclitus's scorn for 'the multitude' is implicitly equated with Johnson's own disdain for popular culture. The *Rambler* essays had been addressed to a discerning audience, 'the learn'd and wise'; 'blockheads' could find their pleasures elsewhere. In the essay, Johnson expands on this theme. He has never, he concedes, 'been much a favourite of the publick,' but this is a source of pride, rather than regret:

> I have seldom descended to the arts by which favour is obtained. I have
> seen the meteors of fashion rise and fall, without any attempt to add a
> moment to their duration. I have never complied with temporary curio-
> sity, nor enabled my readers to discuss the topick of the day. (5:316)

Johnson's aversion to popular culture – his determination to avoid the fashionable, the topical, the current issue – is clearly manifested here. Many of his readers, however, and especially his women readers, were alienated by this lofty indifference to the quotidian.

The Rambler, as Johnson had made clear throughout the length of its run, was not to be another *Spectator*, the daily paper published by Joseph Addison and Richard Steele in 1711–12, which aimed 'to bring Philosophy out of Closets and Libraries, Schools and Colleges, to dwell in Clubs and Assemblies, at Tea-Tables, and in Coffee-Houses' (*Spectator* 1:44). Still less was it intended to build on the success of Eliza Haywood's *Female Spectator* (1744–6), a journal written by a woman and marketed for women. Johnson's concern was not with the immediate appeal of *The Rambler*, or of his other publications, but with the judgment of posterity. As James Boswell noted, the 208 numbers were rapidly reissued in six duodecimo volumes, 'and its author lived to see ten numerous editions of it in London, beside those of Ireland and Scotland' (Boswell 1:212–13). My concern here is not with the later success of *The Rambler* and the process by which it established its place in the canon, but rather with its reception, during the years of its initial publication, by four women readers: Catherine Talbot, Elizabeth Carter, Dorothy, Lady Bradshaigh, and Hester Mulso. All four read *The Rambler* closely and also contributed essays themselves (number 10 by Mulso, 30 by Talbot, 44 and 100 by Carter, and a rejected essay, no longer extant, by Lady Bradshaigh). They all, moreover, had close ties with another major author, the novelist Samuel Richardson, whose own contribution (number 97) forms part of my discussion.[1]

As Betty Schellenberg points out, for bluestocking women such as Talbot and Carter, Johnson's failure to find a wide readership for the *Rambler* essays was a matter of profound regret. Their letters, notes Schellenberg,

> reveal their frustration at the paper's failure to successfully construct a sociable author-reader relationship. They assigned blame on both the producing and the receiving ends: on its author, who stubbornly refused to cater to the tastes of contemporary urban readers, on those readers, who refused to recognize what was good for them, and on the political and social leaders of the day, who did not step forward to endorse the labours of this author for the public good. (4)

Talbot first raised the subject of Johnson's new project in a letter to Carter of 28 April 1750, five weeks after *The Rambler* had been launched. She was planning to meet Carter shortly in Canterbury and indicated that she would bring the published numbers with her from London with the remark, 'I hope you are fond of *the Ramblers*' (*Series of Letters* 1:226). It was apparently during this meeting that the two women resolved to contribute to *The Rambler* themselves. In a letter to Carter of 28 May, Talbot, relaying comments by Johnson himself, told her friend:

> The Vision is much approved with its present preface, and will make an excellent *Rambler*, only it is wished there were something added. Being writ with the sole intention of raising depressed spirits into cheerful gratitude, wrong-headed people may draw inferences from it favorable to a life of mere amusement and good-humour; therefore now that it is intended for general use, something should be mentioned of the serious and active duties of life, and its proper restraints. (*Series of Letters* 1:229)

'The Vision,' the first of Carter's contributions to *The Rambler*, would appear a few months later, on 18 August 1750. In allegorical form, it argues for the superiority of religion, 'the offspring of Truth and Love,' over superstition, 'the child of Discontent' (3:239). This is hardly the stuff of popular culture; Carter had evidently made her essay as serious as Johnson could have desired.

Talbot, however, was aware that Johnson's own essays, which constituted the vast majority of *The Rambler*, were by no means in need of greater sobriety. In the same letter to Carter of 28 April, she remarked that

> the author of the Rambler need not be put upon writing papers of amusement, as he takes to it of himself; but he ought to be cautioned to admit the letters of his correspondents with much care and choice, and if one might say so, not to use over many hard words.

Talbot had been reading *Rambler* 20 (26 May 1750), certainly one of the lighter essays. It was, she wrote, 'a very pretty one indeed,' but with two 'hard words' in a single sentence of the concluding paragraph: 'equiponderant' and 'another so hard I cannot remember it' (*Series of Letters* 1:230).[2] Talbot hoped that Carter, whose own formidable learning Johnson respected, would steer him in the right direction, encouraging him to take a greater interest in popular culture in the manner of his great precursors, Addison and Steele:

when he writes papers of humour, there are many odd clubs, advertisements, societies, meetings, and devices of various kinds, which this
age produces; and London swarms with what would afford as amusing
subjects as any in the Spectator. The Marrying Register, the Threepenny
Club in Essex-street, a most universal nursery of low, infidel orators; the
Threepenny Masquerades, numberless follies and enormities.

But Talbot's belief that 'any hint that is known to come from you will
have great weight with the Rambler' (*Series of Letters* 1:230–1) was surely
mistaken; Johnson had no intention of writing to please, in the manner
of Addison and Steele.

While airing her views on how *The Rambler* could be made more
acceptable to popular taste, Talbot was also putting her ideas into practice. Her own contribution, like Carter's, was accepted shortly after
their Canterbury meeting in May, and published as *Rambler* 30 for 30
June 1750. It takes the form of a letter to the editor, Mr Rambler, written in the persona of 'Sunday,' a sabbath day suffering from the abuse
of its times. As Rhoda Zuk, Talbot's modern editor, observes, this is a
'didactic yet comical narration,' which 'avoids the ponderousness that
[Talbot] perceives in Johnson's own papers' (37). It was, however, to
be Talbot's only *Rambler* paper; with the single exception of Carter, no
contributor was called on twice.[3]

The Talbot-Carter campaign on behalf of *The Rambler* continued for
the rest of the year. In a letter of 4 June 1750, Carter enlisted Susanna
Highmore, another bluestocking woman and friend of Samuel
Richardson. She begins by expressing her hope that Highmore has
been pleased by the periodical: 'Something of this kind seemed greatly
wanted & I heartily wish these papers may meet with the Incourage-
ment they deserve' (Carter 138). In her reply, Highmore apparently
voiced some reservations about *The Rambler*'s lack of popular appeal,
which Carter, in a letter of 9 July, attempted to counter:

> I am every paper more & more charm'd with the Rambler. The objection
> you mention I have heard. But is it not strange that human Creatures
> designed for noble & serious Thought shd. be perpetually calling out for
> something to make them laugh. (Carter 140)

Talbot was also poring over and commenting on Johnson's undertaking.
In a letter to Carter of 28 September 1750, she writes about two recent
issues: 46 (25 August) and 51 (10 September). Both show Johnson's

lighter vein, yet, paradoxically, neither one pleased her. She was not at all impressed by the first, an account of the tedium of country life in the persona of 'Euphelia,' which she found 'far-fetched and unnatural.' The second, a comic account of the rural Lady Bustle's family, she finds more successful, but not *The Rambler* at its best:

> I think this is a paper of much humour, and there might be many more of the same sort in different ways. But what Mr. Johnson most excels in is the serious papers, that seem to flow from his heart, and from a heart amiable and delicate to a great degree. (*Series of Letters* 1:233)

Johnson, it seems, is in a classic bind. If he writes the 'serious papers' that he himself prefers, his readership will be limited to those of refined tastes, but if he tries to broaden his appeal, he will be writing counter to his strengths.

Despite such reservations, Talbot continued to hope that *The Rambler* might recreate itself as an outlet for popular culture, as well as for the moral essays at which Johnson excelled. In a letter to Carter of 20 October 1750, she mentions three recent numbers: 59 (9 October), 61 (16 October) and 62 (20 October). She finds the first of these 'a little exaggerated in the expression,' but enjoys the 'strain of humour' in the second. The third, written in the persona of 'Rhodoclia,' suggests the direction that Johnson could follow. It gives him, writes Talbot,

> an excellent opportunity to introduce humorous descriptions of, and reflections on, the London follies and diversions, of which she may be supposed to write him the sentiments of her full heart, sometimes rejoiced, sometimes mortified and disappointed. Then another should write by way of contrast, who voluntarily spends her's or his in the country, rationally enjoys it, describes its frosty prospects, land or sea, its Christmas mirth, joy, and hospitality. (*Series of Letters* 1:235)

No such papers by 'Rhodoclia' on London follies and diversion materialized, however; Johnson's aims for *The Rambler* were far from those of his admirer.

In a letter to Carter of 17 December 1750, Talbot's concern for the success of *The Rambler* took a new turn. She was now in London for the winter season and was in touch with Samuel Richardson, discussing his third novel, *Sir Charles Grandison*, as well as Johnson's enterprise, of which they were fellow admirers. She had just read *Rambler*

78 (15 December) on human mortality ('what a noble paper his last upon death'), and was more eager than ever for the periodical to attract a wider audience. It was, she suggests, crucial for Johnson to accept judiciously selected submissions from others, such as Hester Mulso, another of Richardson's female correspondents, whose *Rambler* 10 (21 April 1750) had been the first of the non-Johnsonian contributions. The printer and co-proprietor of *The Rambler*, Edward Cave, 'complains of [Johnson] for not admitting correspondents; this does mischief.' Still envisaging a periodical more akin to *The Spectator*, Talbot wondered why Johnson himself would 'not write now and then on the living manners of the times? – The stage, – the follies and fashion.' And if Johnson or another eminent author, such as Lord Chesterfield, would not do so, perhaps Carter might oblige:

> I do really now wish you would write a cheerful paper to the Rambler. Whether on Christmas merriment as laudable; and the town madness, and that of the age of continual joyless dissipation as illaudable – or on the hoops of these days, compared with those of the Tatlers, &c. and so on all sorts of caps, bonnets, aigrettes, colored capuchins, &c. &c. &c. on drums – on the improvement, and misuse of the stage, and the French *comedies larmoyantes*, – or on any thing or nothing. (*Series of Letters* 1:244, 245)

Carter responded swiftly, sending her friend, on 28 December, a 'nonsensical thing,' 'merely to shew you that I had rather make an imperfect attempt than seem to decline making any at all' (*Series of Letters* 1:246).

Carter's paper, entitled 'Modish pleasures,' would appear as *Rambler* 100 (2 March 1751). Ostensibly written for those 'buried in the country,' remote from London's fashionable diversions, it satirizes the 'manners and customs of higher life' with considerable relish (4:169, 170). Much livelier than Carter's previous contribution, it proposes a survey of contemporary leisure pursuits: 'a compleat history of forms, fashions, frolicks, of routs, drums, hurricanes, balls, assemblies, ridottos, masquerades, auctions, plays, operas, puppet-shows, and bear-gardens' (4:170). Talbot's request for a paper on the 'town madness' had been fulfilled, but Johnson, tellingly, was said by Hester Piozzi to have preferred Carter's first *Rambler* paper, although Piozzi herself favoured the second (Piozzi 76).

Talbot might also have been instrumental in persuading Richardson to contribute the paper which appeared as *Rambler* 97 (19 February 1751), 'Advice to unmarried ladies,' ten days before Carter's. Richardson's interest in *The Rambler* can be traced back to 9 August 1750, when he wrote a letter about the periodical to Cave. By this time, *The Rambler* had been running for almost five months and had reached number 41. From this letter we learn that Cave had presented Richardson with the first five numbers, that Richardson has been a regular subscriber for the rest, and that within the last few days he had found time, at last, to read up to number thirteen. He is, he tells Cave, 'inexpressibly pleased with them,' preferring Johnson's even to *The Spectator* papers, and by singing their praises he has 'procured them admirers; that is to say, readers.' Although *The Rambler* papers were published anonymously, Richardson has uncovered their authorship: 'There is but one man, I think, that could write them.' He hopes to hear from Cave that they are finding sufficient readers: 'for I would not, for any consideration, that they should be laid down through discouragement' (Richardson, *Correspondence* 1:164–6).

In his reply of 23 August, Cave confirmed that Johnson was indeed 'the *Great Rambler*,' and had been assisted, to date, in only three of the numbers. As for its circulation, 'the encouragement, as to sale,' Cave regrets, 'is not in proportion to the high character given to the work by the judicious.' Cave is unsure whether readers are deterred by the price, two pence, or by what he terms 'the unfavourable season of their first publication.' He hopes though that *The Rambler* will find more buyers when sold as a set, 'as it is a fine paper, and, considering the late hour of having the copy, tolerably printed' (Richardson, *Correspondence* 1:168–70). Cave concludes his letter to Richardson by remarking that Johnson 'thinks highly of your writings,' a compliment born out by Johnson's brief but memorable introduction to *Rambler* 97. Without mentioning Richardson by name, Mr Rambler tells his readers that they are 'indebted for this day's entertainment, to an author from whom the age has received greater favours,[4] who has enlarged the knowledge of human nature, and taught the passions to move at the command of virtue' (4:153). Inordinately susceptible to flattery, Richardson would have relished such well-turned praise. Enlarging our knowledge of human nature and demonstrating how virtue can subdue our passions were Richardson's overarching aims for his fiction; Johnson here goes to the heart of the Richardsonian enterprise.

Rambler 97 begins, in the same vein as Richardson's letter to Cave, by comparing Johnson's periodical with *The Spectator*, but with a new suggestion: that *The Rambler* should devote more space to depicting female manners. Thus, Richardson declares, 'the *Spectators* may shew to the rising generation what were the fashionable follies of their grandmothers, the *Rambler* of their mothers, and ... from both they may draw instruction and warning' (4:154). Depicting the ways of modern women was Richardson's great strength, and the essay comes to life when he portrays what he regards as an ideal courtship, leading up to the moment of the proposal:

> Her relations applaud her for her duty; friends meet; points are adjusted; delightful perturbations, and hopes, and a few lover's fears, fill up the tedious space, till an interview is granted; for the young lady had not made herself cheap at publick places. (4:156)

This is, in miniature, the story of Harriet Byron in *Sir Charles Grandison*. And like that novel, which concludes with the newlyweds Sir Charles and Harriet about to enjoy marital bliss at Grandison Hall, the *Rambler* passage concludes with the young couple at home, 'the place of their principal delight' (4:157).

Richardson's *Rambler* was also the one that caught the attention of *Sir Charles Grandison*'s great admirer, Jane Austen, who was especially struck by a passage on the proper behaviour of women during courtship. In *Northanger Abbey*, the narrator writes of Catherine Morland,

> if it be true, as a celebrated writer has maintained, that no young lady can be justified in falling in love before the gentleman's love is declared, it must be very improper that a young lady should dream of a gentleman before the gentleman is first known to have dreamt of her. (22)

Austen even provides a footnote, citing 'Mr. Richardson' in *The Rambler* as the celebrated writer in question – one of the very rare occasions on which she annotates her own fiction.

Austen was not alone in her enjoyment of *Rambler* 97. According to John Nichols, it was the only paper 'which had a prosperous sale, and may be said to have been popular' (5:39), the numbers presumably boosted by Richardson's many admirers. The statement can hardly apply to the original folio number since, as David Fleeman notes, there is no evidence that it was reprinted before the collected editions, and the printers were unlikely to have issued an especially large number of Richardson's paper (1:195). But there is firm evidence of its popularity: Roy Wiles observes that it was reprinted in at least eight English provincial newspapers, more often than any other of the *Rambler* essays (166).

Richardson's *Rambler* paper, however, was not universally admired; at least two women objected to what they saw as its antifeminist bias. One of these, intriguingly, was Elizabeth Carter, who in a letter to Talbot of 4 March 1751 displayed some vanity of her own in comparing her newly published contribution with that of Richardson. Her piece, she wrote,

> pleases me better than Mr. Richardson's Rambler. Do you like that paper? and will you be angry with me for not liking it at all? I cannot see how some of his doctrines can be founded on any other supposition than that Providence designed one half of the human species for idiots and slaves. One would think the man was, in this respect, a Mahometan. (*Series of Letters* 1:254–5)

Talbot, in her response of 16 March, defended 'the *Mahometan* Mr. Richardson' from her friend's critique:

> Fie upon you! indeed I see no harm in that poor paper, and must own myself very particularly fond of it. He does not pretend to give a scheme (not an entire scheme) of female education, only to say how when well educated they should behave, in opposition to the racketing-life of the Ranelagh-educated misses of these our days. (*Series of Letters* 1:257)

Talbot urges Carter to reread the essay 'a little candidly,' and wonders 'how you can ever imagine that the author of Clarissa has not an idea high enough of what women may be, and ought to be.' Carter gave the piece another reading and duly recanted; she had, she tells Talbot in a letter of 24 March, 'been too much prejudiced both by the opinions of those who read it before me, and from some of his own notions which I had lately seen on another subject' (*Series of Letters* 1:258). Lady Mary Wortley Montagu, always hostile to Richardson, was also critical of the essay, though perhaps without knowing the author's identity. In a letter to her daughter Lady Bute, she deplored the suggestion that modern women were less decorous than their forbears, adding that she was 'not of the Rambler's mind that the Church is the proper place to make Love in' (3:79).

In late October 1751, Johnson must have told Richardson of his plans for revising the *Rambler* papers, including his friend's contribution, for the six-volume London duodecimo edition that would be published in the following year. Richardson replied, in a letter of 2 November: 'You

are extremely obliging in what you offer, about the paper you favoured
with a place – You will do with it, what you please. The more it is
yours, the worthier it will be of a place among yours' (4:153, n1). In the
event, Johnson did make a substantial change, deleting two sentences
in which Richardson had been especially harsh about the conduct of
modern women and their suitors:

> The young fellows buzz about them as flies about a carcase, and they hear
> with greediness foolish things which they think pretty. They believe the
> men in earnest; and the men, to gratify the pride and conceit which are
> raised by such easy conquests, ridicule them for their credulity. (4:158, n.t)

What no one seemed to know at the time was that this sentence, together
with much of the essay, was first drafted by Richardson in a letter of
some four thousand words to another of his female correspondents,
Frances Grainger, written on 8 September 1750. This discovery was first
made only in 2010 by John Dussinger, who suggests that Johnson 'must
have deemed Richardson's morbid image of the coquette as a stinking
corpse attracting flies to be a bit over the top!' (99).

Richardson's Lancastrian correspondent Lady Bradshaigh, despite
living far from London at Haigh Hall, near Wigan, and having few con-
tacts in the world of letters, was also following *The Rambler*'s progress.
In a letter of March 1751, six weeks after Richardson's *Rambler* was first
published, she wrote,

> A few days ago I was pleased with hearing a very sensible lady greatly
> pleased with the Rambler, No. 97. She happened to be in town when it
> was published; and I asked if she knew who was the author? She said, it
> was supposed to be one who was concerned in the Spectators, it being
> much better written than any of the Ramblers. I wanted to say who was
> really the author, but durst not, without your permission. (*Correspondence*
> 6:108)

She did not, however, tell Richardson that in addition to admiring his
paper, she had ambitions of becoming a contributor to *The Rambler*
herself.

Among the conventions of the English periodical was that unsolicited
contributions would be at least considered, if not accepted, for publication. In the case of *The Spectator*, as Donald F. Bond observes, almost
half of the original series of 555 numbers contain letters ostensibly

from outside contributors, although some of these were written by the editors. In 1725, moreover, a two-volume collection of unused letters designed for *The Tatler* and *The Spectator* was published, and yet more rejected offerings survive in manuscript today (*Spectator* 1:xxxvi–xliii). Given the strength of the tradition, it is not surprising that the publishers of *The Rambler* repeatedly placed newspaper advertisements asking for communications to be sent to them, to be forwarded to the author. Yet in practice, no such offers were accepted; all of the published contributions to *The Rambler* were by friends and acquaintances of Johnson, who needed no newspaper promptings. Some readers did respond to the advertisements, as Johnson acknowledges in *Rambler* 10. Most of this number is taken up by four letters written by Hester Mulso, with some Johnsonian prefatory remarks. His correspondents, he declares, are increasing in number daily, which he takes as a 'proof of eminence.' 'The only pain,' he continues, 'which I can feel from my correspondence, is the fear of disgusting those, whose letters I shall neglect.' 'Not all letters,' Johnson adds, 'which are postponed are rejected, nor all that are rejected, critically condemned' (3:51).[5]

At some point before *The Rambler* ceased publication in March 1752, and probably after reading Richardson's essay in February 1751, Lady Bradshaigh joined the ranks of the would-be contributors. The first mention of her piece in her extant correspondence with Richardson occurs in a letter of 25 September 1753:

> The author of the Rambler I believe did justice to the publick, in *not* Inserting the letter I sent you. but the subject is worthy of his pen. I wish I had given it you sooner. you might perhaps have prevail'd with good Sir Charles to have said something to the hints given. (Bradshaigh f. 42)

This letter clearly takes up a thread begun in earlier, missing correspondence. Lady Bradshaigh must have sent her composition to Richardson, who commended it in his reply. Lady Bradshaigh is now modestly deprecating her rejected contribution, while regretting that she had not sent it to Richardson in time for him to draw on it in *Sir Charles Grandison*.

Richardson's reply tells us as much about Lady Bradshaigh's composition as we are ever likely to know, unless the manuscript itself should come to light. After wondering why Johnson 'did not choose it for a Subject,' Richardson writes, in a letter of 5 October 1753: 'There are two or three Places, in Sir Charles's Conversations, that I could have introduced the Subject, to the Advantage of the particular Conversation.'

Such assistance from 'the Authoress of Determinta' would have been valuable, but it is now too late: 'The unprinted Part of my Story, hurries on the Catastrophe, the strange, perhaps, unnatural Catastrophe, too much, to admit of so cool and instructive a Conversation as is proper to bring in such a Subject' (*Selected Letters* 244). It seems that Lady Bradshaigh's lost offering was written in the persona of Determinta, presumably a determined woman, and that it contained what Richardson regarded as a 'cool and instructive' conversation, unsuited to the dramatic conclusion of *Grandison* that he was then writing.

Another revelation in this letter is that Richardson had recently received a visit from Johnson and read Lady Bradshaigh's contribution to him:

> I ... expressed my Wonder that he had not made a Paper of it, as I thought it would have been a very good one. He remembered it not; and spoke handsomely of it. He made it, he said, pretty much a Rule with him to write his own Papers. He is of Opinion, that most of those directed to the Spectators as Papers of others, were written by the Authors themselves. (*Selected Letters* 247)

Not surprisingly, Lady Bradshaigh found little consolation in Johnson's belated commendation. She would, she claimed in a letter of 27 November 1753, 'have been frighten'd to have seen my self in *print*, tho' with a Veil on,' but she questions why Johnson took the pain 'to let his readers know, where letters to the Rambler were taken in, if he was determin'd not to give anything to the publick but his own?' Of the non-Johnsonian *Ramblers* that were published, she declares, '*one* indeed plainly speaks its author, and towers above the rest.' As for herself, 'do not you think Sir, I am a little piqu'd? I protest I am *not*, that he did not publish the letter, but I am sorry he did not touch upon the *subject*. I think I can scarcely forgive him' (Bradshaigh f. 42). Although Richardson loved to disagree with Lady Bradshaigh, his reply of 8 December supports her position: 'the Author of the Rambler should not have advertised, Where Letters for him should be taken in, if he designed to be so little obliged to Correspondents' (*Selected Letters* 242).

Lady Bradshaigh mentions her abortive essay to Richardson on only one other occasion in their extant correspondence, dismissing it tersely on 25 May 1754 as 'the letter I was so foolish to send to the Rambler' (Bradshaigh f. 98). It is possible though that Richardson's claim that it would have made a 'very good' *Rambler* and Johnson's eventual approval were not merely polite compliments. An extant letter that Lady Bradshaigh wrote for a projected additional volume of *Sir Charles Grandison* shows that she could create lively fictive dialogue with witty turns of phrase.[6] The last 101 numbers of *The Rambler*, from 108 to 208, were written exclusively by Johnson; perhaps room should have been made for Lady Bradshaigh's tantalizing, lost 'Determinta.'

Although Johnson was unwilling to accept any contributions to *The Rambler* in its latter stages, Talbot and Carter remained faithful readers. In a letter of 3 June 1751, Talbot remarks that 'the Rambler is grown very agreeable this summer,' and contrasts it with a daily paper, *The London Advertiser and Literary Gazette*, which had begun publication on 4 March. Talbot cannot commend the paper 'on the whole,' but notes that it 'takes up every one of those subjects that we wished the Rambler to mention. The bakers' club, the public diversions – every thing that relates to the present times and daily occurrences. Some few of the papers lately have been very pretty' (*Series of Letters* 1:268). The past tense here, 'we wished,' is significant; Talbot has by now given up her hope that *The Rambler* would deal with various aspects of popular culture. In a letter to Carter of 14 March 1752, the day on which the final *Rambler* appeared, she discusses *Sir Charles Grandison*, Henry Fielding's *Amelia*, and Charlotte Lennox's *The Female Quixote*, without giving Johnson's periodical a single mention (*Series of Letters* 1:293–4).

This omission led to a final flurry of correspondence between Carter and Talbot on *The Rambler*. In a letter of 30 March 1752, Carter wrote with mock-seriousness:

> I was outrageous at your not uttering a sigh of lamentation over the departure of the Rambler, nor once mention his farewel paper. For some minutes it put me a good deal out of humour with the world, and more particularly with the great and powerful part of it ... it seems mighty absurd that those who govern states and call themselves politicians, should not eagerly decree laurels, and statues, and public support to a genius who contributes all in his power to make them the rulers of reasonable creatures. (*Series of Letters* 1:296)

Talbot concurs, writing to Carter on 22 April: 'Indeed, 'tis a sad thing that such a paper should have met with discouragement from wise, and learned, and good people too – Many are the disputes it has cost me, and not once did I come off triumphant' (*Series of Letters* 1:297). Carter takes up the refrain of an ungrateful world in a letter to Susanna

Highmore of 28 April (Carter 142), and again in a letter to Talbot of 9 May, in which she deplores the 'death of the Rambler' at the hands of 'such formidable enemies' (*Series of Letters* 1:299).

In condemning those who had failed to give *The Rambler* its due, both Talbot and Carter seem to have forgotten their own earlier attempts to steer Johnson's work in a different, more populist direction. It should also be noted that several of *The Rambler*'s 'formidable enemies' were Talbot's and Carter's personal friends. William Duncombe, for instance, remarked in a letter to Carter that the *Rambler* was a 'very rational performance, but . . . wants more sprinklings of humour to make it popular' (Clifford 80). The Marchioness Grey, in a letter to Talbot of 21 June 1750, expressed her dissatisfaction at length:

> I see nothing new or clever in his essays, and the stories and characters he attempts are seldom well hit off or resembling common life: besides that every paper is full of so many hard words as really break my teeth to speak them. I can't say I shall have a much higher opinion of it even though it should be grown fashionable; but I can't readily imagine neither what should make it so, except its being now and then a little unintelligible. (Clifford 80)

More damaging than these waspish remarks is a sustained attack on *The Rambler* by a professed admirer and contributor, Hester Mulso, in a letter to Carter of 11 October 1752. Part of Mulso's critique concerns Johnson's 'too general censures of mankind' and his 'speaking of envy and malice as universal passions' (Mulso 61–2). But the last part of her long letter is more relevant to the concerns of the present collection:

> I have another quarrel with the Rambler, which is for the contemptuous manner in which he generally speaks of women, for neglecting to address his precepts and cautions to them, and for drawing so many bad and ridiculous female characters, and hardly one good one. I believe he would have found us more docile disciples than the men, less prepossessed by vicious habits and passions, and more easily attracted by the claims of virtue and truth. (Mulso 64)

Several recent critics, including James Basker, Annette Caferelli, Isobel Grundy, and Sarah Morrison, have written persuasively on Johnson's sympathetic interest in women. But Mulso's charge cannot be dismissed; she was not one of Johnson's 'blockheads,' and her profound dissatisfaction with *The Rambler* strikes an important counterbalance with Carter's and Talbot's unswerving support. Their claims that *The Rambler* suffered at the hands of the 'great and powerful' make it seem as though a conspiracy were at work to undermine the periodical's success. But Johnson's true adversaries were those, especially women, who felt themselves excluded from *The Rambler*, either because of its style or subject matter, and who expressed their dissatisfaction simply by not subscribing. Addison could boast of daily sales of 3,000 copies of *The Spectator* only two weeks after its first publication (*Spectator* 1:44). Johnson, in contrast, indifferent to the 'meteors of fashion,' wrote for those with 'leisure for abstracted truth, and whom virtue could please by its naked dignity' (5:316). The combined efforts of Catherine Talbot, Elizabeth Carter, Lady Bradshaigh, Hester Mulso, and Samuel Richardson could not persuade him to write in any other way.

NOTES

1 Parts of two other *Rambler* numbers were also written by others: 15 by David Garrick and 107 by Joseph Simpson. See Johnson, *Rambler* 3:xxi, n1.
2 The word that Talbot cannot remember must be 'adscititious,' which Johnson defines in his *Dictionary* as 'that which is taken in to complete something else, though originally extrinsick.'
3 Anthony W. Lee suggests that Johnson's allowing Carter two essays 'indexes his healthy endorsement of her equal footing as writer and intellectual' (205).
4 The 'greater favours' are the four volumes of *Pamela* (1740–1) and the seven of *Clarissa* (1747–8); *Sir Charles Grandison* (1753–4) was still in progress.
5 Steven Lynn contends that by including Mulso's letters in this number, 'Johnson shapes our perception of the desire for *The Rambler* to be more like *The Spectator*. Most obviously, the allusive struggle with his precursor is now brought into the open by these correspondents' (43).
6 See Eaves and Kimpel 412–13. Lady Bradshaigh's letter, written in the character of Lady G., is in the Forster Collection 11, ff. 116–19.

WORKS CITED

Austen, Jane. *Northanger Abbey*. 1817. Ed. Barbara Benedict and Deirdre Le Faye. The Cambridge Edition of the Works of Jane Austen. Cambridge: Cambridge UP, 2006. Print.

Basker, James G. 'Dancing Dogs, Women Preachers and the Myth of Johnson's Misogyny.' *Age of Johnson* 3 (1990): 63–90. Print.

Boswell, James. *Boswell's Life of Johnson.* 1791. Ed. George Birkbeck Hill. Rev. L.F. Powell. 6 vols. Oxford: Clarendon, 1934–50. Print.

Bradshaigh, Dorothy, Lady. MS correspondence. Forster Collection 11. Victoria and Albert Museum Lib., London.

Caferelli, Annette Wheeler. 'Johnson and Literary Women: Demasculinizing Literary History.' *Age of Johnson* 5 (1992): 61–114. Print.

Carter, Elizabeth. *Elizabeth Carter, 1717–1806: An Edition of Some Unpublished Letters.* Ed. Gwen Hampshire. Newark: U of Delaware P, 2005. Print.

Clifford, James L. *Dictionary Johnson: Samuel Johnson's Middle Years.* New York: McGraw-Hill, 1979. Print.

Dussinger, John. 'Samuel Richardson's Manuscript Draft of *The Rambler* No. 97 (19 February 1751).' *Notes and Queries* 57.1 (2010): 93–9. Print.

Eaves, T.C. Duncan, and Ben D. Kimpel. *Samuel Richardson: A Biography.* Oxford: Clarendon, 1971. Print.

Fleeman, J.D. *A Bibliography of the Works of Samuel Johnson.* 2 vols. Oxford: Clarendon, 2000. Print.

Grundy, Isobel. 'Samuel Johnson as Patron of Women.' *Age of Johnson* 1 (1987): 59–77. Print.

Johnson, Samuel. *A Dictionary of the English Language.* London, 1755. Print.

– *The Rambler.* 1750–2. Ed. Walter Jackson Bate. The Yale Edition of the Works of Samuel Johnson. Vols 3–5. New Haven: Yale UP, 1969. Print.

Lee, Anthony W. 'Who's Mentoring Whom? Mentorship, Alliance, and Rivalry in the Carter-Johnson Relationship.' *Mentoring in Eighteenth-Century British Literature and Culture.* Ed. Anthony W. Lee. Burlington, VT: Ashgate, 2010. 191–210. Print.

Lynn, Steven. *Samuel Johnson after Deconstruction: Rhetoric and* The Rambler. Carbondale: Southern Illinois UP, 1992. Print.

Montagu, Lady Mary Wortley. *The Complete Letters of Lady Mary Wortley Montagu.* Ed. Robert Halsband. 3 vols. Oxford: Clarendon, 1967. Print.

Morrison, Sarah R. 'Samuel Johnson, Mr. Rambler, and Women.' *Age of Johnson* 14 (2003): 23–50. Print.

Mulso, Hester. *The Posthumous Works of Mrs. Chapone.* 2 vols. London, 1807. Print.

Nichols, John. *Literary Anecdotes of the Eighteenth Century.* 9 vols. London, 1812–15. Print.

Piozzi, Hester Lynch. *Anecdotes of the Late Samuel Johnson, LL.D. during the Last Twenty Years of His Life. Memoirs and Anecdotes of Dr. Johnson.* By William Shaw and Hester Lynch Piozzi. Ed. Arthur Sherbo. London: Oxford UP, 1974. Print.

Richardson, Samuel. *Correspondence of Samuel Richardson.* Ed. Anna Laetitia
  Barbauld. 6 vols. London, 1804. Print.
– *Selected Letters of Samuel Richardson.* Ed. John Carroll. Oxford: Clarendon,
  1964. Print.
Schellenberg, Betty. 'Manuscript Culture and Women as Patrons of Samuel
  Johnson.' Johnson and Gender. Johnson at 300. Houghton Library,
  Cambridge, MA. 27 Aug. 2009. Address.
A Series of Letters between Mrs. Elizabeth Carter and Miss Catherine Talbot. Ed.
  Montagu Pennington. 2 vols. London, 1808. Print.
The Spectator. 1711–12. Ed. Donald F. Bond. 5 vols. Oxford: Clarendon,
  1965. Print.
Wiles, Roy McKeen. 'The Contemporary Distribution of Johnson's *Rambler.*'
  Eighteenth-Century Studies 2 (1968): 155–71. Print.
Zuk, Rhoda, ed. *Catherine Talbot and Hester Chapone. Bluestocking Feminism:*
  Writings of the Bluestocking Circle, 1738–1785. Vol. 3. London: Pickering &
  Chatto, 1999. Print.

10 'The Most Dangerous Talent': Riddles as Feminine Pastime

MARY CHADWICK

These unnatural stories have the worst possible effects on your minds. The imagination that can produce such things must be extremely gross and barbarous; they mark the Gothicism of the rudest ages, and not only divert your study and attention from real life but embarrass your affections with fictions and ideas not only of no use, but seriously pernicious, as they inflame the passions and tincture both the fancy and the heart with extravagance and romance.

Tell Tale, *The Lady's Monthly Museum* (392)

This opinion, pronounced by a 1798 caricature of a patriarch, will be as easily recognized as an example of anti-novel rhetoric by those who study the literature of the eighteenth century today, as it would have been by those who read such 'pernicious' tales when they first appeared. The next target for his ire, however, might be somewhat less familiar to modern-day readers. His daughter begs forgiveness and, aiming to make amends, shows her father other books: 'As you often say, we must have amusement and cultivate an habit of reading, here are great variety. The contents show we have many nice verses, charades, riddles, enigmas, &c. and these do puzzle us so charmingly' (392). Her ploy fails, and her father informs her that

such reading ... cherishes prying, inquisitive dispositions, which give young minds such a bias to intrigue, as they seldom or never lose ... The whole class of these mystical conceits is ... beneath the attention of a rational, not to say a cultivated, mind. And it really hurts me, after all my pains and expence, that your taste should be still so groveling and vulgar ... For what, then, are they calculated, but merely to excite and strengthen the silly and vicious curiosity of the idle and impertinent? (392–3)

In the late eighteenth and early nineteenth centuries, a fashion for the pastimes of collecting, solving, and composing riddles and enigmas gripped British readers. Word games filled spaces in the pages of newspapers, magazines, and almanacs; enigmas written by such distinguished authors as Hannah More and William Cowper were published in collections of poetry; and a plethora of riddle books appeared. Here, I examine some of the reasons for such a wholehearted condemnation of these works and investigate the ways in which the gap between what was popularly practised and what was preached in Britain at this time was negotiated by those who produced and enjoyed 'these mystical conceits.'

Critics and historians alike have noted the 'strong desire' of eighteenth-century Britons 'to classify and categorise, to affirm clear boundaries: it is the age of the rise of scientific taxonomies and the growth of dictionaries and encyclopedias' (Pearson 9). 'The cardinal ideological distinctions underlying eighteenth-century cultural life' highlighting the 'organizing dialectical schema of eighteenth-century life' (Castle 6) indicate an attachment to binary oppositions, the starkest of classifications, permitting the creation of 'a fiction of the present that allowed [people] to organise the world into binary social, economic, and literary relations' (Ingrassia 7). Hester Thrale compiled her *British Synonymy; or, An Attempt at Regulating the Choice of Words in Familiar Conversation* (1794) with the aim of assisting 'foreigners' because 'as words form the medium of knowledge, so it often happens that they create the mists of error too' (vi–vii). Through their embodiment of contradictions, dualities, and linguistic slippages, it is exactly these boundaries, distinctions, and classifications which riddles disrupt. Elli Köngäs-Maranda writes that 'riddles make a point of playing with conceptual borderlines and crossing them for the intellectual pleasure of showing that things are not quite as stable as they appear' (53). The ways in which riddles and conundrums were presented, read, adapted, and appropriated in eighteenth-century British society blur an array of boundaries. The divisions between polite and popular culture, between private and public reading practices, and between literary genres are all breached by these word games.[1]

Debates surrounding what should, or should not, be considered popular culture and the interaction between the popular and the polite

seem almost as well rehearsed as those focusing on the suitability of
the novel for young women. Given their characteristics, outlined above,
riddles appear to be an ideal medium through which to address the
'contradictory, divided' dynamic(s) of the 'pluralist approach to culture' adopted by those who follow in the wake of Peter Burke and
Tim Harris (Mullan and Reid 3). With reference to the categorizations
mentioned above, this chapter will consider briefly the ways in which
published riddle collections such as *The Aenigmatical Repository; or, New
Fund of Amusement for Young Ladies and Gentlemen* (1772) by one Charles
Crinkum and the anonymously compiled *A New Collection of Enigmas,
Charades, Transpositions, &c.* (1791) fit into these debates before moving
on to a discussion of the literary and social culture in which these riddles
were devised. I argue that riddle collections, being slightly above the
popular, in eighteenth-century terms, form instead part of a 'common'
culture. Using Samuel Johnson's definitions of common as 'belonging
equally to more than one . . . often seen; easy to be had; of little value;
not rare; not scarce . . . Publick; general; serving the use of all,' I suggest
that riddles, in particular those found in the *New Collection*, form part
of a range of 'serial entertainments' (Warner 4), aimed at women of the
middling ranks, which reflect and interact with the conduct literature
which, with varying levels of didacticism, appeared in periodicals and
books throughout the eighteenth century.

Eleanor Cook identifies the significance of 'the distinction between
folk riddles and literary riddles' (114–15). Folk riddles are associated
with the oral transmission of 'traditional material' to a number of 'rid-
dlees' in a public setting. 'The archetypal riddling situation' for literary examples, on the other hand, takes place 'in private, where the
individual reader contends with riddles transmitted in writing' by an
author or a 'conscious literary artist' (Pagis 83). As Dan Pagis points
out, these binaries are by no means unassailable: 'folk riddles have
been handed down from generation to generation in books written
for the entertainment of individuals and families' and in the case of
literary riddles 'the public riddling situation was quite popular' (83).
The social nature of riddling in the eighteenth century provided a
source of censure for women who indulged in the pastime, as I discuss below. Following Alastair Fowler's work on the development of
literary genres, Cook labels folk riddles 'primary' examples and literary riddles 'secondary' with the adjunct that the terms 'have to do with
the continuous historical development of a genre, with no implication
of superiority in either kind' (115). This egalitarian approach was not

taken by eighteenth-century readers who were, as John Mullan and Christopher Reid show, very well able to comprehend a 'division of culture into polarities of high and low,' with regard to the literature which surrounded them, even as, or perhaps because, they were aware that the boundaries 'between the popular and the polite were nego-tiable and, therefore, constantly being redrawn' (17). The terms given by Tell Tale, the pseudonym adopted by the *Lady's Monthly Museum's* riddling correspondent, to the father she depicts, indicate that riddles were not considered 'high' culture but 'groveling and vulgar.' The prefaces to riddle collections show that authors were well aware of the way in which their work was viewed by arbiters of literary taste. Crinkum is typical in apologising for the 'futile' nature of the 'squibs of imagination' contained within the *Repository* while the compiler of the *New Collection* describes her volumes as 'puerile.' Like the novelists who 'strove to assert the value of their own writing by condemning the genre' (Tadmor 165) these editors employ a mask of self-deprecation in the knowledge that however 'low' their genre, their collections would be enthusiastically received by their audience.

The primary and secondary classifications into which today's folklor-ists organize riddles are the inversion of those of the eighteenth century. Isaac Watts condemned 'the conundrums of nurses' as a poor educa-tion for children in his 1795 *The Improvement of the Mind* (102). Crinkum draws a distinction between the 'quibbles' of the 'vulgar' and 'the aenig-matical contrivances' of 'the nobility' (vi). Just as these authors stress the classical and biblical precedents of riddling, the literary puzzles of 'those whose names are most conspicuous in the annals of literary fame' yet who 'have not deemed these bagatelles beneath their notice' are invoked as a means of legitimizing their work (*New Collection* pref-ace).[2] Similarly, editors go to great lengths to reassure their readers that their collections are 'totally free from everything which has an inde-cent, or an immoral tendency' (Crinkum 2). In terms of content, writers looked to all (innocent) quarters – literature, both ancient and modern, livelihoods, composers, everyday objects and virtues were all consid-ered fair game. As an article in the *Monthly Miscellany* observes, 'not a great man ... not fruit, fish, nor flower, [exists] but have been enig-matized' (171). Crinkum is not alone in expecting his readers to pos-sess a degree of awareness of the classics, Shakespeare's work, and the political figures of the time in order to solve his puzzles. This assump-tion about the general knowledge of those who purchased or other-wise acquired his work indicates, to an extent, their social standing and level of education. As Pagis states, the author of the literary riddle takes 'the cultural milieu' of his or her audience as a guide to both the clues and solution of their work (94). Samuel Richardson took themes which 'must have seemed decidedly low' (Mullan and Reid 5) to the polite audience who devoured the comparatively respectable 'didactic novels' *Pamela* (1740) and *Clarissa* (1748) in which they were explored. Conversely, those who chose to meet publishers' demands for riddle collections took care to include only respectable content in work which bridged the blurred line between the popular and the polite.

The most usual consumers for riddle collections were 'the middling social groups' who encompassed a wide range of educational and financial statuses and, like the books they read, 'straddled the world of the elites and the common people.' The 'infinite gradations' (Ingram 95) of both class and literary hierarchies in eighteenth-century Britain are illustrated through a comparison of the different ways in which two households known to have read Crinkum's work approached his puzzles. A family living in Denbighshire, in North Wales, was so well amused by his series of culinary riddles, divided into first, second, and third courses, followed by desserts and liqueurs, that they wrote their own imitative version.[3] In the copy of the *Repository* owned by a clergyman from Yorkshire, however, these puzzles are neglected in favour of those relating to plays, trades and professions, authors, composers, and historians.[4] The answers to these less frivolous riddles have been entered under each rhyming couplet – in pencil rather than ink.[5]

That eighteenth-century Britons, like today's literary historians, made assumptions about character based on the ways in which people used their time is the premise of Sarah Jordan's study *The Anxieties of Idleness*. In relation to female idleness, as the number of leisure hours enjoyed by their wives and daughters came to be seen as a signifier of the status of husbands and fathers, there developed a body of advice literature informing women of the best ways to fill their days. Jordan identifies the apparent contradiction at the heart of this trend. The opportunities to fill their hours constructively were diminished and yet, simultaneously, women were beset by authors of literature guiding and commenting on their conduct who would 'repeatedly proclaim the evils of idleness' (91). Within this paradox, Jordan characterizes woman as 'a cipher ... she was a puzzle, a message in code ... Her meaning had to be deciphered [by] observing how she used her time' (84). The remainder of this chapter situates riddles and riddling within the discourses surrounding the ways in which women who did not work were advised to spend their time.

My starting point is Jane Austen's *Emma* (1816), one of the most well-known literary representations of these activities. Austen depicts her eponymous heroine concocting, solving, and mis-solving puzzles in both the literature she reads and the lives of those who surround her. The ambiguous depiction of the benefits and the evils of 'enigmatizing' are aligned with Austen's well-documented equivocal view of conduct literature. I move beyond these two well-known contexts in order to examine enigmas found within the female-edited *New Collection*, with which Austen may have been familiar (Doody 362), and the writings of contemporary commentators published in periodicals such as *The Lady's Monthly Museum* and *The Female Spectator*. These examples make up part of that body of literature which exhibited varying degrees of didacticism, directness, humour, and wit as it aimed to form and inform ideal eighteenth-century women. For riddles to be soluble they must reflect 'the language of the speakers or their perception of empirical reality and their conception of their social and cultural experience. Both language and reality serve as a pool of terms, objects, actions, ideas, and personalities upon which the riddle solver draws' (Ben-Amos 252). Riddles, like the texts to which they related and the women who perused them, 'read and were read by' the culture in which they operated (Cook 119). These texts reflected and contributed to a 'common' culture which eighteenth-century British women of the social ranks from the newly idle tradesmen's and farmers' daughters and upwards were aware of but not bound by.

John Gregory's *A Father's Legacy to his Daughters* (1774) provides the quotation used in the title of this essay. Gregory warns his readers that 'Wit is the most dangerous talent you can possess. It must be guarded with great discretion and good nature, otherwise it will create you many enemies. Wit is perfectly consistent with softness and delicacy; yet they are seldom found united' (30). The ideal or 'normative Woman,' to adopt Peter Stallybrass's phrase, formed by works such as Gregory's, appears to be the antithesis of a woman of fashion, a being frequently linked, as I show below, to the female riddler. As Jordan points out, ladies of propriety 'were to be passive, not active ... Any sort of self-assertion ... must be sternly excised from a lady's character' (88–9, 95). She should have no desire 'to enter the public realm and be seen there' (95–6). Wit, self-assertion, and a desire for display are all essential to riddling and enigmatizing. Wit unequivocally demands an audience while the very fact that riddles are 'answered' suggests self-assertion and an unfeminine lack of that 'air of deference and doubt' prescribed by Francois Fenelon's *Treatise on the Education of Daughters* (185). 'Clever words' lead Emma Woodhouse to 'discover that her wit is her most dangerous talent: when used with indiscretion . . . it leads her astray' (Byrne 298). It is the incident in which Emma is rude to Miss Bates and draws the reproaches of Mr Knightley, however, that provides the catalyst for her discovery of her true feelings for him and ultimately leads to her marriage, thereby undermining Gregory's advice. Well versed in the advice propounded by the authors of conduct literature that aimed, in theory at least, to create an ideal eighteenth-century woman, Austen and authors such as the compiler of the *New Collection* illustrate and bridge the gap between what was practised and what was preached in late eighteenth-century society.

The extent to which *Emma* illustrates Austen's approval for enigmatic activities has divided critics. Cecily Devereux argues that Emma must abandon her games and her jokes in order to achieve her happy ending in 'her conversion from Miss Woodhouse to Mrs Knightley' (53–4). Joseph Litvak suggests that it is, in fact, Emma's 'little novels of error' to which Mr Knightley is attracted and that he is in no hurry for her to attain the 'perfection' which he appears to desire (771). Austen's attitude toward conduct literature is similarly indistinct. Only the unattractive characters of Mr Collins and 'the pedantic, ignorant Mary' (Pearson 48, Byrne 298) in *Pride and Prejudice* (1813) favour James Fordyce's *Sermons to Young Women* (1766) but Austen appears to have approved of Thomas Gisborne's *An Enquiry into the Duties of the Female Sex* (1797) (Stabler 43). Representations of the efficacy of conduct literature in *Emma* are entwined with depictions of characters enjoying or rejecting enigmas and conundrums. The 'insufferable' and 'common' Mrs Elton displays her knowledge of, and superficial adherence to, the advice of Gisborne and Gregory through her repeated claims to possess the 'inner "resources"' which are prescribed as prevention against both boredom and the temptation to enter the 'public realm' which proceeded from it. 'I honestly said that *the world* I could give up – parties, balls, plays . . . Blessed with so many resources within myself, the world was not necessary to *me*,' Mrs Elton informs Emma upon their first meeting. 'To those who had no resources it was a different thing; but my resources made me quite independent' (221). When an injured horse throws a projected outing 'into sad uncertainty' Austen's comment that 'Mrs Elton's resources were inadequate to such an attack' bitingly undermines both her character and the effectiveness of the literature that aimed to form it (278). Austen's strongest championing of riddles and riddling occurs when the despised Mrs Elton rejects such word games. When puzzles become the order of the day at the Box Hill picnic, Mrs Elton declares them 'all very well at Christmas, when one is sitting round the fire; but quite out of place, in my opinion, when one is exploring about the country in summer ... I do not pretend to be a wit ... [I] have nothing clever to say' (293).

The riddling set pieces in *Emma* – the picnic, for example, and the games played in the Bates's sitting room – take place in mixed company. For conduct book authors such as Hannah More and, therefore, for Mrs Elton, a woman who displayed her wit among mixed company, or even the accomplishments she was urged to acquire, was tantamount to being an actress (Jordan 98). A chasm between the strictures of these authors and the daily activities of eighteenth-century Britons is illustrated by the fact that the majority of riddle collections appear to have been written with the intention of appealing to both sexes even if, as the *New Collection* illustrates, editors were aware that their audiences were more likely to be feminine than masculine. Crinkum offers his *Repository* as a 'New Fund of Amusement for Young Ladies and Gentlemen,' and both Peter Puzzlewell's *Choice Collection of Riddles, Charades, Rebusses, &c.* (1792) and *Hooper's New Puzzle Cap* (1799) include illustrations of 'well-dressed men and women gathered' to enjoy an evening's entertainment (Cook 237). Both men and women compiled and published riddle books, wrote to periodicals requesting solutions to rebuses or offering new conundrums, published poetical enigmas in collections of poetry, and engaged in riddling to while away idle hours.

It was not only young women who were warned to beware of wasting their time on conundrums. Captain Jenkin Jones advises young boys that

> *False-wit*'s an ill-bred, stumbling, stupid dolt,
> *True-wit* a vig'rous, fleet, full blooded colt,
> And would you mount him, shun those spurious jades
> *Conundrums, Quibbles, Riddles,* and *Charades.*   (9–10)

The fact that women, more than men, enjoyed increasing amounts of leisure time, however, ensured that riddle collections and a great deal, although not all, of the disapprobation reserved for them were targeted at 'the ladies.' The editor of a 1775 issue of the *Female Spectator* suggests that men engage in riddling only in order to curry favour with their female acquaintances. In a call for women to recognize the influence that they might exert over their admirers by obliging them 'to become rational creatures before accepting their addresses,' the editor rues the fact that 'while puppet-shews and conundrums take up their attention, no such thing is to be expected. While the women continue to be attached to trifles, the men will also continue to encourage them in the hope of pleasing' (305–6). This is certainly true of Mr Elton, who composes conundrums with Emma and Harriet only until it no longer serves his purpose in pursuing Emma. Once married, he joins his wife in dismissing such pursuits.

Those writers who comment upon the behaviour of women use a diverse range of media, and riddles function in a number of frequently contradictory ways within their work. The *Female Spectator* employs a critique of conundrums in order to advise readers on their actions. In *Emma*, Austen uses a not unfavourable portrayal of riddles to interrogate and undermine the conduct literature that created the 'pictures of perfection' she railed against (Pearson 48). The 'cultural literacy' (Mullan and Reid 15) that women would have acquired from their reading is further illustrated by the enigmas selected by the compiler of the *New Collection*, which blur the boundaries between riddle books and conduct advice. There can be little doubt that the editor knew her audience would be predominantly female. Although her introductory remarks are carefully crafted to apply to both men and women, many of her puzzles are addressed to a female audience. An enigma to which the solution is 'The Devil' for example, interrogates the ladies thus:

> Long before Adam, one there lived,
> And liveth still, as is believed,
> Whose name reversed here you'll see,
> Ladies, pray say, who this may be.   (2:7)

Another enigma is addressed to young women, warning them of one of life's potential sadnesses:

> Young ladies now give ear, I pray,
> To one the most forlorn;
> For share my hapless fate you may,
> And grieve that you were born.

Your lovely image I've display'd,
Possesst of life and breath,
I'm flesh and blood, tho' always made
By the rude hand of death.   (A Widow) (1:3)

Several of the puzzles in the collection reflect the themes and tropes of conduct literature written by authors such as Gregory and Gisborne. Cards and gambling, for example, were a great cause for concern among the writers of conduct books and a target for satire among eighteenth-century authors of a less earnest bent. One Copernicus Courtly puts forward a proposal for a new almanac devoted solely to the needs of 'People of Fashion' who are ill-served by publications which 'direct the vulgar tradesman and mechanic when to open shop' (591). Having established his satirical position by opining that 'riddles ... happily serve to improve the minds of the two sexes, by taking them off from trifling subjects, and fixing their attention upon matters of the last importance,' Courtly goes on to observe that far from attending church regularly, 'people of quality ... know no use of Sunday, but as it serves to call them to the card-table' (591). In her poetical introduction to Crinkum's 1772 *Key* to his *Repository*, Philo Astrea argues that the fruits of 'Crinkum's genius' tread a happy line between 'men of letters' who 'With sines and tangents rack their busy heads, / And Newton-like forget the use of beds' and 'those who waste the midnight oil / In solving problems which they find in Hoyle' (Preface).[6] The editor of the *New Collection* offers her work as an 'innocent' way of passing time 'that might otherwise be sacrificed to cards, which generally excite baneful passions, or devoted to the hateful purposes of detraction and calumny' (vi). These sentiments are echoed by an enigma, once again addressed to a female audience, to which the solution is 'A Pack of Cards':

With prudence us'd, the world may bless my pow'r;
Spleen I prevent, and gild the social hour:
But when my votaries, without this care,
With me engage, retire, ye gentle fair;
Mild joys give place to rage and fell despair.   (1:60)

The enigmatist suggests that card-playing might bring some benefits. Like novels and riddles, which 'kept women from worse pastimes,' cards might prevent boredom and the resulting irritable sniping or malicious conversation (Pearson 84). Without due care, however, a near-innocent pastime is heavy with the potential for those 'baneful passions' and the fear provoked by heavy financial or personal losses. Georgiana, duchess of Devonshire, is a high profile example, in both contemporary and modern-day terms, of just how true this could be. In her biography of the duchess, Amanda Foreman states that 'gaming was to the aristocracy what gin was to the working classes' and notes that Georgiana, unable to refrain from gambling, ran up debts of £3,000, equivalent to £180,000 today, before her second wedding anniversary (36, 126, 42).

Throughout her collection, the editor uses widely known stereotypical examples of womanhood, positive as well as negative, to aid her readers in solving her enigmas. She does not draw explicitly upon the characterization of woman as a riddle which Jonathan Swift enigmatized thus in the 1720s: 'Women, as they are like riddles in being unintelligible, so generally resemble them in this, that they please us no longer when once we know them' (262). A warning of the ease with which innocent card games become purveyors of 'man's vile art,' however, is conveyed through a metaphorical depiction of cards as women of easy virtue and fickle tastes: 'Possess'd you'll find me of the wanton's wiles, / Her patches, paint, and heart beguiling smiles' (1:60). An apparently positive example of femininity is presented in 'Innocence.' Beginning by invoking biblical images of this desired quality, such as paradise before the fall and 'Noah's dove,' the composer of this puzzle then creates not only a series of hints to its solution but a creditable picture of an ideal eighteenth-century woman, not dissimilar to Austen's portrayal of Emma's elder sister, Isabella: 'Passing her life with those she doted on, full of their merits, blind to their faults, and always innocently busy, [Isabella] might have been a model of right feminine happiness' (Austen 120). The enigmatist writes,

My sex is feminine, or poets feign;
I wear a placid and engaging mien:
I'm gentle, mild, benevolent, sincere;
And where I dwell diffusive smiles appear. (1:25)

Placidity is a quality quite lacking in those fashionable ladies who are 'immersed in trifles, and hurrying with impatience, never satisfied, from one scene of diversion to another' (Gisborne 202). Young ladies who peruse riddle collections are similarly harried and apt to 'speak wildly' according to the conservative father quoted at the beginning of this chapter: 'No wise man ever puts such ridiculous compositions into the hands of his daughters. They are calculated for nothing but to nurse that constitutional flutter, or nervous kind of palsey, which seems the radical disorder of your sex' (Tell Tale 389). Harriet, whose somewhat wild answers to Mr Elton's 'Court-ship' riddle draw Emma's exasperation, is also portrayed as being 'in a flutter' more than once throughout the novel. That Isabella is not presented as one who might enjoy solving riddles, or even, as Harriet apparently does, enjoy failing to solve riddles, only adds to her portrayal as a model of the 'feminine happiness' prescribed by conduct books and reproduced in this enigma.

Austen's description of Isabella hinges on the phrase 'innocently busy.' The enigma devoted to 'Indolence' contains the line: 'Virtue 'tis said I oft destroy,' and in the contrasting Woodhouse sisters, Austen illustrates the accuracy of this statement. Isabella is never bored nor idle and, apparently, does not engage in any of the activities thought to threaten a young woman's mind, heart, or reputation as Emma does in her dealings with Frank Churchill. Their shared indolence leads Emma and Frank into behaviour, in their concocting fictions around Jane Fairfax, which is, respectively, unladylike and ungentlemanly. As Devereux observes, these acts, and Emma's mocking of Miss Bates, threaten Emma's 'comfort and security far more seriously than the unrepentant Frank's behavior has threatened his' (52). The inter-related beliefs that indolence leads to a loss of reputation and virtue for women, and that it is they who are most likely to be idle, are apparent throughout this enigma. From the very beginning, the anonymous author indicates not only her knowledge of the themes and concerns of conduct literature with regard to women's lives but also the place of her own work within them. The father whose comments relating to riddles have earned him a recurring role in this chapter enquires of his daughter what purpose such puzzles serve except to feed 'the silly . . . curiosity of the idle.' He answers his own question, asserting that 'publishers find it in their interest to feed this diseased appetite; as pampering a bad taste may be more profitable than exemplifying a good one' (392). This exploitation of the finances of bored young women is implicit in the opening lines of the puzzle: 'Enigmatists try their skill, / How to bring me to their will' (2:10). The link between indolence and a lack of virtue is emphasized by the closing lines:

Goodness hates me as the devil,
Because I oft on her bring evil,

But ladies you must all confess,
I'm generally your patroness.

The final couplet in particular suggests a tone similar to that in which Austen describes Mrs Elton's 'resources.' Austen's irony succeeds in hitting its target because that target is so well known. Similarly, as Pagis points out, 'the riddle must be soluble, not only in terms of its hints but also in the nature of the subject itself [which] must be general and familiar' (94). The familiarity of the ladies who solved the enigmas of the *New Collection* with the discourses surrounding their conduct is likely to have ensured not only the solving of the enigma, but perhaps a wry acknowledgment of its accuracy.

As Cook notes, 'when not perfunctory' the prefaces to riddle collections 'are concerned to justify their pursuit' (236). Peter Puzzlewell's rhyming 'Introductory Address' suggests that 'Enigmas ... youthful minds invite / To drink instruction mix'd with pure delight,' while Crinkum, in a rather more verbose manner, hopes that his work will 'rouse the genius and awaken the inquiry of the puerile' for 'experience has indeed shewn us, that lessons, couched under such a semblance, frequently convey more lasting traces than the persuasives of the preacher, or the instructions of the preceptor' (ii). An awareness that the best hopes of these authors may not be realized is provided by the editor of the *New Collection*: 'how much amusement is sought instead of improvement, I need not point out' (v). The female-oriented nature of this work and the use of the word 'improvement' might suggest the editor's hope that, to paraphrase Crinkum, conduct literature couched in the semblance of enigmas, riddles, and conundrums, may have a more lasting effect upon the minds of those who solve them than the dry persuasives of Fordyce's *Sermons* and their ilk. Just as authors of both novels and riddle collections don a mask of self-deprecation, however, this editor presents an admittedly somewhat flimsy façade of 'improvement' to conceal an intent which better fits the ways in which the 'common' culture I have described was assimilated and acted upon by eighteenth-century women. Enigmatists manipulate the language which leads to their solutions in order to confuse their readers. As with Swift's riddles or Jordan's ciphers, women may manipulate the hints which lead to their categorization as 'good' or 'bad,' or innocent or indolent, and it is in the knowing awareness of this fact that the compiler and authors of these enigmas indicate their subversive potential.

The 'patches' and 'paint' of the harlot in the card analogy cited earlier are overt and highly readable examples of a woman's appearance misrepresenting her actuality. Most particularly in the enigmas 'Innocence' and 'Indolence,' the ambiguities of femininity and the importance of the appearance of virtue as much as the possession of it are exposed. No sooner is innocence linked to femininity than the connection is undermined by the enigmatist's reference to the 'feigning' of poets. The suggestion that the 'placid and engaging mien' of innocence is merely 'worn' suggests that ingenuousness may be exhibited by a woman when necessary but cast off when it is no longer required. The connotations of the word 'mien' are those of superficial appearance, belying depths which bear only a limited resemblance to the face, or façade, presented to the world. In the literature that aimed to form an ideal, 'normative' eighteenth-century woman, there are hierarchies associated with the categories and oppositions which riddles upset. These hierarchies align superficiality with indolence, knowingness, and badness, and depth with industry, innocence, resources, and goodness. In drawing attention to the ease with which innocence may be feigned, and the undeniable association between indolence and femininity from which they themselves profit, the enigmatist or enigmatists responsible for these puzzles highlight the inefficacy of conduct literature to truly influence behaviour.[7]

NOTES

1 For eighteenth-century definitions of each type of word game, see Johnson's *Dictionary*, Crinkum's preface to the *Repository*, or Thrale. For a twenty-first-century explanation, see Cook.
2 See also the preface to Crinkum's *Key:* 'Butler and Swift have both their riddles wrote / And these, tho' riddles, please some men of note.'
3 The Griffith family were not as concerned about the innocence of their compositions as Crinkum. 'A couple of Faronellis roasted' refers to Farinelli, the famous eighteenth-century castrato. The solution is an allusion to nuts. Griffith Family. *An Aenigmatical Entertainment.* c. 1794. National Library of Wales. GB 0210 FL1/1/26.
4 This particular copy is held by Trinity College Library, Cambridge (K.10.80[4]).
5 Riddle books may provide useful evidence in the study of the second-hand book trade in the eighteenth century. As riddles are of little use once solved, the collections are well-suited to systems of reuse or resale.

6 The introduction is titled 'On Mr Charles Crinkum's Aenigmatical Repository.' This passage is a reference to the work of Edmund Hoyle who wrote 'scientifically' on whist, quadrille, piquet, and backgammon during the first half of the eighteenth century and whose works remained popular after his death in 1769. Regarding the choice of the pseudonym Philo Astrea, Jacqueline Pearson suggests that the works of Aphra Behn, who was known as Astrea, had fallen out of favour by the early nineteenth century (22). As the immodest foil to Katherine Philips's virtuous Orinda, however, the connotations of this feminine pseudonym suggest that riddles were not a sober or earnest pursuit, but rather more frivolous, if not worse.

7 Thanks to Rebecca Davies, Tom Davies, Louise Marshall, and Sarah Prescott for reading drafts of this chapter.

WORKS CITED

Austen, Jane. *Emma*. London: Collins, 1969. Print.

Ben-Amos, Dan. 'Solutions to Riddles.' *The Journal of American Folklore* 89.352 (1976): 249–54. Print.

Burke, Peter. *Popular Culture in Early Modern Europe*. Aldershot: Wildwood House, 1978. Print.

Byrne, Paula. 'Manners.' *Jane Austen in Context*. Ed. Janet Todd. Cambridge: Cambridge UP, 2005. 297–305. Print.

Castle, Terry. *Masquerade and Civilisation: The Carnivalesque in Eighteenth-Century English Culture and Fiction*. London: Methuen, 1986. Print.

Cook, Eleanor. *Enigmas and Riddles in Literature*. Cambridge: Cambridge UP, 2006. Print.

Courtly, Copernicus. 'A Dissertation on Almanacks; with the Plan of a New One for the Use of People of Fashion.' *London Magazine, or, Gentleman's Monthly Intelligencer* November 1776: 591. Web. 13 May 2010.

Crinkum, Charles. *The Aenigmatical Repository; or, New Fund of Amusement for Young Ladies and Gentlemen*. Canterbury, 1772. Web. 13 May 2010.

– *A Key to the Aenigmatical Repository*. Canterbury, 1772. Print.

Devereux, Cecily. '"Much, Much beyond Impropriety": Ludic Subversions and the Limitations of Decorum in "Emma."' *Modern Language Studies* 25.4 (1995): 37–56. Print.

Doody, Margaret Anne. 'Jane Austen's Reading.' *The Jane Austen Handbook: with a Dictionary of Jane Austen's Life and Works*. Ed. J. David Grey. London: Athlone, 1986. 347–63. Print.

Female Spectator. 'Book XII.' December 1775: 267–317. Web. 13 May 2010.

Fenelon, Francois. *Treatise on the Education of Daughters.* Trans. T.F. Dibdin. London, 1805. Web. 13 May. 2010.

Foreman, Amanda. *Georgiana, Duchess of Devonshire.* London: Harper Collins, 1999. Print.

Gisborne, Thomas. *Enquiry into the Duties of the Female Sex.* London, 1797. Web. 13 May 2010.

Gregory, John. *A Father's Legacy to His Daughters.* London, 1774. Web. 13 May 2010.

Griffith Family. *An Aenigmatical Entertainment.* c. 1794. National Library of Wales. GB 0210 FL1/1/26. Manuscript.

Harris, Tim. *Popular Culture in England c. 1500–1850.* London: Macmillan, 1995. Print.

Hooper's New Puzzle Cap. London, 1799. Web. 13 May 2010.

Ingram, Martin. 'From Reformation to Toleration: Popular Religious Cultures in England, 1540–1690.' Ed. Tim Harris. *Popular Culture in England, c. 1500–1850.* London: Macmillan, 1995. 95–123. Print.

Ingrassia, Catherine. *Authorship, Commerce, and Gender in Early Eighteenth-Century England.* Cambridge: Cambridge UP, 1998. Print.

Johnson, Samuel. *A Dictionary of the English Language.* London, 1755–6. Web. 13 May 2010.

Jones, Jenkin. *Hobby Horses, a poetic allegory, in five parts.* London, 1798. Web. 13 May 2010.

Jordan, Sarah. *The Anxieties of Idleness.* London: Associated UP 2003. Print.

Köngäs-Maranda, Elli. 'Theory and Practice of Riddle Analysis.' *The Journal of American Folklore* 84.331 (1971): 51–61. Web. 13 May 2010.

Litvak, Joseph. 'Reading Characters: Self, Society, and Text in Emma.' *PMLA* 100.5 (1985): 763–73. Web. 13 May 2010.

Monthly Miscellany. 'Riddles in Real Life.' April, 1774. 171. Web. 13 May. 2010.

Mullan, John, and Christopher Reid, eds. *Eighteenth-Century Popular Culture.* Oxford: Oxford UP, 2003. Print.

New Collection of Enigmas, Charades, Transpositions, &c. London, 1791. Print.

Pagis, Dan. 'Toward a Theory of the Literary Riddle.' *Untying the Knot: On Riddles and Other Enigmatic Modes.* Ed. Galit Hasan-Rokem and David Shulman. Oxford: Oxford UP, 1996. 81–104. Print.

Pearson, Jacqueline. *Women's Reading in Britain 1750–1835.* Cambridge: Cambridge UP, 1999. Print.

Puzzlewell, Peter. *Choice Collection of Riddles, Charades, Rebusses, &c.* London, 1792. Web. 13 May 2010.

Stabler, Jane. 'Literary Influences.' *Jane Austen in Context*. Ed. Janet Todd. Cambridge: Cambridge UP, 2005. 41–50. Print.

Stallybrass, Peter. 'Patriarchal Territories: The Body Enclosed.' *Rewriting the Renaissance: The Discourses of Sexual Difference in Early-Modern Europe*. Ed. Margaret W. Ferguson, Maureen Quilligan, and Nancy J. Vickers. Chicago: U of Chicago P, 1986. 123–42. Print.

Swift, Jonathan. *Miscellanies*. Vol. 2. London, 1747. Web. 13 May 2010.

Tadmor, Naomi. '"In the even my wife read to me": Women, Reading and Household Life in the Eighteenth Century.' *The Practice and Representation of Reading in England*. Ed. James Raven, Helen Small, and Naomi Tadmor. Cambridge: Cambridge UP, 1996. 162–74. Print.

Tell Tale. 'To the Proprietors of the Lady's Monthly Museum.' *Lady's Monthly Museum* November 1798. 389–93. Web. 13 May 2010.

Thrale, Hester. *British Synonymy; or, An Attempt at Regulating the Choice of Words in Familiar Conversation*. London, 1794. Web. 13 May 2010.

Warner, William. 'Licensing Pleasure: Literary History and the Novel in Early Modern Britain.' *The Columbia History of the British Novel*. Ed. John Richetti. New York: Columbia UP, 1994. 2–24. Print.

Watts, Isaac. *The Improvement of the Mind*. London, 1795. Web. 13 May 2010.

11 Comic Prints, the Picturesque, and Fashion: Seeing and Being Seen in Jane Austen's *Northanger Abbey*

TIMOTHY ERWIN

On arriving at Bath, Jane Austen's Catherine Morland is distinguished by her avid gaze. Moving through the streets toward the hotel, writes Austen, 'Catherine was all eager delight; – her eyes were here, there, everywhere' (11). Whatever her shortcomings as Gothic heroine, here she more than meets the mark. The spectacle of Georgian Bath was expected to hold visitors spellbound, and visitors might expect to be keenly observed in return. The *Bath and Bristol Guide* makes it a rule that 'the younger Ladies take Notice of how many Eyes observe them,' adding that the requirement 'does not extend to the *Have-at-Alls*' or indiscriminate observers (22). We can catch a glimpse of the urban scene that Catherine absorbs in the contemporary comic prints, where swollen or languorous visitors nod off at concerts, sink awkwardly into sulfurous waters, or tumble helplessly down manicured lawns, as in *The Comforts of Bath* series of Thomas Rowlandson (1798; BM 9321). The callousness of the comedy is somewhat tempered by the fact that the chief infirmity treated by Bath's waters was a painful inflammation of the joints actually remedied mainly by a change of diet: this is the symptom that brings Mr Allen to town and the subject of James Gillray's well-known print *The Gout* (1799; BM 9448). Austen draws upon the reputation of the city for hosting unusual types in creating the single-minded fashionista Mrs Allen, while the falsehood regarding Catherine's fortune that John Thorpe conveys to General Tilney recalls Henry Bunbury's print, *The Propagation of a Lie* (1787; BM 7230). Comic prints like these reflect the popular culture of the later eighteenth century in the sense articulated by Paula R. Backscheider: a mass-market publication that responds to political crisis or public scandal, or to some other less well-defined cultural novelty or need, often on a scale surpassing the production of elite art. Like whitecaps on a series of distant waves suddenly foaming underfoot, such publications bring a brisk comic spirit to the visual culture of the period and broadcast their earnest whimsy across all ranks of society from patrician to pleb.

Bath attracted the sharp pen of caricature from the earliest examples of the art form. Amelia Rauser has shown how caricature emerged from the private cabinet to the print-shop, shifting rapidly from personal memento to public commentary before opening onto subjectivity.[1] In the mid-1770s, Mary and Matthew Darly began marketing sets of caricatures showing various local species of the imported genus macaroni, including *The Emaciated Bath Macaroni* (see figure 11.1). Caricatures became a powerful vehicle for social unmasking, Rauser argues, for subjective truth-telling about individuals and issues. And as we shall see, Austen is not above reworking their popular sight gags as literary punchlines. More generally, her authorial attitude assumes the detachment of caricature by diffusing irony across a wide array of characters and events. When these events turn inward, her tone remains diffident, though the situation of the heroine all but demands a sympathetic reader. The cultural trajectory of caricature from exaggeration and ridicule toward sympathy retraces a larger polarity. John Brewer describes what he calls the 'spectacularization' (230) of later eighteenth-century visual culture in the invention of new urban media, and at the same time calls attention to the countervailing emergence of sensibility in the depiction of rural life epitomized by Thomas Gainsborough's cottage paintings. The Claude glass of the 1770s introduced a sense of personal experiment into popular visual culture. The device was followed by the eidophusikon or moving picture of Philip de Loutherberg (1781), then by the monumental urban panoramas of Robert Barker, first exhibited at Leicester Square (1792), and later by the kaleidoscope of David Brewster (1817).[2] At a distance, these media, with their novel Greek nomenclature, inform the experimental funhouse atmosphere of *Northanger Abbey*. Austen entertains several different forms of textual vision during the course of the narrative, to be sure, in the frightened stare of Gothic alarm, the conspiratorial glance of adolescence, and the inter-animating look of romantic attraction, and yet the larger narrative arc from spectacle to subjective identity subsumes these other forms. Eventually, these fictive aspects of seeing and being seen merge in a model of consciousness where a shifting strangeness in the quotidian order of experience – a developmental process that sifts unexpected experiences and objects less according to youthful standards of novelty

The EMACIATED BATH MACARONI

Publish'd according to Act Sept.r 7.1772 by M.Darly 39.Strand.

Figure 11.1. Matthew Darly. *The Emaciated Bath Macaroni* (1772), an early example of the English vogue for caricature. Reproduced courtesy of the British Museum.

and more according to the morality of custom – promises to bring about a mature and reliable social knowledge.

Northanger Abbey is often understood to be a hybrid text, at once a keen parody of Gothic fiction and at the same time an admiring act of ventriloquism, indeed a tribute. Its collapsing aesthetic contexts suggest that readers adopt something of the same mixed attitude toward the picturesque. The opening chapters deconstruct the popularly understood opposition of the male sublime and female beautiful for the sake of a bi-gendered characterization we may call picturesque. But no sooner does the aesthetic connection of hero and heroine begin to develop than it collapses in the confusion of the Beechen Cliff episode, where, I will argue, Henry misreads a popular view as picturesque to significant effect. Later on, aesthetic expectation actually blinds Catherine to the reality of her situation at the abbey. One problem common to Gothic sensation and the picturesque gaze alike as they are represented in the novel is that they have become outmoded. Cultural transition operates at several speeds in *Northanger Abbey*, from the passing fad of 'quizzing,' to the sustained vogue for taking in the landscape picturesque through travel, to the widespread adoption of a trend with staying power, like the substitution of muslin for silk in the wardrobe. Austen sets empirical observation the task of sorting out ephemeral novelty from genuine innovation. A second complication with the novelizing of trends in popular culture is that mass phenomena rarely sponsor the individuality that leads to personal development. Austen sketches a solution for both these problems: she indulges the appeal of trend-observant youth culture by staging episodes typical of adolescence, like dancing at the assembly rooms and daytrips into the countryside, but at the same time, she affirms the need for successive generations to improve upon the past. She asks younger readers to reconstitute their own individual vision by looking longest at what bids fair to last. Sceptical of secondhand aesthetics, Austen turns our attention to their basic formative elements instead. And because she recognizes the challenge of bringing worthwhile innovation to culture high and low, her comedy often turns upon a dynamic of frustration.

Visual Motifs and Bath Culture

Austen abstracts three motifs from the basic picturesque experience, with fashion foremost among them. The motif first surfaces when Catherine's tomboy 'love of dirt' gives way to a teenage appreciation of 'finery' (7). A second motif, of travel, is introduced by the sudden appearance of John Thorpe driving a gig recklessly, showing the dangers of male irresponsibility. A third motif is that of books and reading, which includes the central opposition of important male history and frivolous female fiction. Like the diminished beauty of Edmund Burke, which exchanges ancient symmetry for modern smoothness, fashion is gendered female and encompasses both clothing and fabric. Travel or transportation is gendered male, like Burke's sublime, and includes coaches and horses. In the same way that the picturesque blends and blurs aesthetic difference, the interplay of character across gendered motifs allows concerns otherwise exclusive to be shared between the sexes.[3] Travel enlarges personal awareness and extends the comparative representation of character; fashion gradually reveals those aspects of cultural change that continue to wear well. In the third motif, the affinity of history and fiction grants the feminine form of the novel a place of honour in the history of genres (the rightful place that Austen claims for it in chapter 5). Austen's reading list is inclusive enough to admit Gothic sensation as well as the good sense of Frances Burney. Modestly, she grants history pride of place, even as the natural world of plants and flowers is understood to refine individual taste.

Fashion and travel are well represented in comic prints from the mid-1790s, when *Northanger Abbey* was composed. Not long after entering Bath, Catherine notices 'high feathers' (13) dancing above a crowded ballroom. The sight is frustrating because neither she nor Mrs Allen recognizes anyone among the mass of bobbing bodies. In Gillray's *A Modern Belle Going to the Rooms at Bath* (see figure 11.2), one chairman contrives (to the annoyance of another) to protect an ostrich-feather head-dress by raising an umbrella above the cantilevered roof of a sedan chair.[4] Print and passage share a metonymy in which a stylish accessory is taken for the whole. The headdress poses a problem for the chairmen, and the humour of the scene rests in the differing attitudes they take toward its solution, between the complacence of one and the exasperation of the other. [5]Austen gives fashion unusual prominence in these early chapters, and for different reasons all of the women in *Northanger Abbey* are interested in dress. Mrs Allen leads the way. Early on we learn that dress is 'her passion' (12), and as if on cue she comments insistently on the condition of her clothing (14, 20, 24), even when no one is there to listen (57). She is followed by Isabella Thorpe, who possesses an air of 'resolute stilishness' (51) that later will be contrasted to the genuine elegance of Eleanor Tilney. Where Mrs Allen dresses to

Figure 11.2. James Gillray. *A Modern Belle Going to the Rooms at Bath* (1796), a comic print illustrative of the vogues in fashion and travel. Reproduced courtesy of the Huntington Art Collections, San Marino, California.

be au courant, Isabella dresses to compete with other women, pretending to dictate style to Catherine while imitating the taste of her young friend instead.

In female fashion Austen creates a sequestered world of competitive regard open to men only by invitation. Henry waits to give his opinion of Catherine's gown until after Mrs Allen prompts him, and then comments on the durability of the fabric rather than the cut, pattern, or fit of the garment:

> 'It is very pretty, madam' said he, gravely examining it; 'but I do not think it will wash well; I am afraid it will fray.'
>
> 'How can you,' said Catherine, laughing, 'be so –' she had almost said, 'strange.' (21)

The brief exchange is of a piece with the mediation of the picturesque. Henry appears peculiar or odd for venturing halfway across a gendered divide, for taking a step that convention views as unnatural. At the same time he demurs from full engagement with the fashion system. A question meant to turn Henry's attention to Catherine draws an ironic reply that Catherine misunderstands. Before posing her own question in return, she tactfully substitutes amused silence for utterance. In ensuing episodes the narrative continues to ring changes on the word that she avoids saying here, 'strange,' so that it points to her subjective progress toward a mature viewpoint. At first the word describes the unpromising normalcy of the heroine (6), next her innocent surprise at the impoliteness of the Thorpes (86, 98), then her encounter with the atmosphere of the abbey (167–8), until we finally hear it spoken aloud in regard to General Tilney. Catherine learns that his dishonourable behaviour has been motivated by the 'false calculations' (255) of a selfishness that he is too proud to conceal – a 'strange business,' her family agrees, from a 'very strange man' (242). The comment completes a shift from the aesthetic to the ethical portrayal of character.

In the meantime the initial dialogue places personality on dramatic display, strikes a first spark of attraction, and grants the two young people a lasting acquaintance. In due course Catherine will learn to trust her own preferences, to question convention, and to withstand the deluded 'mischief' brought about by the reading she has been enjoying in Bath (205): in short to become more alert to the fine weave of modern experience. Already, she distinguishes among the spotted (or patterned), sprigged (decorated with branching stems and foliage), mull (plain and thin), jackonet (plain and less thin), and tamboured (embroidered) types of muslin (71), distinctions that reveal an easy expertise transferable to other fields. A popular song called 'In My Silver Muslin Gay' speaks to the democratic appeal of the fabric: 'In my silver muslin gay / I shall Blaze, superbly drest; / Frisk and flaunt my hours away, / Strut as proudly as the best' (*Songsters Companion*, 177).[6] For the moment, instead of fixing the irony through indirect discourse, Austen allows it to hover like a question mark over succeeding encounters until we reach the Beechen Cliff.

There is fashion in behaviour as well as dress, and Catherine is quick to sort out Henry's teasing tone from the insulting manner of John Thorpe. Tilney banters with other characters politely, for the sake of sharing information. Thorpe indulges the fad for quizzing in ways thoughtless or cruel: 'Where did you get that quiz of a hat?' he asks his mother. 'It makes you look like an old witch' (44). The habit of policing the appearance of others is captured in the anonymous comic print *College Fun, Or Quizzing the Proctor* (see figure 11.3), and also in the popular song 'The Etymology of Quiz' by Charles Dibdin, a composer Austen admired (Piggott 151):

> The word Quiz is a sort of a kind of a word
> That people apply to some being absurd;
> One who seems, as 'twere, oddly your fancy to strike,
> In sort of a fashion you somehow don't like:
> A mixture of odd, and of queer, and all that,
> Which one hates just, you know, as some folks hate a cat:
> A comical, whimsical, strange, droll, that is,
> You know what I mean, 'tis – in short 'tis a quiz.[7]

A mere villain in training, Thorpe is much less forbidding than the general and for all his bluster fails to frighten Catherine. On helping her into his gig, for example, he warns that his horse 'will ... give a plunge or two' since he is 'full of spirits' and 'playful as can be' (58). Henry Fuseli's painting *The Nightmare* of 1781 had helped to make the horse, along with mountain scenery in general and steep precipices in particular, yet another symbol of the sublime.[8] A comic print by Isaac Cruikshank called *Symptoms of Jolting* (1797; BM 9133) portrays the discomfort of riding over rough roads. Instead of allowing Thorpe to exercise sublime mastery, the placid animal trots off without incident and spares Catherine any alarm.

Figure 11.3. *College Fun, Or Quizzing the Proctor* (1796), an anonymous print illustrating the youthful vogue of exposing others to ridicule. Reproduced courtesy of the Library of Congress. British Cartoon Prints, LC-USZ62-59618.

Tilney by contrast practices just so much horsemanship as necessary. On the way to the abbey Catherine finds herself alone with Henry 'as happy a being as ever existed':

> The merit of the curricle did not all belong to the horses; – Henry drove so well, – so quietly – without making any disturbance, without parading to her, or swearing at them; so different from the only gentleman-coachman whom it was in her power to compare him with! (160)

The two journeys counterpoint one another, anticipate Catherine's departure from the abbey after the veil of Gothic illusion is lifted, and show Henry to marked advantage. He heightens Catherine's imaginative surrender by reciting a frightening catalogue of what to expect at Northanger and yet holds the reins of romance with all the genuine mastery of seeming ease.

The motif of books and reading is broached midway through the novel when Austen transports her heroine and hero, and also his sister

Eleanor, to a viewpoint overlooking Bath. The party is discussing the merits of fiction versus history when Catherine declares that the part of history she most admires is invention. As the threesome climb the Beechen Cliff, Henry instructs Catherine in the appreciation of the modern landscape. 'He talked of fore-grounds, distances, and second distances – side-screens and perspectives – lights and shades,' Austen writes, and 'Catherine was so hopeful a scholar'

> that when they gained the top of Beechen Cliff, she voluntarily rejected the whole city of Bath, as unworthy to make part of a landscape. Delighted with her progress, and fearful of wearying her with too much wisdom at once, Henry suffered the subject to decline, and by an easy transition from a piece of rocky fragment and the withered oak which he had placed near its summit, to oaks in general, to forests, the inclosure of them, waste lands, crown lands and government, he shortly found himself arrived at politics; and from politics, it was an easy step to silence. (113)

The passage deserves the commentary that it has attracted.[9] It proposes that readers bear comic witness to an aesthetic newly imposed upon the countryside. It likens the exertion of climbing a hill to the effort of understanding a new idea and the grasping of that idea to the attainment of an eminence. It also offers a syntactical ekphrasis where distant points of interest are met by the conventional topoi of improvement. All of this earnest tracing of the horizon is guided by the shaky hand of irony, of course, so that Henry's brief lecture traces the downward-sloping graph of its own failure to signify. A long sentence heaves itself with affected ease across the soft footing of ever more implicit prepositions toward a conclusion, when the civil gaze of Whig improvement suddenly encounters the unmentionable object of Tory nostalgia. [10]A blasted oak tree with long-standing Stuart connections raises implicit topics of enclosure, property, and power. While the eye of the ordinary observer may pass quickly from one point of interest to another, the mind moving by way of association never quite knows where it is going, and Henry arrives at the full stop of discursive impasse.

In fact, the view from the Beechen Cliff, though a popular tourist attraction, would not have qualified as picturesque for contemporaries like William Gilpin. Elevation and distance alone, he writes in the *Observations on the River Wye*, cannot make for a picturesque landscape: 'Hence appears the absurdity of carrying a painter to the top of a high hill, to take a view. He cannot do it. Extension alone, though amusing in nature, will never make a picture. It *must* be *supported'* (127–8). By support, Gilpin means the placement of objects in the foreground. The shift of target from Gothic novel to picturesque landscape aligns the novel not with considerations of the landscape picturesque like the Menippean satire of T.L. Peacock's *Headlong Hall* (1815), but rather with *Doctor Syntax in Search of the Picturesque* (1812) by Thomas Rowlandson and William Combe. Henry loses his way much as the wandering curate and schoolmaster does.[11] Both works deride a popular vogue now on its last legs, and both have a larger target in mind. Affirming the traditional value of charity, Combe and Rowlandson mock the zeal for preferment that impoverishes an honest curate, while Austen uses the picturesque to frame a window opening onto the elements of aesthetic perception. She avoids summarizing old debates because she remains serious about the possibility of genuine instruction. Although Henry's lesson is muddled, Catherine takes the idea further than he does and is shown to remain eager to learn more at the abbey, confirming an ongoing theme of education. Fashion alerts Catherine to keep her eye on enduring common values, while travel helps her to sort out worthy suitors from those less worthy, and nature encourages her to trust her developing individual taste. In sum, Austen salvages the basic elements of the picturesque for the sake of preserving the educational uses of a passing visual medium within a popular genre rarely considered instructive.

The Subjective Turn

As the narrative draws to a close Catherine briefly catches sight of the great spire of Salisbury Cathedral, a feature that John Constable would shortly make a picturesque icon. For the moment the steeple conveys only dread at having to explain an unceremonious return home. Where Gilpin admires the way the spire appears to move on the traveller's winding approach, a phenomenon known as motion parallax, Catherine has arrived at what Slavoj Žižek would call a subjective blind spot.[12] An earnest student of the countryside, she must focus her attention elsewhere now, on the secondary meaning to be drawn from primary sense impression. What can she tell her parents about her sudden return? The passage opens onto all the swirling unmapped emotion beneath the failed aesthetic template. As troubling as it is, Catherine may now profit from the situation because she is better able to reflect on what has happened to her. A subjective space has opened for reflection. She is left with 'feelings . . . to be investigated,' as Henry says without irony, addressing the practical imagination, 'that they may know themselves' (213). Among the things she has learned is that her affection for Isabella is not what it was. Isabella represents the power of beauty to conceal insincerity, her brother John the tendency of the sublime to swell into bombast, and neither is half so sympathetic as Henry or Eleanor.

Sympathy was a developing concern of empirical thought, of course, and the period rhetoric goes some way toward describing the turmoil Catherine suffers. Adam Smith describes subjective states of mind as 'internal facts' – that is, as the 'thoughts, sentiments, or designs' that pass through our minds.[13] Internal facts are represented either directly or indirectly, he goes on to say, and indirect demonstration is the more effective. Take the category of the great or sublime, from the perceptual triad that Addison called the great, uncommon, and beautiful. We can either view the sublime directly as a kind of telling, as in Milton's description of Eden in book four of *Paradise Lost*, Smith remarks, or we may view it indirectly, as a kind of showing, as when Edgar persuades the blind Gloucester that he has fallen from a cliff in *King Lear* (4:64). Austen makes use of both direct and indirect representation, and in their visual as well as verbal forms. During the journey home Catherine's dilemma is described in direct fashion as an 'unceasing recurrence of doubts and inquiries' (239). One sleepless night spent at the abbey wondering what the odd written characters she has discovered could mean is replaced by another worrying why General Tilney should ask her to leave when his children wish her to stay. The comparison is instructive, and the answer to the second question worth knowing, not least because it informs the filial freedom the narrator offers as theme in the closing sentence. The journey home reveals the psychological dark side of the narrative, a mixture of social horror and affective dread. Henry is as yet 'unconscious' (238) of her departure, and she agonizes about what his response will be when he learns of it, whether passive acquiescence or active resistance. Once Catherine arrives at Fullerton, the narrative bears indirect witness to her keen anxiety. The solicitous attention of her mother only intensifies her distress, until by chapter 15 she becomes the antithesis of her boisterous former self, withdrawing from conversation in order to imagine Henry's moment-by-moment understanding of her situation. Nor can she recognize herself as the character portrayed in Mr and Mrs Allen's account of their stay in Bath. She knows only that she is neither a Gothic heroine nor the same person who left home only three short months before. Without a story of her own, who can she be?

For Paul Ricoeur self-knowledge develops by moving from recall to agency. We formulate a narrative identity by looking backward to activate memory, and forward to extend the promise of individual ability in new directions (69–149).[14] Ricoeur likens the grasping of a memory trace to the sudden recognition of an image. To create a personal narrative is to bear witness to the picture of a remembered self, a project that leads in turn to a mutual recognition among others and eventually to a shared common identity. When Henry suddenly appears at Catherine's door, all her doubts disappear, and the narrator tells us outright that her state of mind swings round to 'unutterable happiness' (253). Less directly, we have already seen how her 'glowing cheek and brightened eye' (251) replace listless repining as welcome signs that her dilemma is ending. Henry has been in her mind all along, his image so filling her daydreams in Bath that its only rivals are 'castles and abbies' (143). The visual-verbal axis of the novel runs from the sustaining mental image of Henry back through the dawning distrust of a deceptive popular discourse, a way of talking that, to Catherine's great credit, she hardly understands. As she tells Henry, rather like Alice peering into the rabbit hole, 'I cannot speak well enough to be unintelligible' (135).

What I have suggested is that Austen replaces one form of empirical visual culture with another in *Northanger Abbey*. The picturesque is but one pretext among many that might have brought our hero and heroine together, and once the two are separated, the picturesque is powerless to reunite them. The last impediments to happiness are removed not by means of side-screens and perspectives but by a sceptical awareness of character and motive. The word 'nature' retreats from the vegetable frame to recover a human dimension, and the story plays out across familiar causal ground where hidden aims are disclosed and conflicting wishes resolved. Henry undeceives Catherine about his father so that she may see General Tilney for the manipulative parent he is rather than the murderer she imagines. For all his attentiveness, General Tilney becomes a figure of over-charged self-interest, a caricature of parental concern. The general is undeceived about Catherine when Thorpe's information regarding her fortune proves false. Neither needy nor an heiress, she becomes irrelevant to the future of the abbey when the 'obstacle' (258) of paternal disapproval is finally overcome by 'means' (259) of the marriage of Eleanor to a man of consequence. Catherine's awakening from her Gothic 'visions of romance' (210) finally exchanges a slippery knowledge of aesthetics for a grasp of psychology as yet still slim, but promising to become stronger.

The paradoxical appeal of caricature, on the other hand, is that while gliding across the superficial physiognomy of the individual it also delves into a shared human nature. Extending across social rank, it asks not only that the beholder locate a telling distortion of the common human mean in another, but also that the beholder look within to find anything that might appear strange to an outsider. When Henry asks Catherine to consult her observation at the abbey (203), he advises her in effect to extend the visual record of her sense impressions, and from Bath onward narrative events are often accompanied by the stage direction of a visual dialogue. Without a conventional syntax to follow, visual images may prove less articulate than verbal utterance and as a result these looks can be wholly illegible. When Isabella enters the parlour at Edgar's Buildings with 'a look of happy importance' (119) bespeaking a new-found connection to James, for instance, Catherine fails to recognize her meaning and returns 'a look of wondering ignorance' (119). When Catherine silently implores her chaperone to help her refuse an outing with Thorpe, Mrs Allen proves unfamiliar with the language of significant looks (57) and so unhelpful. Moments like these return us to the metaphor of parallax by insisting on the gaze as a personal and subjective phenomenon. The hyphenated construction that portrays our heroine as a 'good-looking girl' (7) is reprised on the Beechen Cliff when the narrator uses the same phrase to say that someone like Catherine 'cannot fail of attracting' (112) a likely young man, and is again recalled in the mention of 'three smart looking females' (24; spoken of the Thorpe sisters), of a 'knowing-looking coachman' (38; spoken of Thorpe), a 'sober looking morning' (80), and of a 'very fashionable-looking, handsome young man' (133; spoken of Captain Tilney). It is precisely because meaningful looks so often misfire and appearances so easily deceive that observation must remain in constant play.

On other occasions the same communicative practice proves eloquent, serving alongside propitious circumstances to bring together our hero and heroine. At a ball, for example, Catherine keeps her eyes 'intently fixed on her fan' until Henry approaches her, and then looks up with 'sparkling eyes' to agree to dance (72). At a play Catherine sits in a box opposite Henry 'for two entire scenes ... without being once able to catch his eye' (92). Austen fuses ekphrasis with the elements of grammar in claiming that though Catherine's eloquence resides 'only in her eyes,' Henry finds them so expressive that the very 'parts of speech' (122) shine out from them. The enamoured gaze is sealed as reciprocal at the assembly rooms when Catherine listens with 'sparkling eyes

Figure 11.4. Isaac Cruikshank. *Attraction* (1794). Reproduced courtesy of the Huntington Art Collections, San Marino, California.

to everything' Henry says, and in 'finding him irresistible' becomes so herself (134). According to Adam Smith, youth is the season of life when a 'propensity to joy' tends to 'sparkle from the eyes' (*Theory* 1:42), a time when fellow-feeling most naturally engages the emotions, diffusing gaiety even to the aged. A preparatory watercolour by Isaac Cruikshank for a comic print called *Attraction* (see figure 11.4) illustrates the idea. Mutual regard courses outward like an electric current from a young couple's joined hands to fix an approving glance across the distinctions of gender, profession, and age. It has been suggested that the print targets the roving eye of the Prince of Wales (Nygren 65), but if so the fluent lines and relative absence of exaggeration make for gentle raillery. A 'droll' rather than a caricature, the print stands in the same relation that a situation comedy does to a series of satiric sketches on television. Despite its public setting the image preserves a delicate sense of interiority for the central female figure, an effect heightened by the two men who crane forward to look at her. Who is she, this young woman of fashion? The caption indicates a general application by quoting Thomas Otway's oft-revived *Venice Preserved* from 1682 – 'Lovely Woman ! ... / There's in you all that we believe of Heav'n' (I i 335, 339) – a drama that Backscheider treats persuasively in this volume and elsewhere as a prime example of the canonical work feminized, and in the minds of some also trivialized, by mass culture (44–53). Catherine rises to meet much the same representational challenge, through all of the shifting tides of taste that Tiffany Potter describes in her preface to this collection, by remaining an Everywoman who continues to place aesthetic assumptions in question. Swept along by a flood of images numbering easily in the tens of thousands (Donald 1), she resists mute anonymity to speak eloquently to the sympathetic power of the popular gaze to bind the affections.[15]

NOTES

1 Rauser sorts out four factors contributing to the development of caricature during the later eighteenth century: the increasing size of print formats; the emergence of a rapid process of etching as opposed to the more elaborate process of engraving; the rise of the commercial gallery and print-shop as markets; and the growing popularity of the caricature artist as a celebrity (96–9). See also Donald 9–15, 44–74, et passim.
2 On the Claude glass, see Maillet. Altick notes that Robert Barker first coined the term 'panorama' to describe the two rotundas built to house his large-scale urban perspectives (128–40). On Barker, see Oettermann 99–141 and Comment 23–8.
3 These motifs serve mainly to link events and mark stages of personal development. They are neither gestural (like the visual motif of Panofsky) nor literary (like the lock of hair in *Sense and Sensibility*) but reflect the basic empirical elements of the picturesque experience.
4 The rules for transporting passengers by sedan chair and the penalties for failing to meet them are found in the *Bath and Bristol Guide* 28–39.
5 For a representative selection of images from Gillray (1756–1815), see Godfrey. The best record of Gillray's European reception is found in Banerji and Donald.
6 See further Lemire: a 'number of circumstances combined in the eighteenth century to encourage and promote the manufacture of ready-made clothing in Britain,' she writes, most notably the 'diffusion of fashion' (185). Lemire

notes that the fabric gained royal sanction when the Princess of Wales appeared at the 1795 Ascot Races dressed in muslin (110).

7 The first song in a musical review called *The Quizzes, Or, A Trip to Elysium* (1792). The song ends with the wish that two hours hence the audience not set the author down for a quiz. For the full text, see Dibdin (3:171–2). The *OED* defines 'quiz' as either 'an odd or eccentric person, in character or appearance' or else 'an odd-looking thing,' citing *Northanger Abbey* for the second sense. Austen makes her dislike of quizzing plain in an 1805 letter to Cassandra, describing a morning visit where there was 'a monstrous deal of stupid quizzing, & common-place nonsense talked, but scarcely any Wit' (Le Faye 104).

8 The painting was parodied in the comic prints on several occasions, notably by Rowlandson in *The Covent Garden Night Mare* (1784; BM 6543), a print deriding the election prospects of minister Charles James Fox, and by George Cruikshank in *The Night Mare* (1816; BM 12817), a satire on attempts to reform public morals. See also Donald 69–73.

9 Austen takes her terms from several texts by William Gilpin: 'fore-ground' occurs in the *Essay on Prints* to mean the near space of an image (53), and in the *Remarks on Forest Scenery* is paired with 'distances' to describe the interaction of wood and heath (1:225); in the *Observations on the River Wye* the term 'second distances' describes the landscape that becomes visible when a forest opens onto groves and glades (147). Gilpin briefly takes up perspective in the *Three Essays* when advising amateurs how to sketch a building or ruin in a landscape (84–5). As is often remarked, Henry's loose, associative syntax owes something to discussions like Knight's *Inquiry into the Principles of Taste*. Knight speaks of picturesque spectators 'whose pre-existing trains of ideas are revived, refreshed, and re-associated by new, but correspondent impressions on the organs of sense' (194).

10 As Bermingham puts it, 'Less aristocratic than simply polite, Gilpin's picturesque aesthetic, in its accessibility, its nationalism, and its appeal to bourgeois moral values, was the essence of the Addisonian Whig landscape' (101).

11 First published as 'The Schoolmaster's Tour' in a verse miscellany (1809–10) and later published separately. Austen writes to her sister Cassandra during the spring of 1814 that she has seen 'nobody in London yet with such a long chin as Dr Syntax' (Le Faye 256). The prolific Rowlandson (1756–1827) illustrated the novels of Sterne, Smollett, and Goldsmith as well as the *Tour of Dr Syntax in Search of the Picturesque* (1812), a series that went through eight editions by 1819 and was rapidly followed by *Dr Syntax in Search of Consolation* (1820), *Dr Syntax in Search of a Wife* (1821),

and *The History of Johnny Quae Genus, the Little Foundling of the Late Dr Syntax* (1822).

12 'Motion parallax' describes the apparent movement of fixed objects as seen by an observer actually in motion. In *Observations on the Western Parts,* Gilpin writes that on approaching Salisbury, 'the lofty spire of the cathedral makes its first appearance, and fixes the spot to which the road ... will certainly carry us at last' (53). Today students of perception call the phenomenon an optic flow pattern, and distinguish between the two sorts of information it provides, environmental information about the object and kinesthetic information about the observer's movement. See Lee. Žižek in turn takes optical parallax to speak to the apparent displacement of the object as grasped by subjective consciousness, locating a hermeneutic 'blind spot' (17) in the divergence between the two.

13 Smith distinguishes internal from external facts (or the 'transactions that pass without us') in *Lectures on Rhetoric and Belles Lettres* (4:63; and cited again in the text). Elsewhere Smith follows Burke in arguing that pain, 'whether of mind or body' (1:44), is a stronger source of passion than pleasure. He adds that human nature is more inclined to share in the pleasure of joy than in the grief of pain (1:44–5), making the honest communication of painful internal facts such as Catherine experiences all the more necessary. On Austen and Smith, see Knox-Shaw, *Austen and the Enlightenment* 129–52, and 'Philosophy' 346–56.

14 Catherine resembles a fictive character in having a certain narrative destiny, Ricoeur would say, but she remains an ordinary human being in not knowing exactly what it is. She is poised between the 'immutable identity of the *idem*,' the same person recognized by her family, and the 'changing identity of the *ipse*' (101), the person that she is coming to recognize in herself.

15 I would like to thank Kelly Malone and Elizabeth Mansfield for hosting a version of this paper on their panel 'Seeing Satire' at the 2009 ASECS meeting, and also Priscilla Finley, Amanda Lahikainen, and John Mulryan for help of various kinds.

WORKS CITED

Altick, Richard D. *The Shows of London.* Cambridge, MA: Harvard UP, 1978. Print.

Austen, Jane. *Northanger Abbey.* Ed. Barbara M. Benedict and Deirdre Le Faye. Cambridge: Cambridge UP, 2006. Print.

Backscheider, Paula R. 'The Paradigms of Popular Culture.' *Eighteenth-Century Novel* 6–7 (2009): 19–59. Print.

Banerji, Christane, and Diana Donald, eds. and trans. *Gillray Observed: The Earliest Account of his Caricatures in London and Paris.* Cambridge: Cambridge UP, 1999. Print.

The Bath and Bristol Guide. 3rd ed. Bath: T. Boddely, 1755. Reprint Kingsmead Bookshop. 1969. Print.

Bermingham, Ann. *Learning to Draw: Studies in the Cultural History of a Polite and Useful Art.* New Haven and London: Yale UP, 2000. Print.

Brewer, John. 'Sensibility and the Urban Panorama.' *Huntington Library Quarterly* 70.2 (2007): 229–49. Print.

Combe, William, and Thomas Rowlandson. *The Tour of Doctor Syntax in Search of the Picturesque.* London: R. Ackermann, 1812. Print.

Comment, Bernard. *The Painted Panorama.* Trans. Anne-Marie Glasheen. 1999. New York: Harry N. Abrams, 2000. Print.

Dibdin, Charles. *The Professional Life of Mr. Dibdin, Written by Himself ... with the Words of Six Hundred Songs.* 4 vols. London: By the Author, 1803. Print.

Donald, Diana. *The Age of Caricature: Satirical Prints in the Reign of George III.* New Haven: Yale UP, 1996. Print.

Freeman, Rosemary. *English Emblem Books.* London: Chatto & Windus, 1948. Print.

Gilpin, William. *Essay on Prints.* London: R. Blamire, 1792. Print.

– *Observations on the River Wye.* London: R. Blamire, 1792. Print.

– *Observations on the Western Parts of England, Relative Chiefly to Picturesque Beauty.* London: Cadell and Davies, 1798. Print.

– *Remarks on Forest Scenery.* London: R. Blamire, 1794. Print.

– *Three Essays: On Picturesque Beauty, on Picturesque Travel; and on Sketching Landscape.* London: R. Blamire, 1792. Print.

Godfrey, Richard. *James Gillray: The Art of Caricature.* Intro. Mark Hallett. London: Tate Gallery, 2001. Print.

Goody, Jack. *The Culture of Flowers.* Cambridge: Cambridge UP, 1993. Print.

Groth, Helen. 'Kaleidoscopic Vision and Literary Invention in an "Age of Things": David Brewster, Don Juan, and "A Lady's Kaleidoscope."' *ELH* 74.1 (2007): 217–37. Print.

Knight, Richard Payne. *Analytical Inquiry into the Principles of Taste.* London: T. Payne and J. White for J. Mercier, 1805. Print.

Knox-Shaw, Peter. *Jane Austen and the Enlightenment.* Cambridge: Cambridge UP, 2004. Print.

– 'Philosophy.' *Jane Austen in Context.* Ed. Janet Todd. Cambridge: Cambridge UP, 2005. 346–56. Print.

Lee, David N. 'Visual Information during Locomotion.' *Perception: Essays in Honor of James J.Gibson.* Ed. Robert B. Macleod and Herbert L. Pick, Jr. Ithaca: Cornell UP, 1974. 250–67. Print.

Le Faye, Deirdre, ed. *Jane Austen's Letters.* London: Oxford UP, 1995. Print.

Lemire, Beverly. *Fashion's Favourite: The Cotton Trade and the Consumer in Britain, 1660–1800.* Oxford: Oxford UP, 1991. Print.

Macleod, Robert B., and Herbert L. Pick, Jr, eds. *Perception: Essays in Honor of James J. Gibson.* Ithaca: Cornell UP, 1974. Print.

Maillet, Arnaud. *The Claude Glass: Use and Meaning of the Black Mirror in Western Art.* Trans. Jeff Fort. New York: Zone Books, 2004. Print.

Nygren, Edward J., ed. *Isaac Cruikshank and the Politics of Parody: Watercolors in the Huntington Collection.* San Marino, CA: Huntington Library P, 1996. Print.

Oettermann, Stephan. *The Panorama: History of a Mass Medium.* Trans. Deborah Lucas Schneider. New York: Zone Books, 1997. Print.

Otway, Thomas. *Venice Preserved.* Ed. J.C. Ghosh. *The Works of Thomas Otway: Poems Plays and Love-Letters.* 2 vols. Oxford: Clarendon Press, 1932. Print.

Piggott, Patrick. *The Innocent Diversion: A Study of Music in the Life and Writings of Jane Austen.* London: D. Cleverdon, 1979. Print.

Rauser, Amelia. *Caricature Unmasked: Irony, Authenticity, and Individualism in Eighteenth-Century English Prints.* Newark: U of Delaware P, 2008. Print.

Ricoeur, Paul. *The Course of Recognition.* Cambridge, MA: Harvard UP, 2005. Print.

Sollors, Werner, ed. *The Return of Thematic Criticism.* Cambridge, MA: Harvard UP, 1993. Print.

Smith, Adam. *Lectures on Rhetoric and Belles Lettres.* Ed. J.C. Bryce. Vol. 4 of *The Glasgow Edition of the Works and Correspondence of Adam Smith.* 6 vols. Oxford: Clarendon, 1976–83. Print.

– *The Theory of Moral Sentiments.* Ed. D.D. Raphael and A.L. MacFie. Vol. 1 of the *Glasgow Edition of the Works and Correspondence of Adam Smith.* Print.

The Songsters Companion. 12th ed. Coventry: Luckman and Suffield, 1800? *Eighteenth Century Collections Online.* Web. 15 June 2010.

Styles, John. *The Dress of the People: Everyday Fashion in Eighteenth-Century England.* New Haven: Yale UP, 2007. Print.

Todd, Janet, ed. *Jane Austen in Context.* Cambridge: Cambridge UP, 2005. Print.

Vanhelleputte, Michel. 'The Concept of Motif in Literature: A Terminological Study.' *The Return of Thematic Criticism.* Ed. Werner Sollors. Cambridge, MA: Harvard UP, 1993. 92–105. Print.

Wolpers, Theodore. 'Motif and Theme as Stuctural Content Units and "Concrete Universals."' *The Return of Thematic Criticism*. Ed. Werner Sollors. Cambridge, MA: Harvard UP, 1993. 80–91. Print.

Žižek, Slavoj. *The Parallax View*. Cambridge, MA: MIT Press, 2006. Print.

PART III

Eighteenth-Century Women in Modern Popular Culture

12   Mother and Daughter in Beryl Bainbridge's *According to Queeney*

MARTHA F. BOWDEN

In considering the eighteenth century's popular culture, it is useful to think of its role in our own, where it continues to be a site of examination and representation. The Tudors will no doubt continue to dominate the fields of costume drama and bodice-ripping sensationalism for some time, although the excesses of Marie Antoinette and Charles II go on providing rich work for the costume department. But the lives of eighteenth-century women contain their own fascination, even without farthingales and beheadings. In part, the interest arises because they are so much nearer to us, yet remote enough to be exotic. Their culture bears many resemblances to ours – novels, newspapers, fashion, shopping, celebrities – but just when we get close we realize that their life choices and constraints are quite different. This tension between the familiar and strange is a fruitful site of comparison between the eighteenth century and the twenty-first, one that Beryl Bainbridge exploits in her novel *According to Queeney* (2001). Its depiction of a fraught relationship between a mother and a daughter has resonances in our own day. The conflicts between need and expectation, both mother's and daughter's, resemble similar tensions in our own society. But the particular context in which the conflicts occur – the constraints under which eighteenth-century women lived – are more remote. In this essay I examine the consequences of this tension in Bainbridge's work, and her qualified success in presenting an eighteenth-century mother-daughter struggle in a twenty-first-century novel.

The novel also illustrates two modifications of the classical form of historical fiction. In the first place, it is a biographical fiction that foregrounds the historically stormy relationship between Hester Thrale Piozzi and her daughter, Hester Maria Thrale, commonly known as

Queeney, played out against the background of the Johnson circle. Biographical fiction, in which all or most of the characters have a historical reality, is a recent development in the history of the form. In Sir Walter Scott's more generically traditional Waverley novels the protagonist is generally a fictional character cast into major historical events, and the historical figures make cameo appearances that intersect with the adventures of the protagonist. In the twenty-first century, however, the biographical novel is rapidly becoming a dominant form. In 1971, Avrom Fleishman, in his survey of historical fiction in Britain from Scott to Woolf, claimed that a novel centred on a historical figure was unlikely ever to be successful:

> The individuals selected by the novelist for heroic (or at least specially marked) status are not likely to be world-historical figures, for such figures are by definition exceptional, since they realize in themselves the tensions and direction of history at a particular time. The typical man of an age is one whose life is shaped by world-historical figures and other influences in a way that epitomizes the processes of change going forward in the society as a whole. (10–11)

Yet in his 2009 review of Hilary Mantel's *Wolf Hall*, which won the Man Booker prize that year, Stephen Greenblatt states categorically, 'In the most fully realized historical novels, the historical figures are not merely background material or incidental presences, but the dominant characters, thoroughly reimagined and animated' (24). Despite this distinction, these recent texts contain many family resemblances to their nineteenth-century predecessors. One significant element is that the protagonist, while a historical figure, tends to be marginal to the events at hand; see, for example, Susan Sontag's *The Volcano Lover* (1992), Emma Donoghue's *Life Mask* (2004), and Philip Baruth's *The Brothers Boswell* (2009). History is decentred and reconfigured: we see the Hamilton-Nelson ménage à trois through the eyes of Sir William Hamilton, the Devonshire House set through Ann Damers and Eliza Farren, and James Boswell and Samuel Johnson largely through the disturbed consciousness of James's brother John. These texts also, like Scott's fiction, participate in the imaginative, sympathetic engagement with their characters that Scott called 'romance.'

But unlike many writers of historical fiction, Beryl Bainbridge does not create broad, sweeping novels in the romance tradition, and this is the second and more striking way in which the text veers from its formal expectations. Her milieu is the portrait, the miniature even, and her voice is acerbic, sardonic, and detached, for which reason the cool, child's eye view of the Johnson circle she presents in *According to Queeney* is a natural subject for her.[1] The historical relationship between Queeney and Hester Thrale[2] contains precisely the kind of emotional tension – uncomfortable, sometimes cruel, often risible, and always on the edge of destructive – that Bainbridge usually portrays. But the novel is not a romance, and it is in many ways less satisfying (although much funnier) than a romance might be. Satire and irony are modes of deliberate objectivity and distance; romance employs interiority and empathy. Most readers turn to historical fiction for precisely these attributes, the direct access to a world long lost. Although Bainbridge speaks sympathetically about her characters in the BBC documentary *According to Beryl*, especially Hester Thrale, and dismisses James Boswell as 'bumptious,' her narrator's voice produces caricature, particularly in the depiction of Hester Thrale, stamping about, losing her temper, and becoming red in the face.

Queeney, Johnson, and Eighteenth-Century Biography

Queeney Thrale, like William Hamilton, Ann Damers, and John Boswell, is a marginal historical figure in a well-documented milieu. She is almost completely absent from Boswell's *Life of Johnson*, the best known of the many biographies to appear after Johnson's death. The index to the Chapman/Fleeman edition of the *Life* contains six references in the entry on Hester Maria Thrale; if we count those places in which she can be assumed to be included, such as references to 'Mrs. Thrale and her daughters,' there are actually eleven. Many of her appearances are in Johnson's letters – reports on her health, her singing master in Bath, Marie Antoinette's noticing her while she is in Paris with her parents and Johnson – that Boswell quotes, and not in Boswell's direct narrative; the letters are generally in the text because they contain other matter of interest, or fill in a scene when Boswell was not there to record it himself. On one occasion he misreads his source (or copies it inaccurately), erasing her existence entirely: 'Queeney on the *Sellette*' in Johnson's diary of the trip to Paris becomes 'Queries on the *Sellette*' (Boswell 648, n4). This exclusion is in keeping with his diminishing of the entire portion of Johnson's life spent with the Thrales at Southwark and Streatham. There is little about the trips to Brighthelmstone (Brighton) or Wales, or about Johnson's role in the Thrale household, especially his participation in the two efforts to retrieve the family fortunes from bankruptcy and his work as one of Thrale's executors. The sale of the brewery after Thrale's death appears in the text in a letter from Johnson to Bennet Langton, although the price for which it sold (135,000 pounds) indicates that it was a significant undertaking, and a crucial one for the futures of the widow and children (Boswell 1132, 1168). Mary Hyde, who transcribes Hester Thrale's *The Family Book* in its entirety, and uses *Thraliana* as the primary text in much of her commentary on it, in *The Thrales of Streatham Park*, demonstrates how active a friend Johnson was to the household, before and after his executorship: he offered legal advice, was a trustee for the Welsh estates, was interested in the children, and even looked in on Sophy and Susanna when they had chicken pox (Hyde 158).

Boswell's dismissive treatment has nothing to do with Queeney herself, and everything to do with his overwhelming desire to establish himself as the sole authoritative biographer of the greatest literary figure of the century. In order to do so, he must undermine in every possible way the credibility of his rivals, especially Hester Piozzi and Sir John Hawkins; a ubiquitous thread in the *Life* is Boswell's corrections to, and aspersions on, these two biographers. As the daughter of one of them, Queeney becomes a kind of collateral damage in the biography wars. But Boswell is also obviously dismayed that Johnson honoured so highly the family of a man who was, despite his wealth and education, a tradesman. After noting that, in 1765, Johnson was 'introduced into the family of Mr Thrale, one of the most eminent brewers in England, and Member of Parliament for the borough of Southwark,' he comments that foreigners are 'not a little amazed' at the idea that tradesmen are 'held forth as persons of considerable consequence.' Boswell is clearly uncomfortable with the idea: 'perhaps, the too rapid advance of men of low extraction tends to lessen the value of that distinction by birth and gentility, which has ever been found beneficial to the grand scheme of subordination.' He quotes at length Johnson's recitation of the rise of the Thrale family, which Johnson himself obviously admired, but in Boswell's context it implies opportunism and overreaching. He concludes by asserting with conviction what he has previously suggested more tentatively, that arguments for a 'new system of gentility' that recognizes accomplishment rather than birth are 'specious, but false' and do not even deserve to be refuted: 'The general sense of mankind cries out, with irresistible force, "*Un gentilhomme est toujours gentilhomme*"' (347–9). Having lowered himself thus far, it is not surprising that Johnson should stoop to creating 'namby pamby rhymes' for 'Mrs. Thrale and her daughter' or that *Easy Lessons*, which Baretti wrote to teach Queeney Italian, should be dismissed as 'ludicrous,' significant only because Johnson wrote the preface (Boswell 129–30, 696, 572). Ian McIntyre writes of Boswell's 'feline thrusts,' but these remarks show little cat-like subtlety (186). Martine Watson Brownley observes that the 'namby pamby' rhymes are evidence of the loving and welcoming atmosphere that Piozzi provided both at Southwark and Streatham, where Johnson enjoyed 'indulging his light-hearted and frivolous side, which few others ever saw' ('Domaine' 74).

Boswell erases this aspect of Johnson's life; he never loses an opportunity to catch Thrale in error, taking particular delight on those occasions when *his* Dr Johnson – the arbiter of all that is good and true – remarks on her general unreliability. He triumphantly quotes one of Johnson's reprimands: 'I told Mrs. Thrale, "You have so little anxiety about truth, that you never tax your memory with the exact thing." Now what is the use of the memory to truth, if one is careless of exactness?' (1033). Meeting Hester Thrale at Johnson's, he 'had conversation enough with her to admire her talents, and to shew her that I was as Johnsonian as herself' (407). Bainbridge's Queeney, surveying such scenes with her usual self-possession and silent scorn, would appear strikingly adult in comparison.

Bainbridge, Queeney, and Twenty-First-Century Fictions

Bainbridge deals with Boswell in short order, reducing him in her fiction to an occasional visitor at Streatham. Her fictional Mr Johnson comments that his transcriptions of conversations will not be accurate, 'for man's compulsion is to replicate himself.' Alone among all the many voices at Streatham, Henry Thrale has the prescience to warn that Boswell should not be discounted: 'Mr. Garrick likened him to the buffoon, Pantalone, and Mr. Goldsmith said he was of no account, but Papa said he should not be so easily dismissed' (Bainbridge 106, 77). Queeney confines her comments on him to her letters to Laetitia Hawkins, themselves masterpieces of redirection. Thus Bainbridge's text executes the decentring ploy common to the genre, undermining the dominant historical voice. Bainbridge also draws attention to Mr Johnson's pleasure in the domesticity of the Thrale household, and to his sympathy with the children, for example, in an early, almost wordless encounter with Queeney:

He was not a fool. He knew full well his presence drew others to Southwark, and if the circumstances had proved different he might have absented himself, in spite of the fine dinners. The satisfaction, however, was not all on one side, for the Thrales had a child, a daughter not much above twelve months old. One afternoon on the stairs, coming face-to-face with his boots on the bend of the stairs, she had neither screamed nor scrambled past, simply stared gravely up at him . . .

'Sweeting,' he had said, and bowed.

'Da-da,' she had crowed, and crawled onwards on hands and knees.

Until that auspicious moment he had always thought of himself as a member of clubs; now, he was inclined to believe he was part of a family. (6)

The significance of the moment becomes clear later on when the conscious Queeney reflects that while she is in competition with him for her mother's attention, he and her mother are also very much alike, 'for both are selfish' (92). Her attempts as a young woman to retrieve her father's character, unjustly smirched through the family's focus on Mr Johnson, remove any hint of sentimentality – as 'Da-da,' Johnson steps into the civil war that is Bainbridge's version of the Thrale household.

Unlike the friends, admirers, and hangers-on still alive when Johnson died, the historical Queeney did not forge into print with a volume, slim or stout, of anecdotes or Life Writ Large. There is thus a gap, the necessary space in which historical fiction can grow. Bainbridge's novel fills in that gap in a manner that retains Queeney's distinctive reticence. Her characterization of Hester Maria Thrale Elphinstone, Lady Keith, is consonant with Hyde's; it may well be that Queeney was silent by choice, and the novel, in which she speaks little but thinks much, emerges out of that silence. Queeney's is the perfect voice for Bainbridge, and the dominant one in the book, a distant, outwardly disinterested, inwardly angry, observer of her world, busily rewriting history in opposition to the many versions chattering around her. Writing back against the Johnson-centred world of the biographers, she insists that her father, not Johnson, originally named her Queeney, and despite her obvious affection for Johnson, she openly resents the time her mother devotes to him. Her self-enclosed nature is highlighted in the text, as it seems to have been in life, by the much more outgoing, impulsive, and dramatic figure of her mother.

Nor is the novel 'according to Queeney' in the expected sense. It is neither in Queeney's own first-person voice nor exclusively from her point of view. Other characters share the stage in turn: Hester Thrale, Samuel Johnson, and Mrs Desmoulins. Nonetheless, much of the perspective of the narrative is through her eyes, and in a voice that is singularly hers, without the usual filters of her mother or Johnson's biographers. When the Streatham Circle is recast in a Bainbridge landscape, the fiction provides a special insight into Queeney's character that traditional biography cannot. The fictional Queeney ultimately controls our view of the world in which the historical one grew up. Because she is channeled through the distinctive gaze of Bainbridge, however, there is much that is satiric here; it is the sympathetic moments that are striking and unexpected. Bainbridge's Queeney is reminiscent of the Jane Austen of the Juvenilia, or the young Mary McCarthy, who apparently reduced one of her high school English teachers to tears (McCarthy 95). And Queeney's triumph comes at her mother's expense; the Mrs Thrale of *According to Queeney* fails to do credit to the historical Hester Lynch Thrale Piozzi. The tensions between the eighteenth and twenty-first century are strongly visible here. While it is possible to see a figure like McCarthy objecting to her mother's desire for display and while many young people have difficulties with parents' second marriages, these objections are not likely to include the new spouse's being Italian and/ or Roman Catholic, as the historical Queeney's did. Bainbridge avoids this historically specific tension by focusing on the more recognizable issues.

That Queeney's visibility will come at the expense of her mother's character is perhaps inevitable, given both their relationship and the Bainbridge style. The character of Mrs Thrale is for the most part a caricature, and a failure of the book, but accurate in that this tempestuous, rather silly woman feels isolated and shut out from her daughter in precisely the way we know she was from both Hester Thrale's own account and from historical scholarship like that of Hyde. The text privileges Queeney's unfairness to her mother, recording Queeney's explanation for the financial crisis at the brewery without the corrective of the historical record: 'owing to my mother's desire for expansion, both at Streatham Park and the Brewery, my father was forced to borrow money at exorbitant rates of interest, a debt he did not shake off for a further nine years – which burden undoubtedly led to a decline in his health' (78). At no point does Bainbridge allow the redemptive historical facts to appear: that Henry Thrale attempted to make beer without hops, that Hester and Johnson between them saved the brewery while Henry was rendered almost paralytic by distress, that Henry brought on his own death by a gluttony that was striking even in an age marked by overeating.[3] Hester's silliness as a character in the fiction, and her historically documented proclivities for display (of herself and her children) and harsh discipline, provide good reasons for Queeney's distaste, but presenting her as a kind of Mrs Bennet figure, loud, embarrassing, calling unwanted attention to her more decorous daughters, is scarcely using the devices of historical fiction in an insightful or useful way. Moreover, Bainbridge appears to concur with Boswell's insistence on her carelessness with the truth. She is not concerned with historical accuracy: 'It is the nub of the story that matters,' she says. Mr Johnson disagrees; Queeney listens judgmentally (90). It tells us less, rather than allowing us to imagine more, than the historical record already provides.

The *Family Book*, the record that Hester Thrale kept of her children's accomplishments and progress, establishes the pull between love and frustration, the kind of family discord that feeds Bainbridge's muse. In January 1777, considering the possibility that she might die in childbirth (and she appears quite prepared to do so in order to produce a son) Hester assumes that Henry will quickly remarry to provide a mother for his children and to produce more, but 'as for Queeney I defy him to find her a Mother [whom] She will appear to like less than her own.' She believes that Johnson 'would have the greatest Loss of me, and he would be the most sensible of his Loss.' Two months later, however, she is in turmoil over Queeney's sudden illness: 'Another agony! ... hers would be a Loss I *could* not outlive' (Hyde 175, 177). In 1772, when Queeney is eight, Hester compares her coldness with Lucy's warm nature: 'Queeney never would be fondled, nor delight in any Caresses I could give her, – She has a Heart wholly impenetrable to Affection as it should seem, & Lucy is softness and kindness itself' (Hyde 57). At the same time, she lauds her daughter's merits, which include self-discipline, prudence, and good judgment; when Queeney is less than nine years old, her mother asks her for advice, and by the age of nine she is assisting in the education of her sister Sophy (Hyde 61, 112). These passages encapsulate much of what forms the tone of the novel, including the comparisons between Queeney and Johnson.

While Bainbridge does capture Hester Thrale's anguish at Queeney's coldness, the ironic distance collapsing on occasion, there is still conflict between maternal desire and her reaction to the child's resistance. In one scene, concerned that some harm might have come to her daughter, she catches sight of her and attempts to hold her: 'She met with resistance; no amount of tugging, or pinching, would budge the child. Face flushed with resolve, Queeney stared defiantly and tightened her grip about Nurse's neck ... Relief replaced with anger, Mrs. Thrale would have slapped her into submission but for the lofty presence of Bennett [*sic*] Langton' (24–5). The mixed impulses to embrace and pinch, to caress and slap, have an authentic tone, and suggest the difficulties in presenting Hester Thrale as a sympathetic character – sympathy and historical accuracy are in tension with each other.

The dialogue between Queeney and her mother soon after Gabriel Piozzi appears on the scene sounds like pure Bainbridge, however, especially in Queeney's acidic tone. When Mrs Thrale claims that the singing master has an intuitive understanding of women (especially compared to Mr Thrale), her daughter answers, 'I allow he flutters his eyelids.' To her mother's contention that she was referring to his understanding, not his eyelids, Queeney answers, 'Last year and all the years before . . . it was Mr. Johnson who knew best what a woman felt.' Her encounter with her daughter leaves Mrs Thrale so rattled that she cannot think straight: 'Mrs. Thrale, endeavouring to extricate herself, found she stammered, even in her head. I have h-harmed Queeney in some way, [. . .] not least by loving her too much . . . and must p-pay for it' (184). Yet nothing in the fiction is more mordant or cruel than the historic eight-year-old Queeney's list of misfortunes that might happen to Hester, recorded in the family register: 'Papa . . . shall die, so shall Gmama [*sic*]; Mr. Johnson shall be affronted & never come here again, Harry shall go to Sea and be cast away, and I shall die – poor Lucy must die too, & you shall have nothing left at all but Susan for your Child, & Kit (that was a poor wretch of a Fellow) for your Man' (Hyde 87).

Hyde argues that Hester's mother's dominating presence in her life may have prevented her from ever establishing a companionate relationship with her husband (18), and that, far from finding that presence cramping, overwhelming, or oppressive, she sought to replicate it with her daughters. The advent of Johnson, of course, brought another equally dominating presence into the household. Interestingly, Hyde claims that Hester quickly felt 'as much at ease with him as she was with her mother' (19), indicating that this new relationship placed another barrier between Thrale and her husband and children. Yet Johnson had misgivings about her closeness to her mother; he thought it 'not right,' in Thrale's own words, that Mrs Salusbury should be the most important person in her life, and not entirely out of a jealous desire to be in that position himself (Hyde 70). Her despairing comments about Queeney's lack of affection, and her turning to her very young daughter for advice, suggest an attempt to make her daughters into the companions that her relationship with her mother led her to believe was both desirable and normative. There is no doubt that the girls resisted these attempts: 'Mrs. Thrale was never to have a child who had any such attachment for her' (Hyde 70). The Queeney of the novel clearly wishes to be the daughter of a woman who behaves as she believes a mother should, one who is affectionate and nurturing, not needy and unpredictable. Bainbridge agrees with most commentators that the final rupture was not caused by the Piozzi marriage, but had been brewing for a long time (*According to Beryl*), caused in part by Thrale's frequent resort to corporal punishment and stringent applications of home medications.

But Bainbridge also creates scenes that allow her to dispute Hester Thrale's historic claims for Queeney's coldness: 'I am not partial to her, Why Should I? She loves me not. And [*sic*] in Truth now her Brother is gone She has I think no great Kindness for any body' (Hyde 165). The novel represents a Queeney for whom that statement is not true – for example, in her relationship with her father – and in doing so it opens up the many misunderstandings that disrupted the household. Once she hides because she wishes for her mother to find her, but because 'Mamma was contrary in all things' she also knew that 'Found, she would be lectured on insolence, then kissed, then, like as not, slapped' (48). When the opportunity comes to be alone with her mother, she is uncharacteristically compliant: 'The rosy prospect of time spent with Mamma free of the younger siblings scratching round her like chicks about a hen filled her with such joy that she stood perfectly still and uttered scarcely a squawk while New Nurse wrenched the tangles from her hair' (49).

But her affection is rarely extended to Mrs Thrale. Some of her gestures of allegiance are as much opposition to her mother as solidarity with the object of affection – for example, when she kicks her mother for striking Old Nurse (who appears to be allowing her to choke on a button [41–2]), and when she identifies with a parrot: 'Other visitors had tried to get the parrot to talk, but it had only opened its beak for Queeney. This, she reasoned, was on account of her not joining in the general pestering; she herself grew stubborn when put on show' (56). She is more often sympathetic to animals than to people, again in contrast to her behaviour toward her mother. On their visit to Lichfield, Mrs Thrale is painfully aware of the difference between Queeney's face when looking at a pony that has been brought to the inn for her to ride, compared with the way she looks at her mother. The pony brings 'a shine on her face, such a pleasing curve to her pink mouth' whereas at 'breakfast the child had gazed at her coldly and when spoken to had twice pretended deafness' (113). Her identification with the animal world is once more evident in her reaction to Mrs Thrale's announcement of her remarriage. Speaking of herself and her sisters, she charges, 'if you must abandon your children, you must. You may turn us out to fend for ourselves, like puppies in a pond, to swim or drown as Providence pleases' (203). Hyde draws attention to the documented solidarity among the historical Thrale sisters, for whom Queeney served as leader and surrogate mother; rather than trusting to Providence, she made sure the puppies did not drown in the pond. The historic Queeney made an extraordinary trip across country in 1797 to attend her sister, Cecilia, who was about to give birth to a child. Her mother, by then Mrs Piozzi, and estranged from most of her daughters, admires her eldest from afar: '285 Miles from the coast of Sussex, with no Companion, no female Servt – nothing but a Groom & Saddle Bags: all the way on one Horse, as People travelled in Days of Yore. They are astonishing Girls' (Hyde 265). The 'Girls' at this time are thirty-three (Queeney) and twenty (Cecilia).

In *According to Beryl*, Bainbridge describes Piozzi as a bright and accomplished woman who needed the intellectual company that Johnson's presence brought into her house. She also believes that Hester's immense spirit countered Johnson's melancholia. Nonetheless, little of that sympathy makes its way into the novel; what little we have is in large part because in this as in all depictions, Henry Thrale comes across as a buffoon. In common with the biographers and historians before and after her novel, Bainbridge is unable to make us understand what Johnson saw in him. She has Johnson express his respect, but telling is not as persuasive as showing. One of the few moments when she evokes any sympathy for Mrs Thrale is when her husband climbs into her bed after a drunken episode, resplendent in his hostess's petticoat (111). Yet the historical Henry's most vicious act, his insistence that the heavily pregnant Hester travel to Southwark to sort out a problem at the brewery, resulting in the journey that caused the stillbirth of a child, is not mentioned, perhaps because this scene is not grotesque but tragic and thus outside the realm of satire. It would nonetheless add another layer of uncertainty, a collision of fact against Queeney's attempted recuperation of his reputation, because Queeney mentions the stillbirth but not the cause. The mordant conversation about Piozzi's sensitivity and eyelids, quoted above, in fact derives from his treatment of Mrs Thrale after the stillbirth, suggesting that Bainbridge is deliberately avoiding a sympathetic depiction.

It may well be that she is a difficult figure to portray; even Ian McIntyre, although he writes with great admiration and sympathy, does not altogether erase the sense of a woman who was raised to expect admiration and is uncomfortable when she does not receive it. The first lines of Piozzi's *Anecdotes of the Late Samuel Johnson* are redolent of the desire to be recognized as a scholar; in a few short pages she refers to *A Midsummer Night's Dream*, Trajan's column, the Telamonian shield, Johnson's lament 'that so little had ever been said about Butler,' 'the first representation of the Masque of Comus,' and the comparative superiority of the Jenisca and Nile rivers:

> the first receives near seventy tributary streams in the course of its unmarked progress to the sea, while the great parent of African plenty, flowing from an almost invisible source, and enriched by any extraneous waters, except eleven nameless rivers, pours his majestic torrents into the ocean by seven celebrated mouths. (3–5)

Such insistence is wearying rather than persuasive or admirable. Hyde, describing her letters to her daughters from Italy as 'amusing and tactless,' claims 'never throughout her life did she have the capacity to put herself in someone else's place' (247).

It is striking how much of Bainbridge's text is direct quotation from the sources, sometimes with startling effect. It is one thing for Hester Thrale to keep her *Family Book* to record her children's accomplishments; it is another to have Queeney's mother spouting these same accomplishments in public. Thrale may well have bragged about her children, but the language of conversation must have been a little more nuanced than the journal checklist, which is ludicrous when given public voice as it is here: 'She knows the compass as perfectly as any mariner upon the sea, is mistress of the solar system and the signs of the Zodiac ... and is thoroughly acquainted with the difference between the Ecliptick and Equator.' Should she have done so, and there is no record of such behaviour, Queeney might well have recoiled, especially if, as Hyde asserts, she was shy.[4] We certainly know that Johnson, who had been a very bright child, disapproved of children being displayed by their parents like performing pets. The words in which Bainbridge describes Mr Johnson in this scene ('She looked at him and saw that he was frowning, and knew the cause, for he had once told her that as a clever child he had suffered much from being put on show by his father') is a close paraphrase of a sentence in *Anecdotes of the Late Samuel Johnson*:

> The trick which most parents play with their children, of shewing off their newly-acquired accomplishments, disgusted Mr. Johnson beyond expression; he had been treated so himself, he said, till he absolutely loathed his father's caresses, because he knew they were sure to precede some unpleasing display of his early abilities. (Piozzi 10)

Mr Johnson, obviously disgusted beyond expression, resorts to wordless communication as the litany continues: 'Mrs. Thrale's last words were rendered almost inaudible by a tremendous clearing of the throat executed by Mr. Johnson ... At this Mr. Johnson gave vent to what could only be described as a warning growl ...[and] turned his back on the room' (32). This passage closely resembles his pronouncement on the pains of being a child of aging parents: the child is treated as 'a little boy's dog' who is 'forced ... to sit up and beg, as we call it, to divert a company, who at last go away complaining of their disagreeable entertainment' (Piozzi 11). But Mrs Thrale cannot be stopped, even by Mr Johnson's disapproval: 'she saw no reason to subdue her motherly pride. Raising her voice, she said, "In the last few months she has learnt to recount, with neat perfect accuracy, the Judgement of Paris and the legend of Perseus and Andromeda."' The other result of the frequent quotation of historical sources (and this material is very well-known, especially amidst the flurry of publications in honour of Johnson's tercentenary) is that the informed reader begins to feel that she is reading not a work of literary imagination, but a synthesis (and a clever one) of what she has already read elsewhere.

Bainbridge claims that Queeney 'had a different perspective about what was going on in the household,' the view of a precocious child, who perhaps felt superior to them all, 'but only because she was in adolescence' (*According to Beryl*). Certainly, the struggle to separate herself from a strong and demanding mother, especially on the part of a shy young woman with no desire to be a child prodigy, has an authentic, teen-angst ring to it. So too does the disgust at discovering her mother to be a sexual being, which must have been part of her objection to the marriage to Gabriel Piozzi, in addition to the fears of what such an alliance would do to her status and marriage prospects. But Queeney was always distant, even as an infant and a toddler, as Thrale's journals quoted above reveal in agonized detail; still, she was twenty-one at the time of her mother's second marriage, well beyond the age where sullen adolescence should be expected. Martine Watson Brownley contends that the daughters 'had in reality been lost from the beginning. All of them disliked her from childhood' ('Women's Images' 71). Johnson's comments, quoted in *Anecdotes*, should have served as a warning: 'You teach your daughters the diameters of the planets, and wonder when you have done that they do not delight in your company' (Piozzi 17). The beatings and home remedies cannot have helped.

The fictional Queeney's version of the story includes the recuperation of her father's reputation, a project Bainbridge handles by employing the child's view through much of the narrative. When Mrs Jackson, a visitor to Streatham, asks about her, her father requests that she be brought downstairs, where she sits on his knee 'quite contentedly,' until sent back to the nursery upon the revelation that she is not yet able to read (31). On another occasion, she is following her mother and Mr Johnson in a tour of the cathedral in Lichfield, but they are arguing and take no notice of her, so that she is left behind: 'At once she turned tail and sped out of the doors in search of her father . . . Papa had a beautiful smile, one that always took away her fright.' In this scene, Queeney appears content, even child-like, in a way that rarely happens in the narrative:

> they lolled companionably together in its golden rays and amused them-. selves with the recitation of nursery rhymes. Though she considered herself far too old for such childish entertainment, Queeney submitted to it for Papa's sake. It was not a chore, for he made her giggle when he stuck his thumb in his mouth and played at being little Jack Horner. (90–1)

There is no lolling or giggling with her mother; when they set off on their tour once more, Mrs Thrale moves so fast that she steps on Queeney's heel. Yet her attempts to restore the image of her father fail; apart from a few playful moments that provide respite from her mother's more coercive attentions, it is hard to see why Queeney, so judgmental about others, could remain fiercely loyal to his memory, except as revenge against her mother, and a strike at the bumptious (and now deceased) Boswell.

The historical Queeney, so devoted to her sisters, had an equally good relationship with her daughter, who, when she was widowed at an early age, willingly returned to her mother and lived with her for the rest of her life, a striking contrast to the Thrale family's cold relations. The Keiths' home at Tullyallan 'represented all the qualities of happiness which Queeney had sought as a young girl – dignity, comfort, and serenity' (Hyde 319); the fictionalized household that Bainbridge describes so vividly certainly contains none of these qualities, and all their opposites. Having refused to raise her daughter 'to be an intellectual prodigy like her mother' (Hyde 319), Queeney achieved instead what her mother longed for: a daughter who was her friend.

The title of Bainbridge's novel is deeply ironic, because Queeney, as becomes clear in the text, does not want her say. Alone among all the compulsive writers, recorders, publishers, and compilers who surrounded her – even Baretti, her Italian tutor, published the dialogues he wrote for her – she did not leave a written record. According to Queeney, it would be best if everyone kept silent and got on with their lives, as she makes clear to Laetitia Hawkins she is doing herself. Her cool attitude toward Laetitia, who is seeking anecdotes about Johnson (although she explains it as developing from childhood hatred, itself an interesting psychological point), seems more deeply rooted in her distaste for display, for being made the centre of attention, for being held up and scrutinized. This dislike of attention is consonant with her known attitudes in life, her almost intentionally bad dancing for example (dancing being a prime method of displaying daughters, as all Jane Austen's mothers know). Hester Thrale complains that, whether because of 'bashfulness or naughtiness,' Queeney's dancing was 'incomparably ill'; Hyde, with typical charity and perception, believes that 'the art of dancing was something Queeney did not choose to conquer, perhaps because it was the one thing she did badly' (170, 113). Bainbridge develops hilarious scenes of resistance to the French dancing master – refusing Sunday lessons, for example, because 'it was against her Christian principles' (145). Later, in a letter to Laetitia, she claims that the dancing master treated her with 'untoward familiarity,' although her mother refused to believe it (150).

But all these examples reveal more about the observers and interpreters than they do about Queeney herself. Only a novelist can enter into that deliberate, possessive silence, because only fiction can give her a voice, especially when the silent are insistently so. In the long run, the romance of biography provides more illumination than its satirical mode, a true amplification and addition to what historians and biographers are allowed to do. Nonetheless, this twenty-first-century imagining of Queeney allows us to imagine how a child and young woman very much of her own class and period would react to such an imposing environment as the Johnson circle – many of her judgments, for example, on her mother and Boswell, reflect those of her day – at the same time as we understand and sympathize with those reactions. Bainbridge creates a character who is fiercely reticent. She effects the representation by portraying a home filled with relentless talk and demands for attention, a mother who wished to exhibit her, and the competitor for her mother's attention, a man whose every word the company is at pains to remember, record, and publish. In this milieu, silence is the ultimate rebellion.

NOTES

1 The minimalist, lapidary structure of her prose is no accident: 'I throw away 12 pages for every one I finish. I cut like mad,' she explained to an interviewer from *Publishers Weekly* (Baker 53). I cite this article with the caveat that Baker describes Hester Thrale as 'Mr. Johnson's landlady' (53).
2 In this essay I alternate between calling the historical Hester Lynch Thrale by that name to indicate her life during her first marriage, and 'Piozzi' after her second marriage. I am using the name 'Mrs Thrale' to indicate the character in the novel, because that is the name by which Bainbridge most often refers to her. In the same fashion, Samuel Johnson, or simply Johnson, indicates the historical person; 'Mr Johnson' is Bainbridge's character.
3 Bainbridge refers to these facts in *According to Beryl*, so it cannot be argued that she was unaware of them. Indeed, it would be difficult to avoid them; Thrale's reckless business practices and gluttony are documented widely in the literature on the Johnson circle.
4 'Queeney was extremely shy because she could not bear to be laughed at' (Hyde 40). According to Valerie Rumbold, Frances Burney describes her as 'shy but likeable' (35). The text Bainbridge quotes in this scene is from Thrale's report on her daughter at two-and-a-half. It begins: 'She cannot read at all, but knows the Compass as perfectly as any Mariner upon the Seas' (Hyde 21).

WORKS CITED

According to Beryl. Directed by Udayan Prasad. BBC Arena Series. 2001. Film.
Bainbridge, Beryl. *According to Queeney*. New York: Carrol & Graf, 2001. Print.

Baker, John F. 'Beryl Bainbridge: Total Immersion in the Past.' *Publishers Weekly* (9 November 1998): 52–3. Print.

Baruth, Philip. *The Brothers Boswell*. New York: Soho Press, 2009. E-book. Digital file.

Boswell, James. *Life of Johnson*. Ed. R.W. Chapman and J.D. Fleeman. New York: Oxford UP, 1970. Print.

Brack, O.M., Jr. Introduction to John Hawkins. *The Life of Samuel Johnson LL.D.* Ed. O.M. Brack, Jr. Athens: UP of Georgia, 2009. xxi–xxxiv. Print.

Brownley, Martine Watson. 'Eighteenth-Century Women's Images and Roles: The Case of Hester Thrale Piozzi.' *Biography* 3 (1980): 55–76. Print.

– "Under the Domaine of *Some* Woman": The Friendship of Samuel Johnson and Hester Thrale.' *Mothering the Mind: Twelve Studies of Writers and Their Silent Partners*. Ed. Ruth Perry and Martine Watson Brownley. New York: Holmes and Meier, 1984. 64–79. Print.

Donoghue, Emma. *Life Mask*. New York: Harcourt, 2004. Print.

Fleishman, Avrom. *The English Historical Novel: Walter Scott to Virginia Woolf*. Baltimore and London: Johns Hopkins UP, 1971. Print.

Greenblatt, Stephen. 'How It Must Have Been.' *The New York Review of Books* 61.17 (5 November 2009): 22–5. Print.

Hyde, Mary. *The Thrales of Streatham Park*. Cambridge: Harvard UP, 1997. Print.

McCarthy, Mary. *How I Grew*. New York: Harcourt Brace Jovanovich, 1986. Print.

McIntyre, Ian. *Hester: The Remarkable Life of Mr. Johnson's 'Dear Mistress.'* London: Constable and Robinson, 2008. Print.

Piozzi, Hester Lynch. *Anecdotes of the Late Samuel Johnson, LL.D., during the Last Twenty Years of his Life*. Ed. S.C. Roberts. 1925. Repr. Westport: Greenwood Press, 1971. Print.

Rumbold, Valerie. 'Music Aspires to Letters: Charles Burney, Queeney Thrale, and the Streatham Circle.' *Music & Letters* 74 (1992): 24–38. Print.

Sontag, Susan. *The Volcano Lover: A Romance*. Picador Books Edition. New York: Farrar, Strauss and Giroux, 1992. Print.

13   The Agency of Things in Emma Donoghue's *Slammerkin*

ELIZABETH KOWALESKI WALLACE

The action of Emma Donoghue's novel *Slammerkin* (2000), an account of the real-life Mary Saunders who murdered her mistress with a cleaver in 1764, begins with one single, very powerful thing – a bit of scarlet ribbon coveted by the then thirteen-year old protagonist. The novel ends with same ribbon, now faded and frayed, tucked into Mary's stays as she jumps from the scaffold to her death by hanging, in retribution for killing her mistress. What, then, does this red ribbon *do*? In asking this question, I am drawing on Bruno Latour's recent assertion that, in the case of things, 'there might exist many metaphysical shades between full causality and sheer existence.' He further explains, 'in addition to "determining" and "serving as a backdrop for human action," things might authorize, allow, afford, encourage, permit, suggest, influence, block, render possible, forbid, and so on' (72). Given Latour's observation, I would like to ask 'how many metaphysical shades can a red ribbon possess?' More specifically, what role does the ribbon play in Mary's movement from infantile craving to adult appetite, from innocence to guilt?

In some ways, *Slammerkin* is the story of the ribbon and all that the ribbon, as a metonym, signifies. Like the larger category of clothing and physical adornment, the ribbon possesses great agency as it introduces the possibility of sensual fulfilment, of tactile and visual pleasure, and of the self transformed in relation to such possibility. The novel charts Mary's path as she comes to understand the power of things. Because women's relationship to popular culture is often accessed through a discussion of the special appeal of things to women, this novel utilizes an actual, historically based form of female consumer activity to tell a modern morality tale. In both London and provincial Monmouth, where the closing action of the novel takes place, fashion disguises and distorts, but also facilitates a large-scale social masquerade. Yet

Donoghue's teenage character possesses an arguably modern psychology as the author endows her character with two equally strong impulses: Mary feels a nearly biological imperative toward a life of things and she is driven to attain those things at all cost; yet she also evinces a late-adolescent psychology that drives her to destroy anything or anyone who reaches toward her, resulting in her own self-destruction. The novel brings the two impulses together in a way that becomes a didactic judgment on the necessity of resisting the lure of things, even while it paradoxically grants things their due. Thus in *Slammerkin* Donoghue returns to an eighteenth-century context both to mine its social history and to explore a pressing contemporary question – namely, how do women understand themselves in a world of things? How do cultural things simultaneously define female subjectivity and yet necessitate moralistic engagement?

From the very first pages of the novel, the ribbon belongs to a world where the 'unnatural' has asserted itself over and above the 'natural.' The novel opens with a prologue set in 1752, when Great Britain first adapted the Gregorian calendar, resulting in the loss of eleven days from 2 September to the 14th. The protagonist's father, a cobbler, experiences the transition as a theft: 'There were eleven days of chiseling shoe leather he'd never be paid for, eleven dinners snatched away before they reached his lips, eleven nights when he was going to be cheated out of the sweet relief of dropping down on his straw mattress' (1). He subsequently joins the calendar riots, and dies of jail fever before being executed.[1] Thus, the novel's first significant pattern of imagery is established: the bodily, lived time of the simple tradesman, which he experiences 'naturally' with relation to physical process, clashes with a man-made, social time that has been superimposed upon corporeal experience. The father rages against the arbitrariness of the new time that seems to cheat and deprive him, but he is ultimately powerless. He finds himself out of step with modern society.

The prologue immediately transitions to Mary, who similarly chafes against an arbitrary measurement that has been imposed on her body, near the end of her brief life in 1763. The jail cell that confines her is 'twenty-two feet long and fifteen feet wide,' dimensions that her own pacing feet have measured (2). If her father found himself out of step with modern time, Mary finds herself literally out of steps, as her execution is scheduled for the next morning. The red ribbon makes its first appearance in the prologue, when a thief attempts to remove the ribbon from its hiding place on Mary's sleeping body, just before she is to be hanged.

Even from the prologue, then, the novel establishes an opposition between the natural rhythms of the body – rhythms to be experienced in working, eating, sleeping, or simply walking – and social restraints that temporally and spatially confine physicality.[2] Thus the urge for things is aligned with an unnatural experiencing of the body. Much of the novel's action unfolds in London, and city life epitomizes a life out of touch with the 'natural.' London pulls in people – like Mary's own mother, who had once had the promise of a stable existence as a seamstress in Monmouth – but it also cruelly transforms them into individuals displaying the most brutal human passions, unleashed and unrestrained. Alienated from her mother, who has remarried and borne an all-important son, Mary is soon alone and vulnerable on the city streets. After she is raped and impregnated by a ribbon peddler at age fourteen, her mother banishes her from home. On her first night on the streets, she is brutally gang raped by a group of soldiers. She is then taken in by a kindly prostitute named Doll who introduces Mary to the trade. She spends some time in the Magdalen Hospital, until she chafes against its strict routines and asks to be released. But she discovers that her old friend Doll has died from illness. Part 2 of the novel unfolds in Monmouth, where Mary presents a letter, forged in her mother's voice, asking that she be taken in by a family of artisans. She begins her new life as a servant and is soon taken into the confidence of the kindly mistress. While Monmouth is free of London's worst excesses, it none-theless possesses its own share of hypocrites and otherwise dishonest types. And so, though Mary can almost see how a provincial life might suit her, in the end the desire for more leads her back into prostitu-tion – and eventually to the heinous crime for which she will be hanged.

As already suggested, the novel opposes 'natural' or corporeal time with socially imposed rhythms that cheat the body and ultimately lead to its destruction. Similarly, the novel opposes 'natural' and arti-ficial expression, and thus construes the agency of things most nega-tively – and conservatively. In particular, Mary observes how fashion 'unnaturally' covers the body beneath – and indeed, throughout the novel, clothing in general disguises and distorts what 'naturally' is, thereby creating a world in which appearances are not to be trusted. Thus clothing talks *to* her. It speaks about the wearer's status and posi-tion, though Mary soon learns that it does not always tell the whole story. When she hears of the example of Nan Pullen, who borrows fine garments from her sleeping mistress to attract customers under the cover of night, Mary recognizes how clothing emboldens the wicked to dupe the gullible (50). Mary quickly perceives that '*Clothes make the woman*' (70) but also '*Clothes are the greatest lie ever told*' (71). Thus Mary's coming of age requires that she become literate in the language of clothes and that she gain competency in manipulating its symbolism.

But clothing also talks *for* Mary. For instance, it announces her entry onto the streets. When Mary is sent out to turn her first trick, Doll reminds her of her bright colourful dress and cheerfully assures her, 'The clothes will speak for you, won't they?' (47). Throughout the novel, Mary herself is conflated with a particular item of clothing, as the very title of the book makes clear: the word 'slammerkin' refers first to a loose dress and then to the wearer of that dress – a loose woman (47). Paradoxically, this conflation of person and things, or of human identity and clothing, also comforts Mary, as it allows her to imagine her actual self as existing elsewhere, beyond the nexus of girl and dress. As a prostitute, she thinks to herself that it is not herself she sells: 'she was sure of that much. She just hired out a dress called skin' (65). Yet where this actual self resides, how it knows itself other than through its coverings, and how it configures itself without recourse to its wrappings is left temporarily unsaid. Moreover, the difficulty of an existence outside of or beyond one's clothing is underscored by a prostitute's necessary and powerful investment in her wardrobe. Without proper dress, a prostitute has diminished economic possibilities. When Mary and Doll spot an impoverished girl trying unsuccessfully to turn tricks, Doll identifies her failure as the fault of her tawdry dress: '"it's not us they want, you dolt," said Doll. "In those rags, the girl can't let on to be anything but herself. Remember, sweetheart, you should go without a week of dinners sooner than pawn your last good gown"' (70). Doll's own death is later presaged by the disappearance of key items from her stock of clothing, as if, without her gaudy clothing, she simply fails to exist.

One of the many strengths of Donoghue's novel is its attention to historical specificity, and in particular its awareness that clothes carry their signifying potential across England's territories. As John Styles illuminates, during the eighteenth century, while commercial society both benefited and victimized the humbler ranks, nonetheless, 'their clothes were the most blatant manifestation of the material transformation of plebian life' (3). Donoghue's novel relies upon this historical fact. So, although one might imagine that fashion would lose both its appeal and power beyond the capitol's reach, in this story clothes have even greater agency among the provincial middle ranks. For the second half of the story, Donoghue chooses as her setting interior spaces where the self comes to be transformed through the magic of the stay-maker and his wife the dressmaker. As Mr Jones begins to let Mary into the secrets of his trade, he explains that '"The French call us *tailleurs de corps*, tailors of the body ... We are artists who work in bone"'(175). He takes great pride in his work, and in particular in his ability to reshape the natural female body into more fashionable forms. He tells Mary, '"I can mould the female form into whatever I like. I aim for an effect of harmonious symmetry, much like the designs of Mr Adam, I'd like to think." (He thought this allusion was probably wasted on the girl)' (253).

In Monmouth Mary learns just how far fashion can go. The clothes that hang in Mrs Jones's dressmaker shop are even more animated than the styles in London, as they appear to take on a life of their own. Her first impression is of 'small space, entirely peopled by clothes. A lady's embroidered bodice, laced up with silver, hung from hooks set in the ceiling. Ruched under-petticoats swayed in the icy draught from the door; Mary had the impression they had just stopped dancing. A quilted petticoat in swanskin flannel was tasseled in ten places. A French sack dropped voluminous pleats of yellow and white silk ... [Mary] had never seen finer work in the shops of Pall Mall' (163–4). The quality is better because of the pride that Mrs Jones takes in her work. She is represented as a highly skilled artisan, someone with an expertise in fashion that belies her provincial circumstances. Like her husband, Mrs Jones takes pride in the idea that she exerts powerful control over her customers: she 'toyed with the notion that the ladies of Monmouth were her puppets: walking advertisements for handiwork' (257). She is an expert, recognizing the smallest variations in the styles of various aspects of a lady's dress, for instance the between 'a fitted casaquin and a caraco' – two types of camisoles – or between 'a palatine and a mantalet and a cardinal, and, most importantly between a round gown and an open gown, not to mention a wrapping gown and a nightgown (which was only worn in the day)' (164).

This kind of attention to subtle yet important sartorial detail enhances Mary's earlier impression that clothes have the power to speak and signify person and occasion, yet it often irritates her to serve customers who lack any natural grace or refinement. Her experience in Mrs Jones's shop enhances lessons learned in London – that clothes make the person and facilitate her ability to navigate a world of social relations: ' Something else Mary was learning: what mattered just as much as what someone wore was how they carried it off. The best silk sack gown could be ruined on a stooping, countryish customer. It was all in the gaze, the stance, the set of the shoulders' (191). So Mary herself begins to mould her body into a shape that will win respect: she learns 'how to move as if the body – in all its damp indignity – was as sleek and upright as the dress' (193). We see, then, in both London and Monmouth, that fashion is both unnatural or artificial and absolutely necessary for an unfolding conversation about class, status, and social location. Without their clothes, the citizens of Monmouth would have difficulty communicating with one another.

In this way, Donoghue (a Cambridge-trained scholar in eighteenth-century studies) taps into a historical preoccupation with the role of dress in provincial English society that has been well-documented by a range of historians, including Amanda Vickery, Beverly Lemire, and John Styles.[3] Historical, archival work supports an impression that is easily gathered from a broad range of eighteenth-century literary texts: fashion was simultaneously celebrated for its capacity to signify and connote internal merit and virtues (think Richardson's *Pamela*) and excoriated for its ability to distract, disguise, or deceive (think Defoe's *Roxana*). In other words, historians and literary critics alike would bear out this novel's message about the agency of clothes, and they would endorse the heroine's sense that the language of fashion was audible and powerful, if also deeply conflicted.

Yet the novel departs from its historical foundations when, through its use of free indirect style, it also affords its protagonist a 'true' subjectivity that is not merely the sum of its signifying surfaces. I have alluded to this idea once before, in the instance where Mary assures herself that it isn't her 'self' that she sells in the act of prostitution. As a character in a modern novel, Mary also has a recognizable psychology.[4] Thus, she experiences appetites that Donoghue registers as 'natural,' or even biological. The things that Mary wants, then, are not merely arbitrary, but are as necessary to her as the air she breathes or the food that nourishes her. Indeed, as a young girl, she experiences physical deprivations that are conflated with a craving for things. Mary's longing for the bit of red ribbon, for example, is depicted as physical. The ribbon itself is unnatural, artificial, and man-made, but it powerfully mimics and evokes nature: it is the 'exact color of the poppies that grew in Lamb's Conduit Fields at the back of Holborn' (7). Later, when Mary sees the coveted ribbon in the hair of a prostitute, it takes on the colour of blood (9).

Here, then, the agency of things gathers new meaning: by taking on the shade of the poppy, the ribbon partakes of nature's aesthetic potential. Moreover, by assuming the colour of blood, it mirrors an elemental physiology. Though they may be artificial, things speak to fundamental, physical urges. The narrative tells us that 'Mary owned nothing with colour in it, and consequently was troubled by cravings' (9). 'Colours [make] her mouth water' (9); she becomes obsessed with 'gaudy colors' (12), and vows never to wear beige (12). For Mary, colour is the same as food. It nourishes and sustains, yet she is deprived of food and colour simultaneously. Conversely, she remembers access to food and to sensual fulfilment in relation to the maternal body, as when she indistinctly remembers her mother feeding her posset with a pewter spoon (15).[5] Mary's turn to prostitution is rationalized as the impulse to 'feed' herself, since life on the streets puts consumer culture within her reach. As a prostitute, she tastes 'rum from Barbados, French wine, lemons from Portugal, and a pineapple so sweet she thought her head would explode' (43).

Mary's failure to reform during her sojourn in the Magdalen Hospital is also linked to sensual deprivation, and in particular to the asylum's hermetic and antiseptic cleanliness. The house is too big, too clean. To Mary's eye, 'This was a silent world of its own, sealed off from the real one. A convent, or a cage' (90). She experiences the grayness of the asylum's uniform as appalling. Though she is adequately fed, her basic needs addressed, the place leaves 'a taste of ash' in her mouth (91), and her appetite is unassuaged. At this point the novel depicts Mary as being incapable of settling for less than full sensual fulfilment. Yet arguably this representation pulls the narrative in two directions: are things powerful, yet unnatural and inhuman agents that disturb and distort what naturally *is*? In other words, are they part of an unhealthy propensity to transform, disguise, and distort a natural order? Or, are they coextensive with biological urges, as necessary as food, as unavoidable as appetite?

As Mary leaves the Magdalen House and travels to Monmouth, the novel appears conflicted on this question, unable to decide exactly which position to take. The novel loses some of its edge – and some of its focus – with the introduction of a new cast of characters in Monmouth. The basic problem is that Donoghue introduces the heroine's key antagonists, the stay-maker and his dressmaker wife, as people who are simply too good, in psychological terms, to be credible, and the narrative flounders as it must establish the motives that will drive Mary to destroy what it clearly meant to be her best chance at happiness. To begin, unlike their counterparts in London, people like the Joneses in Monmouth follow the old time, signalling that they are less out of step with nature's rhythms. 'In the Marches we reckon our dates by the Old Style, which means true Midsummer's not for a fortnight yet,' explains Mrs Jones (308). The master in particular is represented as generous and sympathetic to a fault, even when depicted through Mary's somewhat cynical free indirect style: 'Mary suspected the master would always see to his own wig, even if he had ten thousand pounds a year. She'd never yet heard him say the words I need' (173). The mistress is similarly compassionate and selfless, incapable of duplicity or pettiness. She is completely taken in by Mary's fabricated story that she has come to the Joneses upon the wish of her dying mother. Mrs Jones practises every kindness to Mary, and she demonstrates every faith in Mary's abilities. She treats Mary like a member of her family, until Mary imagines someone would mistake them for mother and daughter (216). Eventually Mary begins to think that her lies can come true and that she can reverse the effects of her time on the streets: 'she could almost believe she was a virgin again' (221).

The battle is pitched between Mary's psychology, resembling as it does the uneven, hormonally driven extremes of a rebellious teenager, and the Joneses. To add to the pathos, the Joneses suffer from a sad affliction, namely Mrs Jones's innumerable miscarriages, which have left the couple without a son to carry on the family business. Yet they remain tenderly devoted to one another and provide an emblem of stability in a world that has, up to this point in the novel, been represented as self-serving and heartless. Also opposing Mary is a would-be suitor, a respectable and upright young man who finds himself drawn to her, despite his intuitive sense that something is a little off. A bookish man, Daffy is also deeply rooted in the natural rhythms of life at Monmouth, and his role is to introduce Mary to 'nature' and to tutor her in the virtues of a life without an addiction to 'things.' Daffy's interactions with Mary seem to assert that her love of objects is unnatural and corrupt, but the implication of moral judgment is blunted by the fact that all the people around her – notably the customers of Mrs Jones's shop – are also so concerned about their 'things.' Donoghue portrays her character as being between two choices which are not depicted as choices for others elsewhere in the novel.

Indeed, Mary begins her slow decline toward her tragic end in the moment when she and Daffy lie among the flowers on a fine spring day and she proves resistant to his saving graces. As Daffy points out the varieties of natural vegetation that surround them, he challenges Mary to find the silk that matches the exact shade of a white anemone (248) – in other words, to duplicate in art what nature has already provided. She responds, 'Mrs Jones and I can cover skirts in glorious flowers, without any need to go out in the mud to see them.' Daffy counters,

'Little neat stunted things, you embroider all the same shape, and flat as thread. That's not nature.' In this dialogue, we are reminded of the binary opposition between the natural and the man-made world, or between the world as it simply exists, and the world as human beings have created it – in other words, between a world where artificial things are unnecessary or superfluous, and a world where man-made objects are generated to simulate and duplicate nature's effects. Daffy and Mary align with the two sides of the binary. He maintains that the things that human beings create are inferior, inadequate – embroidery brilliantly mimics nature's profusions, but it is 'stunted' and flat. Though Mary offers no words against Daffy's assertion, one could certainly argue that the embroidery, when it perfectly renders nature's splendour – has its defences as well. As the famous example of Mrs Delany's needlework (on display at the Yale Center for British Art in the autumn of 2009) suggests, embroidery can represent a high standard of human artistic achievement, and it can testify to a human impulse to capture what is otherwise fleeting in the natural world. That Donoghue gives Mary no recourse against what is perhaps meant to be the 'right' position suggests that she aligns Mary's preference for the stunted and flat, or for the artificial thing, over the three-dimensional real, with her persistent moral depravity.

Daffy then fills Mary's apron with flowers: 'red campion, which isn't red at all, he explained, but pink like the insides of a lip. Bugle, which sounded like music but was made up of little spikes of purple blue. After hooded vetch came a small pale thing he called cuckooflower, though some said lady's smock, and other, milkmaids' (249). Here in his cataloguing of nature's offerings, Daffy implicitly urges Mary to reconsider her addiction to materialism, subtly offering himself as a possible suitor. Under his tutelage, the narrative seems to suggest, Mary might unlearn her preference for the inferior things that culture offers in lieu of nature. Her addiction would disappear, and her cravings might be satisfied in a more wholesome way. With him, she would learn to appreciate a life more in tune with nature's simplicity. But Mary only toys with Daffy: she is perfectly content to have sex with him, but she proves deaf to the language of nature and Daffy's offer of salvation and resistant to the vision of herself and of naturalized femininity that the two imply.

More than rejecting Daffy, Mary persistently gravitates toward the corrupt and the wicked. The narrative throws into the mix a depraved clergyman, Cadwaladyr, whom Mary had tricked into giving her money on the trip from London by pretending to be an innocent girl until he deflowered her. Eventually, partially under Cadwaladyr's influence, Mary returns to prostitution, nightly turning her tricks in the town tavern while the Joneses think she has gone out to fetch beer. Discovered in the act by Mr Jones one evening, she seduces him, to his deep mortification (297). In this way, Donoghue once again raises the question of Mary's true nature. Mary feels herself to be playing a role and queries how she could 'have thought of going into service, even for a short while, a girl who had known what liberty was' (209). In her internal monologue, she further imagines her two options. On one side, she imagines marriage to Daffy: 'To be a wife and mother in a small country town was the life millions led and other millions prayed for' (281). She conjures up a world that offers 'the dull round of domestic duties.' On the other, a life with material satisfaction and aesthetic pleasures might await. But what gives her the right 'to demand a life of silks and gold?' (281–2).

However, here the logic of Mary's thinking is belied by her experience among the provincials in Monmouth: her time in Mrs Jones's shop reveals that a life of domestic duties and fashionable indulgence are not necessarily antithetical. For who would have been the customers for those embroidered bodices, ruched under-petticoats, that French sack 'in voluminous pleats of yellow and white silk' if not some of the same women attached to the 'dull domestic sphere'? To be certain, not all women could afford to dress in the very best or to adorn themselves in the most elaborate styles, yet clearly the shop does a ready business in a wide array of fashionable, well-made garments, enough to keep the business profitable, even in a small city. That Mrs Jones is an apt and ready interpreter of the difference between different camisoles suggests that her customers demand a high level of fashion awareness, and that 'dull' provincial life also offers its moments of sartorial indulgence. Once again, through the free indirect style, we are allowed access to Mary's mind, where the binary opposition between goodness and corruption, between nature and art, satisfaction and dissatisfaction – and between 'no things' and 'things' – persists. In short, Mary associates a life of discipline and order with sensual deprivation, despite the evidence that the opposition between domestic duty and material indulgence is arguably false.

Since the comment appears in free indirect style, perhaps the mistaken perception is Mary's alone: perhaps the author attributes to the teenage protagonist this dualist understanding of the world, in which one is compelled *either* to choose to follow one's duty *or* to follow one's cravings. Perhaps as well Donoghue, with her attention to Mary's intractable desires, means to show us the tragedy of one teenager's immature misunderstanding of the choices she is being offered. But it seems equally possible that the novel displays a deep ambivalence about the nature of things themselves. In short, how much agency do they actually have? This is a crucial question, as it will ultimately determine the reader's modern interpretation of Mary's eighteenth-century murderous act. The passage invites us to consider how things have the power to seduce and mislead. Can they provoke us to behave irrationally and irresponsibly? Does the continual desire for things, especially luxury items like fitted casaquins (or in our time, Dior bags or Jimmy Choo shoes), disrupt our ability to be happy, to rest content with our lot? Does the desire for those things which remain always slightly beyond our reach make it impossible to accept the circumstances in which we find ourselves? If the answer to these questions is yes, then the novel affords terrific agency to consumer culture, to the things that announce its presence – and to its power over human subjectivity. Simply put, *things rule*. Mary's story is 'typical' and generic: she evinces a transhistorical human drive, only differing, perhaps, in the intensity of her response to the things that call out to her.

If this is the case, then a moralistic stance on Mary's crime seems quite possibly irrelevant: Mary is under the power of things. She responds intuitively to their call. Indeed, we can now understand how the red ribbon set her demise in motion, and her heinous crime cannot really be said to be her fault. Yet Donoghue pushes the matter further: far from offering us a heroine who is simply not to blame, she gives us a protagonist who, by the end of the novel, will incur our deepest disapproval, and who will be judged most severely for her pathological inability to draw a very important line between her own self and her things. At the climax of the novel, Mary once again becomes a thing – in this case, an especially stunning dress, a white velvet slammerkin. Here a moralistic discourse, overlaid upon the free indirect style, intrudes and distances the reader from any sympathetic identification with Mary's predicament, so that a tension arises between the first suggestion, that things have ultimate agency over us, and a second interpretation, that it is morally imperative to protect ourselves against their seductive claims.

The denouement unfolds as Mary discovers that Mrs Jones has taken her hidden savings, accrued through her secretive acts of prostitution, and put them in the poor box. Mary becomes incensed; her thoughts rage like those of an out-of-control teenager: 'All of Mary's old griefs welled up now, but rage swallowed them as fast as they would come. Her mouth was bitter, her legs were locked, her hands were sharp. *The bitch is going to get what she deserves*' (346, italics in original). She breaks into the store cupboard and begins drinking Canary. Under the influence of the alcohol, she decides that she cannot run away without resources – and without the clothing that her hidden stock of money would have provided: 'If she went back to London without fine clothes, Mary thought blurrily, she'd be nothing but a beast of the field, a vagabond, shooed along from parish to parish until she ended up in the workhouse with her feet chained to the wall' (346). In fact, both historically and narratively Mary's assessment of her situation makes some sense. As the novel has established, the proper clothes do make a difference, as her society judges individuals, making allowances for some but not others, based on sartorial display. Yet she thinks this idea 'blurrily,' and under the influence of drink, so that the narrative undercuts the idea that Mary proceeds rationally. If anything, she is depicted as desperate and off-kilter.

The next sequence of events tips the narrative away from sympathetic identification with Mary's desperate circumstances and toward moral disapproval of her actions. 'Time seemed to have slowed down now. A long mirror tempted her, so she shucked off her plain brown dress and climbed into [a customer's] white velvet slammerkin' (346). If earlier Mary had resisted the idea that she was her dress, that her subjectivity could be conflated with a thing, here she easily collapses self and dress: 'It was hard to fasten the dress on her own with fingers made clumsy by drink, but she managed. She filled the dress as if it were made for her' (346–7). Despite the fact that the dress was tailored to fit the body of another woman, it becomes her in both senses. Yet the reader's response to this scene is carefully controlled: the wriggling 'little silver snakes' (347) that adorn the long train suggest that we are meant to connect Mary to the story of man's first transgression. Mary displays several of the seven deadly sins as well – pride, to be sure, but also extravagance, greed, and even gluttony all in the same moment. 'Mary stood and twirled in front of the mirror, and the whole world seemed to turn. Enraptured, she grabbed the bottle of wine and toasted herself, from her endless train to her scarlet lips. She'd never seen anything more beautiful' (347). Mary has become Eve, an emblem of woman at her most narcissistic, her most monstrous, and her most depraved. However, this heavily moralistic overlay shifts agency from the dress (which earlier held the ultimate ability to authorize human identity) to Mary herself: for where does the impulse to judge Mary come from, if not from a discourse that perceives human beings as individually responsible for their actions, regardless of their material circumstances? In other words, does it make any sense to blame Mary if she is simply responding to the power of things? The narrative appears conflicted over whether to acknowledge the supreme authority of things over Mary, or whether to judge her for her inability to resist them. Donoghue's novel taps a tension most likely first felt during the dawn of the consumer revolution in the eighteenth century and concurrently reflects an anxiety common in modern consumer society, particularly in regard to women's consumption, economic power, and cultural agency.

When Mrs Jones enters the scene, confronts Mary, and commands her to remove the dress, the protagonist vituperatively reveals the truth of her circumstances – that she had lied about her mother's death, that she has been prostituting herself, and that she has even seduced Mr Jones. Mrs Jones only responds by insisting that Mary take off the expensive dress before she ruins it. Mary freezes on the spot: 'The strange thing was that she could feel the mistresses' words coming true. Her skin soured, leaking poison through every pore, contaminating every stitch of silver embroidery. The velvet hung on her like a snakeskin. She couldn't peel it off now; there'd be nothing left of her' (348). Unquestionably, Mary experiences this corruption as existing within herself, as the dress becomes nothing more than a passive and inert receptacle of all her human error. If the velvet hangs 'like a snakeskin,' she herself is the serpent, the base and animalistic emblem of the human, the very devil himself. Her transformation from human to infernal affects Mrs Jones as well, dragging her down, in the moment of her death, to an inarticulate state: ' Mrs Jones tried to speak. Mary tried to answer. Their lips barely moved. The addressed each other like beasts in a language neither understood' (349).

As the poignancy of the scene crests, no further consideration is given to the agency of things. This is no longer the story of how a red ribbon led one young girl to ruin, but rather a traditional morality tale about how excessive human passion, operating beyond the pale of both divine and human law, led one woman to destroy the very person who might have loved her. The narrative moves quickly here, charting how Mary is caught in flight, how Mr Jones deals with the loss of his wife, how Mary is eventually executed. The novel comes, then, full circle back to the scene with which it opens. What, then, is its final message concerning the agency of things in popular culture during the eighteenth century and now?

As the opening comment from Latour suggests, as modern consumers we can perhaps learn to notice the capacity of things to determine and direct a course of human action – they can indeed 'authorize, allow, afford, encourage, permit, suggest, influence, block, render possible, forbid, and so on.' While we are used to perceiving things as silent and inert, we might usefully begin to listen to what they tell us, and we might begin to grant them the agency that they implicitly possess. *Slammerkin* uses an eighteenth-century backdrop to explore the consequences of Latour's suggestion, as it offers a protagonist who is all too alert to the language of things. However, set at the dawn of the consumer revolution, the novel also demonstrates a level of discomfort over the idea that human agency, better known, perhaps, as free will or even human responsibility, could then – or now – be so easily surrendered to things. Things talk to us, they tell us to do all sorts of things. They are indeed powerful. However, in the end the novel holds its protagonist accountable, and it employs her as a didactic example of what can happen in a world where things are too audible: *Slammerkin* punishes Mary for becoming a thing. The novel paradoxically insists that things are supremely influential over a course of human action and that individuals must be held accountable for their inability to resist that supreme influence. Latour's comment encourages a twenty-first-century meditation, one freed from traditional morality in favour of a playful poststructuralist exploration of how things define us. Donoghue's novel, in contrast, enters a historical world where the nature of things still awaited assessment. Mimetically accurate for its reflection of a conflicted, eighteenth-century response to a rapidly expanding consumer culture, it also mirrors a modern, persistent ambivalence about the agency of things.

NOTES

1 On the calendar riots, see Poole.
2 For a full account of opposing experiences of bodily and mathematical time in the eighteenth century, see Witherbee.
3 While Vickery has explored the meaning behind the purchase and circulation of consumer items, especially clothing, Lemire's research revealed the extensive market in second hand clothing that made fashionable items

available, albeit second or third hand, to the lower ranks. Styles's research, ingeniously done from itemized inventories of clothing lost in one provincial fire, suggests that rich and poor clothing differed in 'numbers, quality, and value,' but not in types of garments (31).

4 See Lynch for an extensive argument on the novelistic creation of 'character.'

5 For more on the theme of maternity, see Morales.

WORKS CITED

Defoe, Daniel. *Roxana*. 1724. Print.

Donoghue, Emma. *Slammerkin*. New York: Harcourt, 2000. Print.

Latour, Bruno. *Reassembling the Social*. New York: Oxford UP, 2005. Print.

Lemire, Beverly. *Dress, Culture, and Commerce: The English Clothing Trade before the Factory, 1660–1800*. New York: St Martin's, 1997. Print.

Lynch, Deirdre. *The Moral Economy of Character*. Chicago: U of Chicago P, 1998. Print.

Morales, Marisol Ladron. 'The Representation of Motherhood in Emma Donoghue's *Slammerkin*.' *Irish University Review: A Journal of Irish Studies* 39 (2009): 107–21. Print.

'Mrs. Delany and Her Circle.' Exhibition. The Yale Center for British Art. New Haven, CT. 24 September 2009 – 4 January 2010.

Poole, Robert. '"Give us our eleven days!" Calendar Reform in Eighteenth-Century England.' *Past and Present* 149 (1995): 95–139. Print.

Richardson, Samuel. *Pamela*. 1740. Print.

Styles, John. *The Dress of the People: Everyday Fashion in Eighteenth-Century England*. New Haven: Yale UP, 2007. Print.

Vickery, Amanda. *The Gentleman's Daughter: Women's Lives in Georgian England*. New Haven, CT: Yale UP, 1998. Print.

Witherbee, Amy. 'The Temporality of the Public in *The Tatler* and *The Spectator*.' *The Eighteenth Century: Theory and Interpretation* 51 (2010): 173–92.

14 'Would you have us laughed out of Bath?': Shopping Around for Fashion and Fashionable Fiction in Jane Austen Adaptations

TAMARA S. WAGNER

'Would you have us laughed out of Bath?' replies fashion-conscious Mrs Allen to the eager heroine's wish to attend society events immediately upon their arrival, unequipped with the latest fashion. In the 2007 ITV production of *Northanger Abbey*, Catherine Moreland 'wonder[s] what their stories are' as she observes the residents of the fashionable watering-place from her window. In dressing up their potential stories in the trappings of popular fiction, she finds herself continuously balked by her chaperon's guiding interest in the prescriptive paraphernalia of fashionable society: they have not yet 'a stitch to wear,' and so 'shops must be visited; money must be spent.'[1] The dresses featured in the film are correspondingly varied and (especially in Mrs Allen's case) suitably extravagant and colourful. It might seem as if the intermittent references to shopping and dressing up in Austen's novel called for such a display. In its invitation to a vicarious consumption of period costumes, however, this display highlights exactly the preoccupation with the popular and the fashionable that is subject to pointed satire in the novel. It is a challenge, of course, to strike the right balance in dealing with Austen's subtle irony in film adaptations, but by juxtaposing Catherine's reading of everyday life through the lens of popular fiction with Mrs Allen's equally narrow attention to dress codes, the latest version of Austen's least-often adapted novel attempts to circumvent costume drama's most common impasses.

Throughout Austen's novels, shopping doubles as a defining marker of satirized society and as a metonymy for changing fashions in fiction. How to transpose such a metonymy onto the screen without reproducing an uncritical appreciation of commodification has long plagued literature adaptations. But in leaving aside mere criticism of minute historical reconstruction (a much deplored bane in adaptation studies), this chapter instead reassesses fashion's changing symbolic significance in Austen adaptations over the decades. The stress with which shopping as a fashionable leisure activity is invested in fast-paced rushes after purchases and, by extension, fortunes (or men with fortunes, to be caught in fashionable attire) can simultaneously reproduce the emergent consumerism of Austen's world and reflect current concerns at the time of each adaptation. Topical issues are transposed across different media, genres, and timeframes in a two-way process. The camera's fond lingering over buildings and costumes in various miniseries of *Pride and Prejudice*, for example, showcases Austen's appropriation by 'heritage industries' (Sales 214–16), generating the often criticized 'romantic nostalgia' of 'heritage pieces' (Wiltshire 135). But such a foregrounding of background material also finds a pointed, if surprising, counterpart in the repackaging of canonical texts as exoticized consumer products in Gurinder Chadha's *Bride & Prejudice* (2004). Targeted at an international market, this Bollywood remake dresses up a classic in newly fashionable issues. It is a no less problematic cultural appropriation. Still, like Mrs Allen's 'most harmless delight in being fine' (21) in *Northanger Abbey*, the consumption and re-production of new fashions in film and fiction may nevertheless be appreciated as fond satire. Shopping thus acts as a catalyst for Austen's complex treatment of popular culture as well as for different attempts to re-present it.

Running Down Bath: *Northanger Abbey*'s Updated Gothic

Late eighteenth-century popular culture receives an ambiguous treatment in Austen's fiction. From the parodied, at times hilariously farcical explosions of fashionable formulae in her juvenilia to the rewriting of an initially failed courtship-plot of the past as 'the natural sequel to an unnatural beginning' (58) in her last finished novel, *Persuasion* (1818), Austen's critical negotiation of competing literary trends at once mocks and, through parody, reshapes fiction. This critical engagement with changing demands faced by popular writers finds its most intriguing realization in the representation of competing fashions. Analogies with fictional formulae bring out a sustained concern with literary developments, elevating an often heavily satirical depiction of fashionable society to a combined social and aesthetic critique. Most prominently, the influential eighteenth-century cults of sensibility and the Gothic are variously reworked – not only parodied – throughout Austen's writing.

Her evocation of Regency shopping culture is equally complex and comparatively underacknowledged. Austen's most satirical stabs at a growing consumer society, in fact, do more than merely reflect what has been termed her 'representation of the shoddiness of the new Regency world,' a shoddiness that has notoriously been edited out in an 'Austen industry' that rewrites her fictional world 'in accordance with the conventions of the Regency reproduction and heritage industries' (Sales 214–16). Retaining her chiefly satirical treatment of fashionable display can solve recurring problems that fissure the translation of Austen's elusive irony.[2]

Offering a vicarious consumption of cultural fashions renders the exploitation of society's common foibles twofold, providing fashionable display and a means to criticize it. This simultaneity is most insightful when it puts Austen's own ambiguous take on popular culture into the foreground. Highlighting the mock-Gothic of *Northanger Abbey*, Austen's first fully fledged novel (written in 1798–9 and published posthumously in 1818), offers perhaps the most straightforward way of conveying this ambiguity. This makes it all the more surprising that the novel has been adapted far less often than any other Austen novel. In part at least, this omission has ironically been due to its overt play with genre paradigms. Austen and the Gothic seem incongruous elements in the general popular imagination, and as a result, her intricate parody of fashionable fictional crazes tends to be sidelined, especially in feature films. There have been stage productions since the late nineteenth century and radio plays since the 1940s, but until 2007 audiovisual versions of *Northanger Abbey* had been limited to one single BBC adaptation in 1986.[3]

As opposed to the 2007 version, the 1986 adaptation makes strikingly little of the novel's Bath scenes, which emphasize the fashionable watering-place's social Gothic. Instead, it concentrates almost exclusively on Catherine's misreading of Gothic trappings at the Tilneys' home. In the novel, Catherine expects the fulfilment of narrative conventions gleaned from popular fiction. While this marks her out as a 'female Quixote,' common in eighteenth-century texts, it ultimately turns out that she reads General Tilney's tyrannical character aright after all.[4] She wrongly – and very embarrassingly so – assumes that he must at least have committed murder or perhaps holds his wife, only presumed dead perhaps, prisoner in a disused part of the abbey. His son Henry consequently scolds Catherine for judging everyday life according to the criteria of Gothic fiction: 'What have you been judging from? Remember the country and the age in which we live' (186). Conventional Gothic is set in remote, exotic places, in picturesquely mountainous, geographically vague parts of Continental Europe. On one level, there is simply a comic effect as Catherine extends Gothic formulae to her interpretation of present-day society, including Bath with its shops, balls, and resort routines.

What is often ignored is that Austen makes very clear that there is enough to the general's social scheming and domestic bullying that Catherine is justified 'to feel that in suspecting General Tilney of either murdering or shutting up his wife, she had scarcely sinned against his character, or magnified his cruelty' (230). This is not the only or even the most significant aspect of the Gothic's partially parodic updating, however. The Bath scenes contain a social Gothic that manifests itself in oppressive crowds, deceitful would-be suitors, and social embarrassments as painful as the supernatural horrors delineated in the novels Catherine consumes. The dichotomous structure of the novel's twisting of Gothic forms, like its split into two main locations (Bath and Northanger Abbey), in fact, is neither incongruous nor simply comical. It stages a twofold intrusion of the Gothic: its paradigms infiltrate Bath through novels and through an unexpectedly apposite updating. Gothic figures include not just the tyrannical general, but also his libertine eldest son, Captain Tilney, who seduces mercenary Isabella Thorpe, who betrays her fiancé, Catherine's brother. The introduction of the Thorpes brings home particularly effectively a domestic bullying that is hardly outdone by the patriarchal general. Group pressure creates not just compromising, but genuinely distressing, situations. Catherine is forced to participate in social events against her inclination as well as in violation of propriety. Breaking an engagement for a country walk with the Tilneys to be instead galloped through town by John Thorpe, Isabella's equally mercenary brother, for example, parodies stock abduction or elopement scenes. The distress it occasions is no less real. Bath's social Gothic anticipates the reinvestigation of traditional Gothic trappings that Catherine more literally embarks on at Northanger Abbey.[5]

It is vital, therefore, briefly to review the novel's intrinsically ambiguous treatment of fictional formulae in order to assess the significance of their representation on twenty-first-century television. Certainly, at first sight the social embarrassments caused by the Thorpes and by Mrs Allen may seem comical. Their very rootedness in the mundane and unheroic is crucial to Austen's updating of clichéd literary paradigms. The mock abduction scene in which Thorpe tricks Catherine into riding in an open carriage parodies Gothic conventions. Paralleling Mrs Allen's preoccupation with the safety of her clothes, his attempt to impress Catherine revolves around fashion-conscious display of his vehicle, 'the merits of his own equipage,' and boasts about his driving skills (63). While it may not be easy to convey the impropriety of this tête-à-tête for a twenty-first-century viewership, in one of the justifiably fast-paced scenes in the 2007 adaptation, Thorpe makes his horses gallop through the streets – rushing not only past the astonished Tilneys (which they do in the novel as well), but nearly over gouty Mr Allen as he is seen to hobble across the street.[6]

Northanger Abbey captures a transitional moment in popular culture. Precisely because of its mixture of parody and updating, the novel invites an adaptation that can combine criticism of social and narrative conventions with an entertaining foray into the emergent consumer society of the eighteenth century. In the 2007 film, Catherine's nightmares (absent from the source text) appear as flashbacks, accompanied by voice-over extracts from novels she is reading. Their adapted passages incongruously include Matthew Lewis's controversial *The Monk* (1796), a book that only the boorish Thorpe enjoys in Austen's novel. In a clichéd evocation of Freudian readings of dreams, visualized intrusions of reading material project unconscious desire. Scenes of abduction and incarceration lifted from Gothic fiction are juxtaposed with a dream in which Henry Tilney raises Catherine up from a bathtub, commenting on her nudity as 'all God's gifts.' This is followed by her innocuous confession of 'hav[ing] such dreams sometimes.' This visualising of an erotic imagination stimulated by an overconsumption of fiction introduces an additional and no less clichéd dimension to the film's updating. Like Austen's own reworking of familiar fictional paradigms, it parodies schematic ways of reading the world.

Spelling out the connection between fashionable reading material and shopping as a leisure activity, the film furthermore adds a significant scene set in a bookstore. The shop gives Isabella Thorpe the opportunity to browse for controversial novels and men. Conversation about books, real-life scandal (invoking Byron's notoriety), and eligible suitors is curiously jumbled. While walking around and ducking behind bookshelves with an abruptness underscored by the camera's dizzying jerks, Isabella takes the opportunity to attract attention. Whereas the novel only briefly references an indiscriminate 'quest' for 'pastry, millinery, or even (as in the present case) of young men' (43), the film stresses that social misdemeanour in a bookstore may precipitate an ultimately embarrassing overconsumption of fiction. The bookstore scene aptly visualizes an underpinning connection in the text, while also extending its guided tour through period details to more shops of the time.

The balking of her desire to get to know 'what their stories are' as Catherine views new acquaintances as potential protagonists of familiar narratives is only the beginning of a parodic parallelism with shopping. If Isabella simultaneously shops around for men and novels, dress is comically evoked as Mrs Allen's 'passion.' In the novel, this passion is slyly declared to be 'harmless': 'Dress was her passion. She had a most harmless delight in being fine; and our heroine's entrée into life could not take place till after three or four days had been spent in learning what was mostly worn, and her chaperon was provided with a dress of the newest fashion' (21). The film's depiction of their purchases culminates in a procession of shop-assistants loading a carriage with parcels. In both versions, Mrs Allen obsesses over her expanding number of gowns as substitutes for a growing family. While Mrs Thorpe (Isabella's mother) lists the accomplishments of her children, Mrs Allen has 'no similar information to give, no similar triumphs ... consoling herself, however, with the discovery, which her keen eye soon made, that the lace on Mrs Thorpe's pelisse was not half so handsome as that on her own' (31). While cutting out some of their deliberately tedious dialogue, the adaptation renders Mrs Allen more of a slapstick character by exhibiting an exaggerated version of her 'inactive good temper' and 'trifling turn of mind' (21). At the same time, the film further accentuates the novel's play with literalized symbolic entanglement by making Mr Tilney more actively involved in tearing a hole in Mrs Allen's favourite gown. In the novel, he simply commiserates (in a tongue-in-cheek fashion) with her victimization by the crowds; in the film, he accidentally tears the dress. The incident precipitates satirized conversations about women's fashion that pivot on the young man's knowledge of their (lack of) practicality: he describes himself as his sister's trusted shopping companion, knows what to pay for the right kind of fabric, and suggests that Catherine's muslin might not 'wash well' (28). A young man who 'understand[s] muslins' (28) makes an unlikely hero, and this is central to Austen's rewriting of clichés.

In contradistinction to the fashionable fiction she sets out to satirize, Austen's own novels seldom delineate her heroines' attire. The one time she supplies more detail, the description is that of an eligible bachelor whose knowledge of women's dress is primarily comical. Only fashion-mad Mrs Allen could possibly be 'quite struck by his genius'; Catherine considers him 'strange' (28). Recent critical discourse on 'fashioning gender' has suggested that Austen's satirical invocation of the young man's talk about women's clothes opens up the 'possibility of gender fluidity' (Wylie 142). Austen 'focuses her subtextual intentions on the vagaries of gender, suggesting that the demands of gender expectations are as manufactured as the muslin that concerns Mrs Allen and Henry Tilney, characters whose purpose is to teach her uninitiated protagonist the consequences of being a heroine' (Wylie 132). Nevertheless, even if dress presents a 'perfect vehicle for subversion,' its most important function in the novel remains Tilney's 'carnivalisation of language' as he turns 'the vestimentary system inside out' (Wylie 130).[7] It further shows how Austen concurrently builds on and undermines narrative conventions and the demands of popular culture that they embody.

Whereas *Northanger Abbey* clearly contains the most direct references to shopping (for books as well as for dresses), Austen's subsequent novels largely restrict descriptions of garments to specific purchases or items. In *Jane Austen Fashion: Fashion and Needlework in the Works of Jane Austen*, Penelope Byrde even maintains that this absence of detail is due to the fact that fashion was 'not considered a suitable or interesting topic for general conversation' (13). This belies the sartorial symbolism of Austen's contemporaries, including Frances Burney and Maria Edgeworth, female novelists whom Austen admired, as well as the Gothic writers toward whom she was admittedly more ambivalent.[8] Increasingly, moreover, the majority of women writers 'kept pace with the etiquette guides,' using dress as a signifier (Langland 36), although at times they simply granted vicarious consumption. Especially fashionable ('silver-fork') novels of the 1820s and 1830s aimed 'to transfer the familiar narrative of Miss Austin [*sic*] to a higher sphere of society' (Gore n.p.). These precursors of modern Regency romances can largely be held accountable for a still prevailing '*mis*understanding or misprision' of Austen's class-location (Tuite 5) and hence also for an often equally misleading costuming on screen. The sheer spectrum of shopping scenes demonstrates the persistence of such misprision and repeated attempts to counteract it.[9]

Pride and Prejudice: Shopping Around for 'Exquisite Young Men'

'[T]oo light, and bright, and sparkling,' as Austen put it (*Letters* 203), *Pride and Prejudice* (1813) is her most often dramatized novel. It provided a good source for a cheerful wartime classic, directed by Robert

Leonard and starring Laurence Olivier and Greer Garson. Anachronistic in sporting the wide sleeves and hoops of the mid-nineteenth century, its strategic deployment of 'numerous and varied Hollywood gowns (glamorous nineteenth-century-style fashions!)' (Richards 112) contributed to a general misperception of Austen as a Victorian writer. Yet, while nostalgically recalling the glamour of a retrospectively enhanced past, the depiction of shopping in the film aptly introduces the marriage-market. Set in a shop, the opening dialogue seamlessly knits together the newest fashions and competition for two 'exquisite young men' arriving in such a carriage that they clearly 'must have come straight from Court!' This alignment is capped by a literalized chase between the Bennets and the Lucases. Competitors in match-making, Mrs Bennet and Lady Lucas speed home to be the first to alert their husbands to the need to make acquaintance with the newcomers. As their carriages are shown to gallop through the landscape, their rivalry literally becomes a race after men. Though close to slapstick, the scene provides a clearly dramatized, easily understood rendering of the competitive marriage-market and specifically of the danger that it might turn women into self-commodifiers.

In subsequent adaptations, such symbolism is often submerged in heritage production. The miniseries of the 1980s and 1990s are notorious for replicating the conspicuous consumption criticized in the novels. Mr Collins's enumeration of costly items could 'allow viewers to feel as if they are wandering through either period locations or museums' (Sales 20). This is indisputably a dubious use of a satirical character. Roger Sales has stressed that, as long as such a dressing up in period costumes predominates, 'the heirs of Mr Collins will always be allowed to hold the camera' (25). Nor is nostalgic reconstruction the only distorting foregrounding of backgrounds. The latest version for the big screen, directed in 2005 by Joe Wright, overcompensates by exaggerating the Bennets' relative poverty: pigs run freely through a markedly dirty household. Shopping scenes are correspondingly confined to a somewhat stale analogy between meat and marriage-markets: the coming of the eligible cousin, Mr Collins, to whom 'the estate passes [instead of] to us poor females,' is discussed among the Bennet sisters as they sidestep meat hung up for display at a market. Elizabeth then rejects Collins's proposal over leftovers at the dinner table – with a partly carved joint interposed between them. More interestingly, an added scene depicting their meeting with Wickham in a milliner's shop characterizes the novel's selfish villain as a superficial fop who boasts of 'having a good taste in ribbons' and sports a ponytail tied up with a baby-blue ribbon. That he then pays for Lydia Bennet's purchase of ribbons – a purchase that may not be extremely extravagant, but is clearly more than she can really afford – moreover foreshadows their later, more problematic shared tastes and passions.

Lydia's wildly exhibited interest in men and millinery has always offered a good point-of-entry into a simultaneously critical and comical display of Regency shopping culture. Although the BBC miniseries directed by Andrew Davis in 1995 partly suffers from the same problems already noted in criticism of earlier Austen adaptations in providing vicarious heritage tours, it also attempts to highlight wasteful consumption. Recurring scenes involving shopping, window shopping, and the 'making up' of bonnets into more stylish versions punctuate the viewer's introduction to Austen's world. More than simply providing opportunities for period paraphernalia, these scenes lift Lydia's voracious consumption of food, fabrics, and young men – metonymical for indiscriminate consumerism at large – into the foreground. She is shown gobbling up chocolates, clamouring for food, and calling loudly for a drink because she 'can scarce draw breath, [she is] so fagged' after romping wildly at a ball.

This painstakingly faithful adaptation dwells on scenes that reveal Lydia's spendthrift and thoughtless behaviour. Impulse buying cuts short funds for a likewise unnecessary 'treat' at an inn, where the conversation swiftly proceeds from a description of consumables to the impending removal of a regiment of officers (the targets of Lydia's flirtations) to the fashionable seaside resort, Brighton. The dialogue is directly lifted out of the novel, but exhibits an additional relish in detailing consumer products. While waiting for their elder sisters, Lydia and Kitty have been 'happily employed in visiting an opposite milliner, watching the sentinel on guard, and dressing a salad and cucumber' (193). That they consequently need to borrow the money for the treat does not prevent them from 'triumphantly display[ing] a table set out with such cold meat as an inn larder usually affords, exclaiming, "Is not this nice? Is not this an agreeable surprise?"' (193). The television version tops this with a double display, both visually and through Lydia's boasts of the spread of 'Cold ham, and pork, and salads, and every good thing!' Replicating the novel's text almost verbatim, it then has Lydia describe her newly purchased bonnet: 'vile, isn't it?' In the original, Lydia simply suggests that she does 'not think it is very pretty' (193). In both versions, she 'shall pull it to pieces [to] see if [she] can make it up any better' (193). What the adaptation leaves out is that this requires additional purchases:

> Oh! but there were two or three much uglier in the shop; and when I have bought some prettier-coloured satin to trim it with fresh, I think it will be very tolerable. Besides, it will not much signify what one wears this summer, after the —shire have left Meryton, and they are going in a fortnight. (193)

What the adaptation does realize is the importance of display. Lydia rearranges current fashions according to her own whims, literalizing a disregard for any conventions. Tearing up bonnets externalizes a wildness that prefigures a violent disruption of social rules and culminates in an elopement that she considers 'good fun' (275).

The miniseries captures Lydia's 'high spirits' by rendering her extravagantly boisterous. A scene that shows her romping half-clad through the house while dressing for a ball is not just a joke at Mr Collins's expense: he futilely endeavours to avert his eyes while Lydia giggles violently. Stressing how TV-serializations of *Pride and Prejudice* 'convey the sexuality of this character' (70), Sue Parrill has compared this scene with the extended discussion of Lydia's lace 'tucker' in the 1980 BBC version. Lydia is meant to tuck some lace around her bodice, but as it keeps slipping down to reveal her bosom, it is strongly suggested that this is not by accident. As Mrs Bennet 'snidely' remarks on other young ladies not needing any lace 'to conceal [their] negligible bosom[s],' it is clear that she favours Lydia and 'that she is rather proud of Lydia's physical assets' (Parrill 70).

This focus on a revealing garment has notably proven an eminently transposable issue in very different 'updates.' The multilevel transposition of Austen's plotline into a present-day context in Chadha's *Bride & Prejudice* substitutes a tank top for the slippery lace. The youngest Bakshi sister, Lakhi, insists on wearing a top her sisters consider 'very vulgar.' She calls it 'killing' and 'what everyone's wearing in Mumbai.' The same adaptation translates the novel's often cited opening that '[i]t is a truth universally acknowledged, that a single man in possession of a good fortune, must be in want of a wife' (1) as '[a]ll mothers think that any single guy with big bucks must be shopping for a wife.' But if shopping metaphors and sartorial symbolism illustrate how minute details can be retained in a transposition into a different cultural context, this transposition unfortunately creates a much more disconcerting impasse in its attempt to link different levels of consumerism, including an exoticism that also constitutes the film's main selling-point.

Bride & Prejudice is itself a product of the cultural selling out that it seeks to criticize. Dealing with – and in – consumerism on three interconnected levels, it exposes and exploits a purchasing of culture: first, shopping, especially abroad, signals both superciliousness (as it does in the novel) and a peculiarly international consumerism; second, buying up heritage is extended to neo-imperialism; and finally, a twofold consumption of popular culture (a literary classic and Bollywood film) is neatly spiced up and yet rendered easily digestible for the international market. A transposition into present-day India, the film turns the Bennets into the Bakshis (who symptomatically reside in a decaying former imperial residence in rural Amritsar), Darcy into an American hotel magnate, and Wickham into a self-indulgent backpacker who sets himself up as the opposite of the foreign businessman, eager to slum it in the Bakshis's home as part of his satirized search for the 'real India.' Most prominently, tacky consumer goods are associated with the caricatured type of the diasporic Asian and especially the self-styled 'Amrikan,' Mr Kohli, the film's version of Mr Collins.

Most of the criticism of the film has perhaps expectedly concentrated on its cultural revision of a classic text. Surbhi Malik has dissected the representation of Kohli as more than just a comical exponent of the Non Resident Indian (NRI). Kohli's empty-headed boasts of his eligibility, of his 'Green Card, new house, big cash,' necessarily presents a problematic engagement with model minorities in the United States (Malik 79). If in period drama Mr Collins is all too often in charge of the camera, as Sales has so pointedly put it (25), the heavy satire of Kohli in *Bride & Prejudice* effectively short-circuits any reductive interpretation of the film. It is neither merely an exotic consumer good nor, alternatively, a straightforward transposition of Austen's familiar plotline into a 'diasporic itinerary' (Malik 83). Immediate reactions to the film have wildly shuttled between praise for its 'multilayered, hybrid form' (Sutherland 357) and condemnation of an underpinning ideological complicity with British or American imperialism (Malik 80). Especially since Kohli occupies a 'scene-stealing role' (Ramachandran 44), the parody of his financial success abroad has been seen as part of an unpleasantly satirical version of an 'American exceptionalism in Indian diasporic popular film' that 'is commensurate with the American racialisation of South Asians as a model community' (Malik 80).[10]

The hilarious parody of his eager consumption of 'the West' finds a more sinister realization in Darcy's ultimately abandoned project to 'turn India into a theme park,' as Lalitha Bakshi, the film's Elizabeth Bennet, puts it. This somewhat blasé exposure of cultural consumption is then further extended to Wickham's equally exploitative foray into what he considers an exotic travel ground. Through this extension and through the parody of Kohli's 'Amrikan' success story, the film succeeds in becoming more than just a rehearsal of postcolonial critiques reapplied to neo-imperialist business ventures. As Wickham presents himself as a swashbuckling, scruffy backpacker – an apt as well as comical translation of Austen's flirtatious officer – Lalita has to overcome her biased opinions of different types of exotic foreign men.

Accentuating the film's intertextual engagement both with Bollywood film and with Austen's novel, the final altercation between Darcy and Wickham takes place in London (the former imperial centre), in the midst of a festival of exotic cultural consumption. They inadvertently mimic an imported Bollywood classic: as Lakhi runs away with Wickham (notably under the guise of a shopping trip), he offers her (and an overseas audience) a tour of London. This tour includes not just the Millennium Wheel, or London Eye, with its view of the Thames and various typified sights of a tourist's London, but also 'that great British bastion, the National Film Theatre,' in the middle of screening Manoj Kumar's *Purab Aur Pachhim* (1970), literally 'East and West' (Ramachandran 44). It is in front of the cinema screen that Darcy and Lalita catch up with Wickham and Lakhi, and their encounter mirrors a fight onscreen. A multilayered critique of neo-imperialist enterprises makes the film more than just a transposition of Austen's plotline across time and space.

This transposition, or updating, of Austen's satirical treatment of shopping and finance notwithstanding, the film cashes in on a thriving market for the vicarious consumption of the 'exotic.' Not surprisingly, given the simultaneous reproduction of Bollywood clichés and an exoticized classic plot, the film has received the doubtful praise of working as a 'tour guide' that aims to '"modernise" Bollywood form and content for non-South Asian audiences' (Gopinath 162). Its double exploitation of updated forms, in which it returns to the dubious play with consumer expectations in costume drama, brings full circle the trajectory of ongoing reworkings. Throughout Austen adaptations, shopping around for fashions in fiction articulates important points about popular culture, past and present. At times such depictions recreate Regency society or, conversely, lay bare its competitive marriage-market; at other times they expose both by establishing links between contemporary and Austen's society.

While neatly costumed courtships set against rolling green land-scapes as well as extensively rolled out, or intriguingly arranged, fabrics have continued to form a main attraction in film and television versions, recent experiments with the limits of literature adaptations have opened up new opportunities for the negotiation of Austen's satirized shopping travails. This is why the popular subgenre of the Austen adaptation forms a revealing case study of the changing treatment of past fashions. Repeated remakes stretch across half a century and cover engagements with a remarkably diverse range of paradigms. From the frantic shopping rivalry that articulates competition in the marriage-market in the opening scenes of the 1940 *Pride and Prejudice* to the hero-ines' exaggerated rushes through Bath in the 2007 *Northanger Abbey*, references to the fashionable and would-be fashionable operate on a symbolic level to dramatize an indiscriminate flirtation with different 'styles' of relationships, including matrimonial speculation, as part and parcel of consumer society. If *Bride & Prejudice* extends this alignment to present-day, global interchanges, it simultaneously sells out culture in more than one way. It builds on and undermines Bollywood clichés and the cultural myths with which Austen, the novel, and its previous adaptations have been associated. Nevertheless, the changing recourse to shopping metaphors crucially informs such otherwise markedly divergent approaches to a consumer society driven by changes to pop-ular culture – fashions in dress, in style and behaviour, in resorts, and at the book-market, and their likewise shifting treatment in fiction as well as its adaptations.

NOTES

1 Produced for television, this film-length adaptation premiered on 25 March 2007 on the UK channel ITV. It was part of the 'Jane Austen Season' that started on 18 March 2007 with the likewise infrequently televised *Mansfield Park* (1814), followed by *Northanger Abbey* and *Persuasion*. A repeat of the 1996 feature-length drama *Emma* was broadcast on Friday 6 April 2007.
2 Sales speaks of 'the ways in which both Austen and the Regency period have become associated not just with the promotion of a general idea of Englishness but also, more specifically, with the marketing of heritage

products' (17). Sutherland refers to Austen's presumed 'Regency production values – a pleasant blur of stately homes, English gardens, and empire-line dresses' (v).

3 Martin Amis's attempt at a screenplay in 2004, written for Miramax Pictures, has so far only been published in *Granta*.

4 *Northanger Abbey* stands in a literary tradition that extends from Cervantes's *Don Quixote* (1605/1615) to Flaubert's famous novel of adultery, *Madame Bovary* (1857). Charlotte Lennox's *The Female Quixote* (1752) has had an important impact on the representation of reading women (Hammond 259).

5 Gilbert and Gubar have further argued that Austen additionally redefines the Gothic by showing that Catherine Morland is 'trapped, not inside the General's Abbey, but inside his fiction, a tale in which she figures as an heiress and thus a suitable bride for his second son. Moreover, though it may be less obvious, Catherine is also trapped by the interpretations of the General's children' (137).

6 This speeding up simultaneously expresses a refusal to linger over Bath's historical buildings as heritage props. Speaking of 'costume drama's characteristic stillness,' Pidduck has remarked that 'Austen's protagonists can never move too quickly' (133). But recent adaptations of her novels sport fast movements and at times dizzying sweeps of the camera. The 2007 versions both of *Northanger Abbey* and *Persuasion* depict their heroines rushing, or being rushed, through Bath. It might be a slightly ridiculous measure in *Persuasion* when Austen's most mature and serenely melancholy heroine is running breathlessly after (news of) her lover. By contrast, an exaggeration of speed and danger suitably dramatizes Austen's updating of Gothic forms in *Northanger Abbey*.

7 See also Reid-Walsh.

8 Compare Copeland on the way in which fashion 'emerges in the last quarter of the century as a certain attraction for women of the middling ranks: in fiction as a focus of comic revelation, as in Frances Burney's novel *Evelina* (1778), and in the *Lady's Magazine*, a popular woman's journal of fashion, fiction, and news that flourished from 1770 to 1832, as a focus of monthly temptations' (3). Whereas Gothic fiction focused on 'the pressing dangers to women from debt,' Edgeworth and Burney stressed 'fictions of active economic engagement' in which '[d]uties of domestic spending grant the heroines of the new decade the keys to the kingdom' (Copeland 7, 10).

9 'Jane Austen Goes Shopping,' an interview with Amy Heckerling, the director of *Clueless* (1995), testifies to common misreadings of Austen's underpinning criticism of consumerism. For Heckerling, shopping is something that Cher, a twentieth-century Californian Emma, does, not Austen's heroines.

Clearly, Austen's heroines do go shopping – and talk about it, often wrongly speculating on the reasons behind it. The misleading speculations on Frank Churchill's anonymous purchase of a pianoforte in *Emma* spring to mind. Unlike the gay character added in *Clueless*, moreover, Austen's Mr Tilney, in *Northanger Abbey*, is a perfect shopping companion and yet also a marriageable bachelor.

10 While Austen scholars have largely endorsed *Bride & Prejudice* as a loose remake of a timelessly powerful plotline, contextualizations of the film in identity politics, racialization, or global marketing processes have been dubious about its play with the clichés it indisputably markets. This denies that different levels of re-orientalization are already satirized in the film itself. Symptomatically, *Bride & Prejudice* was 'simultaneously released in a Hindi dubbed version as *Balle Balle Amritsar to LA*, a title that makes no reference to the Jane Austen text *Pride and Prejudice* on which the movie is based, but foregrounds the diasporic itinerary of the film' (Malik 83).

WORKS CITED

Austen, Jane. *Pride and Prejudice*. 1813. London: Spottiswoodes & Shaw, 1853. Print.
– *Northanger Abbey*. 1818. London: Penguin, 2003. Print.
– *Persuasion*. 1818. London: Penguin, 1985. Print.
– *Jane Austen's Letters*. Ed. Deidre Le Faye. New York: Oxford UP, 1997. Print.
Bride & Prejudice. Dir. Gurinder Chadha. Perf. Aishwarva Raj, Martin Henderson, and Naveen Andrews. Pathé and Miramax, 2004. DVD.
Byrde, Penelope. *Jane Austen Fashion: Fashion and Needlework in the Works of Jane Austen*. Ludlow: Excellent, 1999. Print.
Copeland, Edward. *Women Writing about Money: Women's Fiction in England, 1790–1820*. Cambridge: Cambridge UP, 1995. Print.
Gilbert, Sandra M., and Susan Gubar. *The Madwoman in the Attic: The Woman Writer and the Nineteenth-Century Literary Imagination*. New Haven and London: Yale UP, 1979. Print.
Gopinath, Gayatri. 'Bollywood Spectacles: Queer Diasporic Critique in the Aftermath of 9/11.' *Social Text* 23. 3–4 (2005): 157–69. *Academic Search Premier*. Web. 14 July 2009.
Gore, Catherine. *Pin Money*. London: Colburn and Bentley, 1831. Print.
Hammond, B.S. 'Mid-Century English Quixotism and the Defence of the Novel.' *Eighteenth-Century Fiction* 10.3 (1998): 247–68. Print.

'Jane Austen Goes Shopping.' Interview with Amy Heckerling. *The Times*, 19 October 1995: 35. Print.

Langland, Elizabeth. *Nobody's Angels: Middle-Class Women and Domestic Ideology in Victorian Culture*. Ithaca: Cornell UP, 1995. Print.

Malik, Surbhi. '"UK is finished; India's too corrupt; anyone can become Amrikan": Interrogating Itineraries of Power in *Bend It Like Beckham* and *Bride and Prejudice.*' *Journal of Creative Communications* 2.1–2 (2007): 79–100. *Sage Journals Online*. Web. 12 July 2009.

Mosier, John. 'Clues for the Clueless.' *Jane Austen on Screen*. Ed. Gina Macdonald and Andrew F. Macdonald. Cambridge: Cambridge UP, 2003. 228–53. Print.

Northanger Abbey. Dir. Jon Jones. Perf. Felicity Jones and J.J. Feild. ITV, 2007. DVD.

Parrill, Sue. *Jane Austen on Film and Television: A Critical Study of the Adaptations*. Jefferson, NC: McFarland, 2002. Print.

Persuasion. Dir. Adrian Shergold. Perf. Sally Hawkins and Rupert Penry-Jones. ITV, 2007. DVD.

Pidduck, Julianne. 'Of Windows and Country Walks: Frames of Space and Movement in 1990s Austen Adaptations.' *The Postcolonial Jane Austen*. Ed. You-me Park and Rajeswari Sunder Rajan. London: Routledge, 2000. 116–40. Print.

Pride and Prejudice. Dir. Robert Leonard. Perf. Laurence Olivier and Greer Garson. Metro-Goldwyn-Mayer, 1940. Film.

Pride and Prejudice. Dir. Cyril Coke. Perf. Elizabeth Garvie and David Rintoul. BBC. 1980. DVD.

Pride and Prejudice. Dir. Andrew Davis. Perf. Jennifer Ehle and Colin Firth. BBC. 1995. DVD.

Ramachandran, Naman. Rev. of *Bride & Prejudice*. *Sight and Sound* 14.10 (2004): 43–4. Print.

Reid-Walsh, Jackie. '"Do You Understand Muslins, Sir?": The Circulation of Ball Dresses in *Evelina* and *Northanger Abbey*.' *Material Productions and Cultural Construction/Culture matérielle et constructions discursives*. Ed. Robert James Merrett, Richard Connors, and Tiffany Potter. Edmonton, AB: Academic, 2000. 215–23. Print.

Richards, Paulette. 'Regency Romance Shadowing in the Visual Motifs of Roger Michell's *Persuasion*.' *Jane Austen on Screen*. Ed. Gina Macdonald and Andrew F. Macdonald. Cambridge: Cambridge UP, 2003. 111–26. Print.

Sales, Roger. *Jane Austen and Representations of Regency England*. London: Routledge, 1996. Print.

Sutherland, Kathryn. *Jane Austen's Textual Lives: From Aeschylus to Bollywood*. Oxford: Oxford UP, 2005. Print.

Tuite, Clara. *Romantic Austen: Sexual Politics and the Literary Canon*. Cambridge: Cambridge UP, 2002. Print.

Whelehan, Imelda. 'Adaptations: The Contemporary Dilemmas.' *Adaptations – From Text to Screen, Screen to Text*. Ed. Deborah Cartmell and Imelda Whelehan. London: Routledge, 1999. 3–19. Print.

Wiltshire, John. *Recreating Jane Austen*. Cambridge: Cambridge UP, 2001. Print.

Wylie, Judith. '"Do You Understand Muslins, Sir?": Fashioning Gender in *Northanger Abbey*.' *Styling Texts: Dress and Fashion in Literature*. Ed. Cynthia Kuhn and Cindy Carlson. Youngstown, NY: Cambria: 2007. 129–48. Print.

15 Visualizing Empire in Domestic Settings: Designing *Persuasion* for the Screen

ANDREW MACDONALD
AND GINA MACDONALD

Anne Hollander's *Seeing Through Clothes* observes that, unlike visually rich, film-friendly nineteenth-century writers – Brontë, Dickens, Flaubert, Tolstoy – who fill readers' mental screens with tapestries, carriages, topiaries, and ballrooms, Jane Austen imitates stylistically abstract eighteenth-century models, and sketches socio-psychological milieu through her narrator's inner voice. She thus opts 'almost wholly out of clothes and visual details, relying on other forms ... to carry the social and personal humanity of characters,' rather than their material settings (Hollander 424).[1] Austen, notes Hollander, produced 'incorporeal' characters whom readers must work to visualize, 'however well Austen lets us know them' through their inner voices (439). Despite the lack of visual detail, this prose voice evokes characters of amazing power; however, given their visual medium, film-makers must invent clothing and milieu. Adaptation theorists have been slow to recognize this challenge, possibly because largely nameless film-crew functionaries rather than 'auteurs' or scriptwriters meet it.[2] Purists, in fact, argue that Austen is not truly adaptable: George Bluestone's *Novels into Film* (1959) asserts the disjunction between the linguistic and visual, the conceptual and perceptual, and is echoed in Roger Gard's 'A Few Skeptical Thoughts on Jane Austen and Film' and Patrice Hannon's 'Austen Novels and Austen Films: Incompatible Worlds?' This asserted incompatibility challenges film-makers to create a material correlative to a prose 'voice' that blithely assumes readers know how people and things looked and what these looks meant.

Film-makers must create visual images – landscapes, buildings, animals, servants, costumes, decorations, lighting, and general milieu – that they imagine correspond to Austen's turn-of-the-century realities. Thus, it is not Austen's genius creating what viewers see on screen, but rather the skill and imagination of those responsible for inventing what Austen does not spell out: a costume department doing research and producing drawings, a design team making storyboards defining look and style, and directors actualizing storyboards into camera shots – angles of perception, character groupings, action. Readily available products guide costumers.[3] Set dressers and property masters assemble physical elements. Location scouts scope out viable sets that fit budgets.[4]   Occasionally, film-makers opt for generalized nineteenth-century styles familiar to the audience, as does Patricia Rozema in her *Mansfield Park* (1999), or trade history for modernity as in *Clueless* (1995), a take on *Emma* (1815). Even Regency romance dress conventions have been drafted to serve an ostensible historical authority.[5] Many of these basic film-making decisions have little to do with hewing to Austen's spirit and much to do with the crew's ideas about authenticity issues, about what film-makers imagine viewers might enjoy, about what is available, and about budget limitations.[6] David Mamet's *On Directing Film* convincingly describes the minutiae directors face daily, details that determine respectful adaptation. Yet Hollander reminds us that Austen's textual 'omission' does not 'give historic license to the visual imagination,' for the decor and clothing of her 'very precisely indicated' characters must be 'consistent with her precision' (327) – of character, behaviour, class nuances, and inner voices.

Consequently, locating characters in settings generally appropriate to Austen's period and dressing them in a semblance of late eighteenth-/ early nineteenth-century attire is insufficient to 'translate' or 'adapt' an Austen novel to the screen. Since her writing, though spare in visual adjectives and descriptive detail, is rich in irony, film-makers serious about recreating Austen need also to capture her mocking of the pretensions and manners of the British lower gentry, infusing their adaptation with visuals reflecting her satiric eye.[7] As the criticism suggests, though, adaptation has not always gone well. *Jane Austen in Hollywood* (2000) explores the dichotomy between the Austen of the imagination and Austen on film, arguing that film-makers undercut her strong, independent women. Gina and Andrew Macdonald's *Jane Austen on Screen* (2003) formalizes the debate between literary purists and film-makers for whom the novels are a launching pad for new creations: can film truly capture the wit, tone, and satiric voice of print, and how does translating the abstract to the concrete change the original's nature? Kamilla Elliot's *Rethinking the Novel/Film Debate* (2003) postulates a verbal-visual 'looking-glass' for reducing words to their 'implied images' visually and aurally (215), combining textual cues with cinematic strategies to convey the textually implicit nuances of human interaction. David Monaghan's *The Cinematic Jane Austen* (2008), in turn, highlights Austen qualities that lend themselves to film. In fact, the essential characteristics of the stage – body language, costuming, facial expressions, gestures, lighting, movement, music, placement/ blocking, silences, overhearing, and other overt behavioural expressions of class, inner emotions, and relationships – should join film conventions: alternating sequences, compressed action, a mix of shots and speeds. Brian McFarlane's *Novel to Film* (1996) notes the multiplicity of filmic signifiers (words, sound, sight) transforming linear prose to spatial film.

This paper investigates how three adaptations of *Persuasion* bring Austen's vision to modern viewers, with varying success: director Howard Baker's 225-minute 1971 BBC version, director Roger Michell's 104-minute 1995 BBC/WGBH production (later a Sony Pictures Classic), and director Adrian Shergold's 93-minute 2007 ITV/BBC/ Masterpiece Theatre *Persuasion*. While all three appear to recreate historically authentic settings, the 1971 BBC and 2007 ITV versions lose some portion of Austen's ironic voice. Fashion becomes an end in itself in the 1971 version, and a basically irrelevant historical recreation in the 2007 version, in which romance trumps Austen's satire. In contrast, director Michell's and scriptwriter Nick Dear's *Persuasion* almost uniquely makes fashion – costume, decor, milieu, filmic conventions – a comic and socially satiric instrument that follows Austen's lead, setting the virtues of the British Navy against the extravagance and dissipation of the lower gentry. Examining how Austen's take on eighteenth-century irony is (or is not) conveyed in modern popular film (through costume, set design/milieu, and film conventions) allows us to judge the success of the adaptation, with success measured in the film's closeness to the satiric and thematic intent of the original. The balance is between speaking to a modern cinematic movie-going audience with modern values and retaining the arch eighteenth-century vision that is Austen's enduring triumph and claim to fame. No film can be a book, but like an admirable language-to-language translation of a classic piece of literature, the essential qualities of the text can be conveyed.

Costume: Distinguishing Class, Character and Theme

While all three films recreate a semblance of eighteenth-century fashions, the 1971 BBC and the 2007 ITV *Persuasions* unaccountably celebrate the gentry, whose legitimacy Austen's ironic distance invites her readers to question, while the 1995 Dear/Michell BBC production, in keeping with Austen's social realism, employs costume to distinguish class, define character, and further theme. In the 1971 BBC and 2007 ITV *Persuasions* male attire is indistinguishable: beaver top-hats, high-waisted, high-collared waistcoats and tailcoats, fitted breeches, ruffled shirts, cravats or bow-ties, and, outdoors, greatcoats or capes with velvet trim. In the 2007 version, for example, the dashing young Captain Wentworth and the aging Baronet both sport Beau Brummel cravats and short, dark blue, fitted waistcoats, fashion appropriate for Sir Walter, the poseur, but certainly not for Wentworth. The heir apparent, William Elliot, wears black (1971, 2007), perhaps mourning his deceased wife, but the tall, lanky Tobias Menzies (2007 version) looks like Abraham Lincoln in tall stovetop hat and beard, and at the Pump Room, as the camera pulls back for a wide-angle overview shot, he appears suddenly as one of many so attired, as if his is the fashionable wardrobe choice at Bath. The result in this latter case is sartorial confusion: if fashion, why is this scene the only one in which men other than Elliot are so attired? If satire, does Shergold imply that many of the men in the Pump Room are hypocrites pursuing new wives while in mourning, and to what effect?

Standard female attire in these two adaptations is a high-waisted 'Directoire' empire dress, a high-waisted 'spencer' jacket, and the ubiquitous Indian shawl, in turquoise or lavender, maroon or mustard. Heavy, colourful cloaks and a plethora of bonnets (beribboned, feathered, jeweled, ruffled, rigid stovepipe) complete the picture. In the 1971 version Anne's velvet dress with Mandarin collar and ornate Chinese frog-buttons evokes both colonialism and the 1960s. Although Austen wrote her sister Cassandra about the popularity of 'black gauze cloaks' and 'cambric muslin' bonnets at Bath (6 May 1801) and even detailed a gown being made for herself (Chapman 51), the goal of fashion in the 1971 production is not historical exactitude but sartorial splendour evocative of storybook Regency elegance. Characters channel a fashion show (not quite a *Clueless* California-size computerized wardrobe, but surprisingly large): its extravagant colours, varied finery, and brassieres are for the modern gaze, as are its 1960s beehive hairdos, mandarin collars, and exotic colour combinations. The 2007 fashions are less colourful (plain muslin empire dresses in soft colours – whites, grays, browns).

Most significantly, the 1971 and 2007 versions provide no sartorial signals of hierarchy to distinguish city from country, military from non-military, or one class from another. Only servants' uniforms draw a social line, creating a nameless, faceless caste of outsiders; estate tenants are mentioned, not seen. The vicar dons black episcopal attire, but his déclassé daughter dresses as well as the Miss Elliots. No nuances of dress (or diction) delineate social status, distinguishing the impoverished Widow Smith from the snobbish Viscountess Darymple or the arrogant Elizabeth Elliot. Like a child's pop-up book meant as an earnest tutorial in the quaint fashions of earlier times, costuming here provides almost no signifiers of standing, character, or identity. The clothing remains pristine despite English weather, the absence of paving, and ubiquitous animal droppings. The Navy plays little part except as the means by which Wentworth has become worthy financially and hence an eminently desirable suitor. Ultimately, costuming in both films signals fidelity to the general period 'look' but to little else.

The 1995 Dear/Michell *Persuasion*, in contrast, employs costume as a thematic-satiric statement. Michell makes Sir Walter's fantastic wardrobe visually excessive. Colourful brocades, yellow and blue-grey designs, rich, heavy cloaks in mustard and navy blue, ruffled shirts, and bow-ties confirm him as a vain popinjay at home and abroad, constantly verifying his sartorial perfection in surrounding mirrors (all three productions include mirrors). Despite retrenchment, he cannot resist new finery to mark his self-confirmed superiority. Elizabeth too displays an expensive wardrobe of stylish new gowns and hats to maintain appearances in Bath, in contrast to the moderate Anne in plain muslins and serviceable brown cloak, and, on important occasions, plain unadorned pearl-coloured silk. In fact, the initial image of Anne, burdened by family and Kellynch, is of pale skin, pale dress, and white sheets; only as she regains hope of a future apart from her family does she develop colour in her cheeks and clothing. The more fashionable, form-fitting, copper-coloured dress worn at the card party indicates her greater self-assurance and confidence in being loved by a worthy man.

Costume similarly marks William Elliot as a dandy, a Beau Brummell of fashion (here a character-appropriate association), who has married rich, squandered his wife's wealth, and, penniless with her death, seeks another rich object of prey. His handsome velvet jackets, attractive hats, and flattering attire mark him as a fashion setter. The clothing and behaviour of Sir Walter Elliot, daughter Elizabeth, and cousin William carry satiric significance when writ large, mocking the pretensions of a lower gentry whose rich attire and fine furnishings disguise their financial insecurities. The façade of the heir presumptive is maintained by his highly honed instinct for flattery, pretence to sense and sensibility, impeccable manners, and reliance on the ambitions of others to advance himself. Dear's script has Sir Walter and Elizabeth misread and be manipulated by him because of their own thirst for social recognition; in a lengthy close up William Elliot's facial expression transforming from sugary refinement to glowering anger at Anne's engagement announcement marks him as a scheming, thwarted rogue. Ostentatious finery matches meticulous manners to disguise the real nature of the heir presumptive.

In contrast, whereas neither the 1971 nor the 2007 *Persuasion* attired its naval personnel in uniforms, much less focused on their contributions to the nation, Michell begins and ends with the navy, employs naval uniforms effectively, and has his characters echo Austen's praise of the navy and naval feats with patriotic pride. Austen, whose brothers served in the British navy, made *Persuasion* a tribute to sailors and seamanship,[8] and Michell's adaptation follows this lead. His first scene is nautical: Admiral Croft rowed by his sailors to Captain Wentworth's ship, which he boards by climbing the ropes (unthinkable in the stagey 1971 film but here perfectly justifiable thematically: vigorous physicality in the service of empire is manly and admirable). Topside, impromptu, he inspects sailors and officers, then during officers' mess, announces the war's end, Napoleon Bonaparte confined, the navy demobilized. These sights alternate with bill collectors clamouring for attention at Kellynch (a scene Dear and Michell create), Lady Russell calling for retrenchment, and Sir Walter Elliot asserting, 'I will not have a sailor in my home!' While Anne recounts Admiral Croft's naval merit, her father jokes about 'mahogany faces' and premature aging while admiring himself in a gleaming silver butter knife. The shifting scenes establish both the merit of the naval officers and the false vanity of the Elliots and the social type they represent, with the contrast between functional military attire and extravagant dandyism creating visual satire. It sets the theme that unifies the film: the vigorous, active creators and defenders of British wealth and empire versus the landed gentry who squander their passively received inheritance.

Thematic and historical grounds require naval fashions at the seaport (so that modern viewers must recognize the officers as officers), but Dear explains another, more important reason: 'an old order' (the static order of Sir Walter and the landed gentry) was 'fading . . . into decadence' and a new order based on merit was 'coming to the fore' (ii). Thus, on the quay at Lyme Regis the audience sees officers resplendent in uniform: white pants, high-collared shirts, navy blue wool jackets with gold naval buttons and epaulettes, and huge cocked hats that tower above others. These self-made men have redefined their social status in service of the crown. Paulette Richards says this uniform 'speaks to viewers about British imperialism and naval might and makes its wearer a romantic ... figure' (114). The sight leads Louisa, her eyes shining, to proclaim, 'These sailors have more worth than any men in England.' Yet, they are not mere symbols. Michell signals class distinctions by quality and upkeep of uniform and living quarters and makes these men ring true as competent at sea and on land. In terms of costuming, then, Michell and Dear's adaptation rejects the mere show of fashion in favour of a system of sartorial coding that communicates the economic and political ideology of the novel and its characters without forcing actors into awkward spoken historical exposition.

Set Design and Milieu: Finding Modern Equivalents for Eighteenth-Century Signifiers

John Mosier remarks of Austen's milieu, 'We have no idea whether the house is run-down or well-maintained, whether the servants are few or many, happy or mutinous' (210), yet film-makers must decide how to present these to best accord with a filmic interpretation of the novel. The critical consciousness evident in the use of decor and milieu in the three adaptations of *Persuasion* varies widely, and analysis makes clear the ultimate significance of markers of position that are invisible in Austen, yet known to readers, and thus necessarily made visible in modern media that attempt to communicate Austen to popular audiences, most notably in terms of the representation of servants and the physical settings of Kellynch, Bath, and Lyme Regis.

Though happy indoor servants gather round to wish the Elliots well in Bath, servants are otherwise invisible in the 1971 version. Oddly missing are the tenant farmers referenced in Elizabeth Elliot's reminder to Anne to make the obligatory rounds for the family; likewise, none but gentry people the streets of Lyme Regis and Bath. Where the 1971 version underplays the number of servants, the 2007 film abounds in indoor help. An immobile servant holds an ink container for Anne while she races around the house, a signal of family extravagance that misrepresents the blameless Anne as active in the Eliots' excess.[9] In contrast, the 1995 Dear/Michell version uses the estate staff to draw the

Elliots' character more fully and create a consistent cinematic vision underscoring the irresponsibility of the landed gentry. In addition to household servants such as doormen, housekeepers, and cooks, are groundskeepers, sheep-herders, and grooms. The grim-faced gathering to see the Elliots off to Bath conveys for modern audiences the anxious powerlessness of a group who could be devastated by the Elliots' shirked financial responsibilities.

Baker's 1971 version opts to deny these sorts of grim historical realities, painting a stylish, colourful world of well-dressed servants, striking horses, assorted carriages, and well-furnished, well-maintained dwellings; it is a static, confined, and slow-paced set-piece. The 1971 Kellynch set consists mainly of one large salon, a television stage-set with the camera eye varying little, clearly modelled on a nineteenth-century theatrical set. Except for Nubian statues suggesting the eighteenth century, the sense is of static space removed from time. No visuals indicate extravagance or financial difficulties, but free-standing mirrors assert Sir Walter's vanity. The Hargrave home, though smaller than Kellynch, reflects taste, gentility, and some degree of wealth, a proper place for genteel folk to visit. No Hargrave home appears in the 2007 version, whereas the 1995 Hargrave, though cramped and plain, is also warm and inviting with a cheery fire in the hearth, comrades-at-arms trading stories, and family and friends joining in; despite limited space and limited furnishings, it is made pleasant by its occupants.

Though Sir Walter brags that the Bath apartment is the finest in the city and in Camden Crescent (actually the Royal Crescent in the 2007 film), the only signs of family extravagance in this version are the Nubian statues replicated from the 1971 set, now located at the foot of the staircase; otherwise, the apartment's wallpaper and furnishings indicate little about the overindulgence important to Austen's satiric point. In fact, the declining family fortune and retrenching disappear quickly in this version, with the long sequence on cataloguing, covering, and storing the family possessions (absent in the 1971 version) ending in Anne's very brief report of her retrenchment plan to Lady Russell. Kellynch (the late eighteenth-century Neston Park, Wiltshire, in the film) is a large gray-stone manor, its size emphasized by Anne marching through long hallways, at times almost running, and peeking into large salons, checking off her catalogue of furnishings before the Crofts arrive. The film's ending implies that the wealthy Captain Wentworth will reinvigorate family finances, though only a single line suggests wealth gleaned from naval exploits. In fact, in Shergold's final scene, Wentworth's surprise wedding present for Anne is her family home, though nothing in Austen or the film suggests that the home was ever for sale, especially by a baronet contemptuous of a sea captain even renting his family estate. Instead, the thrust of the novel is for Anne to leave the static and old-fashioned for a more exciting world of travel and movement, not to return to a house with bad memories tied to a failed way of life. Thus, the filmic Kellynch, an adequate representation for untutored viewers, fails to match its significance and function in the novel.[10] The fact of an heir presumptive disappears completely. The movie's streetscapes lack irony or literary significance. Filmic adaptations necessitate scripts that abbreviate original texts and deviate from 'authenticity' of fashion and decor, but if they claim to be 'Jane Austen's *Persuasion*' they might be expected to provide an internal logic that the 2007 version lacks.

The 1995 set depicts the Elliots as landed snobs with pretensions to class and taste but without ready funds. The film viewers' first impression of Kellynch is of Mr Shepherd and his daughter rushing in with dire financial news, their carriage wheels spinning, only to encounter a mob of creditors at the front door, and to find an oblivious Sir Walter within. The interior is a static, cold space, richly furnished, with immobile liveried servants lining an impressive oak table, and a self-admiring Sir Walter, immoveable amid the flurry swirling about him. Later, the house appears sepulchral, its furnishings being stored away or already draped in ghostly white sheets, and Anne, overseeing all, looking haggard and worn except for a candlelit moment storing linens in an attic chest and finding a Wentworth letter. In the 1971 version the Crofts seem out of place at Kellynch, its size and grandeur overpowering, but the 1995 version maintains the theme of merit over heredity, showing the Crofts clearly quite comfortable there and in fact making it a real home, as it clearly was not during the Elliots' residence.

Despite debts and retrenchment, at Bath the 1995 Elliots eat expensive iced sorbets, their table centrepiece adorned with twelve whole pineapples and other exotic fruit. Even the modern eye inured by supermarket excess should process this indulgence as hugely over the top for England two hundred years ago: how did this tropical fruit get here? at what cost? The Elliots' extravagant attire and cold, empty apartment epitomize their nature. Obsessed with Lady Darymple, they view her invitations as a social entrée (as is confirmed by Sir Walter's staircase lecture to Anne, who instead chooses an evening with Mrs Smith). They gush over Lady Darymple's Arab-style indoor tent, a set dressing capturing the period's obsession with the exotic-oriental. Yet the scene is both static and sterile, with submissive social signals (bows and curtseys) but clearly no direct human contact of the type illustrated when Anne visits her disabled friend, whose crowded abode is nonetheless warmly welcoming. Here Michell brings to the screen Austen's satiric image of the empty social conventions of eighteenth-century excess.

Filmic Strategy: Manipulating Film Technique to Define Character

The three films' strategies differ because of time period and film length, with the predictably old-fashioned 1971 *Persuasion* too leisurely to have sharply defined, telegraphic, modern film language. It is scripted to be theatrical rather than realistic. The camera's eye encompasses a whole room, distanced, fourth wall removed. Pairs of characters remain talking heads, speaking theatrically, not conversationally. Though, at 225 minutes, more comprehensive than the later productions, its actions and conversations do little to distinguish class, produce satire, or translate Austen's narrative tone. There are odd pauses, with the camera frozen, the actors silent. At Uppercross a long walk drags on inordinately. At Lyme Regis the camera points at the sky, follows a seagull, and shows distant figures along the quay, wasting time in ways irrelevant to plot and theme. Scenes are generally static. Action comes alive in rare moments, as in the scene between Anne and her former schoolmate, Mrs Smith, once married to a friend of William Elliot, now crippled and ill-served by him. Polly Murch, speaking animatedly in close-up, brings spirit to this role – her facial expressions and gestures nuanced to suggest a good friend withholding painful truths but anxious to share information that could do good. The filmic style shifts briefly. Yet, viewers will be hard-pressed to remember another scene in which the deep passions that Austen reveals from behind the proper façades break through or satire emerges. Such passions can be effectively conveyed onstage, so the theatre-like film set does not excuse the lifelessness of this production. The passivity and voicelessness of Ann Firbank's patient Anne (except with Lady Russell) prevent viewers from sharing in the feelings Austen so effectively renders. Furthermore, characters drawn deftly in the text, with a satiric edge, dwindle into Dickensian caricature, as do the peevish Mary Elliot, the vain, insensitive baronet, and crotchety, gout-ridden Admiral Croft. The initially established decline of family fortune disappears as a concern. Inexperience with film adaptation and lack of previous models may account for the short-comings of this early BBC Austen filmic adaptation.

The 2007 *Persuasion* mimics the 1995 film to some degree (as in some candle-lit group scenes) and concentrates on blocking characters and thwarted romance against the background of Regency romance fashion and decor. With the would-be lovers impeded by Anne's family, Lady Russell, the novel's main blocking character, stands in Anne's dead mother's stead. Modelling decorum and social propriety, she should not only be confident and self-convinced as Anne's support against her family, but should also be her self-appointed older guide to a socially approved, upwardly mobile marriage (as she is in the 1971/1995 versions). Here instead, her role as Anne's close confidante (youthfully whispering conspiratorially as the camera moves close-up, the two in isolated space) shifts the traditional emphasis on her blocking role to make her advocacy of William Elliot seem a betrayal of friendship. A function of selecting some lines from the novel and suppressing others, this shift in Lady Russell's role betrays not a concession to limited running time but a confusion about her function.

Despite their titles, the 1971 and 2007 versions of *Persuasion* focus thematically on passivity versus action rather than on persuasion. Both themes exist in the original text, but foregrounding one over the other may well reflect a modern bias against 'gentle persuasion' and in favour of young women acting forcefully and independently in a way that is assumed to appeal to modern audiences. As a result of this tilt toward passive-active, viewers see no one with sufficient influence to persuade Anne against Wentworth or for Elliot. The 1971 Anne hides her inner life behind a passive acceptance of whatever she is asked to do: stay, go, walk, perform, or sit silently. When Louisa falls, Anne stands immobile, giving advice only when asked. Her few asides toward the film's end are insufficient to suggest action over passivity. The 2007 Anne trudges along, everyone's servant and nursemaid, more voiceless than not. She projects her hidden fears in her vocalized diary (that all is lost, that Wentworth will marry another); like Harriet in *Emma*, she has a memento box of lost love. She weeps copiously with huge upheavals of face and lungs, but despite the device of the voice-over, fails to convey the virtues of character and reason that Austen portrays in Anne. These virtues are unfashionably un-emotive and harder to show on screen, but they are the virtues Austen indubitably valued over weepy theatricality.[11]

To counter Anne's defining passivity, Shergold provides action – but separated from character. Anne indecorously runs from the Royal Crescent to the town centre, across the picturesque Pulteney Bridge, then up the hill to the Crescent once more. She unexpectedly encounters her amazingly cured invalid friend, who reveals Elliot's perfidy and penury, thereby freeing Anne to act against family expectation. Near the Concert Hall, she coincidently encounters the Crofts (bearing a message from Wentworth), then runs breathlessly on until she happens upon her brother-in-law and Captain Wentworth conversing. The chain of coincidental encounters seems like directorial expedience to hurry the ending while promoting Anne's transformation from passivity to action, but not action that confirms steadfastness of character.

Dear/Michell's 1995 production, in contrast, provides a model of how to bring Austen to a modern film audience while remaining true to her intent, creating what is unspoken in the novel but necessary in adaptation to provide both realistic visual detail and thematic congruence with the original. Michell's visualization of Austen's navy men, his use of clothing, decor, and manners to satirize social pretensions, and Dear's compact, pointed script bring to the screen the significant themes that drive Austen's novel. All adaptations are balancing acts, but Michell's is most successful in finding ways to integrate literary text, the visual nature of film, and modern understandings.

Michell maintains the maritime focus, for example, in a long list of scenes: Anne in the attic finding Wentworth's letter folded into a toy boat, the Musgrove children sailing toy boats, the officers in uniform on public occasions, Sophie Croft fascinating her listeners with her tales of shipboard travels to far-flung parts of the empire, Louisa and Henrietta Musgrove consulting the navy list for vessels the admiral and Captain Wentworth served on, the banter of shipmates about past exploits, Charles's whispered observation that Captain Wentworth brought home £20,000 in booty from captured vessels, and an elderly sailor begging on the steps at Bath. The final scene returns to the opening. Bonaparte has raised an army, the nation is again at war, and the navy is mobilized. This time Anne sails with her new husband despite his declaration that he would never permit a woman shipboard. The final shot of the *Bounty*, recognizable only because of the final credit line referencing the clip from the Marlon Brando film *Mutiny on the Bounty*, adds a satiric touch worthy of Austen though outside her novel: the dark underside of naval virtues, the result of harsh punishments and deprivations.

While the *Bounty* clip has been criticized as outside Austen's text, irresistible arguments support the recurring naval elements, including simple historical fact, Austen's personal knowledge of naval matters through her brother, the continual return to naval characters in the text, the rhetorical contrast between the self-sacrificing naval officers and the narcissistic, self-serving Sir Walter Elliot, and a presumably widespread understanding of British self-interest. A primary theme in *Persuasion*, as in all Austen novels, is money; the British navy, though not the source of English wealth, policed the world to safeguard colonial income.

Dear's script enables Michell and his actors to delineate character in accord with Austen through use of specific camera shots and cuts among shots to capture the points of view and perceptions of individual characters. Unlike the 1971 *Persuasion*, the 1995 version moves cinematically, beginning with the alternating navy/Kellynch sequence and continuing with a lively camera that moves from long shots to close ups, for example, capturing a group around the piano, moving to the player's face or hands, then to the dancers from the limited perspective of the piano player, up to Wentworth's face in particular, with close-ups of single dancers or pairs of dancers, and then a long shot again, capturing exchanged glances and reabsorption into the group. The progression in types of shots, angles, and distances changes continually, but always with Anne cut off at the piano, clearly straining to overhear conversations (particularly Wentworth's) as she plays on dutifully while all around her enjoy pleasures long denied her. This is film 'grammar,' fast-paced action with quick cuts shifting in and out, matched with varied sound levels and sound clarity together creating an overall sense of social interacting, blossoming relationships, and hidden passions.

Dear/Michell compress and focus action to create character and carry theme. Unlike the 1971 *Persuasion*, no scene or line exists just because it is in the novel. The economically shot early scene of Anne overseeing covering the furnishings and packing takes far less time than does the 2007 version and ends with Anne finding Wentworth's letter in an attic chest – a painful reminder of loss and of the economic realities behind the leave-taking. Michell compresses the long 1971 sequence of Musgrove family members complaining to Anne into an effective character statement communicated in tableaux, as family members, drinking tea, whisper at Anne in various nooks and crannies as she listens patiently: Mrs Musgrove in a red-and-gold brocade loveseat, Mary next to a cabinet and candlestick, Charles in a leather chair near the fireplace, back to Mrs Musgrove, then Louisa in a window seat, Henrietta against wooden panelling, Mary in a box-window, Charles on the loveseat, and Mary standing, as Louisa plays the harp. Each family member replaces another in quick cuts until Charles sums up what viewers must be feeling, 'Oh, Anne!' Though quite brief, the sequence of shots in varied decors remains in the memory and establishes Anne as a woman valued privately for her usefulness, a quality ignored en famille. Viewers do not overhear every word but need not to understand the point.

While viewers watch Anne care for others – closing up the family home and inventorying its goods, nursing her injured nephew, engaging the mourning Benwick in therapeutic conversation, competently giving orders for the injured Louisa's care, charitably visiting a crippled schoolmate – her self-indulgent family dismisses her as unworthy of attention as her father's query to Captain Wentworth confirms: 'You want to marry Anne? Whatever for?' He and Elizabeth, with her imperious commands and obsession with social prestige, are blind to themselves and others.

Dear/Michell provide further psychological logic. Where the 1971/2007 *Persuasion*s prepare for Louisa's impetuous Lyme quay leap with much style-jumping on the Musgroves' long walk, Michell shows only Louisa's exhilarating flirtation with Wentworth before the dangerous leap, visually framing Louisa quite literally throwing herself at Captain Wentworth, a sexually symbolic scene that John Mosier argues accounts for 'Anne's renewed despair' (236). Anne not only feels an age disadvantage, but, says Mosier, is 'at a keen social and moral disadvantage as well, since she is too well brought up, too moral, to throw herself at Wentworth in public' (236). Michell delineates character where Shergold reiterates only physical leaping.

Novelist-screenwriter Hugh Selby Jr argues that because the screen cannot convey the unspoken voice of a writer, film must be true instead to the essence of the work and seek external means to make visual the psychological (qtd in Macdonald 6). By this standard, the 1971 *Persuasion* fails to translate Austen's voice and intent to a new medium. Likewise, the 2007 *Persuasion*, for all its use of modern filmic techniques to create visual interest, ignores Austen's essential themes, striving instead for a fast-moving romantic tale with modern appeal. Despite Michell's assertion that he adapted a Cinderella story of boy meets girl, loses girl, finds girl (Macdonald 5), Dear's script and Michell's cinematic decisions result in a film that meets Selby's criteria, a visual tale true to Austen's spirit: ironic, satirically edged, praising British navy officers, mocking the pretensions and snobbery of the lower gentry and the whole Bath experience (which Austen despised[12]), and marshalling events in a visually exciting, logical narrative sequence. Dear/ Michell's Anne appropriately embodies the eighteenth-century virtues of restraint, common sense, and propriety, but she also offers the modern viewer relevant modern virtues, a woman of sense and sensibility, who tempers the romantic poets with prose, who has lived in a small, limited world but is open to the potentials of shipboard life. She shares the national pride in naval accomplishments and moves into a male world, ready to embrace her husband's naval experiences for better or worse and to face the possibilities inherent in a new self-vision. Dear/ Mitchell makes her personal triumph over family and circumstance ultimately the heart of their tale[13] and her choice of the self-made captain over the hereditary heir a confirmation of Austen's thesis.

Of the three modern *Persuasion* films, Michell's 1995 version most effectively conveys an interpretively nuanced, but pointed satiric image through fashion, milieu, and film technique, capturing the contrasting pretensions of city and country, the visual signs of social climbing, and the newly minted prestige of British naval uniforms, which elicited pride in imperial accomplishment over the status of birth. It brings to the screen what John Wiltshire calls 'the sense of personal communication having to be made within a crowded complex world in continual danger of being thwarted, interrupted, or twisted by the projects and emotions of others' (81). Michell's version provides an object lesson in intelligent, tasteful adaptation, avoiding the mimetic fallacy of attempting museum-like recreations of the historical past while furthering the literary goals of the source text.

NOTES

1   See also Groenendyk 11 and Murphy 26.
2   See Gay on Austen's built-in signals to staging and production as in the concert scene's approach-retreat movement, 'glances, blushes, averted eyes.'
3   Online at sites like www.smilingfoxforgeli.com. Even YouTube offers sites on making Regency Bonnets.
4   Horton's *Bumstead* provides production drawings, storyboards, and film stills illustrating film technique. See also Landis and Ettedgui.
5   Regency romance writers Georgette Heyer and Clare Darcy provide film costumers 'an eroticism absent in Austen but expected by modern viewers' (Richards 112).

6 Garvie charmingly describes the classic 1980 BBC *Pride & Prejudice* in production: over 100 technicians, prop-men, make-up artists, wardrobe department dressers, design assistants, assistant directors, and runners 'collaborating' (71).

7 See McMaster, Mudrick, and Oldmark on Austen's ironic and satiric voices.

8 See Kindred and Southam on Austen's naval brothers and their influence on *Persuasion*.

9 How this scene is framed for film reveals much about understanding of characters and theme: we should see the essentially frugal Anne dutifully protecting the excessive furnishings of her heedless family while they are off to Bath.

10 The estate so appropriately old-world authentic today would, in Austen's time, have been a fairly new construction. 'Authenticity' of fashion and decor is illusory; the real question is what will pass muster with modern moviegoers, how they will 'read' and process material things. See Nutall.

11 Trilling's introduction to his edition of *Emma* and Harding's essay on Austen's 'regulated hatred' makes Austen's values of restraint, reason, and good sense and her contempt for the maudlin and the sentimental very clear.

12 See Stovel 228.

13 Parrill's discussion of Anne's transformation (152–68) is excellent.

WORKS CITED

Bluestone, George. *Novels into Film*. Berkeley: U of California P, 1957. Print.

Chapman, R.W., ed. *Jane Austen: Selected Letters 1796–1817*. Oxford: Oxford UP, 1986. Print.

Dear, Nick. *Persuasion: A Screenplay*. London: Methuen, 1996. Print.

Elliott, Kamilla. *Rethinking the Novel/Film Debate*. Cambridge: Cambridge UP, 2003. Print.

Ettedgui, Peter. *Production Design and Art Direction* (Screencraft Series). Oxford: Focal, 2000. Print.

Gard, Roger. 'A Few Skeptical Thoughts on Jane Austen and Film.' *Jane Austen on Screen*. Ed. Gina and Andrew F. Macdonald. Cambridge: Cambridge UP, 2003: 10–12. Print.

Garvie, Elizabeth. 'Becoming Elizabeth' and 'Q & A with Elizabeth Garvie.' *Sensibilities* 35 (2007): 66–74, 74–7. Print.

Gay, Penny. *Jane Austen and the Theatre*. Cambridge: Cambridge UP, 2002. Print.

Groenedyk, Kathy L. 'The Importance of Vision: *Persuasion* and the Picturesque.' *Rhetoric Society Quarterly* 30.1 (2000): 9–28. Print.

Hannon, Patrice. 'Austen Novels and Austen Films: Incompatible Worlds?' *Persuasions: The Journal of the Jane Austen Society of North America* 18 (1996): 24–32. Web. 14 March 2010.

Harding, D.W. 'Regulated Hatred: An Aspect of the Work of Jane Austen.' *Jane Austen: A Collection of Critical Essays*. Ed. Ian Watt. Englewood Cliffs, NJ: Prentice-Hall, 1963: 166–79. Print.

Hollander, Anne. *Seeing Through Clothes*. New York: Viking, 1978: 424–37. Print.

Horton, Andrew. *Henry Bumstead and the World of Hollywood Direction*. Austin, TX: U of Texas P, 2009. Print.

Kindred, Sheila Johnson. 'Charles Austen: Prize Chaser and Prize Taker on the North American Station, 1805–1808.' *Persuasions* 26 (2004): 188–94. Web. 4 March 2010.

Landis, Deborah Nadoolman. *Costume Design* (Screencraft Series). Oxford: Focal, 2003. Print.

Macdonald, Gina, and Andrew F., eds. *Jane Austen on Screen*. Cambridge: Cambridge UP, 2003. Print.

Mamet, David. *On Directing Film*. New York: Viking, 1991. Print.

McFarlane, Brian. *Novel to Film: An Introduction to the Theory of Adaptation*. Oxford: Clarendon, 1996. Print.

McMaster, Juliet. 'Class.' *The Cambridge Companion to Jane Austen*. Ed. Edward Copeland and Juliet McMaster. Cambridge: Cambridge UP, 1997: 115–30. Print.

Monaghan, David, Ariane Hudelet, and John Wiltshire. *The Cinematic Jane Austen: Essays on the Filmic Sensibility of the Novels*. Jefferson, NC: McFarland, 2008. Print.

Mosier, John. 'Clues for the Clueless.' *Jane Austen on Screen*. Ed. Gina and Andrew F. Macdonald. Cambridge: Cambridge UP, 2003: 228–53. Print.

Mudrick, Marvin. *Jane Austen: Irony as Defense and Discovery*. Princeton: Princeton UP; London: Oxford UP, 1952. Print.

Murphy, Olivia. 'Books, Bras and Bridget Jones: Reading Adaptations of *Pride and Prejudice*.' *Sydney Studies in English* 31.2 (2005): 21–38. *Project Muse*. Web. 20 March 2010.

Nuttall, A.D. *Shakespeare the Thinker*. New Haven: Yale UP, 2007. Print.

Oldmark, John. *An Understanding of Jane Austen's Novels: Character, Value, and Ironic Perspective*. Oxford: Blackwell, 1981. Print.

Parrill, Sue. *Jane Austen on Film and Television: A Critical Study of the Adaptations*. Jefferson, NC: McFarland, 2002. Print.

Persuasion. Dir. Howard Baker. 1971. Film.

Persuasion. Dir. Roger Michell. 1995. Film.

Persuasion. Dir. Adrian Shergold. 2007. Film.

Richards, Paulette. 'Regency Romance Shadowing in the Visual Motifs of Roger Michell's *Persuasion.' Jane Austen on Screen.* Ed. Gina and Andrew F. Macdonald. Cambridge: Cambridge UP, 2003: 111–26. Print.

Southam, Brian. *Jane Austen and the Navy.* London: Hambledon and London, 2000. Print.

– 'Jane Austen's Sailor Brothers: Francis and Charles in Life and Art.' *Persuasions* 25 (2003): 33–45. Web. 4 March 2010.

Stovel, Bruce. 'Further Reading.' *The Cambridge Companion to Jane Austen.* Ed. Edward Copeland and Juliet McMaster. Cambridge: Cambridge UP, 1997: 227–43. Print.

Trilling, Lionel. Introduction. *Emma.* By Jane Austen. Boston: Houghton Mifflin, 1951: v–xxiv. Print.

Troost, Linda, and John Sayer, eds. *Jane Austen in Hollywood.* Louisville: UP of Kentucky, 2001. Print.

Wiltshire, John. 'Persuasion.' *The Cambridge Companion to Jane Austen.* Ed. Edward Copeland and Juliet McMaster. Cambridge: Cambridge UP, 1997: 76–83. Print.

16 From *Pride and Prejudice* to *Lost in Austen* and Back Again: Reading Television Reading Novels

CLAIRE GROGAN

Jane Austen's status as a cultural icon is indisputable. What is less clear is whether Austen's works should be positioned as part of an elite culture or as part of popular culture since both she and her works travel in fascinating ways on what Stuart Hall terms a 'cultural escalator.' Though her novels have risen steadily in popularity since their first publication in the early 1800s it is the more recent film adaptations that have catapulted first Austen's works and then her person to their current celebrity status. 'Austenmania' can be traced to the mid 1990s: 1995 saw the release of the Ang Lee/Emma Thompson collaborative *Sense and Sensibility*, Andrew Davies's BBC six-hour miniseries of *Pride and Prejudice*, and Robert Mitchell/Nick Dear's film version of the TV series *Persuasion*. Two versions of *Emma* were released in 1996 (Douglas McGrath's Hollywood film and Andrew Davies's television series), and 1999 saw Patricia Rozema's film *Mansfield Park*. Less than a decade later we witnessed another burst of Austen adaptations with Joe Wright's *Pride and Prejudice* and Iain MacDonald's *Mansfield Park* in 2005, then Adrian Shergold's *Persuasion*, Jon Jones's *Northanger Abbey*, and John Alexander's *Sense and Sensibility*, all in 2008. There were also the spin offs: *Clueless* (1996), *Bridget Jones's Diary* (2001), *Becoming Jane* (2006), *The Jane Austen Book Club* (2007), *Bride and Prejudice* (2007), *Miss Austen Regrets* (2008) and *Lost in Austen* (2008).[1] Indeed, as the preface to this collection notes, Austen is the only canonical writer whose name can virtually guarantee a successful film.

Of interest are the curious ways in which these film adaptations link the viewer to the world of Austen and to readers of the original novels, especially if we acknowledge that many now watch Austen but do not read her. How do we understand or accept such treatment of a beloved literary figure and what impact does it all have upon our understanding of her works?

Much energy is expended by film critics in assessing the merits of true or accurate filmic adaptations of the original text as opposed to loose adaptations which allow for modern tastes and methods. Critiques of fidelity invoke a somewhat intangible grading system for determining whether a film adaptation is a true or accurate rendition of the original novel or whether in fact all film representations are derivative and less than the original literary text. George Bluestone's seminal 1957 book *Novels into Film*, in which he argues that the novel and the film are fundamentally incompatible forms of media, established a dominant line of thought that continues to be advanced in the work of later critics such as Paul Willimen and Roger Gard. Such views have been hotly contested most recently by critics such as Brian McFarlane, Thomas Leitch, and Kamilla Elliott, who challenge Bluestone's assumptions, albeit in different ways. Much of this debate hinges on claiming the merits of the reader over the viewer, privileging one medium over the other, championing a 'close' over a 'loose' adaptation. In one attempt to open up the debate, Robert Stam draws up an extensive list of the words available to describe how 'one form emerges out of a creative engagement with another.' This list, which includes 'reading, rewriting, critiquing, translation, transmutation, metamorphosis, recreation, transvocalization, resuscitation, transfiguration, actualization, transmodalization, signifying, performance, dialogization, cannibalization, reinvisioning, incarnation, or reaccentuation' (qtd in Wiltshire 7), attempts to break down the rigid polarity of the two camps of fidelity and antifidelity. However, rather than argue for the merits of one medium over the other or one type of adaptation over another, I wish to assert the interconnectedness between them. Novels and the filmic adaptations are, after all, often enjoyed by the same individuals, alternating between consuming book and film, being reader and viewer. Despite academic snobbery, there is no guarantee that the consumer begins as a reader and moves on to become a viewer. Many viewers of the film adaptations have never read Austen's novels and might be led to read them only after watching the film versions. Certainly that is precisely what is suggested by the slew of new Austen editions and DVDs as well as assorted Austen memorabilia that has flooded the market since the mid 1990s as a direct marketing response to this new 'readership.'

I wish to suggest how a filmic adaptation such as Daniel Zeff's 2008 *Lost in Austen*, while it might tempt some viewers into becoming Austen readers, is primarily directed toward informed Austen consumers. In fact watching this series leads the viewer into an engagement with multiple texts that closely resembles the engagement between novel and reader that Austen herself envisaged when she published her novels in the early 1800s. A four-part series for television, *Lost in Austen* is clearly not a straight filmic adaptation of a specific Austen novel. However, while it is unquestionably a creative rendering of Austen's *Pride and Prejudice* (1813) it does rely upon the viewer being a close adherent of all things Austen. The intertextual references are not limited to those between the novel *Pride and Prejudice* and *Lost in Austen*, but rather the modern viewer of this series is also expected to be an avid consumer of various other film adaptations of Austen novels – specifically the BBC 1995 Andrew Davies *Pride and Prejudice* (starring Colin Firth and Jennifer Ehle) and the 2005 Joe Wright *Pride and Prejudice* (starring Matthew MacFadyen and Keira Knightly).

In this chapter I wish to consider how the movement away from the source novel through various film adaptations to this present television series somewhat paradoxically takes us back to yet another reading of Austen's novel. Therefore, nimbly side-stepping the highly charged debate that rages about the merits of fidelity as opposed to antifidelity, I wish to suggest that the viewer and reader's response to a modern production such as *Lost in Austen* owes as much to its accurate rendition of the original text as to a new creative reworking of that material – a handy combination of both aspects of fidelity and antifidelity. As John Wiltshire notes,

> The mere presence of two or more treatments of the same novel impels the reader towards comparison, and comparison of films impels the viewer towards the source text. The later films derive as much from the earlier films as they do from the novels; they are hybrid or even miscegenated works. (170)

Of interest is how, moving us through years, mediums and adaptations help us to read Austen's 1813 novel and more importantly help to recreate the reading experience that Austen envisaged. While it is generally agreed that Austen's *Northanger Abbey* is the most overtly literary of her works, with its extensive discussion of novel reading and novel readers, all of Austen's fictional works challenge the interpretive skills of the reader. As I argue elsewhere, 'Austen's continual play with social and fictional conventions in *Northanger Abbey* means that our work as reader parallels that of the heroine Catherine Morland herself. As Catherine reads herself in relation to other people, other texts, and other situations, so the modern reader must also situate herself in relation to other works, other genres, and other critics' readings. Reading is shown to be a complicated but enjoyable act for all readers of and within the novel' (Grogan 7–8). Our challenge lies not only in Austen's numerous references to, quotations from, and parodies of other fictional and non-fictional works, but also in the challenge of interpretation itself – the fluidity of language and meaning. Austen demands a sophisticated engagement with the text on the reader's part to untangle the novel's complex intertextual web and to interpret the authorial comments about genres and writing.

Pride and Prejudice is no exception. Oblique references are made to other works of fiction through plot and form, disruptions of reader's expectations, familiar elements of the epistolary, romance, and educational works, and contemporary views about female education and appropriate behaviour. Austen clearly expected her ideal reader to be active rather than passive as she registered such intertextual moments, oblique cultural and historical references, and even inside family jokes. While not all of her readers engage in this manner Austen clearly hoped that some would, and Zeff's success lies in his recreating this challenge for the modern viewer. He delivers what we are familiar with but in a new and stimulating way which is then coupled with original and creative rewritings of Austen's source text. The movement between the film adaptation and the original text becomes an integral part of the interpretative act. Wiltshire explains 'how reference to their source is an inevitable adjunct to the reading of the films' (167). Any creative reworking of a source text relies in large measure upon the viewer's intimate knowledge of that source for parody, imitation, and homage even as it deviates from it to create a new work. Though she is not talking about *Lost in Austen* Adriane Hudelet's observation that adaptations rely upon 'Austen's narrative structure, and some episodes from other films ... to address eminently modern questions' (154) is pertinent here.

Janet Todd, as general editor of the recent *Cambridge Edition of the Works of Jane Austen,* astutely notes that 'Austen wrote to be read and reread,' quoting the remark to her sister Cassandra that 'an artist cannot do anything slovenly' (ix). In a similar manner then to Austen's original reader, I suggest the present day consumer is encouraged to reread and rewatch the various texts (published editions and film versions) multiple times to become conversant with not just the plot lines but all of their varied aspects and filmic nuances. The DVD now, like the literary novel, is something to be purchased with the intention of multiple viewings to create what Wiltshire calls the 'convergence, if not of genres, then certainly of forms' (Wiltshire 162). *Lost in Austen* relies upon the viewer's knowledge of the source text and of other film and television adaptations, not only of *Pride and Prejudice* but also of other Austen novels, which appear in specific techniques, shots, props, scenes, or imaginings. 'Just as films appear to borrow motifs or ideas from one another (or replicate features of the species), they depend to some extent upon each other for their life as commercial entities' (Wiltshire 164). And it is our mental gymnastics between these sources that provides an experience that is both familiar and excitingly novel. 'Moving between a film version and a novel (the dyadic activity which invokes "Fidelity") becomes something different when not one, but two or three versions of the same original are put into play' (Wiltshire 164).

And there are now many film adaptations in play, starting with Aldous Huxley's 1940 MGM screenplay (starring Laurence Olivier and Greer Garson), and more recently the 1980 Cyril Coke television series, the 1995 Simon Langton/Andrew Davies BBC series, and Joe Wright's 2005 film. Intertextuality must be recognized as a marked feature of Austen adaptations. 'Whether consciously or not, they borrow from and allude to each other, so that the viewer of the whole emerging corpus may detect motifs, gestures, even whole sequences as echoes of a previous film' (Wiltshire 163).

Lost in Austen draws upon not only the source novel but also other films as it critiques, imitates, and sometimes parodies these versions. These are clues the viewer is challenged to pick up and relish, and this engagement parallels Austen's own hope, expressed in a letter to her sister Cassandra, that reading should be an exciting challenge: 'I do not write for such dull elves as have not a good deal of ingenuity themselves' (*Letters* 79). As a result, things that happen in *Lost in Austen* but that did not happen in the original novel are not automatically rejected, but cast illuminating light upon or prompt new interpretations of the original work. These connections enhance our enjoyment and set us on what Austen might happily recognize as a challenge of interpretation, literary and filmic allusion, intertextual references mixed in with our wish fulfilment and fantasy. As this chapter will argue, these connections are established in three primary ways: through fidelity to the novel, through references to other adaptations, and through shared fantasies.

Austen's *Pride and Prejudice* is imaginatively complicated in Zeff's *Lost in Austen* by the entrance of modern day woman Amanda Price, who swaps places with the fictional Elizabeth Bennet. While the often uneasy juxtaposition of past and present – as seen when a novel like *Pride and Prejudice*, written some 200 years ago, is read by the modern day audience – provides a backdrop for any reading of a literary work, it is made manifest in *Lost in Austen*. The series opens with Amanda settling down on her sofa after a day's office work to sip a glass of red wine and indulge in a rereading of her favourite Austen novel *Pride and Prejudice*. Amanda chooses to spend some 'time alone with Elizabeth' rather than join her roommate Pirhana out on the town or meet up with her boyfriend Michael. Clearly a few hours' escape into *Pride and Prejudice* allows Amanda to elude her everyday life in Hammersmith and all of its romantic shortcomings. It allows her to escape into a fantasy world where things seem calmer, more ordered and ultimately more romantic. But when Elizabeth Bennet appears in Amanda's bathroom on two separate occasions, Zeff has the two worlds meet as the women swap places. The world into which Amanda enters through the bathroom wall is that of the fictional Bennet home at Longbourn. This world is precisely that of the original novel. We, as viewers, enter the familiar and recognizable in what is a precise filmic rendering of Longbourn and its environs. We enter a Regency period piece which is accurately depicted down to the household, fashion, food, and carriages. No expense has been spared to make this a historically accurate adaptation of *Pride and Prejudice*.

In terms of fidelity *Lost in Austen* is true to the novel in terms of places, characters, and appearances. Where the differences occur is in certain characters' behaviour and the motivations behind such behaviour. True to Austen's novel, Mr Collins is repugnant – Amanda calls him the 'King of the Mingots' – but Zeff has endowed him with numerous brothers to marry all of the Bennet girls! Darcy is suitably proud and austere as Amanda notes ('God, I knew you were abrupt, but that's a bit severe'), Charles Bingley is friendly and ineffectual, his sister Caroline is appropriately beautiful and haughty. All the Bennet family members appear as we expect and anticipate them and this makes it all very familiar. We share Amanda's mounting excitement when she realizes she is there at the beginning. The characters around her do not know what is to happen but we, like Amanda, informed Austen readers (and viewers), do.

We know what will happen and with what results. Or like Amanda, we believe we do from our multiple readings and rereading of *Pride and Prejudice* and/or viewings of film adaptations.

But then there are changes to the novel that the Austen reader immediately notes. These are deviations in the plot line. Amanda's appearance obviously changes things even though she really desires to be a spectator – to see the great romance unfold before her eyes rather than just on the page and in her imagination. Amanda's presence at Longbourn disrupts the plot line, and, rather like disobeying *Star Trek*'s Prime Directive, she invokes what Edward Lorenz, in his work on chaos theory, coined the Butterfly Effect: where 'one storyline diverges at the moment of a seemingly minor event resulting in two significantly different outcomes' (Lorenz 14–15). Amanda's very presence alters events so that things almost immediately begin to spin out of narrative alignment. The fascination lies in how we respond to things going awry. We recognize everything around Amanda but also that things are not as they should be – especially in the misalignment of characters.

What emerges is a fascinating alternative to the original that is curiously true to the spirit of Austen's text. Zeff introduces startling twists. Charles Bingley falls for Amanda rather than for Jane at the Netherfield ball and she has to claim a burning desire for other women to get rid of him. The shocked Charles exclaims 'Oh, so there are people who punt from the other end of the boat!' Amanda ends up temporarily engaged to Mr Collins until Wickham lets slip that her money comes from a fish business, a disclosure that prompts Mr Collins to hastily rescind his offer of marriage. Jane then marries Mr Collins, and as a result Mr Bennet decamps to his study and a despondent and rejected Charlotte Lucas leaves for Africa to be a missionary. Eventually Charles Bingley elopes with Lydia to fulfil his Rousseauistic dreams in Hammersmith – the home of liberation and of their role model Amanda. Caroline expresses her lesbian desires to Amanda and we discover that Wickham has a good side. These changes are noted by the viewer who aligns the series against the novel and waits to see whether these discrepancies will be corrected and whether Zeff (through Amanda) can possibly rescue the plot and bring about the 'right' ending. *Lost in Austen* works on our expectations of fidelity, their apparent fulfillment, and then our excitement and mounting frustration when things start to go wrong. How wrong will they be allowed to go and at what stage will the viewer/reader reject such corruptions of the original plot?

The second type of connection between film and original occurs through intertextual references: those deviations that appear in the introduction of scenes not present in the original novel but found in other film adaptations. As Wiltshire points out, 'More complex issues of intertextuality occur when the issue involves not deleting, but amplifying, reworking elisions or supplying gaps in the original text' (164–5). There are many such changes in the series, but a closer examination of three will illustrate this trait.

The first is the initial proposal scene between Darcy and Elizabeth. The heated argument in *Lost in Austen* between Darcy and Amanda parallels the unsuccessful first proposal of the novel, the BBC Davies proposal, and the Wright proposal, though there are shifts as each adaptation either replicates the novel's interior scene (BBC/Davies) or moves to an exterior scene (Wright). In *Lost in Austen* we return to an interior drawing room scene in which the two characters are drawn to each other, but rather than a proposal and a rejection we have the flat out hostility of mutual repugnance, which of course masks mutual attraction and growing sexual tension. We viewers know what is at stake in *Lost in Austen* because it recalls the former novel and filmic scenes, even if the two protagonists, Darcy and Amanda, do not know what is happening. We see the pattern playing out. We see that Amanda is replacing Elizabeth Bennet in that she has taken her place more than figuratively, and this is one instance where the Zeff series fantasizes about *Pride and Prejudice* from a modern reader's perspective since the modern reader (like Amanda) is able to slip seamlessly into Elizabeth's place. Amanda replaces rather than becomes Elizabeth.

Another pivotal scene from other film adaptations is the meeting between Elizabeth and Darcy's sister Georgiana. In the novel Elizabeth is invited to Pemberley to meet Georgiana, and this is represented accurately in the 1995 Davies BBC adaptation. The 2005 Wright production introduces a clandestine meeting when Keira Knightly as Elizabeth surprises the brother and sister. This prompts an interesting layering of scenes with Georgiana. Wright's filmic version of the incident is then replicated by Zeff to show us brother and sister exchanging heartfelt words in Pemberley as Darcy awaits Amanda's visit. All of these adaptations introduce a slightly new twist on something that is familiar but also distinct. And the manner in which adaptations build upon each other and converse with each other makes such additions as important as the original from the viewer's perspective and enjoyment. For example, we see the specific repetition of the 'peeping tom' shot when Kiera

Figure 16.1. The 'Peeping Tom' shot from Joe Wright's 2005 *Pride and Prejudice*. Used with permission.

Figure 16.2. The 'Peeping Tom' shot repeated in Daniel Zeff's (2008) *Lost in Austen*. Used with permission.

Knightly's Elizabeth discovers Georgiana in the home and then sees Darcy arrive and greet her – an intensely private moment used to reveal his softer inner side. The camera angle heightens the viewers' sense of peeping into Darcy's warmer personal side. As the images reproduced in figure 16.1 and 16.2 make clear, Zeff replicates this 'peeping Tom' shot when Amanda spies Georgiana at play in her room. Zeff further embellishes the moment by having Amanda then enter the room to converse with Georgiana and discover the shocking truth that Georgiana threw herself at Wickham, and when he refused she falsely accused him of ravishing her. This layering makes it more and more difficult to remember that Austen did not write this informal meeting, but the revisions offer what the modern reader might hope to be the case as they flesh out this sibling relationship in an intimate scene. While the reader of 1813 might be content to imagine the relationship, the modern viewer demands more evidence and intimacy.

Last, the 'diving' scene (or what the members of *The Jane Austen Book Club* are able to refer to as 'Darcy in the woods' without need for further explanation) appears to have become a staple of adaptations of *Pride and Prejudice*. No version of this scene ever happens in Austen's novel, but Davies's BBC version, which created 'Firthmania' in Britain during 1995, has burnt its way into so many viewers' minds that many believe that the scene is integral to the work. But why is this addition so necessary, indeed irresistible, to the modern viewer? Perhaps it is because it actualizes what the reader already understands in making explicit the sexual tension between Darcy and Elizabeth. Austen indicates such things through averted eyes, unspoken exchanges, letters, and third person indirect speech but the modern viewer demands further direct proof. Zeff notes the dramatic shift between being attracted and repulsed when he has Darcy cast a brooding look in Amanda's direction for the first time prompting her to exclaim, 'wow smolder alert.'

The visual allusion reproduced in figure 16.3 highlights the connections being drawn between the 1995 diving shot and the later Wright and Zeff adaptations. Wright's film hints at Davies's diving shot in the first Darcy/Elizabeth proposal scene when we see Darcy drenched to the skin from a rain storm. This works to exude sexual tension in large part because the viewer aligns it with the diving moment of the earlier adaptation. A wet shirt connotes Darcy's passions. Zeff explicitly draws attention to this intertextual moment in *Lost in Austen*. When Darcy declares to Amanda, 'You are the one I love,' standing alone with her in the gardens she immediately replies, 'Then do something for me.' It is with shock and delight that the viewer perceives that the next shot shows Darcy emerging from the pond, water dripping off his shirt-clad torso. Her fantasy is to have Darcy emerge from the water in a clear imitation and parody of the Firth dive. Charged with sexual pleasure and delight Amanda clasps her hands and notes, 'I'm having a bit of a strange post modern moment here.' Darcy has no idea what she refers to but we as viewers do. So why does this replica of an invented scene strike us as amusing or even appropriate? To a certain extent I suggest

Figure 16.3. Elliot Cowan as Darcy in Daniel Zeff's *Lost in Austen*. DVD capture. Used with permission.

it is because it confirms our status as Austen aficionados who are picking up such intertextual allusions. The informed Austen viewer aligns this moment with the Davies/Firth dive and not the fountain scene in Wright's *Atonement* – though the ghostly presence of Keira Knightly tempts us in that wrong direction, being the heroine of both Wright productions. The viewer's subsequent sense of knowingness in this moment of antifidelity creates for film viewers much the same pleasurable sense of superior insight that close readers experience in adaptations that privilege textual fidelity.

The third type of connection between *Lost in Austen* and the original novel results from the inclusion of our own fantasies – fantasies which are curiously shared with many other (perhaps predominantly female) consumers of *Pride and Prejudice* and are foregrounded on the DVD cover, which describes Zeff's series as a 'fantasy adaptation.' So we move from issues of fidelity to those of fantasy and the fantasy takes several forms, all of which derive from the triangulation between our reading of Austen's novel, our viewing of film adaptations, and our fantasies about *Pride and Prejudice*.

Certainly this is true when Amanda knees Mr Collins in the groin at the Netherfield ball. Her assault is the realization of what has hitherto been a deep but repressed desire of the female reader. Layered upon

Austen's implicit repugnance to Mr Collins are of course the brilliant portrayals of him by David Bamber in 1995 and then by Tom Hollander in 2005. By 2008 it is impossible not to shudder when Mr Collins minces across the screen. Zeff refers implicitly to these earlier actors by casting Guy Henry as a Mr Collins who, unlike his diminutive predecessors, towers above the others characters. In all of these portrayals Mr Collins cuts a ridiculous figure, but in his male-dominated world intelligent women are subject to his whims and cavils. When a male colleague of mine once commented on how laughable and perhaps loveable Mr Collins was, I could only respond that as a male he had no appreciation of the horror the Collins character evokes in the female reader – he could neither imagine nor fear being forced to marry such a toad. The response of female audiences is invariably one of loathing and disgust. Let us not forget that had the novel's Mrs Bennet not crassly boasted about Jane and Bingley's connection Jane would have dutifully married Mr Collins. In *Lost in Austen* Zeff has Jane make just this sacrifice to ensure her family's financial survival. Zeff is harder hitting than Austen, who allows us the fictional fantasy of Jane's escape. When Zeff binds Jane to Collins he draws attention to the realities of eighteenth-century courtship for women and denies us (albeit only temporarily)[2] any escape from what would no doubt have been the sad reality. So what better than to have Amanda do what many of us have dreamt of – to knee Collins in the groin rather than listen to his simpering boastfulness one second longer. This anachronistic behavior – rather like her ejaculations 'Bum face' to Caroline Bingley, 'Float my boat' when describing Darcy's sexual appeal to Jane, or 'You could park a jumbo here' on entering Netherfield Park by coach – is painfully crass but nevertheless articulates a secret desire. As soon as Amanda knees Collins we know as viewers that it is inappropriate and tasteless – something not to be tolerated – yet it does realize a deep dark secret: one small knee jerk by Amanda one giant gesture on behalf of silenced and oppressed eighteenth-century women.

There are other less substantial changes that Zeff includes through Amanda that make Austen's Elizabeth more understandable to us – most notably in her doting on her father and in her attraction to Wickham. In *Lost in Austen* we see a more active and assertive Mr Bennet than in the novel, which makes it appropriate that he favours Elizabeth: he does not disappoint us as badly as in the novel with his lack of foresight and planning. And we see Wickham as an attractive bounder, racy and cheeky, an outsider who works every situation – but we learn that he has a true and honourable side (what Elizabeth was drawn to) in the inversion of the Georgiana story, when Wickham helps Amanda and then the entire Bennet family rescue Lydia, who has run off with Bingley in this version for philosophical rather than sexual reasons. It is Wickham who helps Amanda, whom he describes as 'a girl a long way from home,' to dress and comport herself appropriately at Rosings. It is also his knowledge of a local surgeon who tends to Mr Bennet's head injury sustained from a fight with Bingley that allows a happy reunion of all the Bennet family.

The biggest change though is when we the viewers see Amanda realize our dream (whether previously articulated or not) to be Elizabeth Bennet – to be the heroine of the drama. She resists as best she can, professing that Darcy must love Elizabeth:

> AMANDA: You must not, you must not.
> DARCY: Wherefore may I not? Who is to judge us?
> AMANDA: Elizabeth, I'm not Elizabeth. The entire world will hate me.
> DARCY: Were that true I would fight the world. You are the one I love.

However, when her resistance falters she rationalizes to herself, 'I love Fitzwilliam Darcy. I love him. Maybe that's what's meant to happen. I'm the understudy, the star has failed to turn up. I have to go on and do the show.'

And last, but not least, Amanda gets to literally take Darcy home – when he follows her through the portal to modern day Hammersmith declaring that he 'would harrow hell to be with [her].' He crosses the historical divide in a similar way to Elizabeth who finally explains her preference for the twenty-first century to Amanda in her assertion 'I was born out of time.' It is a truth, what we have always read and seen: Elizabeth makes do (nicely) with Darcy, but as Austen's novel concludes it is not a future without travail – Elizabeth's nature and personality are curtailed in her marriage. In *Lost in Austen* Elizabeth gets what she really desires – freedom and emancipation. So Amanda returns to Pemberley as mistress, and permanently enters a world of greater reserve and propriety because she also is a woman out of her time. A muted Amanda returns to Pemberley and the modern Elizabeth stays in Hammersmith.

Paradoxically the ostensible 'truth' of the novel's conclusion is maintained in *Lost in Austen* by a strategic mixing of fidelity and fantasy. It is a viewing and reading process that Austen might well appreciate because it engages our interpretive skills while fulfilling expectations.

Lost in Austen is both familiar and new.[3] It not only takes us on a new path – an exciting modern one – but it also leaves the previous path intact. The historical periods are no longer at odds. We have successfully crossed the divide between the eighteenth and twenty-first centuries. Both worlds remain distinct and intact but are imaginatively connected in this adaptation. It is the viewer who brings together the various versions of *Pride and Prejudice*. The act of reading the novel and the act of viewing the film adaptations are united within the same person. In this way a filmic and interpretive symmetry is obtained. The resulting connections between novel and filmic adaptations negate the possibility of categorizing *Pride and Prejudice*'s status as a product only of either elite or popular culture. In this instance Stuart Hall's observation that 'things cease to have high cultural value ... [once] appropriated into the popular' (514) proves inaccurate since *Lost in Austen* requires continual movement on the part of the viewer/reader between the two texts.

The modern viewer of *Lost in Austen* exercises the necessary 'ingenuity' Austen desired as he performs the mental gymnastics required to jump between the original novel and the various film adaptations to see where this series is true to the original, where it deviates, and how. The changes are ultimately acceptable because they enhance our enjoyment of Austen and lead us back to yet another reading and interpretation of her novel, but one concurrently informed by the later film adaptations.

NOTES

1 *The Guardian* reported that work is underway for Sam Mendes to adapt the television series *Lost in Austen* into a Hollywood film. Web. 11 Feb. 2009.
2 In the end Zeff relents when he has Lady Catherine de Bourgh agree to annul Collins and Jane's marriage thus freeing her up to marry Bingley and embark on a new life together in America.
3 Not all adaptations or embellishments of Austen's works aim to capture the spirit of the original. *Pride and Prejudice and Zombies* (2009) and *Sense and Sensibility and Sea Monsters* (2010) are two such examples.

WORKS CITED

Austen, Jane. *Collected Letters*. Ed. Deirdre le Faye. Oxford: Oxford UP, 1997. Print.

– *The Cambridge Edition of the Works of Jane Austen*. Ed. Janet Todd. Cambridge: Cambridge UP, 2006. Print.

Austen, Jane, and Seth Grahame-Smith. *Pride and Prejudice and Zombies*. Philadelphia: Quirk Books, 2009. Print.

Becoming Jane. Dir. Julian Jarrold. Perf. Anne Hathaway, James McAvoy. Miramax, 2007. DVD.

Bluestone, George. *Novels into Film*. Berkeley: U of California P, 1957. Print.

Bride and Prejudice. Dir. Gurinder Chadha. Perf. Aishwarya Rai, Martin Henderson. Pathé, 2004. DVD.

Bridget Jones's Diary. Dir. Sharon Maguire. Perf. Renée Zellweger, Colin Firth, Hugh Grant. Little Bird, Studio Canal, 2001. DVD.

Clueless. Dir. Amy Heckerling. Perf. Alicia Silverstone, Stacey Dash, Paul Rudd. Paramount, 1995. DVD.

Elliott, Kamilla. *Rethinking the Novel/Film Debate*. Cambridge: Cambridge UP, 2003. Print.

Emma. Dir. Doug McGrath. Perf. Gwyneth Paltrow, Jeremy Northam. Miramax, 1996. DVD.

– Dir. Diarmuid Lawrence. Perf. Kate Beckinsdale, Olivia Williams. A&E, 1996. DVD.

– Dir. Jim O'Hanlon. Perf. Romola Garai, Michael Gambon. BBC, 2009. DVD.

Gard, Roger. 'A Few Sceptical Thoughts on Jane Austen and Film.' *Jane Austen on Screen*. Ed. Gina Macdonald and Andrew F. Macdonald. Cambridge: Cambridge UP, 2003. 10–12. Print.

Grogan, Claire. Introduction. *Northanger Abbey*. By Jane Austen. Ed. Claire Grogan. Peterborough: Broadview, 2002. 7–24. Print.

Hall, Stuart. 'Notes on Deconstructing "the Popular."' *Cultural Theory and Popular Culture*. 4th ed. Ed. John Storey. New York: Longman, 2009. 508–18. Print.

Hudelet, Adriane. 'The Construction of a Myth: The Cinematic Jane Austen as a Cross-Cultural Icon.' *The Cinematic Jane Austen: Essays on the Filmic Sensibility of the Novels*. Ed. David Monaghan, Adriane Hudelet, and John Wiltshire. London: McFarland, 2005. 148–59. Print.

The Jane Austen Book Club. Dir. Robin Swicord. Perf. Maria Bello, Emily Blunt, Kathy Baker. Mocking Bird, 2007. DVD.

Leitch, Thomas. 'Twelve Fallacies in Contemporary Adaptation Theory.' *Criticism* 45.2 (2003): 149–72. Print.

Lorenz, Edward. *The Essence of Chaos*. London: University College of London, 1993. Print.

Lost in Austen. Dir. Daniel Zeff. Perf. Jemima Rooper, Alex Kingston, Elliot Cowan, Hugh Bonneville. Mammoth Screen, 2008. DVD.

Mansfield Park. Dir. Patricia Rozema. Perf. Frances O'Connor, Jonny Lee
Miller. Arts Council, 1999. DVD.
– Dir. Iain MacDonald. Perf. Billie Piper, Blake Ritson. Company Pictures,
2007. DVD.
McFarlane, Brian. *Novel to Film: An Introduction to the Theory of Adaptation.*
Oxford: Clarendon, 1996. Print.
Miss Austen Regrets. Dir. Jeremy Lovering. Perf. Samuel Roukin, Olivia
Williams, Greta Scaachi, BBC, 2008. DVD.
Northanger Abbey. Dir. Giles Foster. Perf. Peter Firth. 1987. DVD.
– Dir. Jon Jones. Perf. Geraldine James, Felicity Jones, JJ Field. Granada, 2007.
DVD.
Persuasion. Dir. Andrew Mitchell/ Nick Dear. Perf. Amanda Root,
Ciarán Hinds. BBC, 1995. DVD.
– Dir. Adrian Shergold. Perf. Sally Hawkins, Rupert Perry-Jones.
Clerkenwell, 2007. DVD.
Pride and Prejudice. Dir. Robert Z. Leonard. Perf. Greer Garson, Laurence
Olivier. MGM, 1940. DVD.
– Dir. Cyril Coke. Perf. Elizabeth Garvie, David Rintoul. BBC, 1980. DVD.
– Dir. Simon Langton/Andrew Davies. Perf. Colin Firth, Jennifer Ehle. BBC,
1995. DVD.
– Dir. Joe Wright. Perf. Keira Knightley, Matthew Macfadden. Focus, 2005.
DVD.
Sense and Sensibility. Dir. Ang Lee/Emma Thompson. Perf. Emma Thompson,
Hugh Grant, Kate Winslet. Columbia, 1995. DVD.
– Dir. John Alexander. Perf. Hattie Morahan, Charity Wakefield, Dan
Stevens. BBC, 2008. DVD.
Stam, Robert. 'Introduction: The Theory and Practice of Adaptation.'
Literature and Film: A Guide to the Theory and Practice of Film Adaptation. Ed.
Robert Stam. Oxford: Blackwell, 2005. 1–52. Print.
Willemen, Paul. *Looks and Frictions: Essays in Cultural Studies and Film Theory.*
Bloomington: Indiana UP, 1994. Print.
Wiltshire John. 'Afterword: On Fidelity.' *The Cinematic Jane Austen: Essays on
the Filmic Sensibility of the Novels.* Ed. David Monaghan, Adriane Hudelet,
and John Wiltshire. London: McFarland, 2005. 160–70. Print.

Contributors

Paula Backscheider, Philpott-Stevens Eminent Scholar at Auburn University, is the author of several books including *Spectacular Politics: Theatrical Power and Mass Culture in Early Modern England* and *Eighteenth-Century Women Poets and Their Poetry* (Johns Hopkins) as well as *Reflections on Biography* (Oxford).

Martha F. Bowden, Professor of English at Kennesaw State University, has produced an edition of three novels by Mary Davys (Kentucky), *Yorick's Congregation: The Church of England in the Time of Laurence Sterne* (Delaware), and articles on Sterne, Davys, Fielding, and others. Her current project examines historical fiction.

Mary Chadwick is an AHRC-funded PhD student at Aberystwyth University. Her research focuses on the ways in which members of a particular North Walian family, the Griffiths of Garn, expressed ideas of national identity in poems, riddles, extracts and letters between 1750 and 1820.

Elaine Chalus is Senior Lecturer in History at Bath Spa University. She is the author of *Elite Women in English Political Life c. 1754–1790* (Oxford), and coeditor of *Women's History, Britain 1700–1850: An Introduction* (Routledge) and *Gender in Eighteenth-Century England: Roles, Representations and Responsibilities* (Longman).

Timothy Erwin is Professor of English and former chair of Cultural Studies at the University of Nevada, Las Vegas. He has served as editor for *Studies in Eighteenth-Century Culture* and *Chicago Review,* and enjoys writing on visual topics.

Claire Grogan is a Professor of English at Bishop's University, Quebec. She is the editor of Austen's *Northanger Abbey* with Broadview Press. Her forthcoming book is a study on Elizabeth Hamilton and the politics of genre.

Isobel Grundy, a Fellow of the Royal Society of Canada, is Professor Emeritus at the University of Alberta. She has published widely on Samuel Johnson, Lady Mary Wortley Montagu, and women's writing. With Susan Brown and Patricia Clements she regularly updates the digital resource *Orlando: Women's Writing in the British Isles* (Cambridge).

Berta Joncus is a Lecturer in Music at Goldsmiths, University of London. Her recent publications include *The Stage's Glory: John Rich (1692–1761)*, coedited with Jeremy Barlow, and articles in books and scholarly journals. She is a music critic for the BBC, and designed and directs Ballad Operas Online http://www.odl.ox.ac.uk/balladoperas.

Elizabeth Kowaleski Wallace, Professor of English at Boston College, has published on eighteenth-century women writers; on women, shopping, and business in the eighteenth century; and on the British slave trade in public memory. Recently, she has been writing on contemporary British fiction.

Holly Luhning recently completed a SSHRC postdoctoral fellowship at the Burney Centre, Department of English, McGill University. She has published articles on Eliza Haywood in *Lumen, Age of Johnson,* and Chawton House Library's *Female Spectator.*

Andrew Macdonald, Professor of English at Loyola University, New Orleans, and **Gina Macdonald,** Professor of Languages and Literature at Nicholls State University, Thibodaux, LA, are coeditors of *Jane Austen on Screen* (Cambridge) and authors of various articles on Jane Austen films. Gina Macdonald passed away last year after courageously battling leukemia, completing this article while undergoing chemotherapy.

Robert James Merrett is Professor of English at the University of Alberta. His *Daniel Defoe: Contrarian* is forthcoming from the University of Toronto Press. Other monographs in progress concern eighteenth-century cultural exchanges between England and France, the economic and social history of cooking and cookbooks, and the literary history of wine.

Jessica Munns, Professor of English at the University of Denver, has published widely on eighteenth-century literature and edits the journal *Restoration and Eighteenth-Century Theatre Research*. Her recent publications include *The Clothes That Wear Us: Dressing and Transgressing in Eighteenth-Century Culture* (Delaware).

Tiffany Potter teaches English at the University of British Columbia. She has published books, editions, and articles on eighteenth-century libertinism, gender, theatre, and indigeneity, and is coeditor of the award-winning collection *Cylons in America: Critical Studies in Battlestar Galactica* and *The Wire: Urban Decay and American Television* (Continuum).

Peter Sabor, a Fellow of the Royal Society of Canada, holds the Canada Research Chair in Eighteenth-Century Studies at McGill University and is Director of the Burney Centre. His recent publications include, as coauthor, *Pamela in the Marketplace* (Cambridge) and, as editor, *Juvenilia* in the Cambridge Edition of the Works of Jane Austen.

Tamara S. Wagner works on eighteenth- and nineteenth-century fiction. Her recent books include *Longing: Narratives of Nostalgia in the British Novel, 1740–1890* (Bucknell) and *Financial Speculation in Victorian Fiction: Plotting Money and the Novel Genre, 1815–1901* (Ohio State).

Index